THE GUINNESS WHO'S WHO OF

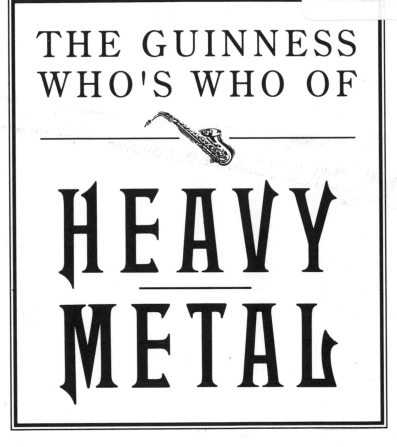

HEAVY METAL

General Editor: Colin Larkin

Introduction by Ian Kenyon

GUINNESS PUBLISHING

Dedicated to James Marshall Hendrix

First published in 1992 by
GUINNESS PUBLISHING LTD
33 London Road, Enfield, Middlesex EN2 6DJ, England

GUINNESS is a registered trademark of Guinness Publishing Ltd

British Library Cataloguing-in-Publication data
A catalogue record for this book is available from the British Library

ISBN 0-85112-581-6

Conceived, designed, edited and produced by
SQUARE ONE BOOKS LTD
Iron Bridge House, 3 Bridge Approach, Chalk Farm, London NW1 8BD
Editor and Designer: Colin Larkin
Picture Editor: Colin Larkin
Editorial and production assistants: Susan Pipe, John Eley, Aileen Tyler, Pat Perry,
Jon Staines, Janice Newman, Johnny Rogan, Jane Ehrlich, Tim Beard
Special thanks to Donald McFarlan and David Roberts of Guinness Publishing
and to Tony Gale of Pictorial Press
Ian Kenyon would like to credit Vivienne;
thank you for all the help, encouragement, love and support during the writing of this project.
Logo concept: Darren Perry. Page make up: Timothy Beard
This book has been produced on Apple Macintosh computers
using Quark Xpress and Microsoft Word
Image set by L & S Communications Ltd

Printed and bound in Great Britain by the Bath Press

EDITORS NOTE

The Guinness Who's Who Of Heavy Metal forms a part of the multi-volume *Guinness Encyclopedia Of Popular Music*. A further 16 specialist single volumes are planned in the near future.

Also available:
The Guinness Who's Who Of Indie And New Wave Music
The Guinness Who's Who Of Sixties Music
The Guinness Who's Who Of Jazz

In compiling this work we have attempted to include as many current, relevant heavy metal bands as possible. During the selection, and following discussions with our heavy metal contributors we have additionally included bands and artists who come under the metal/crossover category. Bands such as Jethro Tull, Status Quo, Queen, REO Speedwagon, Styx are included for this reason, in addition to vital pioneers such as Jimi Hendrix and Led Zeppelin.

The introduction and glossary of terms was written by Ian Kenyon. His knowledge and enthusiasm for the subject will see him develop as a leading authority in the future. Many of the entries were prepared by Ian, in addition to contributions from, Brian Hogg, Johnny Rogan, Colin Larkin, Dave Laing,

Alan Clayson, Peter Doggett, Jeff Tamarkin, Emma Rees, Pam Boniface, Dave Sissons, Pete Wadeson, Michael Burgess, Greg Moffitt, Mark Jones and Michael Barnett.

The vast majority of photographs came from Pictorial Press. Tony Gale, the proprietor has a comprehensive heavy metal library.

For the remaining items we thank: Alex Ogg for Asia, Black Crowes, Blackfoot, Carcass, Cheap And Nasty, Creaming Jesus, Death,Faith No More, F.M., G.W.A.R., Jethro Tull, Legs Diamond, Lillian Axe, Massacre, Gary Moore, Morbid Angel, Napalm Death, Nuclear Assault, Obituary, Paradise Lost, John Parr, Sepultra, Slayer, Sound Garden, Thunder, Wishbone Ash, Xentrix. Ian Kenyon for Chrissy Steele, L.A. Guns, Nazareth.

I would like to thank, in addition to the contributors; John Eley and Susan Pipe for an extraordinary effort in putting it all together at the end, and to Paola Simoneschi, Sallie Collins and Sarah Silvé for their production work. Donald McFarlan takes credit for finding Timothy Beard who took a great deal of the strain away from us. Finally to Laura, Ben, Tom, Dan and Carmen who were still my family at the very end.

Colin Larkin, August 1992

INTRODUCTION & GLOSSARY OF TERMS

The term 'heavy metal' is probably one of the most over-used, abused and misused clichés in the English language. It has expanded, unchecked over and around existing musical genres to become so large and multi-faceted, that a simple description or definition is now totally inappropriate. In time, it has incorporated ever more sub-genres; firstly as a result of musical diversification from the 'initial form' and secondly as a consequence of the acknowledgement of its influences, roots and origins. This has resulted in an ever increasing number of older musical styles being included under the heavy metal umbrella. The gut reaction to the term itself often conjures up images of heavily tattooed band members decked out in studded back leather and spandex trousers with long hair and a macho attitude. In addition, the music is often perceived as being loud, repetitive and aggressive with sexist or satanic elements included in the lyrics. This can be readily qualified if one examines the following dictionary definitions:

'a particularly loud, simple and repetitive form of hard rock'
(*Chambers English Dictionary*, 1990)

'a form of rock music popular during the 1970s and 1980s, basic in form and characterized by shrill guitar solos, repetitive rhythms and high sound levels'
(*Brewers Twentieth Century Phrase And Fable Dictionary*, 1991)

'energetic and highly amplified electronic rock music having a hard beat and usually an element of the fantastic'
(*Webster's Dictionary* 1975)

'simplistic, noisy macho music that appeals to headbanging denim-clad northerners (UK) or beer-swilling Midwesterners (US); the musical equivalent of fantasy's 'sword and sorcery' and game playing's 'dungeons and dragons'
(*Newspeak, A Dictionary Of Jargon*, J. Green 1984)

These definitions are typical of the misrepresentation of heavy metal by the media, as they focus entirely on the shocking or controversial aspects of a small number of performers. Heavy metal has received bad press since its inception, with tabloid newspapers regularly exposing, condemning or ridiculing bands for their outrageous rock 'n' roll lifestyles and stage shows. Over the years, various allegations of sexism, devil worship and the incitement of teenagers to take alcohol, drugs and be promiscuous have all been levelled. In addition, further alienation to the music by the older generations has been aided by the medical reports on the damage that high noise levels and headbanging can inflict on their offspring.

This book attempts to put the record straight. The introduction examines the origins of heavy metal, and its evolution into the complex myriad of sub-genres that exist today. While the book is written primarily for heavy metal fans, it is also designed to be used as a tool for the uninitiated or simply curious. The origins of heavy metal are examined, with reference to both musical and technical innovation. Every facet of heavy metal is considered and each sub-genre is carefully differentiated. A concise glossary of heavy metal terminology is included with brief recommendations and examples given for each sub-genre. The main body of the book provides an A to Z listing of artists. Individual entries give a brief musical history and complete album discography. This is the definitive text of its kind and an essential reference work for anyone interested in music or the music business.

'HEAVY METAL' – WHAT'S IN A NAME?

Heavy metal existed long before the metaphorical term itself was applied to the music. Research suggests that the term was first used by author William Burroughs in his novel *Naked Lunch*, which was published in Paris during 1959 and three years later in the USA. The first musical use of the term was in Steppenwolf's 1968 rebel anthem 'Born To Be Wild'. The lyrics refer to the thrill of burning down the highway on a powerful motorcycle:
'I like smokin' lightnin, heavy metal thunder, racin' with the wind, and a feeling that I'm under'.
In this instance, heavy metal refers to the motorcycle rather than music. However by the end of the 60s, the music press were beginning to use the terms hard rock, progressive rock and heavy rock as descriptive adjectives for the music of Blue Cheer, Cream and the MC5. During the 70s heavy rock was used increasingly as a noun and a new sub-genre of popular music had arrived. This included bands such as Led Zeppelin, Deep Purple, Black Sabbath and Uriah Heep. Progressive, hard and heavy rock diversified rapidly into an infinite number of sub-classes during the early 70s. An adaptive radiation saw the emergence of similar bands in Europe, Canada, USA and

Australia as well as the UK. AC/DC, the Scorpions, Status Quo, Grand Funk Railroad, Golden Earring, Rush and Kiss are among some of the key outfits that came to prominence during this time.

1976-79 represented the nadir of popularity for the hard, heavy and progressive rock movements as punk-rock exploded violently onto the scene in the UK and to a lesser extent everywhere else. Virtually overnight, established artists such as Wishbone Ash, Jethro Tull, Led Zeppelin, Rush and Deep Purple were condemned by a new youth culture as 'boring old farts'. Music was stripped down to the most basic elements again. There had been a traumatic gut reaction to the self-indulgent meanderings of stadium rock bands who played to tens of thousands of people at a time. Their music was delivered with studio-like precision and accuracy and supplemented by ever more expensive and elaborate stage shows. The youth of the day rejected *en masse*, the rock star idiom. Music was back in the clubs once more and there was barely any difference between performers and their audiences. Punk rock was D.I.Y. rock 'n' roll; talent and musical dexterity were secondary requirements over enthusiasm and attitude. For 18 months there was a real revolution and the emergence of important outfits such as the Sex Pistols, the Clash and the Damned. By 1978, the movement was beginning to implode as many bands ran out of steam and were unable to develop or progress musically from their amateurish origins.

Many of the bands that did evolve, became much more competent as musicians and moved into more 'mainstream rock territory'. At the same time, a new generation of young rock bands emerged that combined the aggressive, street-level approach of punk rock but with their stylistic origins rooted firmly in the early to mid-70s hard, progressive and heavy rock scene. In addition, the bands were technically far more competent musicians than those of the preceding punk-rock phenomenon. This was heralded as the New Wave Of British Heavy Metal movement and included bands such as

Diamond Head, Def Leppard, Iron Maiden, Saxon, Angelwitch and Samson. Being labelled as the 'New Wave Of British Heavy Metal' movement suggested that there must have been a 'heavy metal' movement that preceded this new phase. In fact, this was not the case. However, as the new bands cited the Scorpions, Deep Purple, Led Zeppelin, Black Sabbath, Judas Priest *et al* as their main musical influences, the term heavy metal was suddenly applied as a blanket term for all the hard, progressive and heavy rock outfits that had gone before.

The New Wave Of British Heavy Metal (NWOBHM) movement acted as a catalyst for the rapid divergent evolution of many new sub genres, that have also been included under the massive umbrella-like monicker of heavy metal. These subsequent developments have included thrash metal, death metal, power metal, sleaze/glam metal, indie metal, funk metal, neo-classical metal, industrial metal, *avant garde* metal, pop-metal, white metal, black metal, grindcore and crossover. The influences cited by this plethora of sub-genres have, retrospectively, been included as of relevance and interest to heavy metal and its fan-base. Therefore 70s glam-rock bands such as Sweet, Mud, Suzi Quatro, Slade, T. Rex and Gary Glitter suddenly had new significance. Similarly, blues, rock 'n' roll, funk, soul, AOR, punk and even classical music were also rediscovered and their importance and impact re-assessed.

In 1992, 'heavy metal' is a cumbersome term. It is all too often over-used misused or abused, so as to be completely meaningless when considering its original usage. This problem has been accentuated by the music media, and in particular the plethora of glossy colour magazines that have continued to flourish and increase in number since the NWOBHM. With a large number of pages to fill, these publications have had no choice but to feature album reviews, live reviews and interviews with an immense number of bands, no matter how tenuous their links may be with *bona fide* heavy metal. *Kerrang, R.A.W., Metal Hammer, Metal Forces, Hot Metal, Rock Power, Thrash And Burn,* and *Riff*

Raff are all guilty of this. However, with circulation figures between 15,000 and 50,000 copies, it is obviously in their best interests to maximize their potential markets by featuring as wide a range of artists as possible. It is these magazines that have been responsible for the dilution of the term heavy metal. It would be logical to re-classify and re-define the musical sub-genres that exist today, to avoid confusion and gain a new order and understanding of contemporary music. To some extent, the term heavy metal is now redundant as it is so widely used and applied almost indiscriminately to a vast range of musical styles. However, because of inertia, it is here to stay and this book should provide a path through this musical minefield. The reader should emerge with a clearer understanding of heavy metal's development and be able to access the music in which he or she is likely to be most interested. This can be achieved without the often expensive trial and error, hit or miss approach from reading the rather subjective glossy magazines mentioned above.

THE HISTORY AND DEVELOPMENT OF HEAVY METAL

Throughout history, technical innovations have acted as catalysts for experimentation and development. Music is no exception, the first important technical advancement that allowed an adaptive musical revolution, was the introduction of the electric guitar in the late 40s. The Fender Broadcaster, later re-named the Telecaster, launched in 1950, was the world's first 'commercially available electric guitar, with a solid wooden body and bolt on neck. The Fender Precision Bass was launched the following year, to replace the bulky, cumbersome and frequently barely audible acoustic double bass.

Initially, the electric versions of these instruments were played exactly the same way as their acoustic counterparts. The enormous revolutionary potential they possessed was not exploited for several years.

Many artists viewed them as simply more portable alternatives to the acoustic forms. The electric instruments were used purely to amplify the sound and provide sustain on some of the notes.

The rock 'n' roll revolution exploded onto the music scene during the 50s, and the development of electric guitar technique was paralleled by this phenomenon. Some of the earliest innovators, responsible for exploring the potential of the electric guitar were Chuck Berry, Francis 'France' Beecher (of Bill Haley And His Comets), Elvis Presley and Scotty Moore.

In June 1955, Bill Haley And His Comets topped the US *Billboard* singles chart with 'Rock Around The Clock'. This featured a high-energy, 12-bar guitar break from Francis Beecher; achieved by turning the amplifier to maximum volume, so that the notes verged on distortion. The same year, Chuck Berry scored a US Top 5 hit with 'Maybelline'. Berry's style switched between pumping rhythm and punchy lead notes with consummate ease. Economy was his key to success and he subsequently became a very influential role model for future generations of guitarists. He was later to write such classics as 'Roll Over Beethoven', 'Johnny B. Goode' and 'Sweet Little Sixteen' in the same inimitable style. These songs have been covered countless times by successive generations of bands and still feature prominently in many live shows.

Elvis Presley's overtly sexual image, first focused attention on the power of the electric guitar as a phallic symbol. However, Presley merely wore a guitar for decoration, and rarely did anything more than strum along, and pose with it in a provocative manner. It was Scotty Moore in Elvis Presley's backing band that actually provided the inventive lead breaks and red-hot licks on 'Hound Dog' (1956) and 'Jailhouse Rock' (1957). Presley's influence should not be underestimated as he was directly responsible for millions of youths picking up guitars, tennis rackets, broom handles or whatever else came to hand and posing arrogantly in front of the mirror! The youths that progressed to actually playing

their instruments, tried to mimic the sound on Presley's recordings. They were, in the event trying to emulate Scotty Moore's guitar style, rather than the King's.

Following the success and innovation of Fender, other electric guitars started to flood onto the market, notably from the Gibson and Gretsch companies. The Gibson Les Paul 'Gold Top' introduced in 1952, was more craftsman-like, than the mass-produced Fenders. It featured a glued-in neck, ornate fingerboard inlays, heavily carved top and classical symmetrical headstock. Its basic design has remained virtually unchanged throughout its 40-year history. Together, with Fender's Telecaster and later Stratocaster designs, the Gibson Les Paul was the most popular, versatile and frequently copied guitar ever made.

During the late 50s, there was a growing awareness of the real potential of the electric guitar. The distinction between rhythm and lead playing was clearly made and songs were now constructed to include a four or eight-bar break in the middle. A new figure had arrived on the scene - the lead guitarist. Link Wray, originally a country and bottleneck player from North Carolina pioneered a new guitar sound in the late 50s. The breakthrough came with 'The Rumble', an instrumental number which featured fuzzy, semi-distorted chords. This effect was achieved by piercing one of the three speakers of his Premier amplifier with a pencil. Recorded in 1954, 'The Rumble' became a hit in 1958, peaking at number 16 on the *Billboard* US singles chart.

This hard, rough and aggressive sound pre-dated heavy metal by over a decade. It was banned in New York, because of its menacing mood and associations with gangland warfare. This effect is now readily available using a fuzz-box; a foot-controlled device that allows the guitarist to alternate between distorted fuzz-tone and the normal clear sound.

Duane Eddy was the next influential figure to emerge on the scene, with another new and characteristic guitar sound. With the help of radio disc jockey Lee Hazelwood and a

Gretsch 'Chet Atkins' guitar with Bigsby tremelo, he worked on and developed the twangy, reverberating echo effect. Eddy achieved this deep, lazy and seemingly effortless resonance by playing the melody lines on the bass strings, while using the tremolo bar for slight distortion. He clocked up 17 Top 20 hits in the UK between 1958 and 1962, with perhaps 'Peter Gunn Theme', which peaked at number 6 in 1959, being most representative of his unique sound.

A technical innovation in drumming heralded the next phase of rock music's development. In 1957, Remo Belli started supplying plastic, instead of traditional calf leather skins to drum manufacturers. Plastic skins were far more functional. They did not alter their tone with changes in humidity or temperature; they were stronger and also much easier to fit. After initial resistance and criticisms concerning the harder sound that was produced from plastic, traditional leather skins soon became obsolete and the strength and convenience of plastic became paramount. The traditional one-piece bass-drum pedal was replaced by a more efficient two-piece, developed in the USA. This enabled the drummer to keep his heel on the base plate and achieve quick-fire and repeated impacts by merely flexing the ankle. Cymbal quality was also improved, with new specifications being less prone to splitting and cracking than the earlier models.

The improvements in both kit quality and durability meant that the drummers of the late 50s began to attack their kits with more aggression and enjoyed a greater range of sonic flexibility than ever before. Drums as a separate musical form were given more prominence and drum breaks became commonplace on recordings. The Shadows' 'Apache', Sandy Nelson's 'Let There Be Drums' and the Surfaris' 'Wipeout' are clear evidence of the drummer's rise in the ascendancy of rock at this time.

In the early 60s, bands began to capitalize on the benefits offered by recent improvements in technology. In the UK, four and five-piece outfits became the norm, comprising bass, drums, rhythm and lead guitars plus optional keyboards or saxophone. the Animals, the Dave Clark Five, the Beatles, the Kinks and the Rolling Stones all came to prominence during this time. Many of these bands crossed the Atlantic and found immediate success in the USA. As more and more UK outfits established themselves in foreign territory, the whole era was christened the British Invasion in 1964.

It is widely acknowledged that the prototype for heavy metal emerged from the British Invasion bands, with the Kinks' 'You Really Got Me'. Inspired by Link Wray, guitarist Dave Davies lacerated the speaker of his amplifier with razor blades. The distorted signal was then channelled through a larger, more powerful amplifier. This added a dense, raunchy feel to the basic riff; the powerchord had arrived! Drummer Mick Avory assaulted his kit with a manic energy, while vocalist and rhythm guitarist Ray Davies spat out the lyrics with both arrogance and conviction. The single took off and peaked at number 7 on the US *Billboard* chart, while in the UK it hit the coveted number 1 slot in September 1964.

The Rolling Stones, labelled as the 'badboys' of the British invasion did much to initialize the general public's negative attitude to rock music. Formed in 1962 and originally playing covers of blues, rock 'n' roll and R&B numbers Jagger's flamboyant stagecraft added a new visual dimension to the music of the time. Urinating in public, gloating over their sexual conquests along with drug and alcohol abuse added to their ever increasing notoriety. A string of number 1 hits ensued between 1964 and 1966, with 1965's '(I Can't Get No) Satisfaction' being most representative.

The Who exploded onto the British rock scene in 1965. Their outrageous stage show has become the blueprint for countless generations of bands ever since. Lead vocalist Roger Daltrey's lasso-style antics with the microphone, Pete Townshend's flailing, windmill-like guitar style and Keith Moon's demonic drumming, literally stunned audiences into submission. The climax of the show involved complete demolition of their equipment; Townshend scraped his guitar across the amps to generate screeching feedback, before finally destroying it in a display of violent frenzy. The Who's big breakthrough came with 'My Generation' which peaked at number 2 on the UK singles chart. The song related closely to the youth culture of the day, with the unintentionally ironic line 'Hope I die before I get old'. This single phrase epitomized the attitude of the times.

1967 was an important year in the development of rock music. It saw the release of the Beatles' *Sgt. Pepper's Lonely Hearts Club Band*, which marked a growing acceptance of rock as an art form. Bands and audiences became more critical of each other and the displays of hysterical screaming which were commonplace only a few years earlier, were becoming a thing of the past. A much more serious approach was adopted; musicians strove for technical excellence and a mastery over their instruments. Lyrics showed a parallel development, with deeper social, spiritual and religious themes being explored. Audiences now sat quietly analyzing the music instead of dancing on their seats. The message of the lyrics and the musical dexterity of the band became of paramount importance.

The fuzz-box and wah-wah pedal were introduced to give guitarists a greater range of options during their ever longer and more demanding solo spots. The wah wah pedal allowed guitarists to switch from a muted to bright tone, an effect that sounds not unlike the gadget's name. Amplifiers were becoming larger and more powerful, with an ever increasing number of dials, knobs and switches. This facilitated the controlled distortion of the instrument's sound. Drum kits began to expand to include two bass drums, plus a battery of snares, hi-hats and tom-toms. These were the forerunners of the monster kits that appeared during the 70s.

June 1967 saw the Monterey Pop Festival showcase the second generation of rock acts, who had drawn much of their inspiration from contemporary outfits such as the Beatles, the Kinks and the Rolling Stones.

The festival took place on a coastal site midway between Los Angeles and San Francisco and its theme was 'music, love and flowers'. Organized primarily by concert promoter Alan Pariser and John Phillips of the Mamas And The Papas, it became a charity event which raised $200,000. The festival was organized over five separate performances; Friday night, plus Saturday and Sunday afternoon and evening slots. The original intention was to present a wide cross-section of current popular music. However, there was a notable absence of US black outfits on the bill excepting Otis Redding, Booker T. and Lou Rawls. The final line-up was heavily biased towards Californian acts and special guests from the UK. The Grateful Dead and Jefferson Airplane elicited favourable responses, but it was the stunning performances from Big Brother And The Holding Company, with Janis Joplin on vocals, the Who and Jimi Hendrix Experience that sent the 30,000 plus crowd, home speechless. It appeared that the Who's equipment-wrecking finale, complete with smoke bombs and utter carnage could not be surpassed. However, Jimi Hendrix turned in a performance that generated shock waves through the rock cognoscenti. Influenced by American blues-masters such as B.B. King, Chuck Berry and Muddy Waters he added a new dimension to electric guitar technique. Armed with a Fender Stratocaster, he produced a dazzling display of guitar pyrotechnics and extracted all kinds of twisted sounds from the instrument. This involved grinding the neck against the mike stand and amplifiers, playing with his tongue and teeth, playing behind his head and finally setting it alight with lighter fuel as a sacrificial climax. The Who had been upstaged for perhaps the first time in their career.

Hendrix made a massive impact on the rock scene. His style became the blueprint for rock, and later heavy metal guitarists the world over. His untimely death on 18 September 1970, resulted from the inhalation of vomit following excess barbiturate intake. In just four years he had re-shaped the future of popular music and he became acknowledged as the single most influential figure in the development of heavy metal.

The late 60s saw a continuation of the quest for technical excellence and the increasing use of improvised and often lengthy instrumental solos. This approach was epitomized by Cream, a British, blues-rock power trio, comprising guitarist Eric Clapton, bassist Jack Bruce and drummer Ginger Baker. They were also the first 'supergroup' as the three musicians already had an impressive musical pedigree behind them. Clapton had previously played with the Yardbirds and John Mayall's Bluesbreakers, Bruce had just left Manfred Mann and Baker had occupied the drumstool with the Graham Bond Organisation. Formed in 1966, they really came to prominence in 1968 with the release of their third album, *Wheels Of Fire*, which reached number 1 on both sides of the Atlantic. This showcased the two sides of the band; the double album featured one disc of new studio material, while the other was a live recording. The latter showed the band's amazing ability to re-interpret classics such as Willie Dixon's 'Spoonful' and drag it kicking and squealing into the realms of jazz-rock-blues fusion. The studio material saw a more disciplined approach, with the band restricting their songs to a four or five minute maximum; they crashed into the lucrative singles market with 'Wrapping Paper', 'Sunshine Of Your Love' and 'White Room'. As the band's virtuoso performers grew tired of the expected and now obligatory jam sessions, internal conflict led Cream to disband towards the end of 1968. Their career was short but surprisingly important in the development of rock and the influence of their music is still acknowledged by contemporary acts.

With the demise of Cream, a new guitar hero was much sought-after by the media and fans alike. Coincidentally, it was Jeff Beck, who had replaced Eric Clapton in the Yardbirds that first broke from the pack. He established his reputation with the Yardbirds, but quit in late 1966 to pursue his own ideas more fully. Beck helped shape blues-rock,

psychedelia and heavy metal. His groups have been short-lived, but his aggressive style, incorporating high-speed screeching, sustained notes, feedback and distortion has been more influential than his recorded output. He has become, in essence, a guitarist's guitarist. For a short time, Beck was in the Yardbirds with Jimmy Page, another guitarist who was later to have a profound effect on the development of heavy metal. Page originally joined as bassist, but switched to lead guitar on a permanent basis, when Chris Dreja moved from rhythm to bass. By the summer of 1966, Beck and Page were both playing lead guitar, but this line-up was short-lived as Beck quit in November 1966, partly due to ill-health, but also to follow a solo career. By the time Page joined the Yardbirds, their career was already beginning to flag. The band delivered *Little Games* in 1967, an album of mainly old demos and leftover material from earlier studio sessions. This was poorly received and was not even granted a UK release; consequently the band dissolved as a unit in July 1968. Page secured the rights to the name of the band from vocalist Keith Relf, bassist Chris Dreja and drummer Jim McCarty. He formed the New Yardbirds the same year, with Robert Plant (vocals), John Paul Jones (bass) and John Bonham (drums). After a debut tour of Scandinavia in October 1968, they returned to England to record a debut album. At this juncture, they were toying with the idea of a name change for the band; one that might be indicative of their heavy, blues-based musical direction. Keith Moon flippantly suggested the name Lead Zeppelin as he implied they were likely to go down like a lead balloon. The New Yardbirds were immediately taken by the name, and with a slight modification of Lead to Led, the name was adopted. Led Zeppelin entered the studio and recorded their debut album in less than 30 hours.

Led Zeppelin became the role model for other artists to follow. The basic components of their style still represent the essential aspects of heavy metal and they probably rank as the most important influence on the genre. This is an amazing feat considering the band has been defunct for well over a decade. The inspired and emotional style of Plant, Bonham's explosive drumming and the blues-based powerchords of Page combined to startling effect, and became the new blueprint for heavy rock virtually overnight. What really set Led Zeppelin apart from the bands that had gone before was their amazing diversity. They were able to switch styles between slow, brooding blues, to raunchy rock 'n' roll and cajun-like acoustic balladry with consummate ease. In addition, the lyrical elements of the songs were frequently mystical and cryptic in both sentiment and meaning, and often made obscure references to the occult. Accusations of a satanic fascination were borne out by Jimmy Page purchasing the former residence of self-confessed Satanist Aleister Crowley. Rather than resting on their laurels, Zeppelin pushed forward the frontiers of heavy rock by experimenting with and incorporating reggae and even far eastern influences into their blues-based, hard-rock style. Their importance and influence cannot be overstated. One only needs to analyse the primary sources of reference for bands such as Kingdom Come or Mindstorm, whose entire styles are based almost exclusively on Zeppelin's. Led Zeppelin not only broadened the horizons of heavy metal, they made it more respectable and proved that it was a highly marketable commodity. Record companies have been searching for the new Led Zeppelin ever since, but as yet no band has even come close. Each of their albums has sold well in excess of a million copies and eight of them reached the number 1 position on the UK album charts.

At the same time as Cream, Led Zeppelin and Hendrix were making waves throughout Europe, a whole new generation of bands were beginning to emerge out of garages and seedy clubs in the USA. Bands such as the MC5, the Stooges, Steppenwolf, Grand Funk Railroad and Blue Cheer all helped mould the next phase through which rock music would progress. These bands are often referred to as the American garage bands of the late 60s. This term was coined, because many of the bands, did indeed practice in garages and their approach was generally low-tech. The emphasis was clearly on energy and attitude, rather than musical ability. In many texts, the late 60s garage scene is equated with the punk rock explosion which followed in the mid to late 70s. Both marked a radical departure from the previous norm and saw the new youth culture confront and challenge the current musical establishment.

The MC5, or Motor City Five, hailed from Detroit and came to prominence in 1968 as the figurehead of John Sinclair's radical White Panther Party. The soapbox politics of vocalist Rob Tyner, coupled with the incendiary guitar work of Wayne Kramer and Fred 'Sonic' Smith laid waste to audiences across America and shocked and angered parents, politicians and all law abiding citizens in the process. Their debut album, recorded live in October 1968 at Detroit's Grande Ballroom is undoubtedly one of the early milestones in heavy metal. Chaos and anarchy reign supreme and the band introduce the title cut with the rap 'Kick out the jams motherfuckers'! Consequently, it was banned from many high street stores and their record company, Elektra forced them to record a new rap that was toned down to 'Kick out the jams brothers and sisters'. The band never achieved the recognition they deserved, and achieved minimal commercial success. After two studio albums, they disbanded in 1971.

Blue Cheer have often been described as the world's first true heavy metal band. Formed in California 1966, this power trio epitomized the genre's fascination with rebellion and excess. Comprising guitarist Leigh Stephens, bassist Dickie Peterson and drummer Paul Whaley they first attracted attention with a severe mangling of Eddie Cochran's 'Summertime Blues'. Managed by an ex-Hell's Angel named Gut, their press releases stated the band 'were so heavy, they could churn the air into cottage cheese'. They debuted with *Vincebus Eruptum* in 1968, an album which, in retrospect, has been acknowledged as one of the first studio metal releases. They specialized in blues-based hard rock with overamplification, feedback and a total lack of subtlety. The band were plagued by a series of line-up changes during their brief career, and although they released a further five albums before disintegrating in 1971 they never matched the intensity of their debut release.

The Stooges, led by the drug-crazed and self-confessed wildman Iggy Pop, made a considerable impact on the US rock scene between 1968 and 1970. Pop's manic live performances, which included rubbing raw steak over his naked torso, self-inflicted wounding with broken glass and stage diving represent the earliest examples of shock-rock theatrics in metal. The musical backbeat was a loose, but abrasive guitar-dominated onslaught, which was later acknowledged as a forerunner of the punk movement.

The impact of the MC5, Blue Cheer and the Stooges is perhaps now, in the early 90s, more apparent than ever. Contemporary outfits such as Nirvana, Pearl Jam and Soundgarden derive much inspiration from these musical sources. In fact, the grunge-like guitar sound has developed little since its earliest origins in the late 60s.

Following in the footsteps of this first wave of heavy rock innovators came legions of others who utilized the basic approach of Cream, Hendrix, Zeppelin or the MC5, who added individual modifications to establish a whole new range of sub genres. King Crimson's ground breaking debut *In The Court Of The Crimson King* released in 1969 is often cited as the first truly progressive rock album. Progressive rock involves the marrying of blues, rock, classical and even jazz styles into long esoteric compositions with often deep and meaningful lyrics. King Crimson combined elements of Hendrix, Procol Harum and the Moody Blues, and incorporated these styles within both jazz and classical-based frameworks. Other acts materialized in their wake. Innovation, duplication, followed by diversification is the three-tier system through which any new style seems to develop. Consequently, the

progressive rock genre soon expanded with bands such as the Nice, Yes, Van Der Graaf Generator and Vanilla Fudge making an impact.

In addition to the artists above, the years 1967-69 also saw the emergence of Humble Pie, the Allman Brothers Band, Deep Purple, Iron Butterfly, Free, Mountain and Alice Cooper. This collection of artists represented the primary diversification of rock music into a number of distinct sub-genres. Humble Pie and Free, demonstrated the more traditionalist approach; impassioned vocals and a soulful delivery, being the key elements to their style. Steve Marriott and Paul Rodgers respectively were amongst the finest white blues singers, that rock music has ever produced. The Allman Brothers Band, led by Greg and Duane Allman, were instrumental in the establishment of 'Southern Rock'. Blues-based boogie that featured extended dual guitar solos became the band's trademarks.

Alice Cooper's outrageous stage antics saw the inception of rock theatre, where the live show became an integral part and visual extension of the music. Deep Purple incorporated blues, classical and rock influences, with their sound being characterized by Jon Lord's atmospheric organ work and Ritchie Blackmore's stunning guitar breaks. Iron Butterfly, Grand Funk Railroad and Mountain, along with the aforementioned Blue Cheer, are often cited as the originators of true heavy metal. The former, debuting with the appropriately titled *Heavy* in 1967 is dominated by densely mesmeric bass-keyboard interplay delivered with total conviction. Grand Funk Railroad specialized in overamplified and brash, blues-based rock 'n' roll. They were condemned by the critics as dumb and unimaginative, but their albums still sold by the truckload. The group's big breakthrough came at the Atlanta Pop Festival in 1969; waiving their appearance fee, they turned up the sound to overload and literally bludgeoned the crowd into submission. From then on, the band enjoyed repeated stateside chart placings and became the most commercially successful act of the period. Mountain, essentially a Cream-style trio, added some flexibility with the inclusion of a keyboard player. Heavy was an appropriate monicker for this band; lead guitarist Leslie West weighed 250 pounds and went on to become one of the most revered white blues players of the early 70s. West's style was defined by a sequence of staccato phrases, which finally exploded into a long, high volume screech or wail.

All these bands became highly influential, with their distinctly different approaches being modified in an ever increasing number of ways. Between them, they also defined the three basic guitar structures used in rock today. Guitar and bass playing concurrent lines, bass notes supporting guitar chords and call and response. The latter originated from gospel singing, whereby the lead vocalist alternates lines with his back-up singers. In rock music, the call and response system involves guitar alternating with either vocals, keyboards or harmonica. Led Zeppelin, Deep Purple and the Yardbirds respectively were among the early pioneers that eventually honed this style to perfection during the late 60s.

The growth and interest in rock music at this time resulted in a parallel explosion in music journalism. Magazines such as *Rolling Stone*, *Creem*, *Circus* and *Crawdaddy*, and newspapers *Melody Maker*, *Sounds* and *New Musical Express* became highly influential, guiding or misguiding the new youth culture towards or away from bands, based on their journalists' evaluations. The power of the music media should not be underestimated. Album and live reviews undoubtedly have a dramatic effect on both concert ticket and music sales. A percentage of albums have always been purchased purely on impulse with the decision frequently based on a positive review in the music press. This is probably even more widespread today, considering the phenomenal number of album releases each month and the limited radio play that heavy metal actually receives. The music press has become increasingly important, often pontificating on what they consider to be in vogue, old hat, hip, banal or radical.

However, bands deigned unfashionable by the media, have consistently scored impressive chart placings and album sales. Grand Funk Railroad, Mountain and Iron Butterfly prove this beyond any shadow of a doubt. Likewise, artists that have been excessively hyped have not always met with success; early cases in point being the MC5 and the Stooges.

1970 saw the beginning of real exponential growth in the rock industry. The boundaries between blues-rock, psychedelic rock, hard-rock, heavy rock, adult-oriented-rock and progressive rock became increasingly blurred as total musical freedom became a reality. Innovation, improvisation and a more sympathetic audience allowed artists to fully explore and experiment with a myriad of styles and influences. Some of the key artists that emerged at this time included High Tide, Black Cat Bones, Black Sabbath, Black Widow, Uriah Heep, UFO and Blue Oyster Cult. Technical improvements, which allowed greater amplification, cleaner sound and greater flexibility paralleled this stylistic diversification. Monster drum kits became commonplace, with multi tom-toms and snares, dual bass drums and every conceivable arrangement of gongs, cymbals and cowbells. Guitarists now had the option of whole banks of effects pedals, while the use of ever more versatile keyboards to augment the basic sound became increasingly common.

Black Sabbath, Blue Oyster Cult and Black Widow were the pioneers of the 'satanic' or 'black metal' genre. They drew on the occult, witchcraft and Satanism for their prime source of inspiration. The music was characterized by doom-laden lyrics, heavy duty bass-lines and a keen sense of atmospherics. Black Sabbath's eponymously titled debut and Black Widow's *Sacrifice* opened up a whole new concept in rock music.

Uriah Heep and UFO have become British institutions over the past two decades, after starting out under rather inauspicious circumstances. The former have always suffered at the hands of the press, but their 1970 debut *'Very 'Eavy, Very 'Umble'* represents a milestone in heavy metal. The dense guitar-keyboard interplay of Mick Box and Ken Hensley along with David Byron's high-pitched vocal whine gave the band a unique identity. The US rock critic who stated that 'if this group makes it, I'll have to commit suicide' provided probably the most infamous quote in the annals of heavy metal. UFO started out as psychedelic space-rock/boogie specialists but later developed a more mature and dynamic, blues-based approach to hard rock.

The Beck, Clapton and Hendrix-style guitar heroes were soon superseded by a new breed of axemen. Mick Box, Tony Iommi, Michael Schenker, Jimmy Page and Ritchie Blackmore all played their part in taking the guitar as a virtuoso instrument into higher and ever-more experimental extremes of technical sophistication. In addition, bass, keyboards and drums became featured more prominently than ever and no longer simply assumed a supportive role to guitar and vocals. Suddenly there were bass, keyboard and drummer superstars. Roger Glover, Jon Lord and Iain Paice of Deep Purple, representing a single convenient example.

The early 70s, notably 1971-73 saw a growing acceptance by the populist media of hard-rock and heavy metal. Deep Purple, Black Sabbath, Free and Alice Cooper all scored significant hits in the UK singles charts and opened up the genre to a wider audience. From this point onwards, heavy metal ceased to be regarded as a minority interest, and was recognized as an important sub-genre of popular music.

Pop music also underwent a major transformation during the early 70s, with the arrival of glam-rock. This brought the two supposed extremes of 'disposable' pop and 'serious' rock closer together. Pioneered by bands such as Sweet, T. Rex, Gary Glitter, Slade and Suzi Quatro, the glam-rock movement has been highly influential in shaping the development of glam-metal through the last two decades. Three essential aspects transferred to the metal idiom, firstly the garish, over-the-top stage costumes that included platform boots, massive shoulder pads and make-up. Secondly, the music featured simple, often repetitive arrangements that were both anthemic and instantly memorable, with the lyrics focused on sex, rock 'n' roll, partying and law breaking! (The Sweet's 'Blockbuster', 'Ballroom Blitz' and 'Hellraiser', Slade's 'Mama Weer All Crazee Now', 'Gudbuy T'Jane and 'Cum On Feel The Noize' were just some examples that immediately spring to mind.) Finally, the overall sound and presentation were a radical departure from the 'softer' pop that had gone before. The guitars were cranked up to overload and the bands strutted their stuff with a new found confidence and provocatively sexual overtones. Hitting brash powerchords with legs akimbo and lips pouting became the norm, while the stage shows became ever more elaborate and featured monstrous lighting rigs, drum risers and every conceivable effect. Bands such as Queen, Kiss, Rush, Aerosmith, Ted Nugent, Judas Priest, Mott The Hoople, the Sensational Alex Harvey Band, New York Dolls, Thin Lizzy, David Bowie and AC/DC owe much to the glam-rock movement as a source for inspiration and their subsequent utilization and modification of the genre's basic structures into their own individual styles.

Kiss and Ted Nugent took glam-rock's garish image to new heights. Each of the four members of Kiss portrayed a cartoon-like character which necessitated elaborate face make-up and science fiction-like stage attire. Wearing giant platform boots, spiked and studded leather codpieces and even breathing fire, they specialized in formularized and predictable heavy metal glam-rock. Dumb choruses chanted *ad infinitum* over second hand riffs were the order of the day, but America's youth culture took the band to their hearts. The songs became instant teen anthems, with 'Love Gun', 'Rock 'N' Roll All Nite' and 'Hotter Than Hell' being indicative of the band's lyrical strengths. In 1984, 13 years after their inception and a decade after the release of their debut album, the band dropped the make-up and with it lost much of their appeal. Illusions were shattered as underneath the warpaint were a very pedestrian metal outfit. However, their impact on the metal scene remains, particularly image-wise, still paramount. Guitarist Ted Nugent, formerly of the Amboy Dukes, (a blues-based psychedelic outfit) went solo in 1974 with the declaration that 'If it's too loud, you're too old!' Armed only with his trusty Gibson guitar and a mountain of Marshall amps, Nugent quickly established his reputation as the undisputed 'Wildman Of Rock'. Claiming to hunt and kill all his own food with a bow and arrow, wearing just a loincloth on stage and his outspoken and rampaging sexist attitude made excellent copy. However, unlike many of his contemporaries, his outrageous macho claims were fully supported by musical muscle. Ted Nugent and *Free For All* from 1975 and 1976 respectively are two of the most intense, guitar-oriented heavy metal releases of all time. Nugent's style alternates between high-speed fretboard savagery and slower, brooding note-bending atmospherics. Queen and Rush represented, in embryonic form at least, the earliest manifestation of techno-metal. The emphasis was on complex time changes, multi-faceted harmonies and a high degree of musical dexterity. Queen's sound was characterized by the camp vocal style of Freddie Mercury and the unusual guitar sound of Brian May's homemade instrument. Between 1973 and 1979, the band released a string of classic hard rock records, that found favour with both the hard-rock and mainstream audiences. *Queen II* saw the band moving into symphonic rock territory and the following *Sheer Heart Attack* and *Night At The Opera* broke the band on an international level. The latter featured 'Bohemian Rhapsody' one of the most influential and successful rock single releases of all time. From the 80s onwards, the band's direction shifted notably away from heavy rock towards AOR. Their approach became more predictable, but the impact of their early work is still significant.

Rush, a Canadian power-trio were influenced mainly by Cream and Led Zeppelin. The band borrowed, then developed and experimented with their basic ideas, rather than simply duplicating them; Geddy Lee's high-pitched vocal whine, coupled with Alex Lifeson's improvisational guitar technique have become the band's trademarks. *2112*, their fourth album from 1976, was the one that established them on a world-wide scale. Side one is taken up entirely by the title cut, a thematic and conceptual piece based on 'Anthem', the short story by writer Ayn Rand.

Rush have remained highly influential and are highly revered by fellow musicians the world over for their dedication, finesse and musical virtuosity.

The Sensational Alex Harvey Band represent the more eccentric and unconventional side of the metal genre. Led by the manic Glaswegian Alex Harvey, they specialized in blues-based metallic boogie infused with a deranged, but sincere honesty and sense of fun. With guitarist Zal Cleminson, complete in sinister clown make-up, providing the perfect foil to the madman's vocals, they were undoubtedly one of the most original and unpredictable outfits of the mid-70s. *Next*, unleashed in 1973 was the band's finest work and featured the all-time classic metal anthems 'The Faith Healer' and 'Vambo Marble Eye'. In concert, the band set new standards for showmanship; their stage show included spraying graffiti on a polystyrene wall, which was later viciously demolished and thrown to the crowd. Harvey would sing with a pair of tights stuffed into his mouth, whilst cajoling the audience into a carefully controlled frenzy. S.A.H.B. were unique and they are still sadly missed .

Aerosmith, hailing from Boston, Massachusetts, USA metamorphosed the basic R&B and rock 'n' roll structures of bands such as the Faces and Rolling Stones into a new hard-line, infectious metallic form. Steven Tyler and Joe Perry on vocals and guitar respectively became the 'toxic twins' of the 70s as their penchant for drugs and alcohol abuse paralleled their meteoric rise to fame. *Toys In The Attic* and *Rocks*, released in 1975 and 1976, respectively were the albums that saw the band establish themselves on an international level. Instantly memorable hard-rock anthems infused with liberal amounts of blues, funk and soul became the band's trademarks. 'Dream On', from 1973's self-titled debut was re-released as a single in 1976 and became a world-wide hit. This is one of the first of the metal genre's 'power ballads' which realized its immense crossover potential.

AC/DC, formed in Sydney, Australia in 1974, concentrated on raunchy rock 'n' roll and metallized boogie. The band's image and persona were based primarily on Bon Scott's rasping, whiskey-soaked vocal style and Angus Young's powerful, bluesy guitar lines. They built a solid reputation as a live unit, with Young's manic schoolboy image as the major visual focus. Their impact on the development of heavy metal was highly significant.

The New York Dolls formed in 1972 are considered to represent the earliest manifestation of both the punk-rock and sleaze-rock movements. Managed by Malcolm McLaren (later, the manager of the Sex Pistols) the band built upon the ideas and styles of the Stooges, MC5 and Rolling Stones. Excess was the key; the band dressed as semi-transvestites and purveying a sex 'n' drugs 'n' rock 'n' roll image, their phenomenal influence was only acknowledged some time after their demise. The effeminate pouting of lead vocalist David Johansen, combined with the guttersnipe guitar style of the late Johnny Thunders has yet to be equalled in terms of maximum culture-shock overload! Many will never forget their appearance on BBC 2's *Old Grey Whistle Test*, playing 'Vietnamese Baby' and 'Looking For A Kiss' and the bemused and violent reaction of Bob Harris. They oozed attitude, suss and street cred' from every note. Their two-albums are highly flawed masterpieces and a rather unsatisfactory legacy for one of the most influential outfits of the 70s.

1976-79 represents the nadir for heavy metal and hard-rock as the punk movement exploded in every major city in the UK, and later to a lesser extent everywhere else. The punk ethos rejected the rock star idiom, put music back in the pubs and clubs and saw the dissolution of all barriers between fans and performers. Established heavy, progressive and hard-rock acts became instantly regarded as 'Boring Old Farts'. Suddenly, it was highly embarrassing to admit to owning albums by Uriah Heep, Rush, Led Zeppelin, Deep Purple and Pink Floyd. The punk, and later new-wave movement produced a number of bands that have since had a major influence on the subsequent regeneration of heavy metal in the 80s and 90s. The Sex Pistols, the Clash, the Damned, the Stranglers, the Heartbreakers, Television, Bauhaus, Siouxsie And The Banshees, the Dead Kennedys and the Jam are amongst the most important 'first generation' punk outfits. The new movement made excellent copy, with rock journalists, disc jockeys and record company A&R personnel going completely overboard to promote its growth and long-term success. Sounds and later NME in particular completely re-directed their focus away from mainstream rock and concentrated instead on the new, revolutionary and shocking but highly saleable youth-culture phenomenon. At the same time a plethora of local fanzines appeared that covered in detail the local punk and new wave scenes that were erupting in Britain's and America's major cities.

Highly influential and much respected BBC Radio 1 disc jockey John Peel, was also instrumental in the decline of mid-70s metal and its subsequent replacement by punk. Peel openly rejected his previous allegiance to the music of Little Feat, the Faces and Pink Floyd. Suddenly, the main outlet on popular radio for rock music was dominated by shambolic, energetic and often amateurish punk bands. Peel's new heroes became the Undertones, the Fall, the Damned and Siouxsie And the Banshees. The main shift in musical emphasis was shorter songs, a reduction in self-indulgent solos and a lyrical slant that concentrated on contemporary issues such as unemployment, politics, poverty, police brutality and inner city decay. As the movement gained momentum and record companies realized the massive commercial potential of punk, their A & R personnel became like a pack of rabid dogs, driven on by the lure of a quick buck. Never in the history of recorded music, have so many bands been signed to record companies in such a short space of time. Inevitably, the result was a dilution in quality. Within two years the movement was running out of steam and record companies became far more conservative with their cheque books.

Punk and new wave have had a profound influence on the development of rock music ever since. Ironically, since punk's decline there has been an ever growing realization that the punk and metal genres are fundamentally very similar and inextricably linked. The subject matter of many of the songs has much in common, notably anti-establishment sentiments and is a vehicle to vent teenage/adolescent angst and frustrations. The music in both instances is dense, aggressive and loud with highly repetitive chord sequences. In the live-setting, performers concentrate on flamboyant and outrageous stage shows; leather, studs, chains and make-up being a common denominator. Both movements have invoked the wrath of the moral majority. Punk and metal have also both created fanatical fan-based sub cultures, each with their own particular code of ethics and accepted standards of dress and behaviour. Since 1979, the arbitrary boundaries separating these two supposedly distinct musical styles have become increasingly blurred with the subsequent development of hard-core, thrash, industrial, funk-metal, grindcore and indie-metal sub-genres.

The most obvious differences between punk and metal were in the musicians' technical abilities. The punk bands were often amateurish and inexperienced both in the studio and on the stage. However, as time progressed, things began to improve. Consider, for example the later sophistication of Public Image Limited, the Clash, the Stranglers or the Jam! The divide, if one actually exists between punk and metal, is bridged by outfits such as Motorhead, the Ramones, Anti-Nowhere League and the Cult.

The effect of punk was less marked in the USA and bands such as Foghat, Boston, Foreigner, Yes and Z.Z. Top continued to enjoy high levels of commercial success during the late 70s. Nevertheless the punk movement had a cathartic effect on the next generation of rock groups, who adopted a policy of shorter, more direct songs and guitar solos. Van Halen, who exploded onto the US scene in 1978 can be regarded as perhaps the archetypal exponents of this new direction. With the dual focus of flamboyant vocalist David Lee Roth and guitar virtuoso Eddie Van Halen, they single-handedly, re-wrote the heavy metal rule-book virtually overnight. This more economic and powerful style was also clearly manifest in the approach adopted by the new bands to emerge in the UK between 1979 and 1981. Collectively, this is referred to as the New Wave Of British Heavy Metal (NWOBHM). It combines elements of both the punk movement (brevity, attitude and energy) and early 70s heavy rock (technical ability, melody and professionalism). The term itself implies a re-birth, regeneration and renaissance of an earlier musical form that had apparently become extinct. This is far from the case, the music of Black Sabbath, Deep Purple, Rush, Led Zeppelin and Uriah Heep had simply become unfashionable and driven underground once more as the punk movement became fully established. It is also misleading in that the term suggests that the movement was purely revivalist.

A vast number of new outfits appeared, but only a small percentage were actually signed up by record companies; far too many labels had had their fingers burnt during the punk rock explosion and were now extremely cautious in signing new talent. This resulted in a large number of excellent outfits never actually making it on to vinyl. However, bands such as Iron Maiden, Saxon, Def Leppard, Demon, Venom, Raven, Angelwitch, Diamond Head, Tygers Of Pan Tang, Praying Mantis and Samson did overcome record company apathy to make a significant and long-lasting impact. Rather like the first 'British Invasion' of 1964, the

NWOBHM acted as a catalyst for parallel musical developments in the USA, Sweden, Holland, Australia, Germany, Brazil and Japan.

Iron Maiden, Def Leppard and Saxon epitomized the spirit of the NWOBHM and are undoubtedly the three most successful outfits to emerge from it. They combined a heavy-duty, dual-guitar metallic onslaught with instantly memorable hooks, bridges and choruses. Since their inception, both Def Leppard and Iron Maiden have honed this style and have been fully integrated into the mainstream pop-rock market. However, this has been achieved without the sacrifice of artistic integrity and little commercial compromise. By contrast, Saxon have remained faithful to the original sound of NWOBHM despite its limitations.

Angelwitch, Venom and Raven represented the more extreme end of the NWOBHM movement: high-speed metal punctuated by vitriolic guitar bursts and numerous references to the occult. Although, only achieving modest record sales, their impact has been significant and far reaching; later developments in death-metal, black metal, thrash-metal and grindcore are attributable to these origins.

Diamond Head were probably the most innovative band of the entire NWOBHM movement, but surprisingly have only been acknowledged as such, over a decade later. Diamond Head, to quote *Sounds* in 1980 'have more riffs in one song than Black Sabbath have in an entire album'. Carefully executed time-changes, dynamic arrangements and a soulful screecher in Sean Tyler as vocalist made them a unique proposition. Mid to late 80s outfits such as Metallica, Queensryche and Megadeth, cite Diamond Head as a major influence.

At the melodic end of the NWOBHM spectrum were bands such as Magnum and Demon. Utilizing keyboards, they expanded the basic NWOBHM approach with atmospheric, grandiose and at times almost symphonic embellishments. Magnum eventually achieved recognition in the mid-80s with the album *On A Storyteller's Night*, but Demon have remained virtually unknown. Today, Demon are still the prime exponents of underground melodic metal; regularly releasing quality albums such as *The Plague, Breakout* and *Taking The World By Storm*.

The NWOBHM also heralded a growth in the number of female metal outfits. Girlschool, Lita Ford, Joan Jett and Rock Goddess all pedalled pop-rock-metal crossover material, but found it difficult to compete with their male counterparts on a creative level. Girlschool and Rock Goddess deliberately played down the sexual angle and for this, achieved a degree of respect and credibility. However, they were unable to develop musically. Lita Ford and Joan Jett, both ex-Runaways used a sexually provocative style coupled with songs penned primarily by writers outside their bands. They achieved considerable commercial success, but lost some of their original heavy metal following along the way.

1 August 1981 was an important landmark in heavy metal, with the birth of MTV, the 24-hour television music channel. This revolutionized the record industry. Videos were watched by millions of fans daily and they soon began to take effect on record sales. Heavy metal videos allowed the realization and visualization of the music's violent, exciting, sexual, mystical and rebellious imagery. Videos ranged between standard concert performances and concept affairs that elucidated the lyrical content of the songs. This soon resulted in a rapid growth in the number of metal acts entering both the US and UK singles charts, with AC/DC, Van Halen, Def Leppard, Journey, Saxon and Quiet Riot all scoring sizeable hits.

The NWOBHM subsequently acted as a springboard for metal to diversify into a myriad of new styles over the next decade and beyond. Thrash, techno-metal, death metal, grindcore, Christian metal, funk metal, power metal, doom metal and sleaze metal sub-genres either directly or indirectly owe much to the movement as a prime source of inspiration. In the USA, Los Angeles became the centre for new musical developments during the early 80s, with bands such as Motley Crue, W.A.S.P. and Quiet Riot representing the American answer to the NWOBHM.

Thrash-metal was the logical progression from punk in many ways. It combined the energy, aggression and attitude of punk with the technical and musical sophistication of the NWOBHM. Bands such as Blitzkrieg, Raven and Angelwitch were the true pioneers of the genre, but achieved minimal commercial success. Their basic approach was utilized by Metallica, Megadeth, Anthrax and Slayer, who simply amplified, speeded up and improved technically upon this formative style. Thrash involved playing very fast and executing a myriad of complex instrumental time-changes, while the vocals screamed venomously, and at times unintelligibly. These bands progressed rapidly and soon transformed their initial approach into a style that was still uncompromising, aggressive and challenging, but had much wider commercial appeal. This was achieved by introducing a variation of pace, audible, thought-provoking lyrics and innovative production techniques. Suddenly, an added depth and dynamism was apparent in their music, which served to increase their fan-base. Metallica's multi-platinum, self-titled 1991 album represents concrete evidence of the gradual mass acceptance of what was initially considered an obtuse musical style.

Death metal and grindcore represent the extreme, yet logical outposts of the thrash metal sub-culture. The bands are obsessed with the glorification of death, torture, violence, mutilation and putrefaction while the musical backdrop is nothing short of a sonic blur. The songs are incredibly brief, ranging from just a few seconds up to several minutes. The lyrics are generally indecipherable, comprising little more than guttural howls. Napalm Death, Carcass, Obituary and Death are the leading exponents of this sub-genre and have a large and loyal underground following. With enlarged recording budgets, greater experience and a growing musical maturity, it

seems not unreasonable to assume that this at present totally extreme approach will gradually become more integrated into mainstream metal, as thrash did before it.

Faith No More, the Red Hot Chili Peppers, Murdered and the Electric Boys incorporated funk influences into the basic thrash metal formula, to create the sub-genre funk metal. Queensryche and Savatage developed the technical aspect of thrash and concentrated on ambitious concept albums, which resulted in the techno metal moniker.

Guns N'Roses, formed in Los Angeles during 1985 combined elements of punk, thrash and 70s rock with a flamboyant and provocative stage show that was to have a far reaching effect on the development of heavy metal. Oozing attitude, sincerity and aggression, they transcended all metal genre boundaries to become one of the most influential outfits in the development late 80s/early 90s metal.

Thrash-metal also produced a new breed of lead guitarists. They are comically referred to as Widdly-Widdly or less often as New-Age Guitar Gods. Their style is characterized by high-speed melodic lead work and represents the further development of an approach first exemplified by Alvin Lee of Ten Years After. This resulted in a plethora of all-instrumental album releases during the late 80s, with Joe Satriani, Vinnie Moore, Yngwie Malmsteen, Steve Vai and Tony Macalpine being the most innovative exponents.

Kings X and the Galactic Cowboys built on the ideals of the thrash movement, but fused together a whole gamut of styles (pop, rock, blues, funk, thrash, country, R&B and metal), that defied simple pigeon-holing. The result was a form of rock music that ascended to a higher technical, musical and artistic plane. This is sometimes referred to, for want of a more relevant and applicable term, as art rock.

1988-89 saw the explosion of another musical initiative in the UK. It has been referred to as the NWOBHM re-visited, because the bands incorporate influences in common with the original NWOBHM, plus the technical and musical developments that have occurred since. Spearheading the movement are the Almighty, Little Angels, Thunder, the Quireboys, Wolfsbane, Kiss Of The Gypsy, the Wildhearts and Rattlesnake Kiss. At roughly the same time, the Seattle scene began to gain momentum in the USA. This produced a series of bands that played with the technical and aggressive approach of thrash, coupled with musical references that dated back to the garage rock scene of the late 60s. The influences of the Stooges, MC5 and the Velvet Underground are clearly evident in the recorded works of Nirvana, Soundgarden, Pearl Jam, Mother Love Bone and Temple Of The Dog.

Paralleling this was a growth in 'retro rock', a new sub-genre that was based entirely on updated and revitalized late 60s and early 70s rock music; transformed sonically, with the benefit of modern technology. Influences are predominantly British, with the Rolling Stones, the Faces, Cream, Status Quo and the Yardbirds most apparent. Georgia Satellites, Dogs D'Amour, Crybabys, Burning Tree, the Quireboys and the Black Crowes are typical of this approach.

The late 80s and early 90s also saw a revolutionary development in live shows. With the gradual widespread acceptance of cordless, transistorized equipment, performers enjoyed a greater freedom on stage than ever before. Mixing desks, amplifiers, PA systems and lighting rigs had become smaller, more powerful, reliable and flexible; this in turn meant that concerts became more professional, inventive and sonically coherent than had been possible before. Def Leppard performed 'In The Round' with a rotating stage situated in the centre of auditoriums; thus facilitating excellent viewing for the majority of the audience. The most prestigious concert appearance remains the Castle Donington 'Monsters Of Rock' headline spot, the yearly heavy metal one day festival that was inaugurated in 1980 when Rainbow were the main attraction.

Heavy metal has never been in a healthier state; it has never enjoyed such widespread acceptance and popularity as it has during the late 80s and early 90s. Its fan-base continues to increase as successive new generations of youths are added yearly to the long-standing followers. Concert audiences as well as metal performers now comprise three or even four generations, with ages commonly ranging from 10 or 12 to 50 and beyond. Metal can no longer be regarded as music for spotty adolescents and functioning simply as an outlet for their teenage fantasies and frustrations. Initially, most metal fans probably discovered metal in their teens, but have since matured and refined their tastes, in parallel to the musical progression and diversification that has also taken place.

There are no longer class, age, sex or occupational boundaries that isolate heavy metal in the community. Although once predominantly working class, male and adolescent, the movement has gradually branched outwards. The code of dress is no longer paramount; long hair, leather, studs, tattoos and motorbikes are now optional. It is not unusual to observe be-suited businessmen, smartly dressed career women or short-haired, cleanly shaven youths perusing the metal racks in the local record stores. Heavy metal has gradually come of age over the last quarter of a century; it has transcended, infiltrated and incorporated all musical styles to some degree, including classical, jazz, blues, rock, pop, folk and funk. To some extent, the original meaning of the term is now obsolete, although its use as a cliché by the popular media is still often in a derogatory sense. The future of heavy metal offers much promise. There will be a continued acceptance of it as a major musical form and copies of the latest Metallica, Guns N'Roses, Slayer and Def Leppard albums will no doubt be filed carefully alongside those from Dire Straits, the Beatles, Elvis Presley and Frank Sinatra.

Artistic creativity and technical innovation continue apace, and with them the potential for new and exciting musical developments. The growth and diversification of metal has proceeded at an expansive rate over the past 25 years and there is no evidence to suggest that is slowing down.

HEAVY METAL – A GLOSSARY OF TERMS

AOR

Adult-Orientated Rock, Album-Orientated Rock or Album-Orientated Radio? A misleading term for music targeted at a mature, rather than juvenile audience. AOR often encompasses high-pitched, note-perfect vocal harmonies, lightweight guitar work and use of - keyboards. Gimmicks and image are minimal, with the emphasis on a high level of musical dexterity. Arrangement and production techniques are sophisticated. Examples: the Babys, Boston, Kansas, REO Speedwagon, Toto.

ART-ROCK

A term applied to bands that draw their inspiration from important literary or artistic sources. Their ideas and perceptions are frequently explored through complex musical arrangements and thought-provoking lyrics. Examples: Can, Deaf School, Jane's Addiction, Kings X, Last Crack, Warrior Soul.

AVANT-GARDE

Experimental and innovative bands that specialize in the *ad hoc* juxtaposition of seemingly incompatible sub-structures within their songs. They often include highly improvised arrangements and represent one of the most adventurous and challenging outposts of the metal genre. Examples: Celtic Frost, Golgotha, Gong, Henry Cow, Ozric Tentacles.

BLACK METAL

This applies to all bands who use the occult, black magic, Satan, or witchcraft as their prime source of reference or inspiration. Originated during the early 70s as satanic metal, the term was reincarnated with the New Wave Of British Heavy Metal movement in 1979. Now recognized as a sub-genre of speed-metal, in which the songs are predominantly very fast. Many early 80s releases typifying the style were poorly produced. Examples: Angelwitch, Black Widow, Blitzkrieg, Satan, Venom.

BLUES-ROCK

A blanket term for all artists that draw inspiration from blues masters such as John Mayall, B.B. King, Eric Clapton and Jeff Beck. Heavy metal developed as a natural progression from these influences. Further diversification and technical innovation led to the numerous styles that make up the genre today. Examples: Bad Company, Spooky Tooth, Free, Led Zeppelin.

BOOGIE

Simplistic three-chord arrangements form the foundation of the songs. Frequently based on rock 'n' roll or blues riffs, the basic structure is repeated many times, with a lead guitar break in the middle to break the monotony. Often sub-four minute compositions with limited lyrical flair. Sex, drugs and partying are the main source of inspiration. The term was originally derived from the jazz-based boogie-woogie, which refers to a style of piano playing that uses a basic structure of eight-to-the-bar. Examples: AC/DC, Foghat, Spider, Status Quo.

THE BRITISH INVASION

Early exponents of hard-rock, that frequently used two guitarists and a revolutionary, much more abrasive sound. During the mid-60s, a long line of British groups went to the USA and made a considerable impact on the music scene. Hence the term British Invasion. Examples: the Animals, the Kinks, the Rolling Stones, the Who.

CHRISTIAN METAL

The antithesis of Black Metal. As the name implies, the bands spread the Christian message through the proselytizing lyrical content of their songs. Musically, they are characterized by high-pitched vocals, predictable arrangements and an overtly commercial sound. Examples: Barren Cross, Blood Good, Stryper,

CONCEPTUALIZED ROCK/METAL

A label applied to artists that write albums around a central theme or story. Usually complex, both lyrically and musically, the result is that the album as a whole, is usually of greater value, impact or significance, than the sum of its component parts. Examples: Robert Calvert, Genesis, Queensryche, Savatage, Yes.

CROSSOVER

A term applied to any band that incorporates two or more musical sub-genres within their compositions. This increases the chances of commercial success as the potential audience is likely to be double, compared to a more rigidly stylized approach. For example pop-metal and funk-metal. Examples: Bryan Adams, Faith No More, Nirvana.

DEATH METAL

An extreme form of thrash, where the bands are obsessed with the glorification of death, torture, violence, mutilation and putrefaction. Chaotic, high-speed arrangements, complete with gurgling-sewer style vocals. Examples: Death, Obituary, Slayer.

DOOM METAL

One of the sub-genres that subsequently evolved from thrash. Instead of continuing to increase velocity, doom-metallers went in the opposite direction. This song construction was based on slow, brutal, pulsating riffs and aching powerchords. The songs lurch forward menacingly and owe much to the style of early Black Sabbath. Examples: Bathory, Candlemass, Mercyful Fate.

ELECTRONIC ROCK/METAL

A movement during the early to mid-70s, that saw a growth in the use of technical, electronic gadgets in rock music. Synthesizers, with every conceivable range of special effects became the norm. Often, compositions comprised long instrumental passages consisting of little more than electronic hums, buzzes or squeals. Minimalist, *avant garde* and frequently German in origin. Examples: Can, Tangerine Dream, Trace.

EURO-ROCK

A blanket term applied to all commercially minded rock outfits from continental Europe. The vast majority originate from Germany, Sweden, Holland and Denmark. They frequently struggle with English lyrics and model themselves on established British or American bands. Examples: Europe, Golden Earring, Helloween, Scorpions

FOLK-ROCK/METAL

An unlikely crossover style which fuses two seemingly, very strange bed fellows! Folk-like arrangements are transformed using the full range of metal armoury and are also augmented by the use of flute, violin, mandolin and bassoon. Examples: Gentle Giant, Gryphon, Horslips, Jethro Tull, Skyclad.

FUNK-METAL

This crossover style was a growth area during the late 80s and saw the emergence of a number of major new talents. The ball started rolling with Run DMC's link-up with Aerosmith for 'Walk This Way' in 1986. It is difficult to decide whether funk was metallized or metal was funked up. Examples: Faith No More, Red Hot Chilli Peppers, Dan Reed Network

GARAGE ROCK/GRUNGE ROCK

A term first applied to American bands in the late 60s. It was used to describe the lack of technical and musical sophistication in their sound. Aggression, energy and enthusiasm are the key; a rough and ragged approach is dominated by semi-distorted guitar work. Cited as a major influence on the punk movement and also more contemporary outfits such as Nirvana, Pearl Jam and Soundgarden. Examples: Iggy And The Stooges, MC5, Velvet Underground.

GLAM-ROCK/GLAM-METAL

The origins of glam-rock date back to the early 70s, when bands such as Slade, T.Rex, Gary Glitter and the Sweet exploded onto the scene. Playing turbo-charged pop-rock, they wore eye-liner, lipstick, platform boots and outrageous stage clothes. The music often had sexual overtones, a streetwise image and was characterized by repeated, but highly infectious choruses. Since then, this basic style has been transmogrified by successive generations of rock bands into a harder and more powerful form. Examples: Hanoi Rocks, New York Dolls, Poison, Motley Crue.

GOTHIC ROCK/GOTH-METAL

A spin-off genre from punk-rock. The bands initially featured ashen-faced personnel draped in black cloaks, and employing ghostly make-up. The songs frequently had spiritual, sexual or religious overtones. Musically downbeat, sombre and serious, performances were nevertheless full of atmosphere and brooding passion. Examples: The Cult (formative years), Fields Of The Nephilim, the Mission, Sisters Of Mercy.

GREBO-ROCK/GREBO-METAL/ BIKER ROCK

This musical genre was closely associated with bikers and Hells Angels. Many of the songs pay homage to burning down the highway on Harley Davidsons and courting confrontation with the law. Decked out in leather, chains, tattoos and covered in oil, they epitomize the 'bad-boy' rock 'n' roll attitude. The songs are characterized by a raunchy, up-front guitar-style and powerful vocals. Examples: Circus Of Power, Motorhead, Steppenwolf.

GRINDCORE

The most extreme form of heavy metal, which has resulted from the amalgam of thrash, hard-core and punk influences. Songs typically last from just a few seconds up to several minutes and are often lyrically astute. However, the high-speed blur of the delivery renders the sentiments almost unintelligible. Musically, it sounds like somebody emptying the contents of their stomach over the microphone with a razor blades in the food processor-style backbeat. Examples: Carcass,

the Electro Hippies, Napalm Death.

GUITAR-ORIENTATED ROCK

During the mid to late 80s there was an astonishing revival in the use of the electric guitar as a virtuoso instrument. Numerous artists appeared on the scene, combining jazz, rock, blues, metal, classical and funk influences. Wholly instrumental albums became fashionable again, featuring complex time changes, high-speed fretwork and an innate sense of melody. Examples: Yngwie Malmsteen, Vinnie Moore, Joe Satriani, Steve Vai.

HARD-CORE

Hard-core represents the punk ethos taken to its ultimate extreme. Vitriolic and often neo-political vocal tirades cascade over one-dimensional, uptempo musical backdrops. During the 80s, this basic form has been revamped and metallized, increasing both the genre's popularity and credibility. Examples: D.O.A., Dead Kennedys, the Hard Ons, the Stupids.

HARD ROCK

A generalized term applied to differentiate between the softer pop records of the 60s and the less commercial music that began to develop with the emergence of bands such as Blue Cheer, Cream and the MC5. Hard rock incorporates compositions much longer than the three-minute single format and often features instrumental solo spots. The music is less disposable, but more aggressive and technically demanding than the pop music that went before. Most hard rock represents a fusion of blues, pop and rock 'n' roll influences. Examples: AC/DC, the Faces, Montrose, the Who.

HEAVY METAL/HEAVY ROCK

This is now a meaningless blanket term which covers all the sub-genres listed in this article. Originally, it was applied to a section of the hard rock genre that specialized in long, often complex compositions and displayed a high level of musical dexterity. Heavy, as an adjective, was used to describe the sentiments and approach of the musicians involved. It was music to be taken seriously; the artists concentrated on albums rather than singles. Examples: Black Sabbath, Deep Purple, Led Zeppelin, Uriah Heep.

HEAVY METAL ROCK 'N' ROLL

Music with a structure and sentiment based on the ethos of the late 50s and early 60s. Primarily, the songs are rebel anthems souped-up with modern technology for greater impact. Four-minute outbursts of energy written from a brief of the blues and rock 'n' roll. Examples: AC/DC, Georgia Satellites, Status Quo.

INDIE ROCK/METAL

As the Indie movement grew out of punk, it continued to diversify and began to include hard rock, garage-rock and metal elements by the end of the late 80s. A new crossover style was born and the sentiments of the indie ethos were transformed into a more potent style by the addition of metallic power and aggression. Examples: Pearl Jam, Manic Street Preachers, Nirvana, Soundgarden

INDUSTRIAL ROCK/METAL

A fusion of new wave, metal and *avant garde* influences. Often minimalist in approach, industrial metal is cold, intense and thought-provoking. Offbeat song structures are the battleground between lyrical turmoil and off-the-wall instrumentation. Examples: Test Department, Treponem Pal.

JAZZ-ROCK METAL

As the name implies, this is the integration of jazz-style arrangements and nuances within a hard rock framework. Compositions are often long and feature numerous and occasionally self-indulgent instrumental solo spots. In addition, the sound is filled out by the inclusion of additional string, brass and keyboard instruments. Examples: Brand X, the Fire Merchants, the Mahivishnu Orchestra, Baker-Gurvitz Army.

NEO-CLASSICAL ROCK/METAL

The fusion of rock, metal and classical styles. This frequently involves the utilization of classical structures within a hard rock framework. A high level of virtuosity is displayed and the classical input is usually via the electric guitar. Examples: the Great Kat, Golgotha, Yngwie Malmsteen.

NWOBHM (New Wave Of British Heavy Metal)

This acronym was given to the re-generation of hard rock and heavy metal in 1979-81, following the decline of punk. Characterized by a twin guitar approach and generally uptempo numbers, the music drew inspiration from the 'first wave' of heavy rock/metal that included Judas Priest, Deep Purple and Black Sabbath. From this new base, the movement exploded and diversified into the plethora of sub-genres. Examples: Diamond Head, Iron Maiden, Def Leppard, Saxon.

POMP ROCK

A term applied to sophisticated and technically complex rock music, with dynamic arrangements and production techniques. The genre frequently features long, esoteric compositions with classical influences. A high level of musicianship, note-perfect vocal harmonies and virtuoso instrumental passages are vital components of this style. Examples: Queen, Kansas, Journey, Magnum, Marillion, Styx,

POP-ROCK/METAL

A crossover style that fuses the commercial concerns of pop, with the aggressive delivery of rock. Songs are sub-four minute blasts of energy, featuring an infectious chorus and economical guitar break. Examples: Bon Jovi, Europe, Status Quo, Whitesnake.

POWER-METAL

A turbo-charged version of hard rock. As technical innovations during the 80s allowed great improvements in both sound quality and range, bands became equipped with a greater variety of sonic armoury than ever before. Many of the bands given the power-metal monicker were trios, because of the amazing range of sounds produced from what might appear a restrictive line-up. Examples: the Almighty, Drive, the Rods, Tesla.

PSYCHEDELIA

A term applied to late 60s/early 70s bands which derived their inspiration from hallucinogenic substances. Psychedelia is predominantly blues-based rock, but features extended and improvised compositions that have deep sexual, religious or spiritual significance. Bands often assumed strange esoteric names and attempted to convey the meaning of life through their colourful and experimental styles. The genre is highly collectable and is currently about to undergo a major re-issue schedule on CD. Examples: Syd Barrett and early Pink Floyd, the Electric Toilet, T.2., Van Der Graaf Generator.

PUNK

A youth-culture revolution that deconstructed the music industry in the UK, between 1976 and 1979. Brattish, street-level rock 'n' roll with anti-establishment sentiments spread like wild fire and many 70s supergroups were declared redundant virtually overnight. Sub-three minute blasts of vitriol and teenage angst were the order of the day. Without the punk movement, the development of thrash, goth, hard-core and grindcore would not have been possible. Examples: the Clash, the Damned, the Ramones, Sex Pistols.

PUB ROCK

A movement that preceded the punk-rock explosion during 1974-75. Music was back in the bars and clubs once more and the barriers between rock stars and their fans were already being dismantled. Most pub-rock outfits relied on various combinations of R&B, rock 'n' roll and the blues. Examples: Brinsley Schwarz, Ducks Deluxe, Dr. Feelgood, Kokomo.

PROGRESSIVE ROCK

Another term applied to the late 60s and early 70s acts that ventured into long, experimental pieces, often with deep meaningful lyrics. Characterized by complex, multi-faceted arrangements and state-of-the-art production techniques. The style frequently featured synthesizers, electronic gadgets and a dazzling array of special effects. Examples: Eloy, ELP, King Crimson, Yes.

RETRO-ROCK/METAL

A movement which gathered momentum during the late 80s and early 90s. The term applies to bands which derive their main source of inspiration from the music of the Rolling Stones, Mott The Hoople, the Faces, the Kinks, the Animals and the Yardbirds. The sound is totally revitalized with the benefit of modern equipment. Examples: The Black Crowes, the Quireboys, the Crybabys, Thunder.

R'N'B

Rhythm and Blues; a basic fusion of the blues with rock 'n' roll, that forms one of the main foundations on which heavy metal has been built. Simple structures first explored by the likes of Chuck Berry, Bo Diddley, Muddy Waters and B.B. King are still utilized and customized by contemporary outfits. Examples: The Black Crowes, Quireboys, the Rolling Stones.

ROCKABILLY

A form of rock 'n' roll with elements of hillbilly or country music. Many contemporary rock acts incorporate rockabilly with other influences such as blues, funk, jazz, punk or metal. Examples: the Cramps, Stray Cats, Matchbox, Polecats.

ROCK 'N' ROLL

Along with the blues, rock 'n' roll is one of the basic styles on which rock music and heavy metal is ultimately based. High-energy, up-tempo rebel anthems with an irresistible dance beat. Originated in the mid-50s with artists such as Bill Haley And His Comets, Chuck Berry, Little Richard and Jerry Lee Lewis. Examples: Dogs D'Amour,

Quireboys, the Rolling Stones, the Who.

SATANIC METAL

An alternative term for black metal. The occult, witchcraft and Satanism are the prime source of reference. Satanic bands developed during the early 70s and underwent a major revival with the NWOBHM movement a decade later. Examples: Black Sabbath, Black Widow, Blitzkrieg, Satan, Venom.

SHOCK-ROCK/HORROR-ROCK/ THEATRICAL METAL

This form of heavy metal incorporates a strong visual element to accompany the music. Pioneered by Screaming Jay Hawkins, 'horror-rock' was anglicized by Screaming Lord Sutch and later brought to commercial prominence in rock by Alice Cooper during the early to mid- 70s. Cooper combined horror-movie graphics with heavy metal rock 'n' roll. Their stage shows culminated with mock executions by hanging, guillotining or electrocution. Examples: Alice Cooper, GWAR, King Diamond, Lizzy Borden.

SLEAZE-ROCK/METAL/SCUZZ-ROCK

A bastardized form of glam-rock. A streetwise form of metallized rock 'n' roll that oozes attitude and a laid-back image from every note. The songs are frequently based on drinking and sexual exploits, with a high percentage of outfits originating from the Los Angeles bar and club scene. Examples: Faster Pussycat, Guns N'Roses, Skid Row, Shotgun Messiah.

SOUTHERN ROCK/METAL

A blues-based metallic boogie from the USA's Deep South. Whiskey soaked vocals and heavy duty guitar solos predominate, and are delivered with a rare passion, honesty and emotion. Examples: The Allman Brothers, Blackfoot, Black Oak Arkansas, Lynyrd Skynyrd, Molly Hatchet.

SPEED-METAL

This term can readily be applied to the music that provides the natural linkage between the NWOBHM movement, guitar-orientated rock and thrash. Less extreme than thrash, but featuring high-speed metallic rockers, often with a twin-lead guitar approach. Examples: Cacophony, Racer X, Rage.

SYMPHONIC ROCK/POMP ROCK

This term was applied to 70s supergroups that specialized in elaborate arrangements and production techniques. Compositions are often long and feature several sub-themes, strong vocal harmonies and classical structures. Orchestration and keyboards are typical and it represents pomp-rock taken to its ultimate conclusion. Examples: ELP, Genesis, Yes.

TECHNO-METAL

Highly sophisticated heavy metal, which is characterized by dynamic, state-of-the-art arrangements and virtuoso instrumental performances. Complex, but brilliantly executed time-changes help to build an atmospheric musical experience charged with tension and energy. Albums are frequently conceptual. Examples: Be-Bop Deluxe, Crimson Glory Queensryche, Savatage, Rush.

THRASH

Thrash is the bastard hybrid of punk and the NWOBHM movement. The energy, aggression and attitude of the former was combined with the musical accomplishment of the latter, to produce one of the most intense, disturbing and powerful forms of metal. High-speed arrangements, blistering solos and relentless rhythm work formed the basis of a completely new genre; this has subsequently undergone rapid diversification. Examples: Anthrax, Megadeth, Metallica, Testament.

TRASH ROCK/METAL

An ultimately disposable hybrid of glam, punk and rock 'n' roll. Streetwise attitude, with one hand on a bottle and one foot in the gutter is typical. Shambolic, chaotic, but with an underlying sense of fun and suss. Examples: Dogs D'Amour, New York Dolls,

Manitoba's Wild Kingdom, the Tubes.   69.

UNDERGROUND ROCK/METAL

This label applies to the plethora of little-known acts on the small-time bar and club circuit, that do not necessarily follow current or well-established musical styles. In many cases they are regarded as unfashionable, but remain loyal to their own beliefs. Frequently, underground acts break out into the mainstream and launch a whole new fashion or sub-genre of rock music. Marillion and Nirvana could be cited as having origins in the underground scene. Examples: Demon, Fudge Tunnel, New England, Pink Cream

WHITE METAL

An alternative term for Christian metal and as the name implies, the opposite of black metal. Acts are inspired by the work of Christ and pen songs that have moral, religious and spiritual messages. They typically verge on the pop-metal crossover approach and feature high-pitched vocals, slick arrangements and often evangelical lyrics. Examples: De Garmo And Key, Petra, Stryper.

Ian Kenyon, 1992

A

Aaronsrod

Angelo Jensen formed the heavy metal band Aaronsrod in 1984. Hailing from Hawaii, the unit comprised Brian Spalding (guitar), Neil Delaforce (vocals/guitar), Edward Dysarz (bass/vocals) and Gerard Gonsalves (drums). Jensen, originally from Italy, was brought up in a vaudeville family, who spent their time on the stage. Jensen found his debut at six years old an exhilarating experience and was hooked. *Illusions Kill*, released in 1986 was a solid statement, culling influences from Iron Maiden and Def Leppard to a more American sound, typical of Motley Crüe. Despite their promise, Aaronsrod have been unsuccessful; their only major break to date has been as support act to Ratt.
Album: *Illusions Kill* (1986).

Abattoir

Formed during 1983 in Los Angeles, California, USA, this heavy rock group was formed by Mel Sanchez (bass), Mark Caro (guitar) and Juan Garcia (guitar). With the later addition of 'Danger' Wayne (drums) and Rawl Preston (lead vocals), they first performed at the Los Angeles Troubadour. By the time of Abattoir's first studio recordings, Preston had been replaced by an ex-member of Sceptre, John Cyriis. One of these songs from the sessions 'Screams From The Grave', found its way on to the compilation, *Metal Massacre IV*. The result of this was a series of tours supporting some of the top metal acts such as W.A.S.P. and Metallica. However, by this time the personnel had undergone some changes with Danny Amaya replacing Wayne on the drumstool, and a certain amount of disenchantment with Abattoir's progression led to the departure of Cyriis and Garcia, who later re-emerged with their own band, Agent Steel. With the replacements of guitarist Danny Olivero and singer Steve Gaines, the group continued with the recording of their debut album, *Vicious Attack*, on the Roadrunner label. The group suffered yet more personnel changes when Gaines left to join Bloodlust. In his place, Mike Towers' contributions lent a more subdued sound manifested on their second album. By 1988, founder members Mel Sanchez had joined Evildead, signalling the demise of Abattoir.
Albums: *Vicious Attack* (1985), *The Only Safe Place* (1986).

AB/CB

Calling themselves AB/CB, a pun on the Australian group AC/DC, this Swedish rock group was formed by students, Braijan (vocals), Bengus (guitar), Nalcolm (guitar), Clim (bass) and Raijmon Left (drums). They came together in 1986 for a one-off performance at an end of college term party. The resemblance with AC/DC went beyond having a similar name to showing an aptitude for heavy, good-time rock. An astute record producer got them into the studio to record an album, which was subsequently released on the Doremi label. Although the album was well-received and the group obviously talented, fears of court action by the Australians scared off prospective overseas offers. Reluctant to go out under any other name, thus ruining the joke, the group disbanded within a year.
Album: *Victim Of Rock* (1986).

Accept

Accept

This German heavy rock quintet comprised Udo Dirkschneider on vocals, guitarists Jan Kommet and Wolf Hoffman, drummer Stefan Kaufmann and bassist Peter Baltes. Formed in 1977, their power metal sound was characterized by Dirkschneider's guttural howl and the warp speed drumming of Kaufmann. *Restless And Wild* from 1982 epitomized their blitzkrieg style. This had an undeniable influence on the thrash movement which developed during the late 80s. *Metal Heart* adopted a more melodic approach. Unhappy with this style, Dirkschneider quit and formed his own outfit Udo. A series of replacement vocalists came and went, including Rob Armitage, David Reese and Jim Stacey. Three lacklustre albums were released, which received little critical acclaim or commercial success. The band eventually disintegrated in 1989.
Albums: *Accept* (1979), *I'm A Rebel* (1980), *Breaker* (1981), *Restless And Wild* (1982), *Balls To The Wall* (1984), *Metal Heart* (1985), *Kalzoku-Ban* (1986),

Russian Roulette (1986), *Eat The Heat* (1989).

Accuser

This derivative German heavy metal quartet was influenced by Slayer and Metallica. The group was formed in 1986 by vocalist/bassist Eberhard Weyel and drummer Volker Borchert after leaving Breaker. Following a period of trial and error, they finally recruited guitarists Frank Thomas and Rene Schutz to record *The Conviction*. This was a powerful, if unoriginal, album, working to pre-set rules and guidelines that had been drawn up by others. *Experimental Errors*, a mini-album, followed two years later. *Who Dominates Who?* continued the rigidly formularized approach, and their European tour with Mucky Pup the same year was met largely with indifference.
Albums: *The Conviction* (1987), *Experimental Errors* (1988), *Who Dominates Who?* (1989).

AC/DC

This theatrical Australian hard rock band was formed in 1973 by Malcolm Young (b. 6 January 1953, Glasgow, Scotland; rhythm guitar) after the demise of his previous outfit, the Velvet Underground (no relation to the US group).

Young, whose elder brother George had already achieved stardom in Australia as a member of the Easybeats, also enlisted his younger brother Angus Young (b. 31 March 1959, Glasgow, Scotland; guitar). Their sister suggested that Angus wear his school uniform on stage, a gimmick that rapidly became a trademark. The two brothers made their debut appearance in a bar in Sydney, along with Dave Evans (vocals), Larry Van Knedt (bass) and Colin Burgess (drums). In 1974, the Young brothers and Evans moved to Melbourne, where Mark Evans (bass) and Phil Rudd (drums) joined the band. Another immigrant from the UK, Bon Scott (b. Ronald Scott, 9 July 1946, Kirriemuir, Scotland, d. 20 February 1980; vocals), graduated from being the band's chauffeur to becoming their vocalist when Dave Evans refused to go on stage one night. Scott had previously recorded – originally as a drummer – with two Australian pop bands, the Valentines and Fraternity. AC/DC's first two albums, *High Voltage* and *TNT*, were produced by George Young and his writing partner, former Easybeat, Harry Vanda. Neither of them was issued outside Australia, though Atlantic in Britain did issue a selection of material from both records under the title *High Voltage* in 1976 –

0

AC/DC; Angus Young

by which time bassist Mark Evans had been replaced by Cliff Williams. Once AC/DC began to tour outside Australia, the band quickly amassed a cult following, as much for the unashamed gimmickry of its live show as for its furious, frequently risque brand of hard rock. *Let There Be Rock* broke them as a chart act in the UK, but it was *Highway To Hell* in 1979 which established them as international stars. The band's first album with producer Mutt Lange, also proved to be their last with Bon Scott. On 20 February 1980, after a night of heavy drinking, he was left unconscious in a friend's car, and was later found to be dead, having choked on his own vomit. The coroner recorded a verdict of death by misadventure.

Scott's death threatened the band's future, but his replacement, former Geordie lead singer Brian Johnson (b. 5 October 1947, Newcastle, England), proved more than equal to the task. His first album with the band, *Back In Black*, reached number 1 in the UK and Australia, and spawned the hit single 'Rock 'n' Roll Ain't Noise Pollution'. 1981 saw the release of *For Those About To Rock*, plus the band's first headlining appearance at the Castle Donington festival and two Top 20 UK singles. After *Flick Of The Switch* in 1983, drummer Phil Rudd left the band, to be replaced by Simon Wright - who in turn departed to join Dio in 1990. His replacement was Chris Slade (ex-Firm and Gary Moore). In keeping with their superstar status, AC/DC maintained an increasingly relaxed schedule through the 80s, touring to support each carefully-spaced album release. *The Razor's Edge* in 1990 proved to be one of their most successful albums, producing a Top 20 UK hit, 'Thunderstruck'. With Brian Johnson long having buried the ghost of Bon Scott, the band shows no signs of varying its winning musical formula.

Albums: *High Voltage* (1974 - Australia only), *TNT* (1975 - Australia only), *High Voltage* (1976), *Dirty Deeds Done Dirt Cheap* (1976), *Let There Be Rock* (1977), *Powerage* (1978), *If You Want Blood* (1978), *Highway To Hell* (1979), *Back In Black* (1980), *For Those About To Rock* (1981), *Flick Of The Switch* (1983), *Fly On The Wall* (1985), *Who Made Who* (1986), *Blow Up Your Video* (1988), *The Razor's Edge* (1990).

Acid

This Belgian heavy metal band were formed in 1980, and have so far never received acclaim outside their own country; no record company has been prepared to release their material abroad. The band comprises Kate (vocals), Demon (guitar), Dizzy Lizzy (guitar), T-Bone (bass) and Anvill (drums). Their stylistic origins owe much to Previous Page, while their material is derivative

thrash-boogie reminiscent of Motorhead. They showed considerable enterprise and initiative by releasing the three albums on their own Giant label.

Albums: *Acid* (1983), *Maniac* (1983), *Engine Beast* (1985).

Acid Reign

Heavy metal band formed in Harrogate, Yorkshire, England in 198., The band's original line-up consisted of H (vocals), Kev (guitar), Gaz (guitar), Ian (bass) and Ramsey (drums). They wasted no time in recording a demo entitled 'Moshkinstein' which led to them being signed by the Music For Nations subsidiary label, Under One Flag. The band's debut release in 1988, a mini-album also entitled *Moshkinstein*, was well received, being a blend of Anthrax-style riffing with the band's own basic metal sound. The band became popular on the UK club circuit with their quirky stage antics and down-to-earth attitude.

The band's first full length album *The Fear*, released in 1989 is best described as thrash metal with humour. However, all was not well within the band's ranks and shortly after its release Gaz and Ian were replaced by Mac (ex-Holoslade bassist) and Adam (ex-Lord Crucifer guitarist). The band toured Britain extensively including support slots with Nuclear Assault and Exodus in Europe. They then re-recorded 'Humanoi' a track from the previous album, as well as putting out a cover version of Blondie's hit single 'Hanging On The Telephone'. Their second album, *Obnoxious* was a big musical departure, being much more mature. Unfortunately it was not as well received as previous releases and feeling disillusioned, following the departure of Adam and then Kev (now with Lawnmower Deth), the band announced their split early in 1991. As a postscript in the same year Under One Flag released a compilation album entitled *The Worst Of Acid Reign* made up of previously unreleased material, live and demo tracks.

Albums: *Moshkinstein* (1988), *The Fear* (1989), *Obnoxious* (1990). Compilation: *The Worst Of Acid Reign* (1991).

Acrophet

This heavy metal band hailed from Brookfield, Wisconsin, USA and was formed in 1986 by guitarist Dave Pellino. He was joined by Dave Bauman (vocals/bass), Todd Saike (guitar) and Jason Mooney (drums). Technically, they were a competent unit, but originality was not a prominent feature of this thrash metal band. Nevertheless, inspired by Anthrax, Slayer and Megadeth, they managed to release a self-produced demo within a year of formation, and by the autumn of 1988 released *Corrupt Minds*. This received some success and was followed by *Faded Glory* in April 1990. The album showed that Acrophet had progressed into a tighter outfit, but had not yet developed their songwriting capabilities.

Albums: *Corrupt Minds* (1988), *Faded Glory* (1990).

Adam Bomb

This pop-metal outfit was heavily influenced by Bon Jovi and Europe. Self-styled sex symbol cum vocalist Adam Brenner (ex-TKO) persuaded guitarist Jimmy Crespo (ex-Aerosmith), drummer Sandy Slavin (ex-Riot) and bassist Phil Feit to join forces and record *Fatal Attraction* in 1985. *Pure S.E.X.* emerged in 1990 to indifferent reviews. Much of it was leftover material from the first album and was highly derivative.

Albums: *Fatal Attraction* (1985), *Pure S.E.X.* (1990).

Adrenalin

This sophisticated AOR outfit, influenced by Styx, Foreigner and Journey, was put together by the brothers Romeo and Pastoria in 1984. The seven-piece band comprised Marc Gilbert (vocals), Flash (guitar), Michael Romeo (guitar), Jimmy Romeo (saxophone), Marc Pastoria (keyboards), Bruce Schafer (bass) and Brian Pastoria (drums). Adrenalin were signed by MCA and released two quality melodic rock albums. The title track of *Road Of The Gypsy* was included on the *Iron Eagle* film soundtrack. Success eluded the band and they were subsequently dropped by their label in 1987. That year also saw the departure of Gilbert and Flash, with ex-Grand Funk vocalist/guitarist Mark Farner stepping in as replacement. Grand Funk songs started to appear in their live set and the band eventually became known as Mark Farner And Adrenalin. Unable to secure a recording contract and attract media attention, Farner quit the following year, with Joey Hammody taking over soon after as the new vocalist.

Albums: *American Heart* (1985), *Road Of The Gypsy* (1986).

Aerosmith

One of the USA's most popular hard-rock acts, Aerosmith was formed in 1970 when vocalist Steven Tyler (b. Steven Victor Tallarico, 26 March 1948, New York, USA; vocals) joined Joe Perry (b. 10 September 1950, Boston, Massachusetts, USA; guitar) and Tom Hamilton (b. 31 December 1951, Colorado Springs, Colorado, USA; bass) in Chain Reaction, an aspiring New Hampshire-based group. Joey

Aerosmith

Kramer (b. 21 June 1950, New York, USA; drums) and Ray Tabano (guitar) completed the original line-up, but the latter was quickly replaced by Brad Whitford (b. 23 February 1952, Winchester, Massachusetts, USA). Their popularity throughout the Boston area led to a recording deal with Columbia/CBS Records, and in 1973 Aerosmith secured a minor chart place with their self-named debut album. Although its attendant single, 'Dream On', initially peaked at number 59, it became a Top 10 hit when reissued in 1976. *Get Your Wings* introduced a fruitful working relationship with producer Jack Douglas. Nationwide tours established the quintet as a major attraction, a position consolidated by the highly successful *Toys In The Attic*, which has sold in excess of six million copies. A fourth album, *Rocks*, achieved platinum status within months of its release. Aerosmith maintained their pre-eminent position with *Draw The Line* and the powerful *Live! Bootleg*, but despite popular acclaim, failed to gain the approbation of many critics who dubbed the group 'derivative' particularly of Led Zeppelin. Tyler's physical resemblance to Mick Jagger, and his foil-like relationship with guitarist Perry, also inspired comparisons with the Rolling Stones, with whom they shared musical reference points.

In 1978 Aerosmith undertook a US tour of smaller, more intimate venues in an attempt to decelerate their rigorous schedule. They appeared in the ill-fated film of *Sgt. Pepper's Lonely Hearts Club Band*, and although their rousing version of 'Come Together' reached the US Top 30, tension between Tyler and Perry proved irreconcilable. The guitarist left the group following the release of the disappointing *Night In The Ruts* and subsequently founded the Joe Perry Project. Jimmy Crespo joined Aerosmith in 1980, but the following year Brad Whitford left to pursue a new career with former Ted Nugent band member,

Derek St Holmes. Newcomer Rick Dufay debuted on *Rock In A Hard Place*, but this lacklustre set failed to capture the fire of the group's classic recordings.

Contact between the group and Perry and Whitford was re-established during a 1984 tour. Antagonisms were set aside, and the following year, the quintet's most enduring line-up was performing together again. *Done With Mirrors* was a tentative re-embarkation, after which Tyler and Perry underwent a successful rehabilitation programme to rid themselves of drug and alcohol dependencies, synonymous with the group's hedonistic lifestyle. In 1986 they accompanied rappers Run DMC on 'Walk This Way', an Aerosmith song from *Toys In The Attic* and a former US Top 10 entry in its own right. The collaboration was an international hit, rekindling interest in Aerosmith's career. *Permanent Vacation* became one of their best-selling albums, and the first to enter the UK chart, while the highly-acclaimed *Pump*, emphasized their revitalization. Feted by a new generation of acts, including Guns N' Roses, the quintet are now seen as elder statesmen, but recent recordings show them leading by example.

Albums: *Aerosmith* (1973), *Get Your Wings* (1974), *Toys In The Attic* (1975), *Rocks* (1976), *Draw The Line* (1977), *Live! Bootleg* (1978), *Night In The Ruts* (1979), *Rock In A Hard Place* (1982), *Done With Mirrors* (1985), *Permanent Vacation* (1987), *Pump* (1989). Compilations: *Greatest Hits* (1980), *Classics Live* (1986), *Anthology* (1988).

A Foot In Coldwater

This prolific rock band produced four albums during their five-year career. Canadian in origin, they comprised Alex Machin (vocals), Paul Naumann (guitar), Bob Horne (keyboards), Hugh Leggat (bass) and Danny Taylor (drums). Concentrating on a traditional approach to songwriting, their work was characterized by Machin's expressive vocals and Naumann's melodic guitar lines. Leggat went on to form the Rolling Stones-influenced Private Eye, and later a progressive outfit under his own surname.

Albums: *A Foot In Coldwater* (1972), *Second Foot In Coldwater* (1973), *All Around Us* (1974), *Breaking Through* (1977).

After Hours

This British heavy rock quartet was formed from the ashes of XS and Love Attack. Comprising John Francis (vocals), Tim Payne (guitar), Rick Young (keyboards), Martin Walls (bass) and Mark Addison (drums), they specialized in melodic pomp/AOR, but also had rough edges. *Take Off*, their debut, was an excellent collection of songs in the Foreigner/Whitesnake tradition.

Albums: *Take Off* (1988), *After Hours* (1989).

Aftermath

This heavy metal band hailed from Tucson, Arizona, USA. They were formed by vocalist Richard Shayka and guitarist Cliff Finney in 1984. Enlisting the services of John E. January (guitar), Joe Nutt (bass) and Rick Von Glahn (drums), they recorded a self-titled eight-track demo that was rejected by many major labels in the USA. However, newly-formed Dutch label Mushroom signed them in 1988. *Don't Cheer Me Up* materialized the same year; a derivative collection of melodic metal, with the odd anthemic number and power-ballad included.

Album: *Don't Cheer Me Up* (1988).

Agent

This Canadian heavy rock quintet was formed in Vancouver 1981, by the three-man nucleus of Bob Smart (guitar), Craig Zurba (keyboards) and Andre Kunkel (bass). After a series of short-lived line-ups, they stabilized with the addition of vocalist Rick Livingstone and drummer Dave Allen in 1983. They attracted the interest of Virgin Records after winning a 'Battle Of The Bands' style contest and were approached by ex-Doobie Brother, Jeff 'Skunk' Baxter to produce their debut album. Influenced by Foreigner, Styx, Kansas and Loverboy, their style was commercial although derivative.

Albums: *Agent* (1986).

Agent Steel

This heavy metal unit was formed in Los Angeles, California, USA and had been around in various guises since the early 80s. The most popular line-up consisted of John Cyris (vocals), Juan Garcia (guitar), Bernie Versye (guitar), Michael Zaputil (bass) and Chuck Profus (drums). Signing to Combat Records, the band released their debut *Skeptics Apocalypse* in 1985. It was well-received by both music press and the public. However, the group ran into difficulty with both their record label and with the internal band wrangles owing to Cyris's reputed eccentricity. With label problems resolved, the band released an EP entitled *Mad Locust Rising* and quickly followed this up with their finest recording, *Unstoppable Force*. This showed the band playing fast melodic thrash and gelling together much tighter than before. However they experienced further internal problems with Cyris wanting to relocate the band to Florida. As the rest of the group did not agree with this change in locale Cyris carried on with various musicians in his chosen new location but could never quite reach previous standards. Disillusioned with the music business, Cyris dissolved the group in 1988 and has since quit the music business.

Albums: *Skeptics Apocalypse* (1985), *Unstoppable Force* (1987).

Airrace

This British heavy rock quintet was formed in 1983 by vocalist Keith Murrell and guitarist Laurie Mansworth. Recruiting Jim Reid (bass), Jason Bonham (drums) and Toby Sadler (keyboards), they signed to Atlantic Records the same year. The band's most striking feature was the highly accomplished vocal style of Murrell. His powerful Lou Gramm-like warblings led to the obvious Foreigner comparisons, but in a positive rather than critical sense. Their Beau Hill-produced debut released in 1984 was an undiscovered classic of the melodic rock genre. The band split up soon after its release, with Murrell joining Mamas Boys and Jason Bonham forming Virginia Wolf, then later Bonham.

Album: *Shaft Of Light* (1984).

Alaska

This UK heavy rock unit was the phoenix that rose from the ashes of Bernie Marsden's S.O.S. Marsden was joined by Robert Hawthorn (vocals), Brian Badham (bass/piano), and John Marter (drums). The band produced symphonic rock with pomp and circumstance. Hawthorn's vocals contrasted subtly with Marsden's famous blues-influenced style. The band's first big break came in 1984, when they supported Manowar at the Headbanger's Ball in Holland. Sadly, after two albums Alaska disintegrated, with Marsden joining the ill-fated MGM, who split up before releasing any material. Alaska's 'Headlines' was used in a UK television commercial in 1988 for a new sports magazine. The song was issued as a single, but failed to make the charts.

Albums: *Heart Of The Storm* (1984), *The Pack* (1985).

Alcatrazz

This American outfit were heavy metal exponents in the Rainbow/Deep Purple tradition. Formed by ex-MSG and Rainbow vocalist Graham Bonnet in 1983, the initial line-up featured virtuoso guitarist Yngwie Malmsteen, ex-New England members Jimmy Waldo (keyboards) and Gary Shea (bass), plus former Alice Cooper drummer Jan Uvena. *No Parole From Rock 'n' Roll* was chest thumping hard-rock in the David Coverdale/Ronnie James Dio style, complete with

intricately textured and classically influenced guitar breaks. Steve Vai (ex-Zappa) replaced Malmsteen after a disappointing live album to record *Disturbing The Peace*. This was a disjointed affair comprising a mixture of heavy rock and instrumental showcase numbers. Vai joined David Lee Roth's band in 1986, with ex-Axis guitarist Danny Johnson taking over six-string duties. *Dangerous Games* followed but was poorly received, lacking both power and direction. The band split in 1987 with Johnson forming Private Life and Bonnet teaming up with guitarist Chris Impelliteri.

Albums: *No Parole From Rock 'n' Roll* (1984), *Live Sentence* (1984), *Disturbing The Peace* (1985), *Dangerous Games* (1986).

Alien

This melodic hard-rock quartet was formed in Sweden in 1986. Assimilating influences such as Survivor, Styx, Foreigner, Kansas and Journey, they delivered a highly polished, if rather derivative debut in 1988. Original vocalist Jim Gilhead was replaced by the ex-Madison frontman Peter Sandberg soon after the album was released. With a distinct lack of promotion from Virgin Records, they have made little impact outside their native Sweden.

Album: *Alien* (1988).

Airey, Don

Airey is a talented UK keyboards player, who has contributed to a wide range of bands and projects during the 70s and 80s. Unable to make the commitment, or perhaps unable to find the right musicians to work with, he has made short-lived appearances with Colosseum II, Rainbow, Ozzy Osbourne, Whitesnake, Black Sabbath, MSG, Alaska, Jethro Tull and Gary Moore. In 1986 he decided to set some time aside to work on a solo project. *K2* was an ambitious concept album centred on the mystique and dangers of climbing the second highest mountain in the world. With the help of Gary Moore, Cozy Powell and Colin Blunstone, the album came to life, but appealed more to the new-age music aficionados than to serious rock fans.

Album: *K2, Tales Of Triumph And Agony* (1986).

Airraid

This short-lived US quartet specialized in sophisticated and melodic symphonic rock. The band originated in 1980 and featured Arthur Offen (vocals/keyboards), Rick Hinkle (guitar), Tommy Walker (bass) and Rick Brown (drums). Their self-titled debut released in 1981 was strongly reminiscent of Styx and Journey. Technically, the

band were without fault, but they lacked the necessary spark of originality to make any real impact. Failing to attract media attention, they disbanded shortly after the album was released.
Album: *Airraid* (1981).

Alkatrazz

This group was formed in Maidstone, Kent, England in 1980 by vocalist Craig Stevens and guitarist Bob Jenner. Recruiting the services of Gary Bevan (bass) and Nick Parsons (drums), they signed to RCA Records as one of the hopefuls of the New Wave Of British Heavy Metal Movement. *Young Blood* featured hard-rock reminiscent of UFO. Unable to make a breakthrough with this, they switched to an Americanized AOR approach with *Radio 5*. This drive for commercial success also failed and RCA dropped them soon after the album was released.
Albums: *Young Blood* (1981), *Radio 5* (1982).

Alliance

This short-lived, American melodic rock quintet was formed in 1980 by the talented vocalist Mark Bucchare. With guitarist Pat Hand, keyboardist Mark Heckert, bassist Bradley Davidson and drummer David Pridemore completing the line-up, their music was characterized by note-perfect harmonies, razor-sharp arrangements and understated guitar work. Their self-titled debut however, lacked both the image and real direction necessary to elevate them above the plethora of other Styx/Kansas/Journey clones around at the time. Disillusioned by the lack of recognition and label support, they disbanded the following year.
Album: *Alliance* (1982).

Allied Forces

Formed in 1983, Allied Forces was a Dutch hard rock quintet, from the province of Brabant. Featuring Ronnie Gershwin (vocals), Marc Gershwin (guitar), Harold Cucken (guitar), Steven Highwood (bass) and Pete Van de Sluice (drums) they built up a solid reputation touring the European circuit as support for Anvil and TNT. Following a series of delays, *The Day After* was eventually released in 1987 on the German Flametrader label. Produced by ex-Vandenberg bassist Dick Kemper, they acknowledged a variety of influences that included Golden Earring, Scorpions and Europe, but without ever resorting to plagiarism. Highwood and Cucken quit in 1988 with Ferry Schmuter stepping in to take over four-string duties. The band then pursued a more melodic direction, but have yet to provide evidence of this on vinyl.
Album: *The Day After* (1987).

Allies

Allies were formed from the ashes of the religious pomp-rock outfit, the Sweet Comfort Band in 1983. Comprising Bob Carlisle (vocals/guitar), Randy Thomas (guitar, keyboards), Kenny Williams (keyboards, saxophone, vocals), Matthew Chapman (bass) and Jim Erickson (drums), their first two albums are fine examples of melodic Christian rock in a Kansas/Stryper vein. 1987's *Shoulder To Shoulder* saw the band diversifying their approach, with blues, funk and soul influences being given more prominence in their compositions. The album was a disappointment, heavily loaded with nondescript power-ballads. *Long Way To Paradise* tried unsuccessfully to recapture the ground lost by this change in style, but was let down by the material.
Albums: *Allies* (1984), *Virtues* (1985), *Shoulder To Shoulder* (1987), *Long Way To Paradise* (1987).

Almighty

This Scottish hard rock quartet was formed in 1988 by vocalist/guitarist Ricky Warwick (and husband of Vanessa, hostess of *Headbanger's Ball* on MTV), guitarist Tantrum, bassist Floyd London and drummer Stump Munroe. Along with Little Angels, Quireboys and the Dogs D'Amour, the Almighty spearheaded a revival in British rock during the late 80s, drawing their inspiration from bands such as the Cult, Ramones and Motorhead. Signing to Polydor the following year, they released *Blood, Fire And Love* to widespread critical acclaim. The title was changed from *Blood, Fire And Roses* to avoid any possible confusion with Guns N' Roses. This was swiftly followed by a mini-album, which captured the band at their electrifying best; performing live before a hyped-up crowd. The album included a stunning cover of Bachman Turner Overdrive's 'You Ain't Seen Nothin' Yet'. *Soul Destruction* emphasized the group's songwriting abilities. It spawned the UK Top 20 hit 'Free 'n' Easy' and gained them recognition throughout Europe.
Albums: *Blood, Fire and Love* (1989), *Blood, Fire and Love - Live* (1990), *Soul Destruction* (1991).

Alpha Centauri

This exceptionally talented but little-known Canadian heavy rock quintet was formed in 1976 by Kurt Smith (vocals/guitar) and Jesse Redmon (keyboards/vocals). With Garth Hannum (bass/vocals) and Randy Thompson completing the line-up, they specialized in highly dramatic grandiose arrangements, awash with keyboards, but punctuated in places by some fierce guitar work. Their self-titled debut was an undiscovered gem of the pomp-rock genre. Released as a

Anthrax

limited edition, it is still much sought-after by collectors.
Album: *Alpha Centauri* (1977).

Americade

This American hard rock quartet was put together by the De Marigny brothers in 1981. Vocalist P.J. and guitarist Gerard teamed up with ex-Rachel duo Nick Sadano (bass) and Walt Woodman III (drums). Sadano was replaced by Dave Spitz (brother of Dan, the Anthrax guitarist) before any material was recorded. They gained a reputation for covering Van Halen numbers at high-speed. They split in 1984, but Gerard De Marigny resurrected the name in 1989 with ex-Malice vocalist Mark Wcitz, bassist Greg O'Smith (ex-W.O.W.) and Paul Cammarata on drums.
Album: *American Metal* (1982).

Angelwitch

Angelwitch was one of the first rock groups to be associated with the New Wave Of British Heavy Metal movement which originated in 1980. The band, a power trio, put together by guitar virtuoso Kevin Heybourne, featured Kevin Riddles (bass) and Dave Dufort (drums). (Dufort's sister Denise,

occupied the same position in Girlschool.) Their self-titled debut album drew heavily on satanic and witchcraft imagery and combined this with doom-laden riffs and vitriolic guitar breaks. Their only chart success was with 'Sweet Danger' which reached number 75 in the UK chart for just one week in June 1980. Soon after the release of *Angelwitch* the band split up, but Heybourne retained the name and drafted in Dave Hogg and Pete Gordelier on drums and bass respectively, plus vocalist Dave Tattum. After two uninspiring albums they ground to a halt, but Heybourne resurrected the band in 1989 with drummer Spencer Holman and bassist Grant Dennis for a one-off album, recorded live in Los Angeles.
Albums: *Angelwitch* (1980), *Screaming And Bleeding* (1985), *Frontal Assault* (1986), *Doctor Phibes* (1986), *Screamin' Assault* (1988), *Live* (1990).

Anthem

This Japanese group, formed in 1981, specializes in cloning western rock music. The band has been through many personnel changes, with the current line-up comprising Elizo Sakamoto (vocals), Hiroya Fukada (guitar), Nuoto Ski Bata (bass) and Tahamasa Ohuchi (drums). Influenced by the style

and melodies of UFO, Thin Lizzy, Kiss and more recently Megadeth, they have produced a series of identikit rock albums. Their second album was produced by Chris Tsangarides (of Thin Lizzy fame) and was a major success in the Far East.
Albums: *Anthem* (1985), *Tightrope* (1986), *Bound To Break* (1987), *Gypsy Ways* (1988).

Anthrax

This New York-based thrash metal outfit came to the fore in 1982 with a line-up comprising Scott 'Not' Ian (rhythm guitar), Neil Turbin (vocals), Dan Spitz (lead guitar), Dan Lilker (bass) and Charlie Benante (drums). Managed by Johnny Z, head of the independent Megaforce Records, the quintet released *Fistful Of Metal* in 1984. Despite its tasteless sleeve, the album garnered fair reviews and was a small but steady seller. For a time Anthrax co-existed with an offshoot group, Stormtroopers Of Death (SOD), featuring Ian and Lilker. The informality of Anthrax was emphasized by the successive departures of Lilker and Turbin, who were rapidly replaced by Matt Fallon and Joey Belladonna, respectively. In 1985, this line-up issued an EP featuring a lightning-fast reworking of the Sex Pistols' 'God Save The Queen'. A contract with Island Records led to the release of *Spreading The Disease* the following year. During 1987, the group played extensive club gigs and worked with former Kiss and Whitesnake producer Eddie Kramer on *Among The Living*. The latter spawned two UK hit singles, 'I Am The Law' and 'Indians', a testimony to the commercial power of speed metal.
Albums: *Fistful Of Metal* (1984), *Spreading The Disease* (1986), *Among The Living* (1987), *State Of Euphoria* (1988), *Persistence Of Time* (1990).

Anvil

Anvil

Formerly known as Lips, Anvil was a Canadian four-piece from Toronto that made a significant impression on the speed-metal rock scene during the early 80s. It comprised, Lips (vocals/guitar), Dave Allison (guitar), Ian Dickson (bass) and Robb Reiner (drums). The band was technically excellent, playing at breakneck speed and with a demonic intensity that few of their peers could equal. Their first three albums were exemplary, with *Metal On Metal* containing the strongest material. Following a series of legal disputes with their label, as well as internal conflicts concerning musical differences, there was a four-year gap between successive studio albums. *Backwaxed* was a compilation, released against the band's wishes and featured songs they had recorded but rejected. *Strength Of Steel*, released in 1987, was a satisfactory come-back; but it was overshadowed by the concurrent work of Slayer, Megadeth and Metallica. This was ironic as Anvil were acknowledged as having a profound influence on these bands in their formative years. *Pound For Pound* was followed by a compilation of live material, before Allison quit in 1989.
Albums: *Hard 'n' Heavy* (1981), *Metal On Metal* (1982), *Forged In Fire* (1983), *Backwaxed* (1985), *Strength Of Steel* (1987), *Pound For Pound* (1988), *Past And Present-Live* (1989).

Apocalypse

Apocalypse were the most important heavy metal outfit to emerge from Switzerland since Celtic Frost. Comprising Carlos R. Sprenger (vocals), Julien Brocher (guitar), Pierre Alain Zurcher (guitar), Jean Claude Schneider (bass) and Andre Domenjoz (drums) they were heavily influenced by speed-metal bands such as Slayer and Megadeth. Formed in 1984, a series of short-lived line-ups ensued before stability was reached and they secured a contract with Under One Flag. Their debut album was mixed by Metallica-supremo Flemming Rasmussen and featured high-energy power metal, although ultimately flawed with insubstantial vocals.
Album: *Apocalypse* (1988).

Apocrypha

Hailing from Las Vegas, USA, Apocrypha were the brainchild of techno-wizard rock guitarist Tony Fredianelli. Their music was characterized by his intricate guitar work which combined classical and rock styles to startling effect. Formed in 1988, the original line-up featured Fredianelli, Steve Plocica (vocals), Chip Chrovian (guitar), Al Rumley (bass) and Mike Poe (drums). *Forgotten Scroll* and *Eyes Of Time* were excellent speed-metal albums, but lacked variety. Breck Smith and Dave Schiller replaced Rumley and Poe respectively before the band recorded *Area 54*. Released in 1990, it showed that the outfit had matured considerably as songwriters. They are now equipped to compete with artists such as Megadeth and Metallica.

Albums: *Forgotten Scroll* (1988), *Eyes Of Time* (1989), *Area 54* (1990).

Armageddon

This short-lived, mid-70s supergroup specialized in psychedelia-based melodic rock. The band comprised ex-Yardbirds and Renaissance vocalist Keith Relf, guitarist Martin Pugh formerly of Steamhammer, bassist Louis Cennamo and ex-Johnny Winter drummer Bobby Caldwell. Their self-titled debut, released in 1975, graced the US album charts. It featured long esoteric compositions that fused rock, jazz, blues and symphonic influences. This album is now much sought-after by collectors. Relf was fatally electrocuted not long after the album was released, so ending a still promising career. Jeff Fenholt was recruited as the new vocalist, but things did not work out as planned; the band split up after recording tracks for a second album. These have yet to be released.

Album: *Armageddon* (1975).

Armored Saint

This Los Angeles heavy metal quintet was formed in 1981. The band originally comprised John Bush (vocals), Dave Prichard (guitar), Phil E. Sandoval (guitar), Joey Vera (bass) and Gonzo (drums). Gigging incessantly around the LA bar and club circuit led to them being asked to contribute a track to the *Metal Massacre II* compilation album. This, in turn, attracted the attention of Chrysalis Records, which signed them in 1984. *March Of The Saint* appeared the same year to widespread apathy. Poor production resulted in the band's dynamic energy being totally dissipated in a muddy wall of noise. They moved away from the one-dimensional thrash approach on their next two albums, with John Bush's powerful vocal style giving them a strong identity. Sandoval left to form Megattack during the recording of the second album. The band continued as a four-piece for some time, before Jeff Duncan (ex-Odin) was drafted in as replacement. With no commercial success after three albums, their contract with Chrysalis ended. The band returned with an excellent live album on Metal Blade Records, followed almost three years later by *Symbol Of Salvation*, their most accomplished work to date. Duncan was superseded by Alan Barlam (ex-Hellion) in 1989 and Dave Prichard died of leukaemia in February 1990.

Albums: *March Of The Saint* (1984), *Delirious Nomad* (1985), *Raising Fear* (1987), *Saints Will Conquer - Live* (1988), *Symbol Of Salvation* (1991).

Artch

This Norwegian heavy metal quintet was formed in Sarpsborg, Norway during 1982, by bassist Bernt A. Jansen and guitarist Cato Olsen. It took a three-year search to find the right musicians to complete the line-up, with drummer Jorn Jamissen, guitarist Geir Nilssen and vocalist Espen Hoss finally meeting the original duo's requirements. Tragically, Hoss was killed in a motorcycle crash, and a replacement was eventually found in Icelandic-born Eirikur Hauksson. Influenced by Black Sabbath, Candlemass, Celtic Frost and Deep Purple, their debut album assimilated all these elements within a dense melodic framework. Brutal riffs, anthemic choruses and grandiose arrangements were commonplace. The album received a favourable response, but the band were reluctant to promote it with a full scale tour. Little has been heard of the band since.

Album: *Another Return* (1988).

Artillery

This Danish heavy metal band was formed in 1982 by the guitarists Michael and Morten Stutzer. After several trial and error line-ups, vocalist Flemming Rodsdorf, bassist Peter Torsland and drummer Carter Nielsen were recruited. Influenced by Slayer and Anvil, the band specializes in rigidly formularized thrash-metal and have recorded three workman-like albums to date.

Albums: *Fear Of Tomorrow* (1985), *Terror Squad* (1986), *By Inheritance* (1990).

ASAP

The acronym stands for Adrian Smith And Project. This heavy metal unit started off as a sideline interest for the Iron Maiden guitarist. He intended to use it as an outlet for songs that did not fit into the Maiden concept. Recruiting guitarists Andy Barnett and Dave Colwell, bassist Robin Clayton, keyboardist Richard Young and drummer Zak Starkey (son of Ringo Starr), they recorded *Silver And Gold* in 1989. Smith decided to leave Iron Maiden at this point to concentrate fully on his solo career. His work, however, proved uninspiring. *Silver And Gold* sold relatively poorly and was followed by silence.

Album: *Silver And Gold* (1989).

Ashphalt Ballet

This USA heavy metal 'biker-rock' outfit are heavily influenced by the Cult, Lynyrd Skynyrd and Aerosmith. Their name is derived from the description of a motorcyclist crashing and skidding

Asia

along the road at high speed! Fronted by gravel-throated vocalist Gary Jefferies, they soon built up a small but loyal following through incessant gigging on the LA bar and club circuit. Formed in 1988, the line-up is completed by Danny Clarke (guitar), Julius J. Ulrich (guitar), Terry Phillips (bass) and Mikki Kiner (drums). They signed to Virgin in 1991 and their first album was released early the following year. This epitomized their no-nonsense, raunchy rock 'n' roll style, but offered little that had not been heard before.
Album: *Ashphalt Ballet* (1992).

Asia

A supergroup comprised of well-known musicians from British art-rock bands, Asia formed in early 1981 and included John Wetton (b. 12 July 1949, Derby, England; vocals), keyboardist Geoff Downes, Steve Howe (b. 8 April 1947, London, England; guitar) and Carl Palmer (b. 20 March 1947, Birmingham, England; drums/percussion). At the time, Wetton had recently left the English progressive band UK, Howe and Downes had just vacated Yes and Palmer had left Emerson, Lake And Palmer. The group's self-titled debut album was released a year later and, although dismissed by

critics as unadventurous and overly commercial, it topped the US album charts for nine weeks, becoming one of the year's bestsellers. A single, 'Heat Of The Moment', also reached the US Top 5. Neither fared as well in the group's homeland. A follow-up single, 'Only Time Will Tell', was a moderate US success. The group released its second album, *Alpha* in 1983 and although it was a Top 10 hit in the US, as was the single 'Don't Cry', its sales nowhere matched the debut. Wetton then left the group, to be replaced by Greg Lake (b. 10 November 1948, Bournemouth, England), another Emerson, Lake and Palmer alumnus. A live television concert from Japan drew over 20 million US viewers in late 1983. In late 1985 Wetton rejoined the band and a third album, *Astra*, was released. However, its comparatively low chart position precipitated the band's dissolution. By early 1990 Howe had left to join a regenerated Yes, with Pat Thrall, an ex-Pat Travers Band member moving in to take his place. *Then And Now*, released the same year, was a mixture of six earlier recordings and four new songs, however the signs were that the band had peaked long ago.
Albums: *Asia* (1982), *Alpha* (1983), *Astra* (1985),

Then And Now (1990).

Athiest

Formerly known as Ravage, this US heavy metal band changed their name to Athiest in 1987 when the line-up of Randy Burke (guitar), Roger Patterson (bass), Kelly Shaeffer (vocals/guitar) and Steve Flynn (drums) came together. From amateurish origins, the band developed into a powerful and accomplished 'death-metal' outfit. Playing at breakneck speed, their sound is characterized by Shaeffer's gurgling vocal style. They released a debut album in 1990 to favourable reviews and have built up a loyal following in their native state of Florida, USA.
Album: *Piece Of Time* (1990).

Atilla (Netherlands)

This Dutch power-trio was put together in 1984 by former Wells Fargo members Herbie Vanderloo (vocals/guitar) and Arjen Michaels. With the addition of drummer Ton Holtewes, they recorded a mini-album, the following year. Although musically sound, the songs were let down by Vanderloo's amateurish vocal style, which lacked power, range and conviction. Two more thrash-oriented albums followed the same pattern, with 1989's *Triad* containing their strongest material.
Albums: *Weapons Of Extermination* (1985), *Violent Streets* (1988), *Triad* (1989).

Atilla (USA)

This speed-metal trio from New York was assembled by guitarist John De Leon in 1983. Enlisting the services of vocalist/bassist Vincent Paul and drummer A.T. Soldier, they made their vinyl debut with a track on Mausoleum's sampler album, *Metal Over America* in 1985. *Rolling Thunder*, produced by Rods' drummer Carl Canedy, was released the following year, but made little impact. It featured an uninspired fusion of hard-rock and thrash, including a version of the Alice Cooper classic, 'School's Out'. The band disintegrated shortly after the album's release.
Album: *Rolling Thunder* (1986).

Atomkraft

After a series of false starts and four years of frustration, UK heavy metal band Atomkraft finally secured a recording deal with Neat Records in 1985. It was among the first British thrash-metal bands, and built a solid reputation supporting labelmates Venom. The band comprised Tony Dolan (guitar), Rob Matthews (guitar), D.C. Rage (bass), Ged Wolf (drums), and vocalist Ian Swift. By the time *Future Warriors* emerged in 1985, their one dimensional thrashing sounded rather dated in comparison to the new American outfits that had recently appeared. After a further two average releases, Atomkraft split, with Dolan going on to join the revamped Venom in 1989.
Albums: *Future Warriors* (1985), *Queen Of Death* (1986), *Conductors Of Noise* (1987).

A II Z

This band from Manchester, England made a contribution to the New Wave Of British Heavy Metal. (NWOBHM). Formed in 1979, they featured vocalist Dave Owen, guitarist Gary Owen, bassist Cam Campbell and drummer Karl Reti. They landed the support slots to Girlschool and Black Sabbath which introduced them to a wider audience. However, after the release of a poorly produced live-album, their Iron Maiden and Samson-styled material were met with general apathy and they disbanded. Gary Owens went on to play with Tytan.
Albums: *The Witch Of Berkeley - Live* (1980).

Atrophy

This 'speed-metal' outfit hailed from Tucson, Arizona, USA. The band was formed in 1987 by vocalist Brian Zimmerman and guitarist Chris Lykins. Recruiting Rick Skowron (guitar), James Gulotta (bass) and Tim Kelly (drums), they recorded a demo album, *Chemical Dependency* the same year. This attracted the attention of thrash specialists, Roadrunner Records, which immediately recognized them as a band with great potential. *Socialized Hate* was an impressive debut, featuring heavy duty riffing, screaming guitars and interesting lyrics. Their second album saw some musical progression, with the material showing a greater awareness of melody and a slightly less extreme approach.
Albums: *Socialized Hate* (1988), *Violent By Nature* (1990).

August Redmoon

This Californian heavy rock quartet was formed in 1980 by drummer Dave Young. With the addition of vocalist Michael Henry, Greg Winslow (bass) and Ray Winslow (guitar) they adopted a traditional approach to hard-rock. Incorporating Kiss, Van Halen and Aerosmith influences plus an added 'speed-metal' element, they recorded *Fools Are Never Alone* in 1982. Following a long line of management and label disputes, the band changed their name to Terracuda in 1984, but split up before entering a recording studio. Henry, Young and Gary Winslow went on to form Eden.
Album: *Fools Are Never Alone* (1982).

Autograph

Hailing from Los Angeles, USA, rock band Autograph was formed in 1983 by vocalist Steve Plunkett and bassist Randy Rand. With the addition of Steve Lynch (guitar), Steven Isham (keyboards) and Keni Richards (drums), the band signed to RCA the following year. Comprising five exceptionally talented musicians, they delivered a stunning combination of sophisticated and melodic AOR that had enormous pop-metal crossover potential. 'Turn Up The Radio' from their debut *Sign In Please*, became a belated US Top 50 hit in 1985, with the album following suit, eventually peaking at number 29 in the *Billboard* chart. Two further excellent albums were released with 1987's *Loud And Clear* representing the pinnacle of the band's creativity. Isham quit in 1988 to start a new project with ex-Dio guitarist Craig Goldie. Autograph continued as a four-piece, but failed to attract media attention or repeat their initial success. They subsequently became disillusioned and disbanded in 1989, having failed to realize their potential.
Albums: *Sign In Please* (1984), *That's The Stuff* (1985), *Loud And Clear* (1987).

Avalon

This Dutch heavy metal quintet was formed in 1984 by guitarist Jack Pisters and vocalist Richard Muermans. Recruiting Maarten Huiskamp (keyboards), Erik Fox (bass) and Jacques Kraal (drums) it specialized in combining the hard-driving rock style of Iron Maiden with very intricate and off-beat guitar work that at times verged on the *avant garde*. They released an excellent mini-album in 1986 on the independent Dynamo label. This focused attention on the band's imaginative lyrics and futuristic guitar sound. Unfortunately, as soon as the album appeared the band underwent several personnel changes, which resulted in its eventual demise.
Album: *The Third Move* (1986).

Avatar

Formerly known as Metropolis, the heavy metal Avatar were formed in Florida, USA in 1978 by the Oliva brothers. Comprising Jon Oliva (vocals/guitar/keyboards), Chris Oliva (guitar), Steve Wacholz (drums) and Keith Collins (bass), they specialized in hard-edged 'power-metal' with melodic undercurrents. Their sound was characterized by Jon Oliva's soaring vocals and Chris Oliva's razor-sharp guitar runs. They made their vinyl debut with *City Beneath The Surface*, a three-track EP that was brutal and uncompromising metal at its very best. They subsequently changed their name to Savatage and went on to achieve international recognition and success. The EP is now valued by collectors of American heavy metal.
Album: *City Beneath The Surface* (1983).

Avenger (Germany)

This hi-tech thrash metal quartet originated in Herne, West Germany. Formed in 1984, the band comprised Peter Wagner (vocals/bass), Thomas Gruning (guitar), Jochen Schroeder (guitar) and Jorg Michael (drums). Its debut album combined a speed-metal style with intricate Rush-like bridges and interludes. The songs were complex and technically proficient but were let down somewhat by the vocals, which lacked both power and range. After the release of the mini-album *Depraved To Black*, they became known as Rage and went on to receive critical acclaim throughout the European music media.
Albums: *Prayer Of Steel* (1985), *Depraved To Black* (1985).

Avenger (U.K.)

This Newcastle-based, speed-metal outfit was formed by ex-Blitzkrieg duo Brian Ross (vocals) and Mick Moore (bass). With the addition of Gary Young (drums) and Lee Cheetam (guitar) they recorded the single 'Too Wild To Tame' before Ross switched places with Satan's vocalist Ian Swift. *Bloodsports* followed, a prime example of the New Wave Of British Heavy Metal and notable for some inspired guitar work from Cheetam. A series of guitarists arrived and departed in rapid succession, with American Greg Reiter eventually being recruited on a permanent basis. *Killer Elite* was followed by a disastrous American tour. Returning to England, Swift left to join Atomkraft and the band fell apart.
Albums: *Bloodsports* (1984), *Killer Elite* (1985).

Aviary

This short-lived, esoteric art-rock outfit was formed in 1978 by Brad Love (vocals/keyboards) and Toby Bowen (guitar). With the recruitment of Paul Madden (keyboards), Ken Steimonts (bass/vocals) and Richard Bryans (drums) the line-up was complete. Assimilating influences as diverse as Yes, Queen, ELP, the Beatles and classical music, they recorded a pretentious and overblown debut characterized by high-pitched vocals and harmonies. Unable to attract favourable media attention, the band split up soon after the album was released. Brad Love went on to make a solo album in 1982.
Album: *Aviary* (1979).

Aviator

This New York hard rock quartet was formed in 1984 by guitarist Richie Cerniglia and drummer Michael Ricciardelli. With the addition of vocalist Ernie White and bassist Steve Vitale, they signed to RCA in 1986. Influenced by Bon Jovi, Europe and Thin Lizzy their highly commercial debut album was produced by Neil Kernon. The songs were identikit pop-metal, and the band struggled to find their own image. The album sold poorly and was subsequently dropped by RCA. A series of line-up changes ensued, but the band has been unable to secure another recording contract to date.
Album: *Aviator* (1986).

AWBH

After a protracted legal dispute over name ownership, ex-Yes frontman Jon Anderson was forced to concede the name Yes to the Squire/Rabin/White/Kaye line-up. Featuring further ex-Yes members Rick Wakeman (keyboards), Steve Howe (guitar) and Bill Bruford (drums), they had to settle for the awkward acronym AWBH. Their self-titled debut release was a disjointed and unsatisfying album. In places Wakeman's keyboards swamped the songs, and overshadowed Steve Howe's guitar work. The album met with positive reviews, but it is unlikely the four will remain together in a band set up under this name.
Album: *Anderson, Wakeman, Bruford, Howe* (1989).

Axe

Rock band Babyface, comprising Edgar Riley (vocals), Bobby Barth (guitar), Mike Turpin (bass) and Teddy Mueller (drums), recruited Mike Osbourne as a second guitarist in 1979 and changed their name to Axe. Purveying highly-sophisticated pomp-rock, they built up a loyal following in the USA and released a trio of superbly crafted albums. Disaster struck in 1984 when vocalist Riley was killed in a car crash. The band dissolved itself, with Barth joining Blackfoot for a short period in 1985, before re-forming Axe in 1989 with ex-UFO drummer Andy Parker.
Albums: *Axe* (1979), *Living On The Edge* (1980), *Offering* (1981).

Axewitch

This Swedish heavy metal quartet originated in Stockholm in 1981. The initial line-up comprised Anders Wallentoft (vocals), Magnus Jarls (guitar), Mikael Johansson (guitar), Tommy Brage (bass) and Mats Johansson (drums). They started life as a doomy thrash-metal outfit, but, unable to attract press coverage, they decided on a radical change in direction. *Hooked On High Heels* saw the band sporting fashionable clothes, expensive hair-styles and a much more commercial approach similar to Mötley Crüe and Bon Jovi. However, the record-buying public was not impressed and the album sold poorly. The band split up shortly afterwards.
Albums: *The Lord Of Flies* (1983), *Visions Of The Past* (1984), *Hooked On High Heels* (1985).

Axis

This USA power-trio was formed by ex-Derringer duo Danny Johnson (guitar/vocals) and Vinnie Appice (drums). With the addition of bassist Jay Davis, they recorded *It's A Circus World* in 1978. This was a derivative hard-rock album that drew from the early 70s as a source of inspiration. The band disintegrated soon after the album's release, with Appice joining Black Sabbath and later Dio. Johnson replaced Steve Vai in Alcatrazz, then teamed up with Jay Davis again in Private Life.
Album: *It's A Circus World* (1978).

Axxis

This highly competent German hard rock quartet comprised Walter Pietsch (guitar/vocals), Bernhard Weiss (guitar/vocals), Werner Kleinhans (bass) and Richard Michalski (drums/vocals). Their diverse style recalled Boston and Black Sabbath and back again via Europe and the Scorpions. Axxis released *Kingdom Of The Night* in 1986 to favourable reviews and landed the support slot on Black Sabbath's European tour the same year. They could not transform this into album sales however, as the band lacked both image and real direction.
Album: *Kingdom Of The Night* (1986).

B

Baby Animals

This Australian indie-metal quartet were formed in 1990 by vocalist Suzi Demarchi and guitarist Dave Leslie. Recruiting bassist Eddie Parise and drummer Frank Delenza, they signed to the Imago label and debuted with a self-titled album in February 1992. Influenced by Heart, the Pretenders, AC/DC, INXS and Siouxsie And The Banshees, their sound is characterized by Demarchi's provocative growl and the understated guitar work of Leslie. They made a considerable impact in the UK as support act to Bryan Adams on his 1991 tour.
Album: *Baby Animals* (1992).

Bad Boy

The origin of this US rock band date back to the mid-70s, when Steve Grimm (guitar/vocals) teamed up with John Marcelli (bass). The first incarnation of Bad Boy, included Lars Hanson (drums) and Joe Lavie (guitar). The band chemistry was wrong however, and their debut album was a disappointing, half-hearted affair. Things improved with the subsequent release, as the band moved in a heavier direction and made greater use of an up-front guitar sound. Following a period of inactivity between 1978-82, the band hit back with a revamped line-up that saw Xeno (keyboards) and Billy Johnson (drums) alongside Grimm and Marcelli. Unfortunately, they switched back to a melodic pop-rock style once more. Both albums sold poorly and the band split up as a result.
Albums: *The Band That Made Milwaukee Famous* (1977), *Back To Back* (1978), *Private Party* (1982), *Electric Eyes* (1984).

Bad Company

This solid, highly acclaimed UK heavy rock group formed in 1973 with a line-up comprising, Paul Rodgers (b. 12 December 1949, Middlesbrough, England; vocals), Simon Kirke (b. 27 August 1949, Wales; vocals/drums), Mick Ralphs (b. 31 May 1944, Hertfordshire, England; vocals/guitar) and Boz Burrell (b. Raymond Burrell, 1946, Lincolnshire, England; bass guitar). With Ralphs (ex-Mott The Hoople) and Rodgers and Kirke (both ex-Free), Bad Company were akin to a blues-based supergroup. Much of their style was owed to Free, both musically and because of Paul Rodgers' distinct vocals. Their internationally

best-selling self-titled debut album established their style - strong vocals placed beside hard, distinctive riffing. A string of albums through the mid/late 70s brought them chart success on both sides of the Atlantic and a series of arduous, stadium tours maintained their reputation as an exemplary live act. They achieved singles success with a number of powerful songs, well produced and faultlessly played, although lyrically they were often quite pedestrian: 'Well I take whatever I want, and baby I want you' ('Can't Get Enough Of Your Love'), and 'Baby, when I think about you I think about love' ('Feel Like Makin' Love'). A three year hiatus ended with the release of *Rough Diamonds*, which provided another UK Top 20 album success (US number 26). After nearly a decade of extensive gigging and regularly released albums, the group finally dissolved in 1983. A new version of the group with former Ted Nugent vocalist Brian Howe replacing Rodgers came together in 1986 for the reunion album, *Fame And Fortune*. The band's subsequent releases have been mediocre, and are but a pale shadow of their first two albums.
Albums: *Bad Company* (1974), *Straight Shooter* (1975), *Run With The Pack* (1978), *Burning Sky* (1977), *Desolation Angels* (1979), *Rough Diamonds* (1984), *Fame And Fortune* (1986), *Dangerous Age* (1988), *Holy Water* (1990). Compilation: *10 From 6* (1986).

Bad English

Bad English

Towards the end of the 80s a new generation of 'supergroups' emerged from the USA including, Mr Big, Badlands, Damn Yankees, Alias, and arguably the most successful of them all, Bad English. The group was formed in 1988 by ex-Babys vocalist and successful solo artist John Waite, ex-Santana and Journey guitarist Neal Schon, ex-Babys and Journey keyboard player Jonathan Cain, ex-Babys bassist Ricky Phillips, and ex-Wild Dogs drummer Dene Castronovo.

Balaam And The Angel

Their 1989 self-titled debut album was an instant success in the USA combining hard-edged, melodic rock with big ballads. It reached the US Top 10 helped on its way with the Dianne Warren penned 'When I See You Smile' which was a US number 1 hit in 1990 (UK number 61). Success in the UK was not forthcoming and the album barely dented the Top 40, while a similar fate befell the single. 1991's follow up *Backlash* was released, backed up by the single 'Straight To Your Heart'. Internal disagreements struck the band causing them to split soon after its release, with Waite resuming his solo career; Phillips and Castronovo joining the Jimmy Page and David Coverdale project; while Schon and Cain were rumoured to be reforming Journey. Despite their short history, Bad English left behind a legacy of high quality melodic rock which achieved a high degree of commercial success.
Albums: *Bad English* (1989), *Backlash* (1991).

Badlands

This blues-based, UK hard-rock band was put together in 1988 by vocalist Ray Gillen (ex-Black Sabbath and Blue Murder) and former Ozzy Osbourne guitarist Jake E. Lee. With the addition of bassist Greg Chaisson and drummer Eric Singer, they signed to Atlantic and released a self-titled debut album the following year. Using the early 70s as a source for musical inspiration, their music invited comparison with Led Zeppelin, Bad Company, Humble Pie and Free. Singer was replaced by Jeff Martin before the recording of their second album in 1991. *Voodoo Highway* received widespread critical acclaim, with Gillen's classic soulful vocal style contrasting beautifully with Lee's explosive guitar pyrotechnics. The album oozed class, emotion and energy from every note, and included an inspired cover of James Taylor's 'Fire And Rain'.
Albums: *Badlands* (1989), *Voodoo Highway* (1991).

Bad News

This parody of an inept UK heavy metal band (post-Spinal Tap), featured the *alter egos* of the Comic Strip comedy team. They made their first appearance in the *Bad New Tour* television film chronicling the disastrous journey to Grantham for a poorly attended gig, accompanied by a television documentary crew. The members, Colin Grigson (Rik Mayall; bass), Den Dennis (Nigel Planer; guitar) Vim Fuego (Adrian Edmondson;

guitar/vocals) and Spider Webb (Peter Richardson; drums) accurately exaggerated every cliché in the heavy metal handbook. The joke was thoroughly milked when they released an album which included a deliberately out-of-tune cover of Queen's 'Bohemian Rhapsody' plus long-winded banter on the trials and tribulations of recording an album. A short-lived joke, metal fans did not warm to the jibes as the group found when they were 'bottled' off stage when they opened the annual Donington show in 1986.
Albums: *Bad News* (1987), *Bad News Bootleg* (1988).

Bad Steve

This UK speed-metal outfit was put together in 1983 by former Accept members Rubi Rubach (bass), Jan Komet (guitar) and Fritz Friedrich (drums). Recruiting vocalist Phil Magoo (ex-Sin City) and guitarist Akku Becher(ex-Kanaan), they finally landed a deal with Mausoleum Records after being turned down by many major labels in Germany. *Killing The Night* emerged in 1984 and they supported Accept throughout Europe to promote it. The album lacked energy, drive and quality songs and compared unfavourably to Accept's material, the yardstick by which the band were now judged. The album failed to sell and the band disintegrated, with Rubach going on to play with UDO for a short time.
Album: *Killing The Night* (1984).

Balaam And The Angel

This UK rock band included both post-punk gothic and 60s elements in their output. They were originally made up of the three Morris brothers, Jim (b. 25 November 1960, Motherwell, Scotland; guitar/recorder/keyboards), Mark (b. 15 January 1963, Motherwell, Scotland; lead vocals/bass) and Des (b. 27 June 1964, Motherwell, Scotland; drums). They began their career playing working mens clubs as a children's cabaret act in their native Motherwell, encouraged by their father who had insisted they all watch television's *Top Of The Pops* as children. They eventually moved down to Cannock in Staffordshire, where they are still based. An early gig at the ICA in London, 1985, saw a completely different approach to that with which Balaam would become identified. Playing in bare feet and pyjamas, they procured numerous covers of 60s love paeans, and a recorder solo. Somewhat falsely categorized as a gothic group after supporting the Cult on three successive tours, they were, in fact, self-consciously colourful in both appearance and approach. Early in their career they founded Chapter 22 Records, along with manager Craig

Jennings. Their debut came on the label when 'World Of Light' appeared in 1984, although 'Day And Night' was their most impressive release from this period. Their debut *The Greatest Story Ever Told*, was named after the headline under which their first interview in *Melody Maker* appeared. It was apparently intended to be reminiscent of the Doors, though it fell some way short of this. They moved on to Virgin Records and, in September 1988, the band's second album was released after they had returned from support slots with Kiss and Iggy Pop in the USA. A new guitarist, Ian McKean, entered because of the need for two guitar parts on *Live Free Or Die*. They were dropped by Virgin however, and their first tour for over four years took place in 1990. Press speculation that Mark would join the Cult as replacement bass player for Jamie Stewart collapsed as Ian Astbury decided that he was too much of a 'front man'. In 1991, they truncated their name to Balaam, and the first release was a mini-album, *No More Innocence*.
Albums: *The Greatest Story Ever Told* (1986), *Live Free Or Die* (1988), *No More Innocence* (1991).

Balance

This USA melodic AOR group were put together in 1979 by vocalist Peppy Castro and session men Doug Katsaros (keyboards) and Bob Kulick (guitarist and older brother of Kiss' Bruce Kulick). Augmented by other hired hands, they debuted on CBS in 1983 with a self-titled album that came over as a three-way amalgam of Toto, Kansas and Journey. As interest built, the trio signed on bassist Dennis Feldman and former Brand X drummer Chuck Burgi, to stabilize their line-up. *In For The Count* which followed, assumed a harder direction and incorporated Foreigner influences. Attracting an encouraging media response, the album surprisingly failed to take off. Disillusioned, the band went their separate ways in 1982. Bob Kulick subsequently joined Meatloaf's band prior to forming Skull.
Albums: *Balance* (1981), *In For The Count* (1982).

Bangalore Choir

This heavy metal band were named after a torpedo-like explosive device, Bangalore Choir are an ambitious group. They were formed in 1991 by former Accept vocalist David Reece, and the band features ex-Razor Maid guitarists Curt Mitchell and John Kirk, plus Ian Mayo (bass) and Jackie Ramos (drums) who were previously with Hurricane Alice. Their collective pedigree has undoubted potential, but *On Target* failed to reach it. The band are heavily influenced by Bon Jovi, Dan Reed Network and Whitesnake, which is obvious in their work. Reece is a strong frontman, but his phrasing and delivery is so closely modelled on David Coverdale and Jon Bon Jovi that it becomes distracting.

Album: *On Target* (1992).

Bang Tango

Bang Tango

This Los Angeles quintet was assembled in 1987 from the remnants of several Los Angeles club circuit rock bands. Comprising Joe Leste (vocals), Mark Knight (guitar), Kyle Stevens (guitar), Kyle Kyle (bass) and Tigg Kettler (drums) they secured a deal with MCA Records. This followed the release of a highly regarded, live mini-album which the band partly financed themselves. Initially, they concentrated on a sleazy, low-life image and incorporated influences such as Aerosmith and the Cult. This manifested itself on *Psycho Cafe*, a refreshingly honest, but slightly offbeat hard-rock album which was characterized by Leste's laconic vocal style. *Dancin' On Coals* released in 1991, indicated that the band had matured remarkably in two years, both in a creative and performing sense. This album featured a greater degree of musical sophistication, with bluesier and more soulful material being included. Bang Tango are now poised for international success and recognition on a large scale.

Albums: *Live Injection* (1987), *Psycho Cafe* (1989), *Dancin' On Coals* (1991).

Barnes, Jimmy

With the disintegration of the Australian band Cold Chisel in 1982, lead singer Jimmy Barnes embarked on a solo career. He teamed up with ex-Baby Jonathan Cain and produced *Body Swerve* and a self-titled album in quick succession. These were characterized by Barnes's rough and raunchy vocal delivery, and included erudite selections of blues, soul and R&B numbers. *Freight Train Heart* had a much bigger budget, as Geffen Records were hoping to break Barnes in the USA. With

contributions from Journey's Neil Schon, Desmond Child, Mick Fleetwood and Jim Vallence, the result was a classic American rock album. Surprisingly, the album did not take off in the USA and Geffen dropped Barnes in 1988. A credible double live album, appropriately titled *Barnestorming*, was recorded in Melbourne on his 1987-88 tour of Australia. This surfaced on import on the Mushroom label, and eventually led to a new contract with Atlantic Records. *Two Fires* emerged in 1990; yet another quality album of gritty rockers and gut-wrenching ballads. Once again, it made little impact outside Australia. Barnes appears likely to remain a minority interest in Europe and the USA.

Albums: *Body Swerve* (1984), *Jimmy Barnes* (1985), *Freight Train Heart* (1987), *Barnestorming* (1988), *Two Fires* (1990).

Baron Rojo

This Spanish heavy metal outfit was formed in Madrid 1980 by the brothers Armando (vocals/guitar) and Carlos (guitar/vocals) de Castro. With the addition of former session musicians Jose Luis Campuzano (bass) and Hermes Calabria (drums), they specialized in an early 70s approach, redolent of an amalgam of UFO, Uriah Heep and Black Sabbath. Their appeal has been limited in Europe and the USA by the Spanish vocals, but they have made some inroads in South America. In an attempt to widen their audience, they recorded an English vocal version of *Volumen Brutal*, but the result was disappointing due to poor phrasing and an awkward lyrical translation. They make no attempt to follow fashions and are now regarded as an out-dated, but well-respected curiosity on the international rock scene.

Albums: *Larga Vida Al Rock And Roll* (1981), *Volumen Brutal* (1982), *Metal Morphosis* (1983), *Baron Rojo Vivo* (1984), *Tierra De Nadie* (1987), *No Va Mas!* (1988).

Barren Cross

This Christian rock outfit from California was formed by guitarist Ray Parris and drummer Steve Whitaker in 1981. Enlisting the services of Jim Laverde (bass) and Mike Lee (vocals) they initially came over as an amalgam of Iron Maiden and Van Halen. *Rock For The King* featured turbo-charged metallic anthems with fluid guitar work, that were delivered with steely conviction. Lyrically, the band explored themes such as abortion, drug abuse and terrorism, but explained rather than simply condemned these issues. Later releases saw the band afford greater use of melody, but without compromising their ideals or striving for commercial recognition. *Hotter Than Hell* is a

magnificent live album, which fully showcases the band's talents. It provided a much needed shot in the arm for the credibility of Christian metal, which had suffered adverse press coverage for several years.
Albums: *Rock For The King* (1986), *Atomic Arena* (1987), *State Of Control* (1989), *Hotter Than Hell - Live* (1990).

Barth, Bobby
After the disintegration of UK heavy metal band Axe in 1984, lead singer Bobby Barth embarked on a solo career, following a short, but unfruitful association with Blackfoot. Dispensing with the hard-rock style he grew up with, Barth recorded an album of sentimental ballads and middle-of-the-road AOR. The songs featured expansive arrangements, which included swathes of keyboards and a brass section. The album made little impact and it is rumoured that Barth may re-form Axe in the near future.
Album: *Two Hearts-One Beat* (1986).

Bastard
This German quartet was formed in Hanover 1977 by Karl Rothert (bass/vocals) and Keith Kossoff (guitar). With the help of guitarist Uli Meisner and drummer Toto Petticoato, they took the Scorpions, AC/DC and Bad Company as their blueprint for heavy duty rock 'n' roll. Their first two albums are derivative. The live album was an improvement, with the band adding sparkle and character to the songs that sounded dull on record.
Albums: *Back To Nature* (1978), *Tearing Nights* (1978), *Live And Alive* (1980).

Bathory
This Swedish satanic-metal project was masterminded by the enigmatic, multi-instrumentalist Quothorn. The band originally comprised Quothorn (vocals/guitar), Kothaar (bass) and Vvorthn (drums), but the latter two left after recording just a single track for a heavy metal compilation album. Aided by session musicians, Quothorn decided to go it alone and recorded a series of black metal albums during the latter half of the 80s. He attracted a cult following, many of whom were satanists, but refrained from taking his music out on the road. *Hammerheart*, released in 1990 is an ambitious concept album based on Viking legend and his most accessible work to date.
Albums: *Bathory* (1984), *Raise The Dead* (1984), *The Return* (1985), *Under The Sign Of The Black Mark* (1986), *Blood, Fire, Death* (1988), *Hammerheart* (1990).

Baton Rouge
This US hard-rock quintet, formerly known as Meridian, was led by silver-throated vocalist Kelly Keeling. With Lance Bulen (guitar), Scott Bender (bass), David Cremin (keyboards) and Corky McClellan (drums), they delivered a hybrid style of melodic rock that encompassed influences ranging from Heart and Def Leppard to the Scorpions and Van Halen. With the help of Jack Ponti as producer, they have recorded two highly-polished and very accomplished rock albums.
Albums: *Shake Your Soul* (1990), *Lights Out On The Playground* (1991).

Battle Axe
This UK hard-rock quartet was formed in Newcastle, England during 1983 in the slipstream of other north-east outfits, such as Venom, Raven and Satan. Comprising Dave King (vocals), Steve Hardy (guitar), Brian Smith (bass) and Ian McCormack (drums). They made their debut with two tracks on the *Roxcalibur* heavy metal compilation. Signing to Roadrunner Records, they released two competent, albums incorporating elements of Motorhead, the Rods and Samson.
Albums: *Burn This Town* (1983), *Power From The Universe* (1984).

Battlecry
This Christian rock band was formed in California 1984 by Dave Chumchal (vocals/guitar/keyboards) and Doug Morris (guitar). With the recruitment of Robert Kirk Giverink (guitar), Mariko Martinez (keyboards/vocals), Ronald P. Simmons (bass/vocals) and Bret Kik Keys (drums), their sound was heavily laden with keyboards and characterized by high-pitched, note-perfect harmonies. Their sole release was an impressive collection of melodic AOR that paid respect to Yes, Journey and Stryper.
Album: *Red, White And Blue* (1985).

Beau Geste
Beau Geste is the pseudonym of the exceptionally talented US multi-instrumentalist Bryan Hughes. With the aid of session musicians he recorded *Another Night In The City* in 1986. The album was a tribute to Hughes's technical and artistic capabilities, as he took on responsibility for writing the material and contributing vocals, bass, keyboards and guitar parts. However the end result was less impressive, a melodic AOR album lacking character and real energy.
Album: *Another Night In The City* (1986).

Beck, Bogart And Appice

The plan for guitar virtuoso Jeff Beck (b. 24 June 1944, Surrey, England), to form a power trio with the ex-Vanilla Fudge rhythm section was mooted in 1969. Both drummer, Carmine Appice (b. 15 December 1946, New York, USA), and bassist Tim Bogart (b. 27 August 1944, Richfield, New Jersey, USA), were dissatisfied with their present band. The plans were spoiled when Beck was involved in a serious car crash that put him out of action. Meanwhile, Bogart and Appice formed the heavy rock band Cactus, until in 1972 their paths crossed again with Beck and they put together the heavy rock unit Beck, Bogart And Appice. The self-titled commercially successful debut was instrumentally superb, heavy and loud, but suffered from a lack of any songwriting ability and strained vocals. Twenty years later the album sounds ponderous, clumsy and is justifiably disowned by its members.

Albums: *Beck, Bogart And Appice* (1973), *Live In Japan* (1974).

Beck, Jeff

b. 24 June 1944, Wallington, Surrey, England. As a former choir boy the young Beck was interested in music from an early age, becoming a competent pianist and guitarist by the age of 11. His first main band was the Tridents, who made a name for themselves locally. After leaving them Beck took on the seemingly awesome task of stepping into the shoes of Eric Clapton, who had recently departed from the 60s R&B pioneers, the Yardbirds. Clapton had a fiercely loyal following, but Beck soon had them gasping with his amazing guitar pyrotechnics, utilizing feedback and distortion. Beck stayed with the Yardbirds adding colour and excitement to all their hits until October 1966. The tension between Beck and the joint lead guitarist Jimmy Page was resolved during a US tour. Beck walked out and never returned. His solo career was launched in March 1967 with a different sounding Beck on a pop single 'Hi-Ho Silver Lining'. Jeff's unremarkable voice was heard on a sing-along number which was saved by his trademark guitar solo. The record was a sizeable hit and has subsequently demonstrated its perennial appeal to party-goers by re-entering the charts twice in 1972 and 1982. The follow-up, 'Tallyman' was also a minor hit, but by now Jeff's ambitions were in other directions. He retired from being a singing, guitar-playing, pop star and started a career that led him to become one of the world's leading rock guitarists. The Jeff Beck Group, formed in 1968, consisted of Beck, Rod Stewart (vocals), Ron Wood (bass), Nicky Hopkins (piano) and Mickey Waller (drums). This powerhouse quartet released *Truth*, which became a major success in the USA, resulting in the band undertaking a number of arduous tours. The second album *Cosa Nostra Beck-Ola* had similar success, although Stewart and Wood had now departed for the Faces. Beck also contributed some sparkling guitar and received equal billing with Donovan on the hit 'Goo Goo Barabajagal (Love Is Hot)'. In 1968 Jeff's serious accident with one of his hot-rod cars put him out of action for almost 18 months. A recovered Beck formed another group with Cozy Powell, Max Middleton and Bob Tench, and recorded two further albums, *Rough And Ready* and *Jeff Beck Group*. The latter became a sizeable hit. Beck was now fully accepted as a serious musician, and figured highly in various guitarist polls. In 1973 the erratic Beck musical style changed once again and he formed the trio Beck, Bogert And Appice with the two former members of Vanilla Fudge. Only one official album was released and Beck introduced yet another facet, this time forming an instrumental band. The result was the excellent *Blow By Blow*, thought by many to be his best work. His guitar work showed extraordinary technique combining rock, jazz and blues styles. *Blow By Blow* was a million seller and its follow-up, *Wired* had similar success. Having allied himself with some of the jazz/rock fraternity Beck teamed up with Jan Hammer for a frantic live album. Following its release Beck effectively retired for three years. He returned in 1980 with *There And Back*. His loyal fans had not deserted him, and, now rejuvinated, he found himself riding the album charts. During the 80s, Beck's appearances have been sporadic. He has appeared at charity functions and has spent much of his leisure time with automobiles. In one interview Beck stated that he could just as easily have been a car restorer. In the mid-80s he toured with Rod Stewart and was present on his version of 'People Get Ready'. The album *Flash* came in 1985, but proved his least successful to date. Jeff Beck has already ensured his place in the history book of guitarists and his no-nonsense approach to the music industry has earned him considerable respect. The release of a box-set in 1992, chronicling his career, was a fitting tribute to this accomplished guitarist.

Albums: *Truth* (1968), *Cosa Nostra Beck-Ola* (1969), *Rough And Ready* (1971), *Jeff Beck Group* (1972), *Blow By Blow* (1975), *Wired* (1976), *Jeff Beck With The Jan Hammer Group Live* (1977), *There And Back* (1980), *Flash* (1985), with Terry Bozzio and Tony Hymas *Jeff Beck's Guitar Shop* (1989). Compilations: with Rod Stewart *The Late '60s* (1988), *Beckology* (1992).

Becker, Jason

This classically-trained US guitarist first came to prominence in the late 80s with fellow guitar wizard Marty Friedman in the band Cacophony. Combining blues, rock and classical styles he built up a reputation for playing at breakneck speed with a melodic intensity and feel that was reminiscent of Alvin Lee. He took time out between Cacophony albums in 1988 to record *Perpetual Burn*, a solo instrumental showcase for his remarkable six-string acrobatics. After the recording of Cacophony's second album, Becker accepted David Lee Roth's offer to be the permanent replacement for Steve Vai. Becker appeared on Roth's *A Little Ain't Enough* album in 1991, contributing some stunning guitar work, and silenced the critics' premature claims that he would not be able to match his flamboyant predecessor.

Album: *Perpetual Burn* (1988).

Becker, Margaret

This US Christian rock singer first achieved recognition with Steve Camp in 1986. She sang as a duet with Camp on his *One On One* album, with her solo career taking off as a result. Influenced by Heart, Pat Benatar and Elkie Brooks, she concentrated on a melodic and easily accessible pop-rock style, dominated by brooding and atmospheric ballads. Becker has released four quality albums to date, with the vast majority of the songs being self-written. However, she has yet to make a significant impression outside the Christian music scene.

Albums: *Never For Nothing* (1987), *The Reckoning* (1988), *Immigrant's Daughter* (1990), *Simple House* (1991).

Bengal Tigers

This short-lived Australian heavy metal band was formed in Melbourne 1983 by vocalist Gordon Heald and guitarist Barney Fakhouri. Enlisting the services of Steve Tyler (bass) and Mick Egan (drums/vocals), they signed to the Mushroom label and released a mini-album the following year. Influenced by AC/DC, Iron Maiden and Scorpions, they purveyed cliched heavy metal, that lacked both identity and energy.

Album: *Metal Fetish* (1984).

Betsy

In 1988, Bitch, the US, Los Angeles-based sado-masochistic band who were obsessed with leather, whips and chains, decided to clean up their act. They changed their name to Betsy and adopted a less extreme hard-rock image. The band still comprised Betsy (vocals), David Carruth (guitar), Ron Cordy (bass) and Robby Settles (drums), but the sexual side of the band's image was played down. Betsy now performed more like Ann Wilson (of Heart) than Wendy O'Williams (of the Plasmatics). Signing to Roadrunner Records, their sole release was not noticeably different from the old Bitch material; heavy metal with lacklustre vocals. The album sank without trace and they reverted back to Bitch within a year.

Album: *Betsy* (1988).

Big F

This Los Angeles, USA trio comprised Mark Christian (guitar), John Shreve (bass/vocals) and Rob Donin (drums). They unleashed a 'mind-blowing wall of noise', dominated by crashing drums and screeching feedback, while vocalist Shreve screamed incessantly. Psychedelia, Jimi Hendrix, the Stooges, the Cult and avant garde influences appear as reference points, but few bands will ever match the intensity and sheer energy generated by this outfit.

Album: *The Big F* (1990).

Big House

This Canadian quartet specialize in melodic and hard-edged AOR. They were formed in 1987 by drummer Sjor Throndson and vocalist Jan Ek who both wanted to prove that Canada had other things to offer besides Rush and Bryan Adams. Recruiting guitarist K.B.Broc and bassist Jay Scott King, the current line-up was finalized in 1989. After incessant gigging in their native Canada, the band were signed by RCA Records. They debuted in 1992 with a self-titled album that incorporated elements of Bon Jovi, Ratt and Aerosmith, but without being derivative. With time and record company backing, they could develop into a major force.

Album: *Big House* (1992).

Billion Dollar Babies

This short-lived group revolved around Michael Bruce (b. 21 November 1948, California, USA; guitar/vocals), Dennis Dunaway (b. 15 March 1946, California, USA; bass) and Neal Smith (b. 10 January 1946, Washington, USA; drums). Founder members of Alice Cooper, the trio were summarily fired in 1974 by lead singer Vince Furnier, who was known as 'Alice Cooper'. Protracted legal entanglements delayed this riposte, which took its name from one of their former group's best-selling albums. Sessionmen Bob Dolin (keyboards) and Mike Marconi (guitar) completed the line-up, but the resultant album, *Battle Axe* was a major disappointment. Its uncomfortable mix of technology and heavy metal did not prove

Bitch

popular and the quintet was then dissolved. Bruce embarked on a solo career and thereafter temed up with ex-Angel drummer Barry Brandt to pursue a jazz-orientated path. Dunaway and Smith formed the Flying Tigers while Dolin and Marconi reverted to studio work.
Album: *Battle Axe* (1977).

Billy Satellite

This Californian quartet was formed in 1983 by Monty Byrom (guitar/vocals/ keyboards) and Danny Chauncey (guitar/keyboards). With bassist Ira Walker and drummer Tom Falletti completing the line-up, they bridged the musical divide between the commercial radio-rock of Boston, and the bluesy southern-style of Lynyrd Skynyrd. Signing to EMI in 1984, they released a single album before disbanding. Byrom and Chauncey went on to join New Frontier and .38 Special respectively. Eddie Money later covered the band's 'I Wanna Go Back', and scored a minor hit in the USA.
Album: *Billy Satellite* (1984).

Billy The Kid

This brash pop-metal quartet was formed in Los Angeles during 1984 by vocalist Stephen Frederick and guitarist Bill L'Kid. With the addition of Jeffrey Velvet (bass) and Randy Delay (drums), they signed a contract with MCA the following year. Fusing the energy and flamboyance of Van Halen with the commercial sensibility of REO Speedwagon, they cut the impressive and appropriately titled *Sworn To Fun* in 1985. Failing to attract media interest, they disbanded soon after the album's release.
Album: *Sworn To Fun* (1985).

Birtha

Birtha were one of the first USA all-female bands to try and penetrate the exclusively male bastion of heavy rock. Comprising Rosemary Butler (bass/vocals), Sherry Hagler (keyboards), Liver Favela (drums) and Shele Pinizzotto (guitar/vocals), they released two excellent hard-rock albums during the early 70s. They specialized in tight harmonies and a style not dissimilar to that of early Uriah Heep. They were regarded as a novelty at the time, which on reflection is a little unjust. Their tasteless publicity handout during their early 70s UK tour with the Kinks stated 'Birtha has balls'. Along with Fanny they undoubtedly helped to pave the way for future female rockers such as the Runaways.

Albums: *Birtha* (1972), *Can't Stop The Madness* (1973).

Bitch (Switzerland)

Bitch were formed in Zurich, Switzerland in 1979 by the Schmid brothers Eric (vocals), Jimmy (drums) and Geoffrey (guitar). Adding Marc Portman (guitar) and Roddy Landolt (bass), they combined 70s symphonic-rock with a New Wave Of British Heavy Metal approach. Elements of Deep Purple, Krokus, Emerson, Lake And Palmer and Angelwitch were evident in the two albums they released during the early 80s. The band's name was always more provocative than their music, and unable to find an appreciative audience, they disappeared from the scene in 1982.

Albums: *First Bite* (1980), *Some Like It Hard* (1982).

Bitch (USA)

This Los Angeles-based quartet made an impact in 1982 with their debut EP, as a result of their shock value, rather than their originality. Musically, they were derivative of Motorhead. Led by female vocalist Betsy Weiss, they released *Be My Slave*, with David Carruth (guitar), Mark Anthony Wells (bass) and Robbie Settles (drums) completing the line-up. With Ron Cordy replacing Wells, it took a further four years before the appropriately titled *The Bitch Is Back* emerged. Regarded with little affection by the mainstream audience, they relaunched themselves as Betsy in 1988, with a cleaner AOR-like image. This was met with indifference and the band became Bitch again within a year.

Albums: *Damnation Alley* (1982), *Be My Slave* (1983), *The Bitch Is Back* (1987).

Bitches Sin

Formed in Cumbria 1980, during the growth of the New Wave Of British Heavy Metal movement, Bitches Sin comprised Ian Toomey (guitar), Alan Cockburn (vocals), Perry Hodder (bass), Peter Toomey (guitar) and Bill Knowles (drums). Cockburn was later replaced by Frank Quegan, while Mike Frazier took over on bass. Purveying high-energy metallic rock, they combined UFO and Deep Purple influences with modern technology and were reminiscent of Diamond Head in places. Their first single 'Sign Of The Times' achieved success in Holland after it was championed by radio disc jockey Hanneke Kappen. They subsequently contributed a track to a *Heavy Metal Heroes* compilation album, which

helped to further their reputation. A plethora of personnel changes hindered their progress. Subsequently, they released two albums, neither of which fulfilled their initial promise. They had actually disbanded before *Invaders* materialized. The Toomey brothers reappeared in 1988 as Flash Point, and helped finance the release of a debut album themselves.

Albums: *Predator* (1982), *Invaders* (1986).

Black Crowes

Black Crowes

This US, Georgia-based quintet, formed in 1984, comprise Chris Robinson (vocals), Rich Robinson (guitar), Jeff Cease (guitar), Johnny Colt (bass) and Steve Gormon (drums). Their roots are in bar-room R&B and tread a thin musical line between the Rolling Stones (*Exile On Main Street* era) and the Faces and Aerosmith. Sartorially, the group have adopted the styles of the early 70s rock groups as well. Robinson's emotive vocals, oozing attitude and pure soul from every note, while the band coolly pump out simple, but infectious rock 'n' roll riffs in support. With George Drakoulias as producer, *Shake Your Money Maker*, was released, on Def American, to widespread critical acclaim and from the public, who kept the album in the US charts for well over 18 months.

Albums: *Shake Your Money Maker* (1990), *The Southern Harmony And Musical Companion* (1992).

Black 'N' Blue

Formerly known as Boogie Star, Black 'N' Blue were formed in Portland, Oregon, USA in 1981. After a series of line-up shuffles, the band stabilized with Jaime St. James (vocals), Tommy Thayer (guitar), Jeff Warner (guitar), Patrick Young (bass) and Peter Holmes (drums). Relocating to Los Angeles in 1982, they forged a contract with Geffen Records and delivered their self-titled debut album in 1984. Produced by Dieter Dierks, the album was classic hard-rock and surprisingly un-American; shunning the party-metal approach

Black Sabbath

of Ratt and Quiet Riot and having more in common with the Scorpions and Def Leppard. Failing to attract media attention, the band dropped this approach and tried to emulate the style of Kiss and Mötley Crüe from then on. With Gene Simmons (Kiss's bassist) producing their third and fourth albums, the accusations of Kiss imitation grew even stronger. Unable to generate commercial success, the band disintegrated in 1989. Patrick Young went on to Dokken, vocalist James joined Madhouse, Thayer teamed up with Harlow and the remaining pair formed Wet Engine. Black 'N' Blue were an excellent band, who unfortunately compromised their undoubted talents.
Albums: *Black 'N' Blue* (1984), *Without Love* (1985), *Nasty, Nasty* (1986), *In Heat* (1988).

Black Rose

Formed in Newcastle in 1983 by Steve Bardsley (vocals) and Chris Watson (guitar). With the addition of Mick Thompson (bass) and Malla Smith (drums), they followed a musical direction similar to other Englishnorth east bands such as Raven, Venom And Blitzkreig. After contributing tracks to a number of metal compilation albums,

they signed to Bullet Records and released *Boys Will Be Boys* in 1984. Following a tour of the Netherlands to promote the album, Graham Hunter replaced Watson. A second album recorded in 1986 showed that the band had made little musical progression. Yet another change of guitarist saw Pat O'Neill replacing Hunter; but with poorly attended live shows, and an ever-diminishing fan-base, the band folded in 1987.
Albums: *Boys Will Be Boys* (1984), *Walk It, How You Talk It* (1986).

Black Sabbath

Group members Terry 'Geezer' Butler (b. 17 July 1949, Birmingham, England; bass), Tony Iommi (b. 19 February 1948, Birmingham, England; guitar), Bill Ward (b. 5 May 1948, Birmingham, England; drums) and 'Ozzy' Osbourne (b. 3 December 1948, Birmingham, England; vocals) were originally known as Earth, a name they changed to Black Sabbath in 1969. The members of this band grew up together in the musically fertile English midlands, and their name hints at the heavy, doom-laden and yet ingenious music they produced. The name comes from a book by the occult writer Denis Wheatley, and many of

their songs deal with alternative beliefs and ways of life. The title track of *Paranoid* confronts mental instability, and other songs are concerned with the effects of narcotic substances such as cocaine and marijuana. The line-up remained unchanged until 1973 when Rick Wakeman, keyboard player for Yes was drafted in to play on *Sabbath Bloody Sabbath*. By 1977, personnel difficulties within the band were beginning to take their toll, and the music was losing some of its earlier orchestral, heavy metal feel, and in 1978 Ozzy Osbourne left to pursue a solo career. He was replaced by Ronnie James Dio. Dio had been a central figure in the early 70s band Elf, and spent three years with Ritchie Blackmore's Rainbow. Dio's experience with the band was to be short-lived, and he left in 1982. For a while Vinnie Appice, brother of Carmine Appice, had been Sabbath's drummer The replacement vocalist was Ian Gillan. It is this Sabbath incarnation which is commonly regarded as the most disastrous for band and fans alike, *Born Again* failing to capture any of the original vitality of the group. In 1986, the entire line-up was rethought. Iommi was the only original member of the band, which now consisted of Geoff Nichols (b. Birmingham, England; keyboards), Glenn Hughes (b. England; vocals), Dave Spitz (b. New York City, New York, USA; bass), and Eric Singer (b. Cleveland, Ohio, USA; drums).This was an accomplished combination, Singer having been a member of the Lita Ford Band, and Glenn Hughes having worked with such legendary bands as Misunderstood, Trapeze and Deep Purple. In 1986, the surprisingly blues-sounding *Seventh Star* was released, the lyrics and music for which had been written by Iommi. In the first of a succession of personnel changes, Hughes left the band to be replaced by Ray Gillen, an American singer who failed to record anything with them. Vandenburg is the vocalist on the powerful 1987 the *Eternal Idol* and on *Headless Cross,* the album which skilled and renowned drummer Cozy Powell produced and appeared on. By late 1991, Sabbath was suffering from flagging record sales and declining credibility so Iommi recruited their original bassist, Butler, and attempted to persuade drummer Bill Ward to rejoin too. Ward, however, was not interested, Cozy Powell was still recuperating after being crushed by his horse, and so Vinnie Appice became Sabbath's new drummer. After much speculation, a return to the band by Ronnie Dio completed the 1982/3 line-up.
Albums: *Black Sabbath* (1970), *Paranoid* (1970), *Master Of Reality* (1971), *Black Sabbath Vol. 4* (1972), *Sabbath Bloody Sabbath* (1974), *Sabotage* (1975), *Technical Ecstasy* (1976), *We Sold Our Soul*
For Rock And Roll (1976), *Never Say Die* (1978), *Heaven And Hell* (1980), *Live At Last* (1980), *Mob Rules* (1981), *Live Evil* (1982), *Born Again* (1983), *Seventh Star* (1986), *The Eternal Idol* (1987), *Headless Cross* (1989), *Tyr* (1990). Compilations: *Greatest Hits* (1980), *Collection: Black Sabbath* (1985).

Black Sheep

This group was formed in New York in 1974, by vocalist Louis Grammatico and guitarist Donald Mancuso. Recruiting Larry Crozier (keyboards), Bruce Turgon (bass), and Ron Rocco (drums), they signed with Capitol Records the following year. Influenced by Bad Company, Free and Led Zeppelin, they recorded two excellent hard-rock albums, characterized by Grammatico's powerful, yet soulful vocal style. Unable to make an impact, the band split up, with Grammatico changing his name to Lou Gramm and found considerable success with Foreigner. Turgon, after a spell with Warrior, later helped co-write Gramm's first solo album.
Albums: *Black Sheep* (1975), *Encouraging Words* (1976).

Blackeyed Susan

This US Hard-rock quintet were formed in 1991 by ex-Britny Fox vocalist Dean Davidson. With Erik Levy (bass), Rick Criniti (guitar), Tony Santoro (guitar) and Chris Branco (drums) completing the line-up the band soon negotiated a deal with Mercury Records. They debuted with *Electric Rattlebone,* a blues-based set of hard rock songs that paid respect to Aerosmith, Humble Pie, Cinderella and the Rolling Stones in more or less equal portions. Although far from original, the material is delivered with both conviction and real emotion. Their second album will be critical, if they are hoping to emulate the success of fellow retro-rockers the Black Crowes.
Album: *Electric Rattlebone* (1991).

Blackfoot

Southern USA rock practitioners Blackfoot initially comprised of Rick Medlocke (guitar/vocals), Charlie Hargrett (guitar), Greg Walker (bass) and Jakson Spires (drums/vocals). The quartet shared common origins with Lynyrd Skynyrd and in turn offered a similar blues/rock-based sound, centred on Medlocke's confident playing. Session pianist Jimmy Johnson produced Blackfoot's early work at the revered Muscle Shoals studio, but despite this impressive pedigree, the group was unable to translate an in-concert popularity into record sales. *Strikes*, the unit's first release for Atlantic/Atco, offered a heavier

Blackfoot

perspective, while the cream of their early work was captured live on *Highway Song*. Ken Hensley, formerly of Uriah Heep, joined the line-up for *Siogo* and *Vertical Smiles*, but Blackfoot was disbanded following the latter's release.

Albums: *No Reservations* (1975), *Flying High* (1976), *Blackfoot Strikes* (1979), *Tomcattin'* (1980), *Maurauder* (1981), *Highway Song* (1982), *Siogo* (1983), *Vertical Smiles* (1984).

Blackmore, Ritchie

b. 14 April 1945, Weston-Super-Mare, Avon, England. Guitarist Blackmore spent his early career in Mike Dee And The Jaywalkers before joining Screaming Lord Sutch And His Savages in May 1962. Within months he had switched to the Outlaws, a popular, principally instrumental, group which also served as the studio houseband for producer Joe Meek. Blackmore's exciting style was already apparent on his own group's releases, notably 'Keep A Knockin''/'Shake With Me', and on sessions for Heinz and Mike Berry. The guitarist briefly joined the former singer's group, the Wild Boys, in 1964, and completed a suitably idiosyncratic solo single, 'Little Brown Jug'/'Getaway', before forging an erratic path as a member of Neil Christian's Crusaders, the Savages (again) and the Roman Empire. When a short-lived act, Mandrake Root, broke up in October 1967, Ritchie opted to live in Hamburg, but the following year was invited back to London to join organist Jon Lord in the embryonic Deep Purple. Although initially envisaged as an 'English Vanilla Fudge' the group quickly became a leading heavy metal act, with Blackmore's powerful, urgent runs an integral part of their attraction. He left the group in 1975, unhappy with their increasingly funk-based sound, and joined forces with the USA-based Elf to form Ritchie Blackmore's Rainbow. This powerful band became a highly popular hard-rock attraction, but was blighted by

its leader's autocratic demands. Multiple firings ensued as the guitarist searched for the ideal combination, but such behaviour simply enhanced a temperamental reputation. He was nonetheless involved in the Deep Purple reunion, undertaken in 1984, although animosity between the guitarist and vocalist Ian Gillan resulted in the latter's departure. Blackmore's prowess as a guitar 'hero' is undisputed, and his outstanding technique has influenced many current NWOHM bands.

Compilations: *Ritchie Blackmore Volume 1: Early Sessions To Rainbow* (1990), *Ritchie Blackmore Volume 2* (1991).

Blackout

The origins of this Dutch quintet date back to 1983, when Godzilla were assembled from the remnants of the bands Van East and Zenith. Godzilla specialized in mainstream pop-rock material, but switched to 'speed-metal' and changed their name to Blackout in 1984. The band comprised Bas Van Sloten (vocals), Mannes Van Oosten (guitar), Jean Hoffman (guitar), Alfred Dreuge (bass) and Jan Boxem (drums). After securing a deal with Roadrunner Records, they released *Evil Game* the same year. This proved a workman-like collection of songs, constructed around heavy-duty, quick-fire riffs and dual lead soloing. Failing to make any significant impact, they disappeared from the scene within a year of the album's release.

Album: *Evil Game* (1984).

Blackwych

This Irish metal band was put together by the three James brothers in 1985. Comprising vocalist Ciaran, guitarist Declan and bassist Niall, they recruited Bobby Tierney as a second guitarist, plus drummer Chris Andralinus to complete their line-up. Influenced by Thin Lizzy, Mama's Boys and the New Wave Of British Heavy Metal, they made their debut on the Irish sampler, *The Green Metal Album*. They were amateurish and under-rehearsed when they entered the studio to record *Out Of Control*. Consequently, the album was rudimentary, with its flat, tuneless vocals. Reeling from poor reviews, the group split shortly afterwards.

Album: *Out Of Control* (1986).

Blessed Death

This American doom/thrash/hardcore outfit was formed in New Jersey 1984 by vocalist Larry Portelli and guitarist Jeff Anderson. Enlisting the services of Nick Florentino (guitar), Kevin Powelson (bass) and Chris Powleson (drums), they were initially influenced by Black Sabbath, Slayer

Ritchie Blackmore, George Harrison and Ian Gillan

and Anthrax. *Kill Or Be Killed* highlighted the remarkable vocal talent of Portelli whose range extended from a low guttural growl, to a high pitched banshee-like screech. Bass-laden riffs, thunderous drums and vitriolic guitar blasts bridged the ground between the doom and thrash metal factions. *Destined For Extinction* incorporated hardcore nuances reminiscent of the Bad Brains and Jello Biafra. Produced by Alex Perialas and Raven drummer Rob Hunter, it was heralded as a great achievement, combining excellent sound quality with uncompromising and thought-provoking lyrics. Unfortunately, the positive reviews did not translate into commercial success, and nothing has been heard of the band since.
Albums: *Kill Or Be Killed* (1986), *Destined For Extinction* (1987).

Blind Date

This mysterious US 'pop-metal' quartet first came together in 1975 and its members employed strange pseudonyms. Featuring Dane Bramage (vocals/bass/keyboards), Brad Billion (guitar/vocals), Arnie Baddie (guitar/vocals) and Pinky Chablis (drums), their music pays homage to Cheap Trick, Kansas and REO Speedwagon.

Produced by Jeff Glixman, *Blind Date*, released in 1979, actually comprised songs that had been written four years previously. The instrumental 'Twin Engines' gained a certain degree of fame after being used as a theme tune to a European rock radio programme. The band faded back into obscurity after the album's release.
Album: *Blind Date* (1979).

Blind Fury

Formerly known as Satan, these UK purveyors of stereotyped 'black-metal' changed their name, personnel and direction in 1984. Blind Fury comprised Lou Taylor (vocals), Steve Ramsey (guitar), Russ Tippins (guitar), Graeme English (bass) and Sean Taylor (drums). Eighteen months of writing and rehearsing led to *Out Of Reach*, a commercial hard-rock album that played down their previous associations with witchcraft and the occult. Success proved elusive however, and they disbanded in 1986. Taylor had periods of activity with Persian Risk and Tour De Force, while the remainder of the band reformed Satan.
Album: *Out Of Reach* (1985).

Blind Illusion

This group was formed in Richmond, California, USA during 1978, by guitarist/vocalist Mike Biederman and bassist Les Claypool. An extensive series of personnel changes ensued over the next 10 years before the band released any product. With the addition of Larry Lalonde (guitar) and Mike Miner (drums), plus the return of Biederman and Claypool from stints with Blue Oyster Cult and Primus respectively, they finally entered a studio in 1988 to record The Sane Asylum. This was a techno-thrash affair, comparable in places to Megadeth, Queensryche and Metallica.
Album: The Sane Asylum (1988).

Bloodgood

This Christian heavy metal band was formed in Washington, DC, USA in 1985 by guitarist David Zaffiro and bassist Mike Bloodgood. With Les Carlsen (vocals) and Mark Welling (drums) completing the line-up, they were initially strongly influenced by Iron Maiden and Saxon. However, as time progressed, the band matured and diversified their sound considerably, with their latter albums courting Def Leppard, Whitesnake and Van Halen comparisons. Without doubt, the band have been the most credible white metal outfit on the circuit for many years. Kevin Whistler took over the drumstool from Welling in 1989, and guitarist David Zaffiro recorded a solo, The Other Side, the same year.

Blue Cheer

Renowned as one of the world's loudest groups, Dickie Petersen (vocals/bass), Bruce Leigh Stephens (guitar) and Paul Whaley (drums) harboured dreams of a more conventional direction until seeing Jimi Hendrix perform at the celebrated Monterey Pop Festival. Taking their name from a potent brand of the hallucinogenic drug LSD, Blue Cheer made an immediate impact with their uncompromising debut album, which featured cacophonous interpretations of 'Summertime Blues' (US number 14) and 'Parchman Farm'. A second set, Outsideinside, was completed in the open air when the trio's high volume destroyed the studio monitors. Stephens left the group during the sessions for New! Improved, and his place was taken by former Other Half guitarist Randy Holden. Blue Cheer then unveiled a reconstituted line-up of Petersen, Burns Kellogg (keyboards), Bruce Stephens (bass) and Norman Mayall (drums/guitar). Stephens was then replaced by former Kak guitarist, Gary Yoder, for the quartet's fifth album, The Original Human Being. This impressive set featured the atmospheric, raga-influenced 'Babaji (Twilight

Raga)', and is acclaimed as the group's most cohesive work. The band was dissolved during the early 70s, but reformed the following decade following an emotional reunion between Petersen and Whaley. Blue Cheer has continued to pursue the former's bombastic vision and a 1990 release, Highlights And Lowlives, united the group with Anthrax producer Jack Eudino.
Albums: Vincebus Eruptum (1968), Outsideinside (1968), New! Improved! Blue Cheer (1969), Blue Cheer (1970), The Original Human Being (1970), Oh! Pleasant Hope (1971), Blitzkrieg Over Nuremburg (1989), Highlights And Lowlives (1990). Compilations: The Best Of Blue Cheer (1982), Louder Than God (1987).

Blue Murder

Blue Murder

This project was masterminded by ex-Thin Lizzy and Tygers Of Pan Tang guitarist John Sykes, after he left Whitesnake. Enlisting the services of Tony Franklin on bass and Cozy Powell on drums (the latter quickly replaced by Carmine Appice) Sykes decided to record as a three-piece outfit. This followed a long and fruitless search for a suitable vocalist to front the band. The material included on their self-titled debut drew heavily on Sykes's Whitesnake legacy, but featured more extended compositions, with sophisticated arrangements and lengthy instrumental breaks. It was criticised upon its release, perhaps prematurely and unfairly, as it does contain a number of classy songs. Franklin quit in 1991, after the recording of tracks for the band's, as yet untitled second album.
Album: Blue Murder (1989).

Blue Öyster Cult

The genesis of Blue Öyster Cult lay in the musical ambitions of rock writers Sandy Pearlman and Richard Meltzer. Based in New York, the pair put together a group - known variously as the Soft White Underbelly and Oaxaca - to perform their original songs. By 1969 the unit, now dubbed the

Stalk-Forrest Group, had established around Eric Bloom (stun guitar/vocals), Donald 'Buck Dharma' Roeser (guitar/vocals), Allen Lanier (keyboards/guitar), Joe Bouchard (bass/vocals) and Albert Bouchard (drums). The quintet completed a single, 'What Is Quicksand', before assuming their Blue Öyster Cult appellation. Early releases combined Black Sabbath-styled riffs with obtuse lyricism which engendered an 'intelligent heavy metal' tag. Cryptic titles, including 'A Kiss Before The Redap' and 'OD'd On Life Itself' compounded an image - part biker, part occult - assiduously sculpted by Pearlman, whose clean production technique also removed any emotional inflections. 'Career Of Evil' from *Secret Treaties* - co-written by Patti Smith - showed an increasing grasp of commercial hooklines, which flourished on the international Byrds-sounding hit, '(Don't Fear) The Reaper'. Smith continued her association with the band on *Agents Of Fortune*, contributing to 'Debbie Denise' and 'The Revenge Of Vera Gemini', but the release of the live *Some Enchanted Evening* brought the group's most innovative era to an end. Despite a continued in-concert popularity; notably on the *Black And Blue* tour with Black Sabbath, a predictability had crept into their work. Rick Downey replaced Al Bouchard in 1981, while the following year Roeser completed a solo album *Flat Out* as the Cult's own recordings grew noticeably less prolific.
Albums: *Blue Öyster Cult* (1972), *Tyranny And Mutation* (1973), *Secret Treaties* (1974), *On Your Feet Or On Your Knees* (1974), *Agents Of Fortune* (1975), *Spectres* (1977), *Some Enchanted Evening* (1978), *Mirrors* (1979), *Cultosaurus Erectus* (1980), *Fire Of Unknown Origin* (1981), *Revolution By Night* (1983), *Club Ninja* (1985), *Imaginos* (1988). Compilations: *E.T.I.* (1982), *Career Of Evil - The Metal Years* (1990).

Bolin, Tommy

b. 1 August, 1951, Sioux City, Iowa, USA, d. 4 December 1976, Miami, Florida, USA. Tommy Bolin was a highly versatile progressive rock guitarist who successfully branched into fusion with considerable success and respect. Bolin became interested in music after seeing Elvis Presley in concert in 1956. He quickly learned to play Elvis songs on guitar and won local amateur contests. His first groups, Denny and the Triumphs and American Standard, found little or no success, and Bolin took work backing blues guitarist Lonnie Mack. In 1968 he formed Ethereal Zephyr, later shortened to Zephyr. Signed to Probe Records, their debut release was a US Top 50 album in 1969. Following the failure of their follow-up Bolin depated and formed the jazz/fusion group Energy with flautist Jeremy Steig, based in Colorado. Bolin also worked on an unreleased Steig album that also featured Jan Hammer and Billy Cobham. The latter then asked Bolin to play guitar on his *Spectrum* album in 1973 (which reputedly inspired Jeff Beck to try his hand at fusion). Having become a 'name' guitarist he was asked to replace Domenic Troiano (who had replaced Joe Walsh) in the James Gang. Bolin performed on their 1973 *Bang* album and the following year's *Miami*. After contributing to sessions for jazz drummer Alphonse Mouzon's *Mind Transplant* album, he was hired in 1975 by Deep Purple, to replace the departed Ritchie Blackmore. He wrote and co-wrote many songs for the English hard-rock group's *Come Taste The Band*. During the early stages of that band's dissolution in late 1975 Bolin went solo, recording the critically-acclaimed *Teaser* for Nemperor Records and, the following year, *Private Eyes* for Columbia. He toured with the Tommy Bolin Band to promote the albums. In December 1976, Bolin was found dead in a Miami hotel room, the victim of a drug overdose.
Albums: with Zephyr *Zephyr* (1969), *Going Back To Colorado* (1971); with Billy Cobham *Spectrum* (1973); with James Gang *Bang* (1973), *Miami* (1974); with Alphonse Mouzon *Mind Transplant* (1975); with Deep Purple *Come Taste The Band* (1975); solo *Teaser* (1975), *Private Eyes* (1976). Compilation: *The Ultimate...Tommy Bolin* (1989).

Bolt Thrower

Deriving their name from a character in a popular war game story, Bolt Thrower are an extreme 'grindcore' rock band based in Birmingham, England. Comprising Karl Willets (vocals), Gavin Ward (guitar), Barry Thomson (guitar), Jo Bench (bass) and Andy Whale (drums), they gained a recording contract on the strength of their session for BBC disc jockey John Peel, which was broadcasted on Radio 1 in 1987. A year later, their debut album emerged, featuring an aggressive fusion of hardcore and thrash with indecipherable vocals. They have slowly built up a loyal following of fans who crave their amelodic wall of noise.
Albums: *In Battle There Is No Law* (1988), *The Peel Sessions* (1988), *Realm Of Chaos* (1989), *Warmaster* (1991).

Bombers

This Australian-based, hard-rock/boogie group were formed in 1989 by ex-Status Quo bassist Alan Lancaster. Recruiting John Brewster (guitar/harmonica), Steve Crofts (slide guitar), Tyrone Coates (vocals/saxophone) and Peter

Heckenberg (drums), they signed to Polydor and their *Aim High* came in 1990. Musically, they meander through AC/DC, Status Quo territory, with Coates's pumping saxophone and Crofts's slide guitar adding some individuality to the material. They remain a quality band they have largely been ignored outside Australia.

Album: *Aim High* (1990).

Bonfire

Bonfire

This heavy metal band was formed in Ingolstadt, Germany. They came together in 1985 from the ashes of Cacumen which featured Claus Lessmann (vocals) and Hans Ziller (guitar). Other early members included Horst Makr Thorn (guitar) and a nameless drummer, who was sacked and replaced temporarily by Ken Mary from House Of Lords. Edgar Patrik (ex-Sinner, Tyran Pace and Paul Samson) joined in time for their third album, while Thorn was replaced by Angel Schaeffer (ex-Pretty Maids and Sinner) in 1988. An early introduction to UK audiences was convened at 1988's Reading festival. Afterwards they completed recording for their third album, *Point Blank*, produced by Michael Wagner, which gave them critical and commercial success in the UK and Europe. Despite this, Ziller departed leaving the line-up into the 90s comprising of Lessmann, Schaeffer, Patrik, Michael Voss (guitar) and Jorg Deisinger (bass). Despite working in a similar vein to the Scorpions they have so far failed to achieve the same sort of crossover appeal.

Albums: *Don't Touch That Light* (1986), *Fireworks* (1987), *Point Blank* (1989), *Knockout* (1991).

Bonham

This heavy rock band was founded by Jason Bonham (b. 1967, England), who was given his first drum kit at the age of four by his father, Led Zeppelin's John Bonham. After playing in local groups, Jason Bonham toured and recorded in 1987 with Jimmy Page and, after his father's death, performed with the surviving members of Led Zeppelin in New York in 1988. He next formed his own band with ex-Robert Plant Honeydrippers guitarist Ian Hatton (b. 1962, Kidderminster, Worcestershire, England), John Smithson (b. 1963, Sussex, England; keyboards/bass) and Daniel McMaster (b. 1968, Barrie, Ontario, Canada; vocals). In 1990, the group released its first single, 'Wait For You', produced by Alice Cooper's producer Bob Ezrin.

Album: *The Disregard Of Time Keeping* (1990).

Bon Jovi

This commercial hard rock band was formed in New Jersey and fronted by Jon Bon Jovi (b. John Francis Bongiovi Jnr, 2 March 1962, Perth Sayreville, New Jersey, USA; vocals). His four co-conspirators were: Ritchie Sambora (b. 11 July 1959; guitar), David Bryan (b. David Rashbaum, 7 February 1962, Edison, New Jersey, USA; keyboards), Tico Torres (b. 7 October 1953; drums) and Alec John Such (b. 14 November 1956; bass). Bongiovi, of Italian descent, met Rashbaum at Sayreville High School, sharing a mutual interest in rock music. They soon joined eight other musicians in the R&B cover band Atlantic City Expressway. When Rashbaum moved to New York to study at the Juilliard School of Music, Bongiovi followed. Bluffing his way into the Power Station recording studios, he performed menial tasks for two years before Billy Squier agreed to produce his demo tape. One track, 'Runaway', was played on local radio and appeared on a local artist compilation album. Reunited with Rashbaum, they acquired the services of Sambora, an established session musician, Such (ex-Phantom's Opera) and Torres (ex-Knockouts). By July 1983, they had a recording contract with Polygram and support slots with Eddie Money and ZZ Top, the latter at Madison Square Gardens. Jon Bon Jovi's looks attracted immediate attention for the band, and he turned down the lucrative lead role in the dance film *Footloose* in order to concentrate on his music. Their debut album preceded a headline tour and supports with the Scorpions, Whitesnake and Kiss. *7800 Degrees Fahrenheit* was greeted with cynicism by the media, which was already reticent at the prospect of the band's manicured image and formularized heavy rock. A mediocre album only fuelled their scorn. The band responded with style. *Slippery When Wet* was the biggest selling rock album of 1987, although it originally appeared at the end of 1986. Two of its tracks; 'You Give Love A Bad Name' and 'Livin'On A Prayer', were US hits. Headlining the Monsters Of Rock shows in Europe, they were joined on stage by Gene

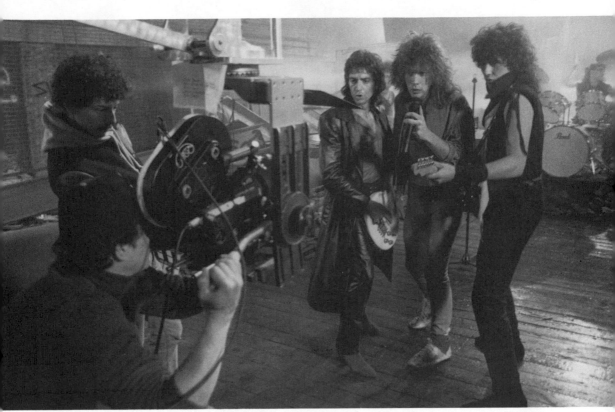

Bon Jovi

Simmons and Paul Stanley (Kiss), Dee Snider (Twisted Sister) and Bruce Dickinson (Iron Maiden) for an encore of 'We're An American Band'. It emphasized the fact that they had reached the top of the rock league in a very short space of time. The tour finally closed after 18 months in Australia, while the album sold millions of copies. When *New Jersey* followed, it contained 'Living In Sin', a Jon Bon Jovi solo composition which pointed to his solo future, although the song owed a great debt to his hero Bruce Springsteen. The rest of 1989 was spent on more exhaustive touring, before the band temporarily retired. As Jon Bon Jovi commented, it was time to 'Ride my bike into the hills, learn how to garden, *anything* except do another Bon Jovi record'. He has since concentrated on his solo career, and appeared in his first movie, *Young Guns II*.
Albums: *Bon Jovi* (1984), *7,800 Degrees Fahrenheit* (1985), *Slippery When Wet* (1986), *New Jersey* (1988).

Bootsauce

This Canadian funk/rap/metal crossover quintet were formed in Montreal in 1989. Comprising, Drew Ling (vocals), Pere Fume (guitar), Sonny (guitar), Baculis (bass) and Rob Kazenel (drums), they have often been compared to a three-way hybrid of Earth Wind And Fire, Red Hot Chili Peppers and Weather Report. At times they verge on avant garde and jazz-rock, but possess an irreverent sense of humour and fun, that sets them aside from the mainstream. They also include a interesting cover of Hot Chocolate's 'Everyone's A Winner' in their live set.
Album: *The Brown Album* (1991).

Borich, Kevin

b. New Zealand. Regarded as one of Australia's leading guitarists, Borich came to Australia with the New Zealand band La De Das in 1976. After a tour of the UK in 1980 other members left, leaving Borich as lead guitarist in a trio which he eventually renamed the Kevin Borich Express. The Express earned a reputation as one of the hardest working groups in the country, touring and playing incessantly. His style was influenced by Jimi Hendrix and Robin Trower, and his excellent guitar work overshadowed his ordinary vocals and songwriting. On album his talent has not been adequately explored, although his guitar playing on the La De Das' version of 'All Along the Watchtower' was exemplary. An involvement with the hugely popular Party Boys cover band led to the gradual dissolution of his own band from 1983 onwards.

Albums: *Celebration* (1976), *The Lonely One* (1977), *Live* (1979), *No Turning Back* (1979), *Angels Hand* (1980), *Kevin Borich Express* (1980), with Renee Geyer *Blues Licence* (1979), with Dutch Tilders *The Blues Had A Baby And They Called It Rock And Roll* (1981). Compilation: *The Best Of Kevin Borich* (1977).

Boulevard

This Canadian band was formed in 1984 by saxophonist and ex-session musician Mark Holden. With the addition of David Forbes (vocals), Randy Gould (guitar), Andrew Johns (keyboards), Randy Burgess (bass) and Jerry Adolphe (drums), the six-man line-up was complete. Initially, they pursued a highly melodic AOR direction, similar to Toto and REO Speedwagon. *Into The Street* marked a move towards a more hard-rock approach, with Foreigner, Bad Company and Bon Jovi influences. They have established a solid fan base in their native Canada, but this success has yet to be translated elsewhere.

Albums: *Boulevard* (1988), *Into The Street* (1990).

Bow Wow

The name translates literally into 'Barking Dog'; a fitting title for Japan's finest exponents of melodic heavy metal. Formed in 1976, the band comprised Kyoji Yamamoto (vocals/guitar), Mitsuhiro Saito (vocals/guitar), Kenji Sano (bass) and Toshiri Niimi (drums). They incorporated classical Japanese musical structures within a framework of westernized hard-rock. Influenced by Kiss, Led Zeppelin and Aerosmith, they released a sequence of impressive albums during the late 70s. Characterized by explosive guitarwork and breathtaking arrangements, the only disappointment was the Japanese vocals, which without doubt, restricted their international appeal. On *Asian Volcano*, their eleventh album released in 1982, the vocals were sung in English for the first time, but the band sounded uncomfortable with the awkward lyrical translations. They played the Reading Festival the same year and were well received. Two subsequent shows at London's Marquee Club were recorded for the live album *Holy Expedition*, which followed in 1983. At the end of 1983, the band changed their name to Vow Wow, adding an extra vocalist and keyboard player to pursue a more melodic direction. Lead guitarist Yamamoto

has released two solo albums to-date, which represent an instrumental fusion of classical, rock and jazz styles; *Horizons* and *Electric Cinema* in 1980 and 1982 respectively. Outside the Far East, success has continued to elude this first-class rock outfit.

Albums: *Bow Wow* (1976), *Signal Fire* (1977), *Charge* (1977), *Super Live* (1978), *Guarantee* (1978), *The Bow Wow* (1979), *Glorious Road* (1979), *Telephone* (1980), *X Bomber* (1980), *Hard Dog* (1981), *Asian Volcano* (1982), *Warning From Stardust* (1982), *Holy Expedition* (1983).

Boyzz

Influenced by Steppenwolf, Black Oak Arkansas and Lynyrd Skynyrd, the US-based Boyzz combined hard-driving rock 'n' roll, with southern-style boogie. With a strong leather-clad, biker image, their sole album *Too Wild To Tame*, featured Dirty Dan Buck (vocals), Anatole Halinkovitch (keyboards), Gil Pini (guitar), Mike Tafoya (guitar), David Angel (bass) and Kent Cooper (drums). Unable to transform media interest into record sales, the band disintegrated soon after the albums release. Halinkovitch, Tafoya and Angel later went on to form B'zz.

Album: *Too Wild To Tame (1978)*

Brats

This Danish quartet was formed in Copenhagen 1979 by guitarists Michael Denner and Hank Sherman. Recruiting Yens (bass/vocals) and Monroe (drums), they signed to CBS and recorded a debut album the following year. Appropriately titled *1980*, it featured a dozen hard-rock tracks, punctuated by some dazzling guitar work from Denner. The band fell apart shortly after the album's release, with guitarists Denner and Sherman joining forces with King Diamond (vocals), Timmy Grabber (bass) and Kim Ruzz to become Mercyful Fate. This corresponded with a change in direction towards satanic heavy metal.

Album: *1980* (1980).

Brave Belt

This Canadian quartet was formed in 1970 by ex-Guess Who duo, Randy Bachman (guitar/vocals) and Chad Allen (keyboards). With the addition of drummer Rob Bachman and bassist C.F. Turner, they made one album of blues/country influenced rock. In 1972, Tim Bachman replaced Chad Allen and Brave Belt became known as Bachman Turner Overdrive. The band then pursued a much more aggressive style of hard-rock boogie.

Album: *Brave Belt* (1971).

Britny Fox

Breathless

This six-piece melodic AOR band was formed in the USA's mid-west in 1978. Breathless was assembled by ex-Michael Stanley Band vocalist Jonah Koslen who, after a successful search, completed the line-up with Alan Greene (guitar), Mark Avsec (keyboards), Bob Benjamin (bass) and drummers Rodney Psycka and Kevin Valentine. They signed to EMI in 1979 and released two albums in the space of 18 months. Their lightweight, Kansas meets Toto-style melodic compositions failed to win an appreciative audience. The band split in 1981, with Koslen releasing a solo album, *Aces*, two years later.
Albums: *Breathless* (1979), *Nobody Leaves This Song Alive* (1980).

Breslau

This German hard-rock quartet was formed in 1981 by vocalist Jutta Weinholt and guitarist Alex Parche. Adding Zweibel Truhol (bass) and Cay Wolf (drums), they recorded their first and only album the following year. Influenced by Iron Maiden, Scorpions and Kiss, *Volksmusik* was notable for Weinholt's powerful and unusual vocal style. The music was derivative, however. Unable to generate any interest, the band disintegrated a few months later. Weinholt reappeared in 1988 as lead vocalist with Zed Yago.
Album: *Volksmusik* (1982).

Briar

This pop-rock quartet was formed in Birmingham, England during 1983 by Kevin Griffiths (vocals/bass) and Daren Underwood (guitar). With Dave Fletcher (guitar) and Dean Cook (drums), they released a self-financed single, that was given considerable airplay by BBC Radio 1 disc jockey, Peter Powell. A Radio 1 live session was followed by a recording contract with Heavy Metal Records. *Too Young* emerged in 1985, an over-produced affair that was full of lightweight guitar, high-pitched harmonies and inoffensive lyrics. The album flopped and the band were forced to return to the club circuit. *Take On The World*, a self-financed cassette was released in 1986, which eventually led to a new contract with CBS. Half the album comprised a selection of cover versions that included Richie Valens's 'La Bamba' and Sister Sledge's 'Frankie'.
Albums: *Too Young* (1985), *Take On The World* (1986), *Crown Of Thorns* (1988).

Bricklin

This American, six-piece rock band was founded by the Bricklin brothers in 1986. Featuring Brian Bricklin (guitar/keyboards), Scott Bricklin (vocals/keyboards), Ian Cross (guitar/keyboard/vocals), James Goetz (bass/vocals) and Eddie Bader (drums), the band secured a contract with A&M Records in 1987. Adopting a commercial approach, their music was comparable in style to Toto, Loverboy, It Bites and Kansas. Although technically excellent and superbly produced, their two albums to date lack individuality and distinction.

Albums: *Bricklin* (1987), *Bricklin II* (1989).

Britny Fox

This American 'glam-metal' quartet was formed in Philadelphia 1987 by vocalist 'Dizzy' Dean Davidson (ex-World War III drummer) and former Cinderella guitarist Michael Kelly Smith. With the addition of bassist Billy Childs and ex-Waysted drummer Johnny Dee, they signed to CBS and released their debut album the following year. This was an amalgam of AC/DC, Mötley Crüe and Quiet Riot influences. Characterized by Davidson's raucous snarl, it included an inspired cover of Slade's 'Gudbuy To Jane' plus nine originals. *Boys In Heat* saw the band mellow a little; the make-up was discarded and replaced with a rough, street-wise rock 'n' roller image. Davidson's vocals were considerably refined and the material edged, significantly, towards Cinderella's style. Britny Fox toured with Bon Jovi and Alice Cooper, but were unable to convert successful concert performances into album sales. Davidson quit in 1990 and went on to form Blackeyed Susan, with Tommy Paris being drafted in as his replacement almost a year later. *Bite Down Hard* emerged in 1991, with the songs following a much heavier direction. Against expectations, the band had made a triumphant return, and were poised for greater success in the second phase of their career.

Albums: *Britny Fox* (1988), *Boys In Heat* (1989), *Bite Down Hard* (1991).

Broken Bones

This British hardcore band was formed in Stoke-on-Trent, England during 1983 by ex-Discharge guitarist Tony 'Bones' Roberts. Recruiting brother Terry on bass, vocalist Nobby and drummer Cliff, they closely followed the metal/punk crossover approach of Bones's former group. With controversial lyrics and a rigidly formularized approach, they have progressed very little since their inception. After a period of inactivity, they returned in 1989 with Quiv and D.L. Harris as new faces on lead vocals and bass respectively. *Losing Control* appeared shortly afterwards; a vitriolic blast of angst-ridden hardcore.

Albums: *Dem Bones* (1984), *Live 100 Club* (1985), *Seeing Through My Eyes* (1985), *Bone-Crushers* (1986), *F.O.A.D.* (1986), *Losing Control* (1989), *Stitched Up* (1991).

Bronze

This band were the first to be launched on the US market by Bronze Records. The five musicians that co-operated in this marketing ploy were from Bath, England and comprised ex-Nightwing vocalist Max Bacon, guitarists Chris Gouldstone and Shaun Kirkpatrick, bassist Paul Webb and drummer Carl Matthews. In spite of using four producers and an embarrassingly large budget, their debut album was a ramshackle affair that was inferior to the well-established outfits of the genre. After one album, the band split, with Bacon going on to achieve success later with GTR.

Album: *Taken By Storm* (1984).

Bruzer

Bruzer were a short-lived collaboration of established US musicians playing a mixture of hard-rock and techno-pop in the style of Cheap Trick. The line-up comprised Paul Frank (vocals), Jeff Steele (bass), Vinnie Appice (drums, ex-Derringer, later Black Sabbath), Mitchell Froom (keyboards, later of Gamma) and Rick Ramirez (guitar, ex-Striker). *Round One*, released in 1982 was well received, but the band splintered, before the interest shown could be consolidated into commercial success.

Album: *Round One* (1982).

Buffalo

Buffalo emerged in Sydney, Australia in 1970 and soon picked up a healthy following of heavy rock fans. Signed by the prestigious Vertigo label, the band's albums sold slowly but steadily enough to retain the interest of the label. The group received bad press owing to the overtly sexist nature of the covers of their first three albums and also for some of the song lyrics (eg 'Skirt Lifter'), which perhaps limited their appeal. Buffalo were an anomaly among bands in Australia during the 70s in that they were as popular in Europe, particularly France, as they were in their homeland. The outfit were musically akin to the likes of Black Sabbath and Deep Purple while retaining their own rock sound, enhanced by Norm Roue's slide guitar playing and the powerful performances of vocalist Dave Tice. Eventually the dearth of original members lead the band to split, after recording five albums. Interestingly the first album went gold three years after initial release. Bassist Pete Wells, played slide guitar in Rose Tattoo with Angry Anderson, while Tice joined original drummer, Paul Balbi, in the Count Bishops in the UK.

Albums: *Dead Forever* (1972), *Volcanic Rock* (1973), *Only Want You For Your Body* (1974), *Mother's Choice* (1976), *Average Rock And Roller* (1977). Compilation: *Best Of* (1980).

Bulldozer

This death-metal trio was formed in Milan, Italy during 1984 by classically trained guitarist Andy Panigada and bassist/vocalist A.C.Wild. With the recruitment of drummer Don Andras, they recorded *The Day Of Wrath* in 1985. This comprised of frantic thrash, with out-of-phase vocals and a muddy production. They built up a small but loyal cult following, gaining notoriety for their extreme style and proverbial bad taste. Two more albums followed a similar pattern, except that 1988's *Neurodeli* played down the satanic emphasis in the lyrics. Presumably no more will be heard from Bulldozer with Wild's appointment as Metal Master's label representative. Albums: *The Day Of Wrath* (1985), *IX* (1987), *Neurodeli* (1988).

Bulletboys

This American hard-rock quartet was formed in 1987 by Mick Sweda (guitar, ex-King Kobra) and Marq Torien (vocals, ex-Ratt). They were joined by Lonnie Vincent (bass) and Jimmy D'Anda (drums) and took their musical brief from AC/DC, Van Halen and Montrose. Championed by producer Ted Templeman, they signed to Warner Brothers and recorded their self-titled debut album the following year. Torien's flamboyant persona courted comparisons with David Lee Roth, while Sweda's guitar histrionics were based on a style first made famous by Eddie Van Halen. *Freakshow* saw the band broaden their musical horizons and incorporate blues and funk influences into the basic hard-rock structures. Albums: *Bulletboys* (1988), *Freakshow* (1991).

Burning Tree

Hailing from Los Angeles, USA this three-piece specialize in early 70s blues-based power rock. Marc Ford (guitar/vocals), Mark Dutton (bass/vocals) and Doni Gray (drums) re-invent, re-hash and re-interpret the riffs, licks and solos first unleashed by artists including Eric Clapton, John Mayall and Jimi Hendrix. In essence they are revivalists using Cream as a musical blueprint to work from. They celebrate rather than simply duplicate, breathing new-life into well-worn

arrangements by a combination of sheer conviction and the latest technology.
Album: *Burning Tree* (1990).

Burtnick, Glen

After working with Helmet Boy, Jan Hammer and Neil Schon, Glen Burtnick (b. USA; vocals/guitar/keyboards) declined the offer to join Bon Jovi, in favour of working on a solo career. Securing a deal with A&M Records, he employed session musicians to help record the debut *Talking In Code*. A sophisticated and highly-polished selection of pop-rock anthems, the album was infused with elements of funk and soul. On *Heroes And Zeroes*, Bruce Hornsby, Anton Fig and Neil Schon made guest appearances, but the songs covered mainly the same format as before. In 1990 he joined Styx in place of Tommy Shaw, to record their comeback album *Edge Of The Century*.
Albums: *Talking In Code* (1986), *Heroes And Zeroes* (1987).

Bush, Stan

This US singer first came to prominence with country/rock band Boulder. Bush went solo in 1983, recording a self-titled album that invited comparisons to the sophisticated pop-rock style of Billy Squier and John Parr. He linked up with the occasional band Barrage in 1987 to pursue a more hard-rock direction.
Albums: *Stan Bush* (1983), *Stan Bush & Barrage* (1987).

Byron, David

b. David Garrick, 29 January 1947, Essex, England, d. 28 February 1985. Byron began his music career as vocalist with the Stalkers, an Essex-based act which, by 1969, had evolved into Uriah Heep. Although subjected to critical denigration, the group became one of the 70s leading hard rock/heavy metal attractions, thanks in part to the singer's powerful delivery. In 1975, Byron completed a solo album, *Take No Prisoners*, as excessive alcohol consumption put his position within the line-up under increasing pressure. He was fired the following year, but hopes of an artistic rebirth with Rough Diamond proved ill-founded and this highly-touted attraction featuring Dave Clempson broke apart within a year. Bereft of a regular group, he completed *Baby Faced Killer*, but the set appeared during the height of the punk boom, and was not a commercial success. A similar fate befell the ensuing Byron Band whose ill-focused *On The Rocks* did little to further the leader's progress. They folded soon after its release after which the disconsolate vocalist attempted to maintain his career. He died in 1985 as a result of a heart attack.

Albums: *Take No Prisoners* (1975), *Baby Faced Killer* (1977), *This Day And Age* (1980), as the Byron Band *On The Rocks* (1981), *Bad Widow* (1984).

Bystander

This American melodic rock quartet was formed in 1981. Influenced by Loverboy and Kansas, the band comprised Andy Kiely (vocals/bass), Bucky Naughton (guitar/vocals), John E. Allison (guitar/vocals) and Jimmy Callaghan (drums). Allison and Callaghan arrived after the release of their album, replacing Mike Weaver and Stanley Steele. The self-financed *Not So Innocent*, was an admirable debut and surpassed the efforts of many of the more well-established acts in the genre.

Album: *Not So Innocent* (1987).

B'zz

Formed from the ashes of heavy metal 'biker-band' Boyzz, this group featured Michael Tafoya (guitar), David Angel (bass) and Anatole Halinkovitch (keyboards). With the recruitment of Tom Holland (vocals) and Steve Riley (drums), they rejected their previous Hells Angels image and concentrated instead on pop-metal crossover material. Their debut album released in 1982, fused elements of Kiss, Cheap Trick and Foreigner, but met with little success. The band disintegrated when Holland left to form a new outfit under his own name. Riley subsequently went on to play with W.A.S.P.

Album: *Get Up* (1982).

C

Cacophony
This speed-metal band was formed in the USA in 1986 and built around the nucleus of up-and-coming guitar wizards Marty Friedman and Jason Becker. Recruiting drummer Atma Anur and ex-Le Mans vocalist Peter Marrino, they debuted with *Speed Metal Symphony*; a predominantly instrumental album, that fused classical, blues and hard-rock styles. Friedman and Becker then went on to record individual solo albums in a similar vein, before commencing work on another band project. *Go Off*, released in 1989, saw the arrival of Jimmy O'Shea and Kenny Stavropoulos on bass and drums, respectively. This album reinforced the band's hi-tech instrumental approach, and featured complex passages where the guitars of Friedman and Becker duelled for supremacy. The album was a commercial failure and subsequently Cacophony was dissolved in 1990, with Stavropoulos joining Starship, Becker teaming up with David Lee Roth and Friedman being recruited by Megadeth.
Albums: *Speed Metal Symphony* (1987), *Go Off* (1989).

Candlemass
This Swedish doom-metal quintet formed in 1985. Comprising Messiah Marcolin (vocals), Lars Johansson (guitar), Mats Bjorkman (guitar), Leif Edling (bass) and Jan Lindh (drums), their style combined elements of Black Sabbath, Black Widow and Mercyful Fate. Marcolin's eccentric appearance gave the band a visual focus; dressed in a monk's habit, his deep bellowing tones added a touch of mystique to their live performances. *Nightfall*, their most accomplished work, fused intense and crushing rhythms with delicate, classical-like interludes to startling effect. *Tales Of Creation* saw the band afforded a larger recording budget with new label MFN. However, their approach had become rather formularized by this stage, and although the album was technically superior to earlier efforts, the songs left a distinct feeling of *déjà-vu*. A live album followed in an attempt to recapture lost ground. It appears that the band are trapped in a creative conundrum, while their initial followers continue to move on to other things.
Albums: *Epicus, Doomicus, Metallicus* (1986), *Nightfall* (1987), *Ancient Dreams* (1988), *Tales Of Creation* (1989), *Live* (1991).

Cannata
Jeff Cannata first came to prominence under the name Arc Angel in 1983. Following five years of producing, arranging and guesting on a variety of projects, he finally took enough time out in 1988 to record *Images Of Forever*. Being responsible for the vocals, guitar, keyboards, bass and drums, the album was a stunning achievement and a testimony to the man's remarkable musical ability. The material invites comparisons with the best works from Boston, Starcastle and Angel.
Album: *Images Of Forever* (1988).

Captain Beyond
Based in Los Angeles, this Anglo-American 'supergroup' was formed in 1972 around Rod Evans (b. 19 January 1947, Slough, Berkshire, England; vocals, ex-Deep Purple), Bobby Caldwell (drums, ex-Johnny Winter) and two former members of Iron Butterfly, Larry 'Rhino' Rhinehardt (b. 7 July 1948, Florida, USA; guitar) and Lee Dorman (b. 15 September 1945, St. Louis, Missouri, USA; bass). Although *Captain Beyond* established the unit's hard-rock style, this initial line-up proved incompatible and Caldwell was replaced by Marty Rodriguez for *Sufficiently Breathless*. The departure of Evans precipitated a lengthy period of inactivity but in 1976 the remaining trio was joined by Willy Daffern (vocals), Reese Wynans (keyboards) and Guille Garcia (percussion). This final version broke up following the release of *Dawn Explosion*.
Albums: *Captain Beyond* (1972), *Sufficiently Breathless* (1973), *Dawn Explosion* (1977).

Carcass
This British hardcore/death metal group was formed in 1987. The band, all vegetarians, comprise Jeff Walker (vocals/bass, ex-Electro Hippies), Bill Steer (vocals/guitar, ex-Napalm Death) and Ken Owen (drums). The line-up was later enlarged with the addition of a second guitarist, Michael Amott. Their approach is characterized by morbid death-grunts over a barrage of chaotic, bass-dominated music. Carcass's lyrical content deals primarilly with mutilation, vomiting, putrefaction, intestinal rupturing and steaming entrails - all dealt with in strict medical and ananomical terminology - ie; 'Intenacious, intersecting/Reaving fats from corporal griskin . . . Skeletal groats triturated, desinently exsiccated' They appear likely to remain of cult interest, appreciated by an army of loyal followers in Europe and the USA.
Albums: *Reek Of Putrefaction* (1988), *Symphonies Of Sickness* (1989), *Necrotism-Descanting The Insalubrious* (1991).

Carcass

Carl, Max

Formerly known as Max Gronenthal, he first came to prominence as a member of Energy during the early 70s, which also featured future Deep Purple guitarist Tommy Bolin. In 1979, Carl embarked on a solo career and released two melodic AOR albums, similar in style to the music of Toto, Kansas and Michael Bolton. *The Circle*, his third solo album, released in 1985, saw the name change but not the musical direction. After being dropped by MCA Records, he replaced Don Barnes in .38 Special.
Album: *The Circle* (1985).

Carnivore

This American heavy metal band was formed by ex-Fallout duo Louie Batteaux alias Lord Petrus T. (drums) and Peter Steele (vocals/bass) in New York 1983. With the addition of guitarist Keith Alexander, they attracted media interest by basing their image on a Mad Max II/post apocalyptic scenario. They dressed in animal skins and achieved a degree of notoriety with their racially naïve lyrics. Their self-titled debut comprised of thrash metal with little originality. Marc Piovanetti replaced Alexander on 1987's *Retaliation*, which resulted in a marked improvement in the band's guitar sound. However, this was not sufficient to enable them to compete realistically with the first division acts such as Slayer, Testament or Anthrax. Piovanetti left in 1988, to join the Crumbsuckers.
Albums: *Carnivore* (1986), *Retaliation* (1987).

Celtic Frost

Formed in Switzerland in 1984 from the ashes of the thrash metal-inspired band Hellhammer, Celtic Frost consisted of Thomas Gabriel Warrior (guitar/vocals), Martin Eric Ain (bass) and Isaac Darso (drums). The first album emerged in 1984 with drummer Stephen Priestly, and was a thrash metal landmark. Reed St. Mark became drummer in 1985 for *Emperors Return*. Martin Ain was replaced by bassist Dominic Steiner for *To Mega Therion*, only to return for *Into The Pandemonium*, which became Celtic Frost's 'avant garde thrash'; a major work. *Cold Lake* was much more mainstream and featured Tom Warrior along with Stephen Priestly (drums), Curt Victor Bryant (bass) and Oliver Amberg (guitar). It was too much of a departure from their true sound to be a success. The band's popularity slid dramatically, with a slight resurgence after *Vanity/Nemesis* which was much improved, and saw the return of Martin Ain.
Albums: *Morbid Tales* (1984), *Emperor's Return* (1984), *To Mega Therion* (1985), *Into The Pandemonium* (1987), *Cold Lake* (1988),

Celtic Frost

Vanity/Nemesis (1990).

Centaurus

This US, blues-based rock quartet was formed in 1977 by guitar virtuoso Nick Paine. Enlisting the services of Nick Costello (bass), Louis Merlino (vocals) and Joey Belfiore (drums), they took their musical lead primarily from Led Zeppelin and Aerosmith. Paine's guitar work was structured on the style made famous by Jimmy Page. Their sole release is noticeably derivative, but the excellent production and rawness of the band's delivery makes it more than worthwhile. They split soon after the album hit the racks, with Costello going on to join Toronto.
Album: *Centaurus* (1978).

Chain Reaction

This Canadian hard-rock/techno-pop quartet was formed in 1981 by Warren Barvour (guitar) and Phil Naro (vocals). Recruiting Ray Lessard (bass) and John Livingston (drums), they secured a contract with Attic Records the following year. Influenced by Van Halen, REO Speedwagon and Foreigner, they recorded *X Rated Dream*; a collection of pop-rock anthems, lifted only, enlivened by some explosive guitar bursts from Barvour. Naro left to work with Talas in 1983 and

Cheap And Nasty

the band subsequently disintegrated.
Albums: *X Rated Dream* (1982).

Champion

When David Byron quit Rough Diamond in
1977, the remaining band members recruited US
vocalist Garry Bell as replacement and
subsequently changed their name to Champion.
With former Humble Pie guitarist Dave
Clempson, ex-Wings drummer Geoff Britton plus
Damon Butcher (keyboards) and Willy Bath (bass)
completing their line-up, Champion's music never
lived up to the promise suggested by their
impressive pedigree. Picked up by Epic Records,
they released a self-titled album in 1978 of blues-
based rock. Failing to attract media attention, they
disbanded shortly after the disc was released.
Album: *Champion* (1978).

Chastain, David T.

This highly productive, new-age guitar virtuoso
emerged from Cincinnati, USA. As well as
releasing solo albums under his own name, he
recorded with CJSS and Chastain, to provide
outlets for the vast amount of material that he
composes. After leaving Spike in 1984 with bassist

Mike Skimmerhorn, the duo formed the two
semi-permanent outfits CJSS and Chastain, with
the latter being a vehicle for the faster, louder and
heavier material. With the help of ex-Rude Girl
vocalist Leather Leone and drummer Fred Coury,
Mystery Of Illusion was recorded under the
Chastain monicker in 1985. The predominantly
uptempo approach, with raunchy vocals and fluid
guitar work, was well received by the critics, and
consequently Chastain became David's major
concern. A series of albums followed in quick
succession, each one an identikit version of the
debut. Eight high-speed rockers and two ballads
were the typical formula. Ken Mary (ex-Alice
Cooper) took over the drumstool in 1986 as
Chastain's work rate reached overload. *Instrumental
Variations* and *Within The Heat* indicated a move
towards a jazz-rock style. *For Those Who Dare* saw
Chastain, the band, back in the studio again. It
comprised the same formularized approach as
before. There is no doubt that David Chastain has
sacrificed much of his original credibility in
repeatedly releasing average material.
Albums: *Mystery Of Illusion* (1985), *Ruler Of The
Wasteland* (1986), *The 7th Of Never* (1987),
Instrumental Variations (1987), *The Voice Of The*

Cult (1988), *Within The Heat* (1989), *For Those Who Dare* (1990).

Cheap And Nasty

This melodic UK rock 'n' roll quartet were formed in 1990 by former Hanoi Rocks guitarist Nasty Suicide. Recruiting Alvin Gibbs (bass), Timo Caltio (guitar) and Les Riggs (drums), they signed to China Records the following year. Debuting with *Beautiful Disaster* the band lacked image and direction, and Suicide seems uncomfortable in his dual role of guitarist and vocalist. They currently specialize in mid-paced rockers, which rely heavily on vocal harmonies to carry the melody lines.

Album: *Beautiful Disaster* (1991).

Cheap Trick

Formed in Chicago, Illinois, USA in 1973. Rick Neilsen (b. 22 December 1946, Rockford, Illinois, USA; guitar/vocals) and Tom Petersson (b. Peterson, 9 May 1950, Rockford, Illinois, USA; bass/vocals) began their careers in various high-school bands, before securing a recording deal as members of Fuse. This short-lived attraction folded on completing a debut album, and the duo subsequently formed a new group with Thom Mooney and Robert 'Stewkey' Antoni from the recently disbanded Nazz. Mooney was subsequently replaced by drummer Brad Carlson aka Bun E. Carlos (b. 12 June 1951, Rockford, Illinois, USA), and with the departure of 'Stewkey', the initial Cheap Trick line-up was completed by vocalist Randy 'Xeno' Hogan. He in turn was replaced by Robin Zander (b. 23 January 1952, Loves Park, Illinois, USA; guitar/vocals), a former colleague of Carlson in the short-lived Toons. Relocated to America's mid-west, the quartet followed the gruelling bar-band circuit before a series of demonstration tapes secured a recording deal. Although *Cheap Trick* is generally regarded as a disappointment, it introduced the group's inventive flair and striking visual image. The heart-throb good-looks of Zander and Petersson contrasted Carlos' seedy garb, while Neilsen's odd-ball costume - baseball cap, bow-tie and monogrammed sweater - compounded this unlikely combination. Having spent a frenetic period supporting Queen, Journey and Kiss, Cheap Trick completed a second collection within months of their debut. *In Color* offered a smoother sound in which a grasp of melody was allowed to flourish and established the group's ability to satisfy visceral and cerebral demands. It contained several engaging performances, including 'I Want You To Want Me', 'Hello There' and 'Clock Strikes Ten', each

Cheap Trick

of which became in-concert favourites. *Heaven Tonight* consolidated the group's unique approach while 'Surrender' contained the consummate Cheap Trick performance, blending the British pop of the Move with the urgent riffing of the best of America's hard rock. *At Budokan* followed a highly-successful tour of Japan, and this explosive live set became the quartet's first platinum disc, confirming them as a headline act in their own right. However, *Dream Police* added little to the sound extolled on the previous two studio releases, and indeed the title song was originally recorded for the Trick's debut album. Producer George Martin did little to deflect this sterility on *All Shook Up*, while *Found All The Parts*, a mini-album culled from out-takes, suggested internal problems. A disaffected Petersson left the group in 1982, but although Pete Comita initially took his place, the latter quickly made way for Jon Brandt. Neither *One On One*, nor the Todd Rundgren produced *Next Position Please*, halted Cheap Trick's commercial slide, but *Standing On The Edge* offered hopes of a renaissance. A 1986 recording, 'Mighty Wings', was used on the soundtrack of the successful *Top Gun* film, while the return of Petersson the same year re-established the group's successful line-up. *Lap Of Luxury* achieved multi-platinum status when an attendant single, 'The Flame', topped the US chart in 1988 while *Busted* scaled similar heights, confirming Cheap Trick's dramatic resurrection as a major US act.

Albums: *Cheap Trick* (1977), *In Color* (1977), *Heaven Tonight* (1978), *Cheap Trick At Budokan* (1979), *Dream Police* (1979), *Found All The Parts* (1980), *All Shook Up* (1980), *One On One* (1982), *Next Position Please* (1983), *Standing On The Edge* (1985), *The Doctor* (1986), *Lap Of Luxury* (1988), *Busted* (1990). Compilation: *Greatest Hits* (1992).

Child, Desmond, And Rouge

This US, commercially minded and chart-oriented

soft-rock outfit was formed in 1975 by keyboardist Desmond Child, backed by an array of musicians. With college friends Maria Vidal, Myriam Naomi Vaille and Diana Graselli completing the line-up as vocalists, they attracted the interest of Kiss guitarist Paul Stanley. Signing to Capitol Records, their debut album released in 1978 was a pot-pourri of styles, that included elements of pop, rock, funk, blues and soul. The follow-up, *Runners In The Night*, adopted a more hard-rock stance, but was also met with indifference. The band became redundant as Child decided to concentrate on writing and production, rather than actually playing. He has composed for Cher, Michael Bolton, Bon Jovi, Alice Cooper, Kiss and Jimmy Barnes among others. 'You Give Love A Bad Name' and 'Livin' On A Prayer' co-written with Bon Jovi and the Kiss million-seller 'I Was Made For Loving You' have been his greatest successes to date. Child made a return to recording in 1991 for Elektra Records, which despite the competent performance failed to set the charts alight.
Albums: *Desmond Child And Rouge* (1978), *Runners In The Night* (1979), *Desmond Child Discipline* (1991).

China

This melodic rock band was formed in Switzerland during 1987 by guitarists Freddy Laurence and Claudio Matteo. Recruiting Math Shiverow (lead vocals), Marc Lynn (bass) and John Dommen (drums), they signed with Phonogram the following year. Influenced by Thin Lizzy, Europe and Scorpions, their self-titled debut appeared in 1988 to a positive media response. It was characterized by Shiverow's high-pitched but note perfect vocals and the dual guitar attack of Matteo and Laurence. *Sign In The Sky*, recorded two years later, saw ex-Krokus guitarist Patrick Mason take over on vocals, and Brian Kofmehl replace Lynn on bass. It was a more mature album in several respects and the songwriting displayed greater depth and the production, courtesy of Stephan Galfas. A live mini-album followed but, as yet, China have failed to receive the recognition that their talents deserve.
Albums: *China* (1988), *Sign In The Sky* (1990), *Live* (1990).

China Sky

This group was formed in Florida, USA in 1987 by ex-Danny Joe Brown and Molly Hatchet guitarist John Ingram. With the addition of vocalist Ron Perry and bassist Richard Smith, they specialized in rough-edged AOR, with a distinctly southern influence. They recorded a self-titled debut in 1988, which attracted attention due to the fact that 'The Last Romantic Warrior' was reminiscent of Derek And The Dominos' 'Layla'. The band split up soon after the album's release.
Album: *China Sky* (1988).

Chinatown. This UK band started life as a glam-rock outfit known as Chinastreet and comprised vocalist Steve Prangell, guitarists Pat Shayler and Danny Gwylym, John Barr (bass) and Steve Hopgood (drums). In 1981 they changed their name to Chinatown and switched to a hard-rock style similar to Thin Lizzy and UFO. Their sound was characterized by Prangell's stratospheric-like vocals and the dual guitar interplay of Shayler and Gwylym. After one album, recorded live, the band split up with only drummer Steve Hopgood resurfacing later. He went on to play with Persian Risk and Paul Di'Anno's Battlezone.
Album: *Play It To The Death* (1981).

Choirboys

This heavy rock group was formed in Sydney, Australia in the late 70s and comprised Brad Carr (guitar), Ian Hulme (bass), Mark Gable (vocals) and Lindsay Tebutt (drums). The band was promoted as the heirs apparent to AC/DC who by then were well-established outside Australia. The band did not achieve any national success until a single and album charted in 1983. Unfortunately Mark Gable damaged his vocal chords that same year and the band was put on hold until 1987 and the release of its second album, which revealed a mature band capable of writing commercial pop-rock radio songs which also carried over well in-concert. The albums spawned several singles, all of which reached the Australian Top 40.
Albums: *The Choirboys* (1983), *Big Bad Noise* (1987).

Chrissy Steele

This Canadian 'heavy metal goddess' is influenced by Led Zeppelin, Bon Jovi, AC/DC, Pat Benatar, Heart and Motley Crue. Linking up with former Headpins guitarist/songwriter/producer Brian MacLeod she produced *Magnet To Steele* in 1991. The album was recorded on Macleods power yacht whilst cruising along the coast of British Columbia! Steele has a powerful and characteristic style, but the derivative and commercial structure to the material did her no favours. The bravado and sexual imagery of the press releases appeared more interesting than the actual music.
Album: *Magnet To Steele* (1991).

Chrome Molly

This hard-rock/thrash quartet was formed in Leicester, England, during 1984, by vocalist Steve

Chrissy Steele

vocals coupled with Ricky Beck-Mahler's grungy guitar riffs are the band's trademarks, whilst Gary Sunshine (bass) and Ryan Maher (drums) provide the necessary ammunition in the rhythm section. Distilling influences such as the Cult, AC/DC, Motorhead and white blues guitarists like Johnny Winter and Rick Derringer, they purvey solid, raunchy rock 'n' roll, underpinned by a keen sense of melody and dynamics. With three albums behind them and a successful support slot on Black Sabbath's 1990 tour, they still remain relatively unknown ouside their native New York.

Albums: *Circus Of Power* (1988), *Still Alive* (1989), *Vices* (1990).

Cirith Ungol

Taking their name from one of the towers in *Lord Of The Rings*, this gothic heavy metal outfit materialized in 1980. Hailing from Ventura, California, USA, the band comprised ex-Titanic duo Jerry Fogle (guitar) and Robert Garven (drums), ex-roadie Tim Baker (vocals) and Greg Lindstrom (bass), the latter eventually replaced by Michael Flint. Characterized by high-pitched vocals and complex, at times cumbersome arrangements, their style is morbid. Their debut *Frost And Fire* has often been referred to as 'The Worst Heavy Metal Album Of All Time!' They did progress however, improving the dynamics and introducing some up-tempo numbers to break the monotony. Nevertheless, success continues to elude them, as they struggle to find an audience for this extreme and somewhat out-dated style of metal.

Albums: *Frost And Fire* (1981), *King Of The Dead* (1984), *One Foot In Hell* (1986).

City

This Californian quintet specialized in sophisticated rock, with a distinctly commercial pop-edge. Formed in 1986, the band comprised Bill Trudel (vocals), Stuart Mathis (guitar), Peter Mclan (keyboards), Wade Biery (bass) and Jerry Speiser (drums). Strongly influenced by Toto, Kansas and Mr. Mister, they debuted in 1987 with *Foundation*, but split up immediately after the album was released. Trudel went on to work with ex-Jeff Paris musician Michael Thompson, while Mclan handled production duties for Men At Work.

Album: *Foundation* (1987).

CJSS

This US group was a part-time side project of virtuoso guitarist David T. Chastain. Ably assisted by Mike Skimmerhorn (bass), Les Sharp (drums) and Russell Jenkins (lead vocals), CJSS is an outlet

Hawkins and guitarist John Antcliffe. With the addition of Nick Wastell (bass) and Chris Green (drums), they recorded the debut *You Can't Have It All* the following year. This was a competent collection of mid-paced rockers. Mark Godfrey replaced Green on drums and Tim Read took over from Antcliffe on lead for the recording *Angst*. This album was recorded with a bigger budget, as the band had been picked up by the I.R.S. label. It included an excellent cover of Squeeze's 'Take Me I'm Yours', but the remainder of the album was much as before. They landed the support slot on Alice Cooper's 1988 UK tour, but this did little to stimulate album sales, and they were subsequently dropped by their label. Far from disheartened, they began writing new material and eventually secured a contract with MFN. *Slaphead* appeared in 1990, to yet another flat response from the music media despite its evident quality.

Albums: *You Can't Have It All* (1985), *Stick It Out* (1987), *Angst* (1988), *Slaphead* (1990).

Circus Of Power

Crawling from the gutter of New York's late 80s lower East Side, this heavily tattooed quartet deliver a unique and uncompromising brand of bluesy heavy metal. Alex Mitchell's paint-stripping for Chastain's melodic and more accessible compositions. They recorded two albums during the mid-80s, characterized by impeccable musicianship and inventive guitar work. In theory, the material still retained enough rough edges to appeal to rock fans but, at the same time, was sophisticated enough to crossover to a mainstream audience. In practice, this did not work out and the band have been inactive since 1987.

Albums: *World Gone Mad* (1986), *Praise The Loud* (1986).

Clarke, 'Fast' Eddie

b. 5 October 1950, Isleworth, Middlesex, England. Eddie Clarke first came to prominence in 1976, when he was recruited by Motorhead as a second guitarist. Plucked from obscurity, he was previously a member of blues-rock no-hopers Curtis Knight. He appeared on all Motorhead albums between 1977's self-titled opus, up to 1982's *Iron Fist*. He undoubtedly helped establish the Motorhead trademarks, but departed on less-than amicable terms. He could not accept the musical direction that Lemmy was pursuing at the time; particularly the collaboration with Wendy O'Williams on the country classic 'Stand By Your Man'. Clarke teamed up with former UFO bassist Pete Way in 1982 and formed Fastway. This partnership was very short-lived as Way soon took up the offer to join Ozzy Osbourne's band. Nevertheless, the name was retained and with a rarely stable line-up, they have recorded six albums to-date. Surprisingly, Clarke has moved away from heavy, blues-based boogie, in favour of a more lightweight, melodic approach.

Cloven Hoof

Formed in 1979, this UK band were strongly influenced by early Kiss. The personnel took on the pseudonyms of Air, Fire, Earth and Water and dressed in appropriately ridiculous stage costumes. Specializing in kitsch glam-metal, with an underlying satanic element, they recorded two amateurish, but naively charming albums before the original line-up and band concept fell apart. The only remaining member, bassist Lee Payne, reformed the band in 1987 with Russell North (lead vocals), Andy Wood (guitar) and Jon Brown (drums). Ditching the old image in favour of a hard-rock/thrash approach, they signed to FM Revolver Records. *Dominator*, produced by Guy Bidmead (of Motorhead fame) materialized in 1988 but was derivative of Iron Maiden, Judas Priest and Metallica. *A Sultan's Ransom*, which moved towards a thrashier style, fared little better and was universally slated in the music press, but the band have continued, undaunted by such setbacks.

Albums: *Cloven Hoof* (1984), *Live…Fighting Back* (1987), *Dominator* (1988), *A Sultan's Ransom* (1989).

Cobra

This US hard-rock quintet was formed in 1982, by ex-Krokus guitarist Mandy Meyer and former Target vocalist Jimi Jamison. With the recruitment of Jack Holder (guitar), Tommy Keiser (bass) and Jeff Klaven (drums) they were soon signed by CBS Records. Their music was a fusion between the blues-rock approach of Whitesnake and Bad Company and the heavier, power-metal style of Van Halen and Iron Maiden. Legal and contractual problems were instrumental in the band's demise after just one album release. Meyer joined Asia, Jamison teamed up with Survivor and Keiser later appeared in Krokus.

Album: *First Strike* (1983).

Company Of Wolves

This US hard-rock group, formed in the late 80s, comprise Kyf Brewer (vocals), Steve Conte (guitar), John Conte (bass) and Frankie Larocka (drums). They were highly competent, but arguably derivative. Showing a wide range of influences encompassing Kiss, Aerosmith, Bad Company, Led Zeppelin and David Bowie, these are re-processed with such frantic energy and a enthusiastic attitude that they are almost convincing!

Album: *Company Of Wolves* (1990).

Coney Hatch

This Canadian quartet was formed in 1981 by vocalist Carl Dixon and guitarist Steve Shelski. Taking their name from the district of Coney Hatch, the line-up was stabilized with the addition of Andy Curran (bass) and Dave Ketchum (drums). They debuted in 1982 with a self-titled album, produced by Max Webster supremo Kim Mitchell. It still remains their essential work, featuring a variety of styles from blues-rock to *avant garde* jazz via heavy metal. Dixon's vocals are outstanding, with Shelski's eclectic guitar bursts providing the perfect foil. Barry Connors took over the drumstool after *Outta Hand*, a disappointing and lacklustre follow-up, which was not helped by a lifeless production. *Friction* marked a slight return to form, but the band disintegrated before they could capitalize on its success.

Albums: *Coney Hatch* (1982), *Outta Hand* (1983), *Friction* (1985).

Cooper, Alice

b. Vincent Damon Furnier, 4 February 1948,

Detroit, Michigan, USA. Alice Cooper became known as the 'master of shock rock' during the 70s and remained a popular hard-rock artist into the 90s. The Furnier family moved to Phoenix, Arizona where Vincent began writing songs while in junior high school. Inspired by a dream to become famous by bands such as the Beatles and Rolling Stones, Furnier formed a group in the early 60s called the Earwigs. By 1965 their name had changed to the Spiders and then the Nazz (no relation to Todd Rundgren's band of the same name). Both the Spiders and Nazz played at local dances and recorded singles that were moderately popular regionally. In 1968, the Nazz, which also included Mike Bruce (lead guitar), Dennis Dunaway (bass), Glen Buxton (guitar) and Neal Smith (drums), changed its name to Alice Cooper, reportedly due to Furnier's belief that he was the reincarnation of a 17th century witch by that name. The name Alice Cooper was also attached to Furnier, who invented an androgynous, outrageously attired character to attract attention. The band played deliberately abrasive rock music with the intention of shocking and even alienating those attending its concerts.

In 1969 the Alice Cooper band found a kindred spirit in Frank Zappa, who signed them to his new Straight Records label. The group recorded two albums, *Pretties For You* and *Easy Action*, before switching to Warner Brothers Records in 1970. By that time Cooper had taken on more extreme tactics in his live performances, using a guillotine and electric chair as stage props and a live snake as part of his wardrobe. Cooper wore thick black eye make-up which dripped down his face, giving him a demonic appearance.

As the group and its singer built a reputation as a bizarre live act, their records began to sell in greater quantities. In 1971, the single 'Eighteen' was the first to reach the US charts, at number 21. Cooper's commercial breakthrough came the following year with the rebellious 'School's Out' single and album, both of which made the US Top 10 as well as topping the UK chart. A streak of best-selling albums followed: the number 1 *Billion Dollar Babies*, then *Muscle Of Love*, *Alice Cooper's Greatest Hits* and *Welcome To My Nightmare*, all of which reached the US Top 10. The last was his first true solo album, as during this period, the band fractured and Cooper officially adopted the Alice Cooper name as his own. In contrast to his professional image, the offstage Cooper became a Hollywood celebrity, playing golf and appearing on television talk shows. In the late 70s, Cooper began appearing in films such as *Sextette* and *Sgt. Pepper's Lonely Hearts Club Band*. In 1978 Cooper admitted chronic alcoholism and

entered a New York hospital for treatment. *From The Inside*, with songs co-written by Bernie Taupin, reflected on the experience. Cooper continued recording into the early 80s with diminishing results. In 1986, after a four-year recording absence, he signed to MCA Records, but none of his albums for that label reached the US charts. A 1989 album, *Trash*, his first on Epic Records, returned him to the Top 40 and yielded a Top 10 single, 'Poison', his first in 12 years. A tour during 1990 found Cooper drawing a new, younger audience which considered him a heavy metal pioneer. *Hey Stoopid* found him accompanied by Joe Satriani, Steve Vai and Slash and Axl from Guns N' Roses. This collection showed Cooper singing with as much energy as his work of more than 20 years ago.

Albums: *Pretties For You* (1969), *Easy Action* (1970), *Love It To Death* (1971), *Killer* (1971), *School's Out* (1972), *Billion Dollar Babies* (1973), *Muscle Of Love* (1973), *Welcome To My Nightmare* (1975), *Alice Cooper Goes To Hell* (1976), *Lace And Whiskey* (1977), *The Alice Cooper Show* (1977), *From The Inside* (1978), *Flush The Fashion* (1980), *Special Forces* (1981), *Zipper Catches Skin* (1982), *Dada* (1982), *Constrictor* (1986), *Raise Your Fist And Yell* (1987), *Trash* (1989), *Hey Stoopid* (1991). Compilation: *Alice Cooper's Greatest Hits* (1974).

Craaft

This German melodic rock quartet was formed in 1984 by guitarist Marcus Schleicher and ex-Krokus bassist Tommy Keiser. Adding Tom Schneider (drums), Franz Keil (keyboards) and Klaus Luley (vocals and ex-Tokyo), they provided a breath of fresh air to the mid-80s teutonic rock scene, which was totally dominated by identikit 'speed-metal' bands. Surprisingly, the band sounded more American than German, combining Nightranger, Whitesnake and Toto influences to great effect. Luley is a highly talented vocalist, using his considerable range and power to carry the melody lines, while the use of keyboards to fill out the sound is achieved in a subtle and understated fashion. They have released two excellent albums to date, but have received little recognition outside Germany.

Albums: *Craaft* (1986), *Second Honeymoon* (1988).

Crash 'N' Burn

This Anglo-German hard-rock quartet were previously known as Riff. Formed by vocalist William Lennox in 1991, with members Becking (guitar), Thomas (bass) and Brendel (drums). Signed by RCA, they debuted with *Fever* in 1991, a blues-based heavy rock album that utilized state-of-the-art recording technology. Their debut

Creaming Jesus

album showed considerable flair and energy and they are likely to win over the most hardened cynic.

Album: *Fever* (1991).

Crawler

This UK heavy rock group was an off-shoot of Back Street Crawler, the band that had featured the late and legendary Paul Kossoff. Crawler comprised Terry Wilson Slesser (vocals), Geoff Whitehorn (guitar), John 'Rabbit' Bundrick (keyboards and ex-Free), Terry Wilson (bass) and Tony Braunagel (drums). They released two blues-rock albums during the late 70s, which were ignored amid the punk rock explosion at the time. The group disbanded in 1978, with Whitehorn going back to session work and Slesser reappearing later in Charlie.

Albums: *Crawler* (1977), *Snake, Rattle And Roll* (1978).

Creaming Jesus

This satirical UK hardcore/metal quintet were formed in 1987 by vocalist Andy and guitarists Richard and Mario. With the addition of drummer Roy and bassist Tally, they signed to the independent Jungle label. Chainsaw guitars collide with machine-gun drumming, whilst the lyrics deal with contemporary issues such as television evangelists, sexual perverts, childhood anxieties and warmongerers. The musical equivalent of a poke in the eye with a sharp stick!

Albums: *Too Fat To Run, Too Stupid To Hide* (1990), *Guilt By Association* (1992).

Creed

This US blues-based boogie outfit was formed in 1977 by vocalist Steve Ingle and guitarist Luther Maben. Enlisting the services of Hal Butler (keyboards), James Flynn (bass) and Chip Thomas (drums) they were soon signed by Asylum Records. Their self-titled debut appeared in 1978 and was notable for 'Time And Time Again', an epic southern-style guitar work-out, comparable in stature to Lynyrd Skynyrd's 'Freebird'. Unable to attract enough media attention, the band split up soon after the album's release.

Album: *Creed* (1978).

Creek

Hailing from North Carolina, USA, this hard rock band shortened their name from Sugarcreek in

1986 to avoid any association with the country music scene. Comprising Jerry West (guitar/vocals), Rick Lee (keyboards/vocals), Mike Barber (bass), Tim Clark (vocals/percussion) and Lynn Samples (drums), they specialized in highly melodic pomp-rock, making extensive use of four-part vocal harmonies. Influenced by Styx, Kansas and Journey they have released two exceptional albums on shoestring budgets. John Harwell and Robbie Hegler replaced Samples and Barber on drums and bass respectively in 1987. If the MFN label are prepared to invest in Creek, they could end up with an exceptionally commercial act on their hands.
Albums: *The Creek* (1986), *Storm The Gate* (1989).

Crimson Glory

Formerly known as Pierced Arrow and Beowolf, this US, Florida-based heavy metal quintet settled on the name Crimson Glory in 1982. Comprising Midnight (vocals), Jon Drenning (guitar), Ben Jackson (guitar), Jeff Lords (bass) and Dana Burnell (drums), they spent a full three years writing material and developing a band. They emerged in 1986 with a self-titled debut on Roadrunner Records, which fused the techno-rock of Queensryche with the uncompromising power-metal of Iron Maiden. The band sported silver masks to add an element of artistic mystique to their identity. *Transcendence* was an ambitious concept album, which explored the themes of destiny, religion and philosophy. It received widespread critical acclaim and put the band on the launching pad to international recognition. Internal disputes led to a line-up reshuffle with Jackson and Burnell ousted. Ravi Jakhorta was recruited on drums and the band continued as a four-piece. They eventually discarded the masks on *Strange And Beautiful*, their third and most complete work to date. Here they incorporated a wider range of influences, added organ and acoustic bridges and showed an increased awareness of dynamics. It maybe only a matter of time before the Midnight/Drenning songwriting partnership, achieves success.
Albums: *Crimson Glory* (1986), *Transcendence* (1988), *Strange And Beautiful* (1991).

Cro-Mags

This US thrashcore band was formed in 1984 by bassist Harley Flanegan. After a series of false starts, vocalist John Joseph, drummer Mackie and guitarists Doug Holland and Parris Mitchell Mayhew were recruited to cement the band's line-up. They specialized in the fusion of thrash, hardcore and heavy metal and the influences of Motorhead, the Dead Kennedys and Metallica

were quite apparent on their debut, *The Age Of Quarrel*. They built up a small, but loyal cult of supporters and regularly headlined major hardcore events at New York's CBGB's during the mid to late 80s. In early 1988, the band members went their separate ways.
Albums: *The Age Of Quarrel* (1987), *Best Wishes* (1990).

Cross

After two individual solo albums, Roger Taylor (b. 26 July 1949, Norfolk, England; vocals/guitar) needed a new challenge outside the confines of Queen. He formed the Cross in 1987 with Clayton Moss (guitar), Spike Edney (keyboards), Peter Noone (bass) and Josh Macrae (drums) and concentrated on a low-key pop-rock approach. They debuted with *Shove It* in 1988, a nondescript collection of half-hearted rockers, that lacked distinction, partly due to Taylor's limited vocal ability. *Mad, Bad And Dangerous To Know*, a title inspired by the poetry of Byron, was somewhat a misnomer. It featured safe, mainstream AOR, with a nod towards Jimi Hendrix via Taylor's guitar work. Following the death of Queen vocalist Freddie Mercury, further extra-curricular work for Taylor seems likely.
Albums: *Shove It* (1988), *Mad, Bad And Dangerous To Know* (1990).

Crumbsuckers

This New York 'thrashcore' quintet was formed in 1983, by vocalist Chris Notaro and guitarist Chuck Lenihan. With the addition of Gary Meskill (bass), Dave Wynn (guitar) and Dan Richardson (drums), they signed to Combat Records and cut *Life Of Dreams* in 1986. This was an uncompromising blast of hardcore angst with metallic undercurrents, which helped establish a large cult following for the band. *Beast On My Back* saw Wynn replaced by Ronnie Koebler, and moved away from their hardcore roots, into the thrash metal domain. Marc Piovanetti and Joe Hegarty replaced Lenihan and Notaro respectively in 1989, with the band subsequently changing their name to Heavy Rain. Since then, the band's transition to Metallica and Slayer-like metal has been fully completed.
Albums: *Life Of Dreams* (1986), *Beast On My Back* (1988).

Crybabys

This bluesy rock 'n' roll quartet from the UK, were formed in 1991 by former Boys' guitarist 'Honest' John Plain. Recruiting Darrell Garth (guitar/vocals), Mark Duncan (bass) and Robbie Rushton (drums) they signed with Receiver

Records the same year. Drawing inspiration from Mott The Hoople, Hanoi Rocks and the Georgia Satellites, the Crybabys successfully bridge the gap between punk and rock 'n' roll. Shambolic, chaotic and full of stamina, they debuted with *Where Have All The Good Girls Gone?* This compares favourably with the best that either the Dogs D'Amour or Quireboys have produced.
Album: *Where Have All The Good Girls Gone?* (1991).

Cryptic Slaughter

This US speed-metal quartet was formed in 1985 by vocalist Bill Cook and guitarist Les Evans. Enlisting the services of Rob Nicholson (bass) and Scott Peterson (drums), they specialized in short, abrupt songs that were carried along by warp-speed drumming and hell-for-leather riffing. They recorded three albums for the Metal Blade label between 1986-88, which compare favourably with the best works of D.R.I., Suicidal Tendencies and Gang Green. The band split up in 1990.
Albums: *Convicted* (1986), *Money Talks* (1987), *Stream Of Consciousness* (1988).

Cua, Rick

Former Outlaws bassist, Rick Cua became a born-again Christian in 1982 and embarked upon a solo career. Ditching the southern-rock style of his former band, Cua aimed his music directly at the AOR audience. Releasing six albums to date, he has become progressively more commercial and moved further and further away from his original hard-rock roots. *Can't Stand Too Tall* and *Midnight Sun* features sentimental ballads and pop-rock anthems in the style of Michael Bolton.
Albums: *Koo'Ah* (1982), *You're My Road* (1985), *Wear Your Colours* (1986), *No Mystery* (1987), *Can't Stand Too Tall* (1988), *Midnight Sun* (1989).

Culprit

This Seattle, USA-based hard-rock quintet was formed in 1980, from the ashes of Orpheus and Amethyst. Comprising John DeVol (guitar), Scott Earl (bass), Bud Burrill (drums), Jeff L'Heureux (vocals) and Kjartan Kristoffersen (guitar), they combined the power-metal style of Iron Maiden with the intricate melodic arrangements of Rush. Signing to Mike Varney's Shrapnel label, they debuted with *Guilty As Charged* in 1983. This was favourably received by the music media, and they built a large following throughout Washington state. However, success was short-lived as the band was beset by drug problems and internal musical disagreements. The band finally disintegrated in 1985, and a planned reunion in 1987 failed to reach fruition.

Album: *Guilty As Charged* (1983).

Cult

Formerly known as Southern Death Cult, the band were formed by lead singer Ian Astbury (b. Ian Lindsay, 14 May 1962, Heswell, Merseyside, England) in Bradford 1981. With the line-up eventually stabilized by Jamie Stewart (bass), Les Warner (b. 13 February 1961; drums) and ex-Theatre Of Hate guitarist Billy Duffy (b. 12 May 1959, Manchester, England), they were born out of the new wave/punk movement, and initially adopted a gothic-like image. Signing to Beggars Banquet Records, they debuted with *Dreamtime* in 1984. This featured material that was low-key, atmospheric and verged on the surreal. The legacy of the late 70s was being played out as the band dressed all in black, had pale complexions and wore love beads. The band's big break came with *Love* in 1985, which comprised more hard-rock song structures and pushed Duffy's raunchy guitar lines to the fore. It spawned two UK Top 20 hit singles in the epical 'She Sells Sanctuary' and 'Rain'. *Electric* saw the band's transition to heavy rock completed. The songs drew inspiration from Led Zeppelin, AC/DC and Bad Company. Produced by Rick Rubin, *Electric* was a bold and brash statement of intent, that oozed energy and pure rock 'n' roll from every note. It became a success on both sides of the Atlantic, peaking at number 4 and 38 in the UK and US charts respectively. Two years later, *Sonic Temple* emerged, which consolidated the band's success, reaching number 10 on the *Billboard* album chart and number 3 in the UK. The band were now down to a three-piece following the departure of Warner. Mickey Curry was hired to fill in on drums, and the album combined the atmospheric passion of *Love*, with the unbridled energy of *Electric*. Bassist Stewart quit in 1990, with the core of the band reduced to just a duo comprizing Astbury and Duffy. *Ceremony* was released in 1991, with the help of Charley Drayton (bass) and Curry. This was a retrogressive collection of songs, that had more in common with *Love*, than their previous two albums. Nevertheless, having already established an enormous fan-base, success was virtually guaranteed. The Cult remain one of the most revered acts working within their particular genre.
Albums: *Dreamtime* (1984), *Love* (1985), *Electric* (1987), *Sonic Temple* (1989), *Ceremony* (1991).

Curry, Cherie

Former lead vocalist of the Runaways, Cherie Curry embarked on a solo career after quitting the all-girl group in 1977. Continuing in the same

vein as her former band, she specialized in undistinguished three-minute pop-rock anthems. Employing a variety of talented session men, including Toto members Steve Lukather (guitar) and Mike Porcaro (bass), the songs were hindered by Curry's limited range and vocal dynamics. *Messin' With The Boys* featured sister Marie and pursued a more hard-rock direction, but once again had very little to recommend it. It appears that the initial accusations of Curry being a 'talentless bimbo', may have some foundation.
Albums: *Beauty's Only Skin Deep* (1978), *Messin' With The Boys* (1980).

Cyclone

Formerly known as Centurion, the band were formed in Vilvoorde, Belgium by vocalist Guido Gevels and guitarist Pascal van Lint in 1981. With the addition of Johnny Kerbush (guitar), Stefan Daamen (bass) and Nicholas Lairin (drums), they initially took their cue from the New Wave Of British Heavy Metal. They later switched to a more thrash-oriented approach, styling themselves on Anthrax. They negotiated a one-album deal with Roadrunner Records and debuted with *Brutal Destruction* in 1986. Roadrunner neglected to renew the group's contract and Cyclone disbanded the following year.
Album: *Brutal Destruction* (1986).

D

D.A.D.

Originally known as Disneyland After Dark, the band came together in Copenhagen, Denmark 1985. Comprising Jesper Binzer (vocals/guitar), Jacob A. Binzer (guitar), Stig Pedersen (bass) and Peter L. Jensen (drums), they combine high-energy metallic rock 'n' roll with an irreverent sense of humour and fun. Imagine a four-way collision between Cheap Trick, Z.Z. Top, AC/DC and Duane Eddy and you'll begin to appreciate where these four 'lunatics' are coming from. After two entertaining and musically competent albums on the independent Mega label, they were signed by Warner Brothers in 1988 and marketed as the next big thing. Their energetic and eccentric live performances were highly impressive, but they could not generate the same intensity in the studio. Consequently, *No Fuel Left For The Pilgrims*, did not live up to Warner Brothers' advance promotion. *Riskin' It All* emerged in 1991 and showed that the band had not been disillusioned by all the adverse press coverage. A hard rock album, that sparkled with offbeat energy and their own particular tongue-in-cheek style. They have built up a large and loyal following in their native Denmark, but have made little impact elsewhere.
Albums: *Call Of The Wild* (1986), *Disneyland After Dark Draws A Circle* (1987), *No Fuel Left For The Pilgrims* (1989), *Riskin' It All* (1991).

Daisy Chainsaw

Contrived, but fun, pop-punk outfit whose sudden appearance brightened-up the UK independent scene of the early 90s. Led by fragile singer Katie Jane Garside, the band also comprised Richard Adams (bass), Vince Johnson (drums) and Crispin Grey (guitar). They debuted with the *LoveSickPleasure* EP, which spiralled into the UK Top 30, aided by the highly colourful video for the lead track 'Love Your Money'. BBC's Radio 1 had picked up on the song's frenetic pace, and the music press were impressed by Garside's similar stage performances, but most importantly it was her visual image as a bedraggled, barefoot waif, in dirty torn dresses and petticoats - occasionally sucking on a baby's bottle, that attracted the most attention. Garside's allusions and references in interviews of having a past of sexual abuse and psychological disorder backfired slightly on the group, but there is little doubt that the band's presentation is disturbingly resonant of the child as victim. The success of the EP encouraged them to sign with larger independent One Little Indian, despite tantalizing offers from the major record labels.

Dakota

This US melodic rock outfit was formed in 1979 by vocalists/guitarists Jerry Hludzik and Billy Kelly. Recruiting Lou Crossa and Jeff Mitchell on keyboards, Bill McMale (bass) and John Robinson (drums) they based their style on the music of Styx, Toto and Kansas. Heavily dominated by keyboards and watertight vocal harmonies, the band released two quality studio albums, before disbanding in 1984.
Albums: *Dakota* (1980), *Runaway* (1984).

Damien Thorne

This American heavy metal quintet was formed in Chicago 1985 by vocalist Justin Fate and guitarist Ken Starr. The group took their name from the Anti-Christ in the book/film *The Omen*. After enlisting the services of Michael Monroe (guitar), Sanders Pate (bass) and Pete Pagonis (drums), they concentrated on a dual guitar approach similar to Judas Priest. They signed to Roadrunner Records and debuted with *Sign Of The Jackal* the following year. This incorporated Iron Maiden, Def Leppard and Metallica influences, but these were not sufficiently modified or re-interpreted, to give the band an identity of their own.
Album: *Sign Of The Jackal* (1986).

Damn Yankees

Formed in 1989, the Damn Yankees were one of several supergroups, which included Bad English, to emerge in the USA towards the end of the decade. Ex-Styx guitarist/vocalist Tommy Shaw had been writing with the larger-than-life guitarist and solo artist Ted Nugent and they were soon joined by Jack Blades on bass/vocals (from the recently demised group Nightranger) and Michael Cartellone, a previously unknown drummer. Warner Brothers beat Geffen Records in the race to sign the band, and the self-titled debut album was released in 1990. The music was hard-edged melodic rock much heavier than the style Styx and Nightranger were noted for, with Shaw and Blades handling the bulk of the vocal duties, while Nugent contributed lead vocals to the outrageous 'Piledriver'. The album went Top 10 in the US, with the help of a Top 5 single - the power ballad 'High Enough'. Damn Yankees, however, were not a record company manufactured creation. They proved they could produce sparkling live performances too, gaining a great reputation for

their shows. These included tantalizing snippets from the respective back catalogues of Styx, Nightranger, and Ted Nugent's solo work. The melodic influence of Shaw and Blades combined with the over-the-top antics of Nugent created a highly successful band in terms of both critical acclaim and commercial success.
Album: *Damn Yankees* (1990).

Danger Danger

Danger, Danger

This melodic and atmospheric hard rock band were formed in 1988 by former Michael Bolton bassist Bruno Ravel. Enlisting the services of Ted Poley (ex-Prophet vocalist), Kasey Smith (keyboards), Steve West (drums) and Tony Rey (guitar), their style lies somewhere between White Lion and Bon Jovi. They were picked up by Imagine Records and debuted with a self-titled album in 1989. Produced by Lance Quinn and Mike Stone, this featured an impressive collection of infectious rockers and dynamic power-ballads. Rey quit to concentrate on his other project, Saraya, in 1989, and was replaced by Andy Timmins. Signing to Epic, they released *Screw It* in 1992, which built on the solid foundations of their debut, but included a greater element of arrogant street attitude. Danger, Danger have considerable crossover potential and with careful management should develop into a major force.
Albums: *Danger, Danger* (1989), *Screw It* (1992).

Dangerous Toys

This group was formed by ex-Onyx members Scott Dalhover (guitar), Mike Watson (bass) and Mark Geary (drums) in Texas 1987. With the recruitment of ex-Watchtower vocalist Jason McMaster, the band signed to CBS and debuted with a self-titled album in 1989. This revealed strong Guns N' Roses and Aerosmith influences alongside their previous techno-thrash style. Danny Aaron was added as second guitarist, shortly after the album was released to add greater

Dangerous Toys

lexibility on the road. They scored minor successes in the US singles market with 'Teas'n, Pleas'n' and 'Scared', the latter a tribute to their idol, Alice Cooper. Collaborating with Desmond Child, they recorded 'Demon Bell' for the inclusion on the soundtrack to the horror film *Shocker*. They subsequently supported the Cult and Bonham on a lengthy US west coast tour.
Album: *Dangerous Toys* (1989).

Daniel Band

This Canadian, Christian heavy metal band was formed in 1981 by vocalist/bassist Dan McGabe and guitarist/keyboardist Bill Findlay. The line-up, which has remained remarkably stable over the years, was completed by Tony Rossi (vocals/guitar) and Matt Delduca (drums). Taking their cue from April Wine, Triumph and Y&T, they specialized in melodic hard rock, that featured extended guitar and keyboard passages. Unlike many Christian rockers, the religious message seemed subservient to the excellent music.
Albums: *On Rock* (1982), *Straight Ahead* (1983), *Run From The Darkness* (1984), *Rise Up* (1986), *Running Out Of Time* (1987).

Danzig

This Satanic rock 'n' roll quartet, was put together

Dare

by ex-Misfits vocalist Glenn Danzig in 1987. Enlisting the services of guitarist John Christ, bassist Eerie Von and drummer Chuck Biscuits, they negotiated a contract with Rick Rubin's Def American label the following year. Their self-titled debut was characterized by Glenn Danzig's howling vocal tirade and a spartan, but atmospheric backbeat. Somehow, they had successfully fused 50s rock 'n' roll with contemporary influences such as the Cult and Metallica. *Danzig II - Lucifuge*, which emerged in 1990, represented a significant leap forward in their songwriting. It incorporated a greater variety of styles and tempos, yet had the band's strangely compelling persona, indelibly stamped on every track. Danzig ignore passing trends and fashions; instead, they remain loyal to their own ideals and beliefs. They have produced some of the most inspired music since Metallica appeared on the scene. However, they have yet to transcend the confines of cult status.
Albums: *Danzig* (1988), *Danzig II - Lucifuge* (1990).

Dare

This UK, melodic rock quintet was formed in

1987 by ex-Thin Lizzy keyboard player, Darren Wharton. The band's name was derived from Wharton's christian name, a suggestion from Lemmy of Motorhead. Relocating in Manchester after Lizzy's demise, it took Wharton six months to find musicians on his own wavelength. He eventually teamed up with Vinny Burns (guitar), Shelley (bass), James Ross (drums) and Brian Cox (keyboards), taking on vocals and additional keyboards himself. They debuted with *Out Of The Silence* in 1988, a grandiose keyboard-dominated album, reminiscent of Giuffria, Journey and House Of Lords. The follow-up, *Blood From Stone*, released three years later, adopted a more hard-rock approach and featured up-front guitar along with much improved vocals from Wharton. The band are heavily tipped to make a significant impact on the international rock scene.
Albums: *Out Of The Silence* (1988), *Blood From Stone* (1991).

Dark Angel

Formed in Los Angeles, California, USA, in 1983 Dark Angel specialize in 'ultra-heavy thrash metal'. The original line-up consisted of Don Doty (vocals), Jim Durkin (guitar), Eric Meyer (guitar),

Rob Yahn (bass) and Jack Schwarz (drums). Early demos saw the band sign to Axe Killer Records resulting in the release of *We Have Arrrived* in 1984. Unfortunately this was a clumsy effort which at times made them sound unrehearsed. Soon after its release, Rob Yahn and Jack Schwarz left to be replaced by Mike Gonzalez (bass) and Gene Hoglan (drums). The band signed a new deal with Combat Records and released the album *Darkness Descends*. This brutally fast, heavy album showed the band had now developed into a tight cohesive unit. There was a lull in recording career until they reappeared in 1989 with *Leave Scars*. If anything, this release was even heavier than previous efforts, showing the band unwilling to compromise. Featuring new vocalist Ron Rinehart, it also contained a cover version of Led Zeppelin's 'Immigrant Song'. The band then embarked on a European tour recording a live mini-album *Live Scars,* which was released in 1990 as a stop-gap until the next studio album. Before commencing the next album the band underwent another line-up change replacing Jim Durkin with ex-Viking guitarist Brett Eriksen. The band then recorded *Time Does Not Heal*, a turbulent vortex of twisted riffs and savage drums. Due to subject matter dealt with in the lyrics and the brutality of the music, Dark Angel are definitely not a band for the faint-hearted.

Albums: *We Have Arrived* (1984), *Darkness Descends* (1986), *Leave Scars* (1989), *Live Scars* (1990), *Time Does Not Heal* (1991).

Dark Lord

This guitar-oriented, hard-rock outfit was formed in Venice, Italy in 1984 by six-string virtuoso Alex Masi and drummer Sandro Bertoldini. With the addition of vocalist Gable Nalesso and bassist Al Guariento, they released a self-titled mini-album that showcased the talents of Masi, a classically trained guitarist in the style of Yngwie Malmsteen and Steve Vai. *State Of Rock*, another mini-album followed, which saw the arrival of new bass player Randzo Zulian and vocalist Emanual Jandee. Masi quit and relocated to Los Angeles soon after the album's release, joining Sound Barrier, who later became Masi. After two years of inactivity, Jandee and Bertoldni re-enacted *Dark Lord* with Paolo Mufato (guitar) and Alex Favaretto (bass). *It's Nigh' Time* was the result, but it lacked the sophistication and experimentation of Masi's era, and consequently made little impact outside Italy.

Albums: *Dark Lord* (1984), *State Of Rock* (1985), *It's Nigh' Time* (1988).

Dark Star

Formerly known as Berlin, the band were formed in the British Midlands in 1980, during the heyday of the New Wave Of British Heavy Metal movement. Dark Star comprised Rick Staines (vocals/synthesizer), David Harrison (guitar), Robert Key (guitar), Mark Oseland (bass) and Steve Atkins (drums). They debuted with 'Lady Of Mars', a track on EMI's compilation, *Metal For Muthas Volume II*. Stylistically, they alternated between true heavy metal and US pomp-rock and consequently found it difficult to win supporters from either camp. The band ground to a halt shortly after the release of their self-titled debut in 1981. Six years later, Staines, Harrison and Key reformed the band. With the help of session musicians they recorded *Real To Reel*, but were unable to attract media attention, they disbanded.

Albums: *Dark Star* (1981), *Real To Reel* (1987).

Deaf Dealer

This heavy metal band was formed in Jonquiere, Canada in 1980. The original line-up consisted of Andy La Roche (vocals), Ian Penn (guitar), Marc Hayward (guitar), J.P. Forsyth (bass) and Dan McGregor (drums). Due to some early demos the band quickly gained popularity on the underground tape-trading scene and also had a track included on the *Metal Massacre IV* compilation album, released on the Metal Blade Records label in 1983. The band then disappeared from the scene until resurfacing in 1985 as Deaf Dealer with a new vocalist Michael Flynn. The band made several false starts on the recording of their debut album until it was finally released on Roadrunner Records in 1986. *Keeper Of The Flame* was a worthy power metal release but in a sea of such releases it sank without trace. The band tried to carry on but in the face of such adversity folded in 1987.

Album: *Keeper Of The Flame* (1986).

Death

Death

Primarily the brainchild of vocalist/guitarist Chuck

Schuldiner the band was formed in Florida, USA in 1983. Chuck Schuldiner is the godfather of the 'death metal' movement, and due to some early demos recorded with various local musicians, he gained a recording contract with Combat Records in America, with the provision that the product would also be released in Europe on the Music For Nations subsidary label Under One Flag. Playing some of the fastest most aggressive noise ever to be recorded, the band, Death, was formed. It is here the story becomes complicated due to the number of different musicians that have joined and left the Death ranks. For the bands debut 1987 *Scream Bloody Gore* the line-up consisted of Chuck Schuldiner (vocals/guitar/bass) and Chris Reifert (drums). The album, as the name implied, was a pure deathly noise experience and put the band firmly on the map as the originators of the death metal movement and definite purveyors of musical extremities. On *Leprosy* (1988), the band's line up now consisted of Chuck Schuldiner (vocals/guitar), Rick Rozz (guitar), Terry Butler (bass) and Bill Andrews (drums). By the time of *Spiritual Healing,* Rick Rozz had left the band to be replaced by James Murphy. Also at this time the band toured Europe as support to Kreator but on the eve of their departure, mainman Chuck Schuldiner left the band. Against all the odds they decided to carry on and undertake this, their most important tour. His replacements for the duration of the tour were ex-Devastation drummer Louie Carrisalez handling vocal duties and ex-Rotting Corpse guitarist Walter Thrashler on guitar. Both had previously been members of Death's roadcrew. The tour was not a great success as the European fans refused to accept a Death without Chuck Schuldiner. On the band's return to America they soon went their separate ways with both drummer Bill Andrews and bassist Terry Butler going on to re-form their original band, Massacre. It is at this point that Chuck Schuldiner decided to resurrect Death to record what is considered to be their best work. Joining him in this new incarnation of the band were Cynic guitarist Paul Masvidal, Sadus bassist Steve DiGiorgio and Cynic drummer Sean Reinert. The album entitled *Human* was released in 1991 and was well received, as the material on offer was much more varied than on the band's previous releases - even going as far as to include a melodic instrumental track entitled 'Cosmic Sea', something previously unheard of in the death metal scene. After its release Chuck Schuldiner promised to put together a full-time unit from the musicians who had played on the album with the intention of a European tour sometime in 1992.
Albums: *Scream Bloody Gore* (1987), *Leprosy* (1988), *Spiritual Healing* (1990) *Human* (1991).

Death Angel

This group was formed in San Francisco, California, USA, the home of the Bay Area 'thrash' phenomenon in 1982. The band consists of five cousins, namely Mark Osegueda (vocals), Rob Cavestany (guitar), Gus Pepa (guitar), Dennis Pepa (bass) and Andy Galeon (drums). Their debut *The Ultra-Violence* was a brutal blend of high speed thrash riffs and thunderous drums. The band quickly followed it up with *Frolic In The Park* in 1988. This album showed the band had progressed both musically and lyrically. The group then experienced internal problems but managed to pull through signing to Geffen Records and releasing the highly-acclaimed *Act III* in 1990. Unfortunately, the band ran into futher problems with the departure of vocalist Mark Osegueda.
Albums: *The Ultra-Violence* (1987), *Frolic In The Park* (1988), *Act III* (1990).

Death Mask

Formed in New York, America in 1985 this heavy metal band consisted of Steven Michaels (vocals), Benny Ransom (guitar), Chris Eichhorn (bass) and Lee Nelson (drums). All the band had been members of various New York street gangs, and taking it off the streets they channelled their aggression into the music. They attracted the attention of Jon-Mikl Thor, the muscle-bound vocalist of the band Thor, who produced their debut album. The band signed to the Killerwatt Records label and released their debut entitled *Split The Atom* in 1986. Production duties were handled by Thor, and guitarist Steve Price. Unfortunately the music on offer did not reflect the band's tough street image, being a mixture of mediocre thrash metal and hard rock. Even though Thor included one of the album tracks, entitled 'I'm Dangerous', on the soundtrack to his film *Zombie Nightmare* the band failed to make any impact and soon sank without trace.
Album: *Split The Atom* (1986).

Deep Purple

Deep Purple evolved in 1968 following sessions to form a group around former Searchers' drummer Chris Curtis (b. 26 August 1942, Liverpool, England). Jon Lord (b. 9 June 1941, Leicester, England; keyboards) and Nick Simper (bass), veterans, respectively, of the Artwoods and Johnny Kidd And The Pirates, joined guitarist Ritchie Blackmore (b. 14 April 1945, Weston-super-Mare, England) in rehearsals for this new act, initially dubbed Roundabout. Curtis dropped out within days, and when Dave Curtis (bass) and Bobby

Deep Purple; Roger Glover and Joe Lynn Turner

Woodman (drums) also proved incompatible, two members of Maze, Rod Evans (vocals) and Ian Paice (drums), replaced them. Having adopted the Deep Purple name following a brief Scandinavian tour, the quintet began recording their debut album, which they patterned on USA group Vanilla Fudge. *Shades Of Deep Purple* thus included dramatic rearrangements of well-known songs, including 'Hey Joe' and 'Hush', the latter of which became a US Top 5 hit when issued as a single. Lengthy tours ensued as the group, all but ignored at home, steadfastly courted the burgeoning American concert circuit. *The Book Of Taliesyn* and *Deep Purple* also featured several excellent reworkings, notably of 'Kentucky Woman' (Neil Diamond) and 'River Deep Mountain High' (Ike And Tina Turner), but the unit also drew acclaim for its original material and the dramatic interplay between Lord and Blackmore. In July 1969 both Evans and Simper were axed from the line-up, which was then buoyed by the arrival of Ian Gillan (b. 19 August 1945, Hounslow, Middlesex, England; vocals) and Roger Glover (b. 30 November 1945, Brecon, Wales; bass) from the pop group Episode Six. Acknowledged by aficionados as the 'classic' Deep Purple line-up, the reshaped quintet made its album debut on the grandiose *Concerto For Group And Orchestra*, scored by Lord and recorded with the London Philharmonic Orchestra. Its orthodox successor, *Deep Purple In Rock*, established the group as a leading heavy-metal attraction and included such now-established favourites as 'Speed King' and 'Child In Time'. Gillan's powerful intonation brought a third dimension to their sound and this new-found popularity in the UK was enhanced when an attendant single, 'Black Night', reached number 2. 'Strange Kind Of Woman' followed it into the Top 10, while *Fireball* and *Machine Head* topped their respective chart. The latter included the riff-laden 'Smoke On The Water', now lauded as a seminal example of the hard rock oeuvre, and was the first release on the group's own Purple label. Although the platinum-selling *Made In Japan* captured their live prowess in full flight, relations within the band grew increasingly strained, and *Who Do We Think We Are?* marked the end of this highly-successful line-up. The departures of Gillan and Glover robbed Deep Purple of an expressive frontman and imaginative arranger, although Dave Coverdale (b. 22 September 1949, Saltburn, Lancashire, England; vocals) and Glenn Hughes (late of Trapeze, bass) brought a new impetus to the act. *Burn* and *Stormbringer* both reached the Top 10, but Blackmore grew increasingly dissatisfied with the group's direction and in May 1975 left to form Rainbow. USA guitarist Tommy Bolin, formerly of the James Gang, joined Deep Purple for *Come Taste The Band*, but his jazz/soul style was incompatible with the group's heavy metal sound, and a now-tiring act folded in 1976 following a farewell UK tour. Coverdale then formed Whitesnake, Paice and Lord joined Tony Ashton in Paice Ashton And Lord, while Bolin tragically died of a heroin overdose within months of Purple's demise. Judicious archive and 'best of' releases kept the group in the public eye, as did the high profile enjoyed by its several ex-members. Pressure for a reunion bore fruit in 1984 when Gillan, Lord, Blackmore, Glover and Paice completed *Perfect Strangers*. A second set, *House Of Blue Lights*, ensued but recurring animosity between Gillan and Blackmore resulted in the singer's departure following the in-concert *Nobody's Perfect*. Former Rainbow vocalist, Joe Lynn Turner, was brought into the line-up for *Slaves And Masters* as Purple steadfastly maintained their revitalized career.

Albums: *Shades Of Deep Purple* (1968), *The Book Of Taliesyn* (1969), *Deep Purple* (1969), *Concerto For Group And Orchestra* (1970), *Deep Purple In Rock* (1970), *Fireball* (1971), *Machine Head* (1972), *Made In Japan* (1972), *Who Do We Think We Are?* (1973), *Burn* (1974), *Stormbringer* (1974), *Come Taste The Band* (1975), *Perfect Strangers* (1985), *House Of Blue Light* (1987), *Nobody's Perfect* (1988), *Slaves And Masters* (1990). Compilations: *Purple Passages* (1972), *24 Carat Purple* (1975), *Made In Europe* (1976), *Last Concert In Japan* (1977), *Powerhouse* (1978), *Singles: As & Bs* (1978), *When We Rock We Rock When We Roll We Roll* (1978), *Deepest Purple* (1980), *Live In London: Deep Purple* (1982), *Anthology: Deep Purple* (1985), *Scandinavian Nights* (1988), *Knebworth '85* (1991).

Def Leppard

This supremely popular hard rock band was formed in Sheffield by Pete Willis (b. 16 February 1960, Sheffield, England; guitar), Rick Savage (b. 2 December 1960, Sheffield, England; bass) and Tony Kenning (drums) as Atomic Mass. They assumed their current name when Joe Elliott (b. 1 August 1959, Sheffield, England; vocals) joined the band. The quartet initially hired a tiny room in a spoon factory, which served as a rehearsal area, for £5 per week. Early in 1978, Willis met another young guitarist, Steve Clark (b. 23 April, 1960, Sheffield, England), and invited him to join the band. Clark agreed only on condition that they would play some 'proper' shows, and in July that year Def Leppard debuted at Westfield School before an audience of 150 children. After several gigs, the band voted to dismiss their drummer, replacing him with Frank Noon, who was working with another Sheffield group, the Next Band. In 1979 they recorded a debut EP for Bludgeon Riffola Records, which included 'Ride Into The Sun', 'Getcha Rocks Off' and 'The Overture'. Shortly after its release, Noon returned to the Next Band, and Rick Allen (b. 1 November 1963, Sheffield, England) became Def Leppard's permanent drummer. Later that year the band supported Sammy Hagar and AC/DC on short U.K. tours. This generated considerable interest and were then offered a deal by Vertigo Records. Their Tom Allom-produced debut, *On Through The Night*, was issued in 1980. The band subsequently staged their first headlining tour of Britain and also visited America for the first time - something which prompted fans to accuse them of 'selling out', making their displeasure known by throwing cans at the band during their appearance at the Reading Festival that summer.

Pyromania in 1983 saw the first change in the band's line-up since 1979. After missing many pre-production meetings and turning up drunk for a recording session, Pete Willis was sacked and replaced by ex-Girl guitarist Phil Collen (b. 8 December 1957, Hackney, London, England). The album was Def Leppard's most successful to date, but they were unable to build on that momentum. On New Year's Eve 1984, tragedy struck when drummer Rick Allen was involved in a car crash in which he lost his left arm. The band maintained faith with their percussionist, and did not resume work until Allen had learned to play a specially designed drumkit which made it possible for him to play most of the drums with his feet. His recovery severly delayed the recording of *Hysteria*, which was finally released in 1987 and eventually sold a staggering 15 million copies worldwide. It topped both the British and American charts, and produced two Top 5 US singles, 'Armageddon It' and the anthemic 'Pour Some Sugar On Me'. To promote the album, the band embarked on a 14-month world tour, which ended at the Memorial Arena, Seattle in October 1988. This was destined to be Steve Clark's last show with the band. As the band began work on their belated follow-up to *Hysteria*, Clark was found dead in his London flat on 8 January 1991, after consuming a mixture of drugs and alcohol. The rest of the band subsequently revealed that they had spent years trying to dissuade Clark from his self-abusive lifestyle. Faced once again by tragedy, Def Leppard soldiered manfully through

Def Leppard

the recording sessions for their fifth album, *Adrenalize*, which was released in March 1992 and immediately scaled the charts, topping the US list almost on release. The album was greeted with the usual mixture of critical disdain and public delight, and the band celebrated by performing at the Freddy Mercury tribute concert at Wembley Stadium.

Albums: *On Through The Night* (1980), *High 'N' Dry* (1981), *Pyromania* (1983), *Hysteria* (1987), *Adrenalize* (1992).

Further reading: *Animal Instinct*, David Fricke.

Demon

This midlands-based quintet were formed in the early 80s by vocalist Dave Hill and guitarist Mal Spooner in the halcyon days of the New Wave Of British Heavy Metal Movement. After two albums, they had outgrown the formularised approach of this genre and diversified into more melodic and mature rock music, fired with passion and a keen sense of dynamics. *The Plague* was the musical equivalent of Orwell's *1984*, a powerful statement of intent on both a musical and lyrical level. *British Standard Approved* and *Heart Of Our Time* followed, which consolidated the band's position as the UK's leading exponents of underground melodic rock. Following the tragic death of Mal Spooner in 1985, keyboardist Steve Watts teamed up with Dave Hill as the band's new writing force. Augmented by Scot Crawford on drums and guitarists Steven Brookes and John Waterhouse, they have released a string of highly polished, atmospheric studio albums and a double live set recorded in Germany. After 11 years, they are still struggling to achieve widespread recognition and exposure.

Albums: *Night Of The Demon* (1981), *The Unexpected Guest* (1982), *The Plague* (1983), *British Standard Approved* (1985), *Heart Of Our Time* (1985), *Breakout* (1987), *Taking The World By Storm* (1989), *One Helluva Night-Live* (1990), *Hold On To The Dream* (1991), *Anthology* (1991).

Des Barres, Michael

The former lead vocalist with 70s glam-rockers Silverhead. Before going solo, he was also a short-lived member of Detective and Chequered Past, and made a guest appearance on Kiss' Gene Simmons' solo album in 1978. He replaced Robert Palmer as the vocalist in Power Station in 1985. Both of his solo albums have been erratic, featuring an ad hoc collection of styles and ideas that are not easily pigeon-holed into one particular genre.

Albums: *I'm Only Human* (1980), *Somebody Up There Likes Me* (1986).

Destiny

This Swedish melodic rock quintet was formed in 1980 by bassist Stefan Bjornshog. Following a plethora of short-lived line-up changes, the band finally stabilized in 1984 with Bjornshog plus Magnus Osterman (guitar), John Proden (guitar), Peter Lundgren (drums) and Hakan Ring (vocals). They debuted the following year with *Beyond All Sense*, which comprised an uninspiring collection of identikit Eurorock numbers. Attracting little media interest, Osterman, Proden and Ring quit the band and were replaced by Jorgen Pettersson, Floyd Konstatin (ex-King Diamond) and Zenny Hanson respectively. This line-up recorded *Atomic Winter*, which was more aggressive and leaned towards the thrash genre. Nevertheless it fared little better than its predecessor. Konstatin and Pettersson quit shortly after the album was recorded, and the band reverted to a four-piece with the addition of Gunnar Kindberg. *Destiny*, released in 1990 is their finest work to-date, but the band are virtually unknown outside their native Sweden.

Albums: *Beyond All Sense* (1985), *Atomic Winter* (1988), *Destiny* (1990).

Destroy All Monsters

This Detroit-based group revolved around ex-Stooges guitarist Ron Asheton and former MC5 bassist Michael Davis. Such experience ensured attention in the new group's fortunes, particularly in the light of the concurrent punk rock explosion. With the group also comprising Niagara (vocals), Larry Miller (guitar), Ben Miller (saxophone) and Rob King (drums) Destroy All Monsters made its recording debut in 1978 with 'Bored'/'You're Gonna Die', issued in the UK by the independent Cherry Red label. The same outlet released a further two singles, while in the US the band completed two privately pressed EPs, *Live* (1979) and *Black Out In The City* (1980). The group was then disbanded, following which Asheton formed New Race with another former MC5 member, drummer Dennis Thompson.

Albums: *November 22nd 1963 - Singles And Rarities* (1989), *Live* (1989). Compilation: *Bored* (1991).

Detente

This heavy metal band with a punk attitude were formed in Los Angeles in 1984, by vocalist Dawn Crosby and drummer Dennis Butler. Recruiting guitarists Caleb Quinn and Ross Robinson, along with bassist Steve Hochheiser through small-ad columns, the line-up was complete. They signed to Roadrunner Records and debuted in 1986 with *Recognize No Authority*. Produced by Dana Strum (now of Slaughter), the album was characterized by Crosby's vitriolic vocal tirade and the heavy-duty riffing of Quinn and Robinson. The album sank without trace and subsequently Hochheiser and Robinson left to form Catalepsy. Detente continued with Greg Cekalovich (guitar) and George Robb (bass) and later ex-Abattoir guitarist Mike Carlino. They lost their contract with Roadrunner in 1988 and the band have been inactive since.

Album: *Recognize No Authority* (1986).

Diamond Head

Diamond Head

Formed in Stourbridge, England in 1979 the original line up comprised of Sean Harris (vocals), Brian Tatler (guitar), Colin Kimberley (bass) and Duncan Scott (drums). The band were one of the pioneers of the New Wave Of British Heavy Metal and their debut single 'Sweet And Innocent', was a catchy melodic rocker showing the bands bluesy influences and Harris's impressive vocal talents. After gigging extensively, the band recorded a session for the Friday night rock show on BBC's Radio 1. 'Play It Loud' and 'Shoot Out The Lights' were both released in 1981 to minor critical acclaim. The press even went as far as to hail the band as the new Led Zeppelin. Owing to the interest being shown towards them they decided to self-finance their debut *Lightning To The Nation*. This was quickly snapped up by the German-based Woolfe Records in the same year, and released on import. The album was full of catchy melodic rock, soaring vocals and tasteful guitar work, and attracted the attention of several major record companies. As a stop-gap, the band released a 12-inch EP *Diamond Lights*, again on DHM Records in 1981, before signing to MCA Records. Their first release for the label was an EP *Four Cuts* which was quickly followed up by their most popular album to date, *Borrowed Time*. Again the material was Led Zeppelin-style hard rock, and the band also included a couple of re-recorded tracks that had originally appeared on their first album. During the recording of the following album *Canterbury*, both Kimberley and Scott left the band. They were quickly replaced by ex-Streetfighter bassist Merv Goldsworthy (member of F.M.) and drummer Robbie France. The album was a brave change of direction for the band, still melodic but much more inventive and unconventional. Unfortunately, this change in style was not well received and despite a very successful appearance at the Monsters Of Rock Festival it flopped, and the group split up in 1985. Tatler then re-mixed their debut album, dropped two of the original tracks and added four previously released single tracks. This was then released under the new title of *Behold The Beginning* (1986). Tatler went on to form Radio Moscow and Sean Harris teamed up with guitarist Robin George in the ill-fated Notorious band and album project. Even though Diamond Head were no longer in existence, they retained a healthy press profile owing to the acclaim levelled at them by Metallica drummer Lars Ulrich, who made no secret of the fact that the band were one of his main influences and inspired him to begin his musical career. Metallica subsequently recorded a cover version of Diamond Head's old stage favourite 'Am I Evil'.

Early in 1991, both Harris and Tatler, reformed Diamond Head with newcomers Eddie Nooham (bass) and Karl Wilcox (drums). The band undertook a short low-key UK club tour using the name Dead Reckoning, then declared officially that they had reformed. The first release from this new incarnation of the band was a limited edition 12-inch single 'Wild On The Streets'. Released on the newly relaunched Bronze Records label in 1991 it showed the band had returned to fine form and rediscovered the spirit they had lost in 1985. The band planned an extensive club tour to promote the mini-album *Rising Up*.

Albums: *Lightning To The Nations* (1981), *Borrowed Time* (1982), *Canterbury* (1983), *Behold The Beginning* (1986), *Rising Up* (1992). Compilation: *Am I Evil* (1987).

Dianno

This British band was formed in 1982 by Paul Di'Anno (vocals), John Wiggins (guitar), Peter J. Ward (guitar/vocals), Mark Venables (keyboards/vocals), Kevin Browne (bass/vocals), and Mark Stewart (drums). Originally they were known as Lonewolf and spent their first year touring Europe playing their American style melodic AOR rock. In 1983 John Wiggins was replaced on guitar by Lee Slater and Lonewolf signed to FM Records. Soon after the contract was signed Lonewolf had to change their name

following complaints from a group of the same title. On their debut album *Dianno*, the unit came across as an English band trying to sound American. Their version of Cliff Richard's 'Heart User' was a surprise cover. The album did not sell well and at the end of the year Dianno fell apart with Paul Di'Anno going on to form Paul Di'Anno's Battlezone.
Album: *Dianno* (1984).

Di'Anno's, Paul, Battlezone

When Paul Di'Anno was unceremoniously 'asked to leave' Iron Maiden he set about forming his own band. After playing in the American-influenced Lonewolf and Dianno, he put together the first incarnation of the band known as Paul Di'Anno's Battlezone in London, England in 1985. Joining Di'Anno in this venture were ex-Deep Machine, Tokyo Blade guitarist John Wiggins, John Hurley (guitar), Pete West (bass) and Bob Falck (drums). The band signed to the Raw Power Records label and released their debut album *Fighting Back* in 1986. It was a welcome return to the style of music Di'Anno plays best, hard fast power metal in the British tradition. Tours took the band through Europe (where the band appeared at the Dynamo Open Air Festival) and America. At the end of the American tour, Falck left the band to join Overkill. Around the same time Hurley also left the band. Their replacements were drummer Steve Hopgood and guitarist Graham Bath, both ex-Persian Risk band members. The band then changed labels and it was time for album number two. *Children Of Madness* was released by the Powerstation Records label in 1987. Slightly Americanized, and harking back to Di'Anno's Lonewolf days, the material was not as strong as the band's previous release. After its release the band soon fell apart leaving Paul to reform the band. The band's last line-up consisted of Di'Anno (vocals), Graham Bath (guitar), Randy Scott (guitar), Mel Gibbons (bass) and Wayne Hewitt (drums). The band gigged but never managed to secure a recording contract and subsequently folded. Di'anno later turned up as guest vocalist with the re-formed Praying Mantis on a Japanese tour.
Albums: *Fighting Back* (1986), *Children Of Madness* (1987).

Dickinson, Bruce

b. Paul Bruce Dickinson, 7 August 1958, Worksop, Nottinghamshire, England. Former public school-boy Dickinson left the heavy metal group Samson to join pioneering contemporaries, Iron Maiden replacing Paul Di'Anno in 1981. By the following year Dickinson had fully established himself within the line-up by his performances on the road and on the UK number 1 *Number Of The Beast*. 1990 was a busy year for Dickinson's solo pursuits. His aspirations to become a novelist were realized in his comic-novel, a sub-standard attempt at the style of Tom Sharpe, *The Adventures Of Lord Iffy Boatrace*. However, legions of Iron Maiden fans propelled the book into the best-seller ratings. Also that year, Dickinson's solo album, *Tattooed Millionaire* reached number 14, while the title track climbed into the UK Top 20. A version of Mott The Hoople's 'All The Young Dudes' also reached the UK Top 30. As a keen amateur fencer and swordsman, Dickinson has at one time been ranked seventh in the men's foils for Great Britain.
Album: *Tattooed Millionaire* (1990).

Die Kreuzen

This heavy rock band was formed in Milwaukee, USA, in 1981. Their name derived from the German for the crosses. The band, featuring Dan Kubinski (vocals, Brian Egeness (guitar), Keith Brammer (bass) and Eric Tunison (drums) started life with a highly regarded album of embryonic thrash. Since that debut their material has revealed a much stronger inclination towards traditional rock. However, they were still widely congratulated for bringing intelligence and lyrical diversity to the heavy metal sphere. Signed to Chicago independent Touch And Go, their last album was produced by Butch Vig (Killdozer, Tad, Nirvana), while they retraced their punk roots with a recent cover of Wire's 'Pink Flag'.
Albums: *Die Kreuzen* (1986), *Century Days* (1988), *Gone Away* (1989), *Cement* (1991).

Dio, Ronnie James

b. Ronald Padavona, c.1940, New Hampshire, USA. Dio was raised in New York, USA and served his musical apprenticeship in the late 50s with school-based bands like the Vegas Kings, Ronnie And The Rumblers and Ronnie And the Redcaps. From 1961-67 he led Ronnie Dio And the Prophets, not solely as a vocalist, but also playing the piano, bass guitar, and even trumpet. Multi-talented musically, he also acted as a record producer. In 1967, with his cousin, David Feinstein, he formed the Electric Elves, a band which, in the early 70s, changed its name to Elf. In the middle of 1970, the entire band was involved in a car-crash, in which guitarist Nick Pantas died. Dio took on lead vocals in Elf and played the bass, the rest of the line-up comprised, Feinstein (guitar), Mickey Lee Soule (keyboards) and Gary Driscoll (drums). Elf was noticed by Roger Glover and Ian Paice of Deep Purple in 1972, and a production and recording deal was arranged, with

Ronnie James Dio

Elf supporting Deep Purple on two American tours. In 1973, Elf recruited bassist Craig Gruber, allowing Dio to concentrate on vocals. The guitarist, Feinstein, gave up touring and was replaced first by Doug Thaler, previously keyboard player for the Elves, and then Steve Edwards. From 1974 Mark Nauseef played percussion for the band. In 1975 Glover gave Dio the opportunity to appear on his project *The Butterfly Ball,* and this gave Dio the widespread recognition he desired. After leaving Deep Purple in May 1975, having already recorded one track with Elf, Ritchie Blackmore edged-out Steve Edwards to create Ritchie Blackmore's Rainbow. Here Ronnie James Dio developed from the honky-tonk influence of Elf to the harder rock of Blackmore and Rainbow. Dio's tendency to write about supernatural events, thoughts and fantasies also began to emerge at this stage, combining with the succession of often excellent musicians in Rainbow to produce four albums of high quality and enduring appeal. In 1979 Dio left Rainbow, taking his gift for singing and songwriting to Black Sabbath, where he built on the previously phenomenal, but waning success of the band, doing much to rejuvenate the flagging supergroup.

Heaven And Hell arrived with the so-called New Wave Of British Heavy Metal, outclassing most of its rivals with its tight, solid, bass-dominated sound and science fiction lyrics. After an acrimonious world tour in 1983, Dio left to form his own band, Dio, which was comprised of Vinny Appice (drums), Jimmy Bain, former bassist with Rainbow, Vivian Campbell (guitar) and Claude Schnell (keyboards). Together, they recorded four albums, with Dio taking on all the lyrics and songwriting himself, allowing his creative interests a completely free rein. While the subject matter remained in other worlds, times and beings, the style ranged from anthemic to epic. A lack of direction led to stagnation, and by 1987 the band was failing. In 1991 Dio renewed his acquaintance with Black Sabbath, recording an album with them, which was due to be released 1992.

Albums: With Ronnie Dio And The Prophets *Dio At Dominos* (1963). With Elf *Elf* (1972), *Carolina County Ball* (1974), *Trying To Burn The Sun* (1975), *Live* (1976). With Rainbow *Ritchie Blackmore's Rainbow* (1975), *Rainbow Rising* (1976), *Live On Stage* (1977), *Long Live Rock And Roll* (1978), *Live In Germany* (1976, 1990). With Black Sabbath *Heaven And Hell* (1980), *Mob Rules*

(1981), *Live Evil* (1982). With Dio *Holy Diver* (1983), *The Last In Line* (1984), *Sacred Heart* (1985), *Intermission* (1986), *Dream Evil* (1987), *Lock Up The Wolves* (1990).

Dirty Looks

Founded in the early 80s by Dutch-born Hendrik Ostergaard, Dirty Looks released three albums on three different independent labels before achieving a major deal with Atlantic Records in 1987. Ostergaard handled both vocals and guitar, ably supported by Paul Lidel (guitar), Jack Pyers (bass) and Gene Barnett (drums). Their debut, *Cool From The Wire*, showed the band as purveyors of straight-ahead, no nonsense power metal very much in the AC/DC mould. Indeed, in both the crushing style of guitar riffing and the vocal delivery of Ostergaard comparisons with the Australian supremos were inevitable. However, such was the energy and commitment the band brought to recording and live performances that any comparisons paled into insignificance. The follow up, *Turn Of The Screw*, was not quite as successful despite critical acclaim. Their 1991 release, *Bootlegs* saw the band presenting the same style of relentless power boogie, albeit now with a return to a smaller label.
Albums: *Dirty Looks* (1985), *I Want More* (1986), *In Your Face* (1987), *Cool From The Wire* (1987), *Turn Of The Screw* (1988), *Bootlegs* (1991).

Dirty Tricks

This blues-based UK heavy rock outfit were formed in 1974 by vocalist Kenny Stewart and guitarist John Fraser Binnie. With bassist Terry Horbury and drummer John Lee completing the line-up, they drew inspiration from Bad Company, the Faces, Black Sabbath and Deep Purple. They never graduated from support status, because their attempt to bridge the divide between hard-rock and heavy metal was sabotaged by weak material. They released three albums on Polydor during the mid-70s, which failed to reflect the energy they generated in the live setting. In 1976 Andy Beirne took over the drumstool, but the band were soon overwhelmed by the growing punk movement. Beirne later joined Grand Prix, Terry Horbury teamed up with speed metal outfit Vardis and guitarist John Fraser Binnie was recruited by Rogue Male in 1984.
Albums: *Dirty Tricks* (1975), *Night Man* (1976), *Hit And Run* (1977).

Dirty White Boy

This 'supergroup' was put together by Earl Slick (ex-guitarist with David Bowie, John Waite and John Lennon bands) and Glenn Eisley, former vocalist of Giuffria. Adding ex-Autograph drummer Keni Richards and bassist F. Kirk Alley to the line-up, their style and approach is the total antithesis of what one might expect from their collective pedigrees. Throwing caution to the wind, they went for a no-holds-barred, down-and-dirty rock 'n' roll approach on their debut album. Produced by Beau Hill (of Ratt) *Bad Reputation* finds these seasoned musicians rediscovering their roots and really enjoying themselves in the process.
Albums: *Bad Reputation* (1990).

Dixie Dregs

Formed in 1973, the instrumental Dixie Dregs fused rock, jazz, classical and bluegrass with seamless musicianship, and one of their alumni, guitarist Steve Morse (b. 28 July 1954, Hamilton, Ohio, USA) is regarded as one of the most technically proficient players of that instrument. The group was formed by Morse, electric violinist Allen Sloan, bassist Andy West (b. 6 February 1954, Newport, Rhode Island, USA) and drummer Rod Morgenstein while attending the University of Miami School of Music in Florida, USA. Morse and West had played in the Augusta group Dixie Grit. They met Sloan, from Miami, and Morgenstein, from Plainview, New York, at the university and the four formed a group, adding Steve Davidowski on keyboards. For college credit, the quintet, now calling itself the Dixie Dregs, produced and recorded an album called *The Great Spectacular*, later privately issued in 1976 and long out of print. After graduating from college, the group moved to Augusta and began playing live dates. They were signed by Capricorn Records in December 1976 and moved to Atlanta, Georgia. Their debut album for the label, *Free Fall*, was released in spring 1977, and Mark Parrish replaced Davidowski that autumn. Their next two albums, *What If* and *Night Of The Living Dregs*, received critical acclaim and charted (as did the rest of their albums), the latter including one side of live performances from the Montreux Jazz Festival. After completion of that album, Tee Lavitz replaced Parrish. The group switched to Arista Records for *Dregs Of The Earth* and remained there for their last two, *Unsung Heroes* and *Industry Standard*. By the time of *Unsung Heroes*, they had shortened their name to the Dregs and for *Industry Standard*, had replaced Sloan with violinist Mark O'Connor, who stayed for about a year and later went on to record several solo albums of virtuoso bluegrass and jazz. The Dregs carried on as a quartet for several months and disbanded in 1982, and Morse's highly-acclaimed solo career began with the 1984 release of *The*

Dixie Dregs; Steve Morse

Introduction. Rod Morgenstein later joined the pop-heavy metal band Winger. Some of the members of the Dixie Dregs reunited for a tour in 1988 but no albums were released.

Albums: *The Great Spectacular* (c.1976), *Free Fall* (1977), *What If* (1978), *Night Of The Living Dregs* (1979), *Dregs Of The Earth* (1980), *Unsung Heroes* (1981), *Industry Standard* (1982).

981), *Industry Standard* (1982).

D'Molls

This Chicago-based heavy metal band features Desi Rexx (vocals/guitar), Billy Dior (drums), S.S. Priest (guitar) and Lizzy Valentine (bass). Their 1988, self-titled debut album caused quite a stir at the time of its release, with its self-assured Aerosmith-meets-Poison-type approach. However, the songwriting on the follow-up *Warped* was weak, being rigidly formularized and lacked the cutting edge of its predecessor. With poor reviews and sales to match, they disbanded in 1991.

Albums: *D'Molls* (1988), *Warped* (1990).

DNA

This band was a short-lived collaboration between guitarist Rick Derringer and drummer Carmine Appice. With the assistance of Duane Hitchings (keyboards) and Jimmy Johnson (bass), they released *Party Tested* in 1983. This featured a wide range of styles that included jazz, rock, funk, blues and pop. The playing was beyond criticism, but the songs were devoid of soul, and the album as a whole lacked unity and cohesion. Failing to win support in the media, DNA disintegrated when Carmine Appice accepted the offer to join Ozzy Osbourne's band. Appice subsequently went on to form King Kobra.

Album: *Party Tested* (1983).

Dogs D'Amour

This hard rock outfit originally formed in Birmingham, England during 1983 with a line-up comprising Tyla (guitar), Ned Christie (vocals), Nick Halls (guitar), Carl (bass) and Bam Bam (drums). After making their London debut in April 1983 they underwent a rapid series of personnel changes. Halls, Bam Bam and Christie departed prompting Tyla to assume lead vocal responsibilities. He and Carl recruited replacements, Dave Kusworth (guitar) and Paul Hornby (drums). They relocated to Finland where their hard rock style won them an underground following. After returning to the UK in 1985, further changes in the line-up were underway, with Bam Bam replacing Hornby, while Kusworth departed in favour of the elegantly named Jo-Dog.

Later that year, the procession of changes continued with the departure of Carl in favour of Doll By Doll bassist Mark Duncan, who lasted until 1987 when Steve James arrived. The group finally broke through with the minor hit 'How Come It Never Rains' and the mini-album, *A Graveyard Of Empty Bottles*. The follow-up 'Satellite Kid' also reached the UK Top 30 as did their album, *Errol Flynn*. The latter met some resistance in the USA where it was forcibly retitled *The King Of The Thieves*. Having at last stabilized their line-up, Dogs D'Amour have yet to establish themselves in the top league of hard rock acts but they continue to tour extensively.

Albums: *The (Un)Authorized Bootleg* (1988), *In The Dynamite Jet Saloon* (1988), *A Graveyard of Empty Bottles* (1989), *Errol Flynn* (1990).

Dokken

Dokken

This Los Angeles band was put together by vocalist Don Dokken. His first break came when producer Dieter Dierks recruited him to supply back-up vocals on the Scorpions' *Blackout* in 1982. Dierks then allowed Dokken the left-over studio time to produce some demos. These rough recordings impressed Carrere Records enough to secure a contract, and he enlisted the services of guitarist George Lynch, drummer Mick Brown and bassist Juan Croucier (who later left to form

Ratt and was replaced by Jeff Pilson) to form Dokken, the band.

Essentially Dokken's music is an intimate fusion of hard rock, melody and atmospherics. It was these qualities that Elektra Records saw in the band when they signed them in 1982. They re-mixed and re-released their Carrere debut *Breaking The Chains* and it made the lower end of the US *Billboard* album charts. From this point on, Elektra allowed the band a substantial recording budget, with producers Michael Wagener, Geoff Workman, Tom Werman and Roy Thomas Baker being used at different times. The band recorded three excellent studio albums for Elektra before internal disputes between Lynch and Don Dokken led the band to split in 1988. A farewell live album, *Beast From The East* followed, and is a fitting epitaph to a fine band. Lynch went on to form Lynch Mob, while Don Dokken negotiated a solo deal with Geffen Records and released *Up From The Ashes* in 1990.

Albums: *Breaking The Chains* (1982), *Tooth And Nail* (1984), *Under Lock And Key* (1985), *Back For The Attack* (1987), *Beast From The East* (1988), *Back In The Streets* (1989).

Dominique, Lisa

Dominique was a former beautician and sister of talented guitarist Marino. She started her career in the UK singing in Marino's band, but came to prominence through the pages of *Kerrang* magazine, appearing regularly as a pin-up. With interest already generated, she decided on a career in the music business and was signed by Heavy Metal Records. With the help of Marino (guitar), Pete Jupp (drums) and other session musicians, she debuted with *Rock 'N' Roll Lady* in 1989. The album was universally slated by the music media, and Lisa was subsequently dropped by her label. Undaunted by such a setback, she signed to Castle Communications and delivered *Gypsy Ryder* in 1991. The work was not well-received in the heavy metal fraternity.

Albums: *Rock 'N' Roll Lady* (1989), *Gypsy Ryder* (1991).

Doro

Dorothy Pesch, the leading light and vocalist of the German heavy metal band Warlock, dissolved the unit after the release of 1987's *Triumph And Agony*. Retaining only bassist Tommy Henriksen, she embarked on a solo career under the Doro moniker. To complete the new line-up she recruited guitarist John Devin and drummer Bobby Rondinelli. Using Joey Balin as a writing partner *Force Majeure* was a departure from her previous heavy teutonic style, moving towards a more mainstream AOR approach in an attempt for commercial success. It featured an embarrassing cover of Procol Harum's 'A Whiter Shade Of Pale' as the opening track and it fared badly. Ditching the entire band in favour of hired hands, she recorded Doro with Gene Simmons (of Kiss) as producer. Musically, this was even further away from her roots, as she compromised on every level to achieve chart success. *Rare Diamonds* was a compilation of older material, giving Doro time for a radical re-think about her next career move.

Albums: *Force Majeure* (1989), *Doro* (1990). Compilation: *Rare Diamonds* (1991).

Dr. Mastermind

Formed in the USA during 1986, Dr. Mastermind were one of the first new-style guitar orientated bands. Comprising Kurt James (ex-Steeler and Driver guitarist), Deen Castronovo (drums) and the enigmatic Dr. Mastermind on bass and vocals, they were a power trio in every sense of the word. Frenetically paced songs, that never degenerated into tuneless thrash, were punctuated by high-octane and complex guitar breaks. After the release of their debut album, Castronovo joined Cacophony, and James left for Turbin. Rick Hosert and Pete Lachman were drafted in as replacements on drums and guitar respectively, but as yet this new line-up has yet to record.

Album: *Dr. Mastermind* (1986).

Dragon

Along with Split Enz, Dragon are considered one of New Zealand's finest rock exports. Formed in 1972 and based around the Hunter brothers (Mark and Todd), the band has been together for nearly two decades. Their early influences were English rock-based bands and they released two albums in New Zealand, but by the time the band emigrated to Australia in 1975, its leanings were towards silky-smooth, soul-inspired melodies, highlighting the songwriting of Paul Hewson. Hits such as 'April Sun In Cuba' and 'Are You Old Enough' were in the middle of a run of seven Top 10 singles and four Top 20 albums. They were highly popular with the young teenage audience, and yet the band also had a rapport with the older generation. The group were not short of publicity, with frequent newspaper stories on the excesses indulged by the band and the arrogance of its members. Despite the deaths of Hewson and early drummer Neal Storey due to drug overdoses, the band toured extensively but eventually imploded in1979 due to friction between members. Marc Hunter released a solo album and Top 20 single 'Island Nights', which encouraged him to form his own band to tour and promote the album. 1990 saw him record an album of jazz covers. Todd Hunter collaborated with Johanne Piggott, in the bands XL Capris and Scribble, which received some attention. Dragon re-formed in 1982, releasing several hit singles (co-written with Piggot), again illustrating the talent of the band, which currently consists of the Hunter brothers, who add musicians when needed.

Albums: *Universal Radio* (1973), *Scented Gardens For The Blind* (1974), *Sunshine* (1977), *Running Free* (1977), *Ozambezi* (1978), *Powerplay* (1979), *Live* (1984), *Dreams Of Ordinary Men* (1986), *Bondi Road* (1989).

Dream Theatre

Formerly known as Majesty, Dream Theatre appeared on the US techno-rock scene in 1988. Comprising Charlie Dominici (vocals), John Petrucci (guitar), Kevin Moore (keyboards), John Myung (bass) and Mike Portnoy (drums), their material incorporates elements of Rush, Queensryche, Kansas and Yngwie Malmsteen. Dynamic, multi-faceted hard-rock, characterized by countless slick time changes and impeccable musicianship are the band's trademarks. Signed by MCA, they debuted in 1989 with *When Dream And Day Unite*. This received a favourable response from the music media, but was strangely ignored by the record-buying public. Dismayed at the poor album sales, MCA terminated their contract and vocalist Charlie Dominici quit shortly afterwards.

Albums: *When Dream And Day Unite* (1989).

DRI

This heavy metal band were formed in Houston, Texas USA in 1982. The band's original line-up consisted of Kurt Brecht (vocals), Spike Cassidy (guitar), Dennis Johnson (bass) and Kurt's brother Eric Brecht (drums). Originally calling themselves Dirty Rotten Imbeciles, they shortened it to DRI and signed to Roadrunner Records in 1983. Their first album for the label, *Dirty Rotten LP,* was released in the same year. It quickly established the band at the forefront of the crossover movement with its vicious mixture of punk, hardcore and thrash metal. However, on the next album, *Dealing With It,* founder member Eric Brecht left the band to be replaced by Felix Griffin. The band continued in the same vein, even going as far as to call their third album *Crossover,* which was released in 1987. However, they were moving into a more traditional thrash metal style and by the release of *Four Of A Kind* in 1988, it was clear the band were taking a more mainstream thrash metal direction. Perhaps to remind their fans of their 'roots', the band re-mixed and re-released the *Dirty Rotten LP* in the same year, also including on this album an extra four tracks which had originally been released as an EP *Violent Pacification* back in 1984. Shortly after this the band hit problems on a short tour of Mexico as new bass player John Menor was viciously attacked and robbed. However, this did not deter the band from producing their most accomplished album to date. Entitled *Thrash Zone*, it was released late in 1989. By now the band had fully crossed over into the thrash scene.

Albums: *Dirty Rotten LP* (1983), *Dealing With It* (1985), *Crossover* (1987), *Four Of A Kind* (1988), *Dirty Rotten LP* (+ 4 extra tracks, re-mixed/re-released)(1988), *Thrash Zone* (1989).

Driver

This short-lived, Canadian power-trio were formed in 1976 by vocalist/guitarist Peter Glinderman. With the addition of bassist Dennis Coats and drummer Stephen Rexford, they signed to A&M the following year. *No Accidents*, their only album release remains today, one of the undiscovered classics of the hard-rock genre. It features an inspired collection of high energy blues-based rockers, saturated with infectious hooks, bridges and choruses. Ideas were explored and exhausted in just three minutes. 'Lookin' For A New Way To Say I Love You' became a modest US hit. Since then the band have disappeared into oblivion.

Album: *No Accidents* (1977).

E

Earthshaker.

This Japanese heavy metal band was modelled on the styles of Y&T, Deep Purple and Van Halen. Formed by guitarist Shinichiro Ishihara in 1981, its name was taken from Y&T's third album. After a series of false starts the band was completed with the addition of Masafumi Nishida (vocals), Takayuki Kai (bass) and Yoshihiro Kudo (drums). Relocating to San Francisco in 1983, it utilized the talents of ex-Gamma keyboardist Mitchell Froom on the following year's *Fugitive* opus. As a consequence the band's sound became less aggressive and highlighted their obvious limitations. They have continued to release albums as a four-piece, but have made little impact outside their native Japan.
Albums: *Earthshaker* (1983), *Fugitive* (1984), *Midnight Flight* (1984), *Live* (1985), *Over The Run* (1986), *Treachery* (1989), *Live Best* (1990).

Electric Sun

This German group was formed by Uli Jon Roth (guitar/vocals) after he left the Scorpions. At first he was assisted by Ule Ritgens on bass and Clive Edwards on drums. He was quickly signed by the Brain Label and released *Earthquake* in 1979. This was a highly spiritual record and at times resembled Jimi Hendrix. The jazzy rock music with occasionally unusual guitar parts was let down by Roth's vocals. On *Firewind*, released in 1981, Clive Edwards was replaced by Sidhatta Gautama. The music improved and now contained oriental influenced pieces, but the vocals remained the same. The next release, *Beyond The Astral Skies* took four years to make, but when finally released, it showed a great leap forward by Roth. In addition to the jazz rock pieces, there were also classical parts which let Roth demonstrate his religious beliefs and his musical ability to the full. On the opening verse he sang 'The astral skies shall open wide/The night the master comes/And all the mountains will step aside'. The biggest improvement was in the vocals, with Roth still singing lead but having the support of seven other singers. Little has been heard of Uli Jon Roth since.
Albums: *Earthquake* (1979), *Firewind* (1981), *Beyond The Astral Skies* (1985).

Electro Hippies

This eccentric grindcore outfit were formed in 1988. Specializing in low-technological studio techniques they have issued four albums to date. In each case, a distorted, bass-laden barrage is over-ridden by stomach-churning vocals that lack both finesse and cohesion. Chaotic and extreme, Electro Hippies criticize the whole recording industry.
Albums: *The Only Good Punk Is A Dead One* (1988), *Electro Hippies Live* (1989), *The Peaceville Recordings* (1989), *Play Loud Or Die* (1989).

Elf

This UK heavy-rock unit was formed in 1970 by vocalist Ronnie James Dio (b. Ronald Padavona) with Steve Edwards (guitar), Mickey Lee Soule (keyboards), Craig Gruber (bass), Gary Driscoll (drums) and Mark Nausseef (percussion). Delivering a mixture of hard-rock, boogie and blues, they impressed Deep Purple's Roger Glover enough for him to offer them his production skills and a deal with Purple Records. They supported Deep Purple on their 1974 tour, promoting their newly released *Carolina County Ball*. This was undoubtedly their finest work and is still highly regarded by metal aficionados today. After the erratic *Trying To Burn The Sun*, Elf became redundant as Ritchie Blackmore hired Dio, Soule, Gruber and Edwards to help record his solo album *Ritchie Blackmore's Rainbow*.
Albums: *Elf* (1972), *Carolina County Ball* (1974), *Trying To Burn The Sun* (1975), *Live* (1976).

Elixir

This UK heavy metal quintet, was formed in the late 80s and featured ex-Iron Maiden drummer Clive Burr, guitarists Phil Denton and Norman Gordon, Paul Taylor on vocals and bassist Mark White. Their stylistic origins date back to the New Wave Of British Heavy Metal, utilizing twin lead guitars to alternate between circular power-riffs and intricate solos. Early Iron Maiden and Def Leppard were strong influences, with their lyrical content split roughly 50/50 between mythology/epic struggles and the equally cliched sex/violence/drugs themes.
Album: *Lethal Potion* (1990).

Enuff Z'Nuff

This Chicago USA based pop-metal crossover quartet comprised Donnie Vie (vocals), Derek Frigo (guitar), Chip Z'Nuff (bass) and Vikki Fox (drums). Influences such as Cheap Trick and the Beatles were apparent through the band's extensive use of three-part harmonies, which carried the melody line in many of the songs. On a visual level, they initially appeared as multi-coloured fashion casualties from the early 70s, sporting an ambitious and often dazzling array of sunglasses, waistcoats, boots and accessories. This image has since been played down with the release of *Strength*, an impressive and mature musical offering that combined infectious hooks, abrasive guitar work and a sparkling production to dramatic effect.

Albums: *Enuff Z'Nuff* (1989), *Strength* (1991).

Epitaph

Epitaph's career comprises two distinct phases, linked together by founder member and guitarist/vocalist Cliff Jackson. The first two albums had little to do with their later hard-rock style and featured MOR, jazz-tinged AOR. The band disintegrated in 1975, but Jackson resurrected Epitaph in 1979 with Heinz Glass (guitar), Harvey Janssen (bass), Michael Karch (keyboards) and Fritz Randow (drums). *Return From Reality* adopted an aggressive approach, characterized by the heavy-duty guitar work of Glass. Karch was fired after the album was released, and surprisingly, *See You In Alaska* which followed, was rather lightweight compared to its predecessor. *Live*, redressed the balance and saw the band in top shape once more. However, internal disputes resulted in the departure of Glass, Randow and Janssen soon after the album's release. Klaus Walz, Norbert Lehmann and Bernie Kolbe were drafted in as replacements on guitar, drums and vocals respectively, to record *Danger Man* in 1982. Unable to generate renewed interest, the band folded in 1983. Kolbe and Jackson went on to Kingdom, while Randow joined Victory.

Albums: *Outside The Law* (1974), *Stop, Look And Listen* (1975), *Return From Reality* (1979), *See You In Alaska* (1980), *Live* (1981), *Danger Man* (1982).

Ethel The Frog

Featuring P. Sheppard (vocals), Tognola (guitar), Hopkinson (bass) and Paul Conyers (drums), they first came to the public's attention via a track on EMI's *Metal For Muthas Vol. I* compilation in 1980. This album was intended to introduce mostly unsigned British heavy metal bands and is most notable for boasting two early Iron Maiden tracks. Indeed the concept was very much designed to develop the New Wave Of British Heavy Metal of which Ethel The Frog was a part. Their track, 'Fight Back' is basic heavy metal. Soon after, they recorded and released their debut, *Ethel The Frog*. Unfortunately, they did not capture much public interest and met with little critical acclaim. Disillusioned they split in 1980.

Album: *Ethel The Frog* (1980).

Europe

Europe

A Swedish heavy rock band, Europe found international success in the late 80s. In 1982, Joey Tempest (19 August 1963, Stockholm, Sweden; vocals), John Norum (guitar) and John Leven (bass) founded Force in the Stockholm suburb of Upplands-Vasby. After winning a national talent contest, the group recorded two Rush-influenced albums for the Swedish market before signing to Epic in 1986. By now Norum had left and the renamed Europe included guitarist Kee Marcello (ex-Easy Action), Michael Michaeli (keyboards) and drummer Ian Haughland. With English-language lyrics, the first Epic album was produced by Kevin Elson and included hits with 'Carrie', 'The Final Countdown' (a UK number 1), 'Rock The Night' and 'Cherokee'. Europe's success in Japan and the USA was assisted by the group's lengthy world tours. Later hits included 'Superstitious' (1988) from the Ron Nevison-produced second album, but *Prisoners Of Paradise*, with Beau Hill as producer, sold poorly.

Albums: *The Final Countdown* (1986), *Out Of This World* (1988), *Prisoners In Paradise* (1991).

Every Mother's Nightmare

This US 'sleaze-rock' band was formed in 1989 by vocalist Rick Ruhl and guitarist Steve Malone.

With the addition of bassist Mark McMurty and drummer Jim Phipps, they signed a deal with Arista in 1990. Their self-titled debut, released the same year, combines Kiss, Aerosmith, Tesla and Bon Jovi influences to startling effect. Their energetic dynamism and ability gives the songs a cutting edge that transcends any accusations of plagiarism.

Album: *Every Mother's Nightmare* (1990).

Excalibur

This group was formed in Bradford, England in 1981 by Paul McBride (vocals), Paul Solynskyj (b. 27 October 1966, England; guitar), Martin Hawthorn (bass), and Mick Dobson (drums). The band got together while they were still schoolboys and sometimes they would fall asleep in class after a heavy night's gigging. On leaving school, Excalibur continued to tour heavily, while its members tried also to hold down day jobs. Conquest Records signed the band in 1985 after one of their employees heard Excalibur one night by accident. *The Bitter End* mini-album was released in 1985. This contained slightly melodic heavy metal. In 1986 Excalibur expanded to a five-piece with the addition of Steve Blades (b. 20 May 1968, Scotland; guitar/keyboards). This was followed by a session for the BBC's Radio I *Friday Rock Show* which was broadcast in July 1986 and again in September. The four tracks that the band recorded were later released by Clay Records as the *Hot For Love* EP in 1988. Also in 1988 Excalibur appeared on a BBC television programme, *On A Personal Note*, where they performed 'Hot For Love' and 'Running Scared'. The programme also featured Def Leppard and Little Angels. 1988 saw Dobson being replaced by Dave Sykes on drums. In support of the *Hot For Love* EP, Excalibur supported Uriah Heep for most of their UK tour. In 1989 the band signed to Active Records and immediately began recording their first full album. The first taste of the album was a track called 'Carole Ann', which had the band being described as Britain's answer to Bon Jovi, simply because the track was an acoustic number. After *One Strange Night* was released to critical acclaim, Excalibur headed out on their first full headlining tour of the UK in February 1990. They supported Saxon on a UK and European tour. Meanwhile there were personnel changes. Livermore had replaced Martin Hawthorn in 1989, and he now left to make way for Dean Wilson (b. 5 March 1966, England; bass). *One Strange Night* sold in Europe and the band also had some success in America, with their melodic form of heavy metal. In 1991 Excalibur were in the studio recording their follow-up album, when

Paul McBride announced that he was leaving the band.

Albums: *The Bitter End* (mini-album 1985), *One Strange Night* (1990).

Exciter

Formed in Ottawa, Canada in 1979 as a three-piece outfit, the band's original line-up consisted of Dan Beehler (drums/vocals), John Ricci (guitar) and Allan Johnson (bass). An impressive demo attracted the attention of Shrapnel Records which as well as featuring the band on an early *U.S. Metal* compilation also released the demo as an album entitled *Heavy Metal Maniac* in 1983. This was fast powerful Motorhead-influenced power metal and quickly gained the band a strong following in Europe. They then changed labels and released *Violence & Force*, on Roadrunner Records in 1984. Produced by ex-Rods drummer Carl Canedy, it was a much better release benefiting from better production and higher quality material. By the next release, the band had changed European labels once again. Their third album, *Long Live The Loud*, appeared on the Music For Nations label in 1985. Recorded and produced in London with producer Guy Bidmead, this album did not seem as immediate as previous releases and the band seemed to have lost some of their early raw power. However, this did not deter the band from undertaking an extensive European tour in support of the release. After touring, guitarist Ricci left the band. His replacement was Brian McPhee, an old friend of the band, who added a new dimension which could be heard on the fourth album, *Unveiling The Wicked*. Unfortunately, even Brian McPhee's excellent guitar work could not alleviate the tiredness in the music, and after a short tour of Brazil the band decided to add a vocalist/frontman to give them a stronger identity. This resulted in the recruitment of Rob Malnati. Once again the band changed labels, signing to the small, Canadian independent Maze Records. Their last album, *Exciter* failed to sell and shortly after its release the band sank into obscurity playing on the local club scene.

Albums: *Heavy Metal Maniac* (1983), *Violence & Force* (1984), *Long Live The Loud* (1985), *Unveiling The Wicked* (1986), *Exciter* (1988).

Exodus

Formed in San Francisco, USA, in the early 80s, Exodus was one of the earlier thrash metal bands. Their line-up at one time included Metallica guitarist Kirk Hammett. Their first album was an important landmark in the thrash arena, with its highly aggressive music and lyrical approach, dealing with all manner of extreme and brutal

Exodus

violence. It was recorded by the line-up of Paul Baloff (vocals), Gary Holt (guitar), Rick Hunolt (guitar), Rob McKillop (bass) and Tom Hunting (drums). Vocalist Steve Sousa replaced Baloff for the recording of *Pleasures Of The Flesh*, which was marginally mellower, but successful nonetheless. Even after the subsequent departure of Hunting, who was replaced by John Tempesta, Exodus continued to record worthy material, but failed to match the commercial success of contemporaries such as Metallica and Anthrax. They have steadfastly refused to compromise or waver from their straightforward thrash style, and have managed to maintain a level of popularity sufficient to gain a major label record deal.

Albums: *Bonded By Blood* (1985), *Pleasures Of The Flesh* (1987), *Fabulous Disaster* (1989), *Impact Is Imminent* (1990), *Good Friendly Violent Fun* (1991).

Export

This British rock band was formed in 1980 by former Hardstuff vocalist Harry Shaw and guitarist Steve Morris. Enlisting the services of bassist Chris Alderman and drummer Lou Rosenthal, they specialized in Americanized AOR. Their material is characterized by note-perfect harmonies, sterling guitar work and infectious hooklines similar to Kansas, Starz and REO Speedwagon. After a well-received self-titled debut in 1981, they were picked up by Epic, who recognized the enormous potential they possessed. Two albums were delivered, with Lance Quinn (of Bon Jovi) at the production helm for 1986s *Living In Fear Of A Private Eye*. Surprisingly, the band failed to take off in the USA and Epic dropped them due to poor sales figures. Steve Morris produced Torino's debut album in 1987, but Export continue to search for a new contract.

Albums: *Export* (1981), *Contraband* (1984), *Living In Fear Of A Private Eye* (1986).

Extreme

This Boston quartet comprised Gary Cherone (b. 26 July 1961, Malden, Massachussets, USA; vocals) Nuno Bettencourt (b. 20 September 1966, Azores, Portugal; guitar) Pat Badger (b. 22 July 1967, Boston, Massachussets, USA; bass) and Paul Geary (b. 24 July 1961, Medford, Massachussets, USA; drums). After changing their name from the Dream, a recording contract with A&M Records was soon secured and the inevitable self-titled debut album followed. Encompassing elements of pop, metal, funk and blues, their songwriting powers were still in their infancy at this stage and although competent, the album met with widespread critical indifference. *Pornograffitti* was a stunning second release, being an ambitious concept affair, sub-titled 'A Funked Up Fairy Tale' based on the life and times of the album's central character. The big breakthrough came when the simple acoustic ballad 'More Than Words', reached number 1 and number 2 in the US and UK singles charts respectively. The band's music was now characterized by Bettencourt's innovative guitar work, intelligent lyrics and a diverse style that transcended a variety of musical genres. Extreme are now on the brink of huge stardom and are likely to have a significant impact on the shaping of rock music during the next decade. Their appearance at the Freddy Mercury concert gave them considerable exposure beyond the heavy metal fraternity.

Albums: *Extreme* (1989), *Pornograffitti* (1990).

Ezo

This Japanese band relocated to Los Angeles immediately after their formation in 1985. This move was deemed necessary in order to achieve wider international exposure. Featuring Masaki (vocals), Shoyo (guitar), Taro (bass) and Hiro (drums) they are retro-rock specialists, drawing heavily on the legacy of Led Zeppelin, UFO and Kiss for their inspiration. Signing to Geffen Records and linking up with Kiss bassist Gene Simmons as producer was a promising start. However, the resulting debut was less than impressive. The follow-up *Fire, Fire* dropped many of the blatant reference points of its predecessor, but ultimately lacked direction, with the band struggling to find its own identity.

Albums: *Ezo* (1987), *Fire, Fire* (1989).

Extreme

F

Faithful Breath

This German, progressive heavy metal band have a long and chequered history, that dates back to 1974. The initial nucleus of the band comprised Heinz Mikus (guitar/vocals), Horst Stabenow (bass) and Uwe Otto (drums). Influenced by King Crimson and Deep Purple, their debut album was *Fading Beauty* in 1974. This featured intricate arrangements and keyboards, but lacked both melody and memorable hooks. After a lengthy gap and the ditching of keyboards, the band concentrated on guitar oriented hard-rock. Three competent albums followed, but suffered from inexperienced self-production. Successful appearances at two Dutch rock festivals in 1983, attracted the attention of Mausoleum Records. Jurgen Dusterloh took over the drumstool and Andy Bibi Honig was added as a second guitarist for the recording of *Gold 'N' Glory*. Produced by Michael Wagener, it remains the band's finest recorded work. Further line-up changes ensued and the band moved towards the thrash end of the hard-rock spectrum. In 1987, the band changed its name to Risk, with only Mikus surviving from the original line-up.

Albums: *Fading Beauty* (1974), *Back On My Hill* (1980), *Rock Lions* (1981), *Hard Breath* (1982), *Gold 'N' Glory* (1984), *SKOL* (1985), *Live* (1986).

Faith No More

Formed in San Fransisco in 1983, Faith No More were among the first outfits to experiment with the fusion of funk, thrash and hardcore styles into a new musical sub-genre. The band initially comprised Jim Martin (guitar), Roddy Bottum (keyboards), Bill Gould (bass), Mike Bordin (drums) and Chuck Mosely (vocals). This line-up recorded a low-budget, self-titled debut on the independent Mordam label, followed by the ground breaking *Introduce Yourself* on Slash, a subsidiary of London Records. It encompassed a variety of styles but exuded a rare warmth and energy, mainly through Mosley's 'over the top' vocals and was well received by the critics. Internal disputes led to the firing of Mosely on the eve of widespread press coverage and favourable live reviews. Against the odds, Mosely's replacement Mike Patton was even more flamboyant and actually more accomplished as a singer. *The Real Thing* that followed was a runaway success, with the single 'Epic' denting the UK Top 20 singles chart. Their style was now both offbeat and unpredictable, yet retained enough melody to remain a commercial proposition. *Live At The Brixton Academy* was released as a stop-gap album, while the band toured on the back of the worldwide success of their last studio album.

Albums: *Faith No More* (1984), *Introduce Yourself* (1987), *The Real Thing* (1989), *Live At The Brixton Academy* (1990), *Angel Dust* (1992).

Fandango

American, melodic hard rock outfit formed in 1976 by, vocalist Joe Lynn Turner and guitarist Rick Blakemore. Enlisting the services of Larry Dawson (keyboards), Bob Danyls (bass) and Abe Speller (drums), they signed to RCA the following year. They produced four albums in four years, with each successive release featuring more accomplished and memorable compositions. Influenced by Kiss, Deep Purple, Journey and Styx, their style was rigidly formularized and totally geared to US FM radio playlists. The band disintegrated in 1981, with Turner embarking on a solo career. His first release was *Fandango*, which comprised tracks from the band's four albums. Turner subsequently went on to play with Rainbow, Yngwie Malmsteen's Rising Force and Deep Purple.

Albums: *Fandango* (1977), *One Night Stand* (1978), *Last Kiss* (1979), *Cadillac* (1980).

Fates Warning

Formed in Cincinatti, Ohio USA, in 1982 the original line-up consisted of John Arch (vocals), Jim Matheos (guitar), Victor Arduini (guitar), Joe DiBiase (bass) and Steve Zimmerman (drums). Owing to a couple of early demos the band were invited to contribute a track to the *Metal Massacre V* compilation album released on the Metal Blade Records in 1984. The label signed the band immediately to a long-term recording agreement and released the band's debut album entitled *Night On Broken* in the same year. The album was very reminiscent of early Iron Maiden due to the song compositions and John Arch's vocal style. Shortly after its release guitarist Victor Arduini left the band to be replaced by Frank Aresti. The next two albums, *The Spectre Within* and *Awaken The Guardian*, released in 1985 and 1986 respectively, showed the band's music to be much more progressive and complex. However, vocalist John Arch was unhappy with the musical direction that Fates Warning had begun to take and left, but he was soon replaced by Ray Alder, whose voice was better suited to the band's material. This was most noticeable on their, *No Exit*, released in 1988, and

Faith No More

it is widely recognized as being the band's best work to date. The album was mainly Queensryche influenced hard rock plus the added bonus of a great overall album sound, thanks to the producer Max Norman. Soon after its release drummer Steve Zimmerman left the band to be replaced by Mark Zonder. *Perfect Symmetry*, was released in 1989 after the band had completed a couple of rather uneasy European tours. The result was an album that in some places sounded orchestral in its arrangements and featured ex-Dream Theater keyboard player Kevin Moore as a guest musician. Come the next album, *Parallels*, released in 1991, the band returned to their earlier Queensryche techno-pomp metal influences. It was very well received by the press, showing the band had a lot to offer and that they deserved a lot more recognition than had previously been awarded them.

Albums: *Night On Broken* (1984), *The Spectre Within* (1985), *Awaken The Guardian* (1986), *No Exit* (1988), *Perfect Symmetry* (1989), *Parallels* (1991).

Fast Forward

This one-off side project from former Stories vocalist Ian Lloyd, came to fruition in 1984. With the help of producer Bruce Fairbairn (of Loverboy and Bon Jovi fame) and a series of highly regarded session musicians, the end result was *Living In Fiction*. A highly polished melodic rock album, featuring razor-sharp harmonies, swathes of keyboards and an infectious pop sensibility. Guest appearances included Mick Jones and Lou Gramm from Foreigner and Beau Hill (Ratt producer) on keyboards. Songwriting contributions from Bryan Adams and Jim Vallance added further interest to the project, yet surprisingly, it was a commercial flop. Consequently, plans to record a second album were abandoned.

Album: *Living In Fiction* (1984).

Femme Fatale

This American quintet formed in Alberquerque, New Mexico in 1987. However, it did not take long before they relocated to the bright lights of Los Angeles in the quest for wider exposure and A&R attention from record companies. Fronted by Lorraine Lewis, they were quickly snapped up by MCA Records and assigned Jim Faraci (of L.A. Guns fame) as producer. Musically, they strived to corner the same market as Bon Jovi, relying on a pop-metal/hard-rock crossover approach. The band, completed by Mazzi Rawd (guitar), Bill D'Angelo (guitar), Rick Rael (bass) and Bobby Murray (drums), recorded a self-titled debut album which played on the vocalist's raunchy and overtly sexual image. This approach often overshadowed Lewis's genuine ability, and although it was received favourably by the critics, it was quickly consigned to the bargain bins and disappeared without trace.

Album: *Femme Fatale* (1988).

Fire Merchants

This hi-tech, power trio of well-seasoned session musicians, was put together by ex-Andy Summers bassist Doug Lunn. Enlisting John Goodsall (ex-Brand X and Peter Gabriel) on guitar and keyboards, the line-up was eventually completed following a long search for the right drummer. Ex-Frank Zappa and Genesis' drummer Chester Thompson was drafted in, and the band stabilized in October 1987. Released two years later, their self-titled debut album was an all instrumental affair, comprising an eclectic fusion of jazz, rock and blues.

Album: *Fire Merchants* (1989)

Fist

This Canadian heavy rock quartet were formed in 1978 by vocalist/guitarist Ron Chenier. After several false starts and numerous line-up changes the band stabilized with Chenier, plus Laurie Curry (keyboards), Bob Moffat (bass) and Bob Patterson (drums). Influenced by Triumph, Rush and Led Zeppelin, they released six albums of generally average hard rock between 1979-85, with *In The Red* from 1983, being undoubtedly the strongest. This featured the highly talented Dave McDonald on lead vocals instead of Chenier, who lacked both range and power. In order to prevent confusion with the British band Fist, their albums were released under the name Myofist in Europe.

Albums: *Round One* (1979), *Hot Spikes* (1980), *Fleet Street* (1981), *Thunder In Rock* (1982), *In The Red* (1982), *Danger Zone* (1985).

5X

This Japanese hard-rock band were founded in 1981 by ex-Midnight Cruiser guitarist George Azuma and former Oz vocalist Carmen Maki. With Kinta Moriyama (bass) and Jun Harada (drums) completing the line-up, they adopted a style that incorporated elements of Motorhead, Van Halen and AC/DC, which veered towards thrash metal at times. By their third album, they had moved into mainstream rock territory, and it appeared that vocalist Carmen Maki was striving to become the Japanese equivalent of Heart's Ann Wilson.

Albums: *Human Target* (1982), *Live X* (1982), *Carmen Maki's 5X* (1983).

Flotsam And Jetsam

This 'thrash metal' band was formed in Phoenix, Arizona, USA, in 1984 by drummer David Kelly Smith and bassist Jason Newsted. Adding vocalist Eric A.K. and guitarists Mike Gilbert and Ed Carlson, they debuted with tracks on the *Speed Metal Hell II* and *Metal Massacre IV* compilations. This led to a contract with Roadrunner Records and the release of *Doomsday For The Deceiver* in 1986. Hard, fast and punchy riffs were the band's trademarks, but their progress was hampered by the departure of Newsted to Metallica, shortly after the album's release. Eventually, Troy Gregory was recruited as a permanent replacement and *No Place For Disgrace* emerged in 1988. This indicated that the band had progressed little in two years, as the new material lacked imagination. In an attempt to break into the singles market, they recorded a cover of Elton John's 'Saturday Night's Alright For Fighting', which failed commercially. Dropped by Roadrunner, they were eventually signed up by MCA in 1990 and released *When The Storm Comes Down*. Produced by Alex Periallis (of Testament and Anthrax fame), it was aggressive and powerful, but suffered from an overall monotony of pace.

Albums: *Doomsday For The Deceiver* (1986), *No Place For Disgrace* (1988), *When The Storm Comes Down* (1990).

F.M.

F.M.

Formed in 1985 from the remnants of Samson and Wildlife, this British quintet quickly established themselves as a superior AOR outfit with a relentless touring schedule. Supporting Magnum, Status Quo and Meatloaf they soon built up a small, but loyal fan base. Comprising Steve Overland (guitar/vocals), Chris Overland (guitar), Didge Digital (keyboards), Merv Goldsworthy (bass) and Pete Jupp (drums) they specialize in lightweight harmonic rock characterized by Chris Overland's high-pitched, and at times almost sterile-sounding vocals. *Indiscreet* was well received by the critics, being a well produced, glossy and easily accessible debut, but surprisingly it sold poorly. After a three-year gap, a serious re-think, and the use of outside writers, *Tough It Out* emerged. The album built on their previous strengths, but adopted a slightly harder style. Epic Records declined to give the album the necessary promotional back-up to push the band towards major status. Disillusioned and frustrated, they disbanded in 1990, but re-formed the following year. Signing to the independent Music For Nations label, they released *Taking It To The Streets*, which represented a back to basics approach.

Albums: *Indiscreet* (1986), *Tough It Out* (1989), *Taking It To The Streets* (1991).

Forbidden

Originally going under the monicker of Forbidden Evil, this band was formed in San Francisco, California in 1985. The band's original line-up consisted of Russ Anderson (vocals), Glen Alvelais (guitar), Craig Locicero (guitar), Matt Camacho (bass) and Paul Bostaph (drums). They quickly gained a strong following playing numerous support slots with more established Bay Area bands such as Testament and Exodus. Owing to some early demos the band signed to Combat Records with the agreement that recorded product would be released in Europe on the Music For Nations subsidiary label, Under One Flag. Shortening the name to Forbidden, the bands debut *Forbidden Evil* was released in 1988 to critical acclaim. The album was a mass of power laden thrash. The band toured Europe in support of the album during 1989, appearing at the Dynamo Open Air Festival in Holland. The gig was recorded and the subsequent live album *Raw Evil At The Dynamo* was released the same year. During preparation for their next studio album Glen Alvelais left the band, but was fortunately quickly replaced by ex-Militia guitarist Tim Calvert in time for the recordings. This next album *Twisted Into Form* released in 1990 was again received well by the media. The album was full of hard-hitting thrash metal, cleverly structured songs and excellent metal guitar virtuosity.

Albums: *Forbidden Evil* (1988), *Raw Evil At The Dynamo* (1989), *Twisted Into Form* (1990).

Ford, Lita

b. 23 September 1959, London, England. Ford was one of the original members of the Kim Fowley-conceived Runaways. This all-girl Californian group rode on publicity generated from the UK punk explosion. A disagreement

Lita Ford

within the ranks of the group in 1979 over musical direction led to the Runaways break-up, and subsequently Ford explored a solo career on the US glam/metal circuit. Her debut album was recorded for Mercury with the assistance of Neil Merryweather on bass. *Dancin' On The Edge* made a minor impact on the US album charts and reached number 66. Almost four years later in 1988, *Lita*, released on RCA, reached the Top 30 and spawned the US number 12 hit 'Kiss Me Deadly' and a Top 10 hit on the duet with Ozzy Osbourne, 'Close My Eyes Forever'. Later that year she married W.A.S.P. guitarist Chris Holmes. *Stiletto* continued to display Ford's commitment to the formula rock format prevalent in the USA in the 90s.
Albums: *Out For Blood* (1983), *Dancin' On The Edge* (1984), *Lita* (1988), *Stiletto* (1990).

Foreigner

This band gets its name from the fact that its original members come from both sides of the Atlantic, and this mixture of influences is much in evidence in its music. Mick Jones (b. 27 December 1944, London, England; guitar/vocals) formed the band in 1976, having spent the early 70s working with musicians such as Johnny Halliday. The line-up consisted of Ian McDonald (b. 25 June 1946, London, England; guitar/keyboards/horns/vocals), formerly of King Crimson, Lou Gramm (b. Lou Grammatico, 2 May 1950, Rochester, New York, USA; vocals), who had played with Black Sheep in the early 70s, Dennis Elliott (b. 18 August 1950, London, England; drums), Al Greenwood (b. New York, USA; keyboards) and Edward Gagliardi (b.13 February 1952, New York, USA; bass). In 1977 the band released *Foreigner*, and in a poll conducted by *Rolling Stone* magazine, Foreigner came out as top new artists. Jones and Gramm wrote most of the band's material, including classic tracks such as 'Feels Like The First Time' and 'Cold As Ice'. Despite playing at the Reading rock festival in England twice in the 70s, Foreigner had more consistent success in the USA. In 1979 Rick Wills (b. England; bass) replaced Gagliardi, having served a musical apprenticeship with King Crimson and Peter Frampton. 1980 saw the departure of McDonald and Greenwood which led to the guest appearances of Thomas Dolby and Junior Walker on *4*. 'Waiting For A Girl Like You' was the hit single from this album, and it demonstrated the band's musical accomplishment, taking the form of a wistful yet melodious ballad. It was another epic AOR song, 'I Want To Know What Love Is', which was Foreigner's greatest success. It topped the charts on both sides of the Atlantic and featured the New Jersey Mass Choir backing Gramm's vocals.
In the mid-80s, the members of Foreigner were engaged in solo projects, and the success of Gramm's *Ready Or Not* in 1987 led to widespread speculation that Foreigner were about to disband. However, this was not the case, as the 1988 *Inside Information* proves, although in 1989, Gramm had success with another solo project, *Long Hard Look*. Hugely successful, they epitimized the classic sound of 'adult orientated rock' better than anybody.
Albums: *Foreigner* (1977), *Double Vision* (1978), *Head Games* (1979), *4* (1981), *Records* (1982), *Agent Provocateur* (1984), *Inside Information* (1987), *Unusual Heat* (1991). Compilation: *The Very Best Of* (1992).

Four Horsemen

This heavy metal rock 'n' roll outfit was formed in 1991 by former Cult bassist, Haggis. Recruiting Frank C. Starr (vocals), Ken 'Dimwit' Montgomery (drums), Dave Lizmi (guitar) and Ben Pape (bass), they negotiated a deal with Rick Rubin's Def American label. With Haggis on rhythm guitar, their music draws heavily from AC/DC, the Cult, the Black Crowes and the Georgia Satellites. Their debut album *Nobody Said*

It Was Easy, was a monstrously powerful collection of heavy duty rockers that were based on loud riffs and infectious chorus lines. They exaggerated every cliche in the book, yet this made them sound relevant and fun. The Four Horsemen have no pretensions.

Album: *Nobody Said It Was Easy* (1991).

44 Magnum

This Japanese heavy metal outfit were formed in 1977 by vocalist Tatsuya Umehara and guitarist Satoshi Hirorse. With the addition of Hironori Yoshikawa on bass and Satoshi Miyawaki, they existed for many years in the shadow of other Japanese bands such as Loudness, Earthshaker and Vow Wow. They eventually secured a record contract in 1982 and debuted with Danger the following year. Although the playing is competent, their ideas and style are often influenced from British and American acts such as Van Halen, Deep Purple, Led Zeppelin and Whitesnake.

Albums: *Danger* (1983), *Street Rock* (1984).

Free

Formed in the midst of 1968's British blues boom, Free originally included Paul Rodgers (b. 12 December 1949, Middlesbrough, Cleveland, England; vocals), Paul Kossoff (b. 14 September 1950, London, England, d. 19 March 1976; guitar), Andy Fraser (b. 7 August 1952, London, England; bass) and Simon Kirke (b. 28 July 1949, Shrewsbury, Shropshire, England; drums). Despite their comparative youth, the individual musicians were seasoned performers, particularly Fraser, a former member of John Mayall's Bluesbreakers. Free gained early encouragement from Alexis Korner, but having completed an earthy debut album, *Tons Of Sobs,* the group began honing a more individual style with their second set. The injection of powerful original songs, including 'I'll Be Creeping', showed a maturing talent, while Rodgers' expressive voice and Kossoff's stinging guitar enhanced a growing reputation.

The quartet's stylish blues/rock reached its peak on *Fire And Water.* This confident collection featured moving ballads; 'Heavy Load', 'Oh I Wept' and compulsive, uptempo material, the best-known of which is 'All Right Now'. An edited version of this soulful composition reached number 2 in the UK and number 4 in the US in 1970, since when the song has become one of pop's most enduring performances making periodic appearances in the singles chart. A fourth set, *Highway,* revealed a mellower perspective enhanced by an increased use of piano at the expense of Kossoff's guitar. This was due, in part, to friction within the group, a factor exacerbated

when the attendant single, 'The Stealer', failed to emulate its predecessor. Free split up in May 1971, paradoxically in the wake of another successful single, 'My Brother Jake', but regrouped in January the following year when spin-off projects faltered, although Kossoff and Kirke's amalgamation (Kossoff, Kirke, Tetsu And Rabbit) proved fruitful.

A sixth album, *Free At Last,* offered some of the unit's erstwhile fire and included another UK Top 20 entrant, 'Little Bit Of Love'. However Kossoff's increasing ill-health and Fraser's departure for the Sharks undermined any newfound confidence. A hastily convened line-up consisting of Rodgers, Kirke, John 'Rabbit' Bundrick (keyboards) and Tetsu Yamauchi (b. 1946, Fukuoka, Japan; bass) undertook a Japanese tour, but although the guitarist rejoined the quartet for several British dates, his contribution to Free's final album, *Heartbreaker,* was muted. Kossoff embarked on a solo career in October 1972; Wendel Richardson from Osibisa replaced him on a temporary basis, but by July the following year Free had ceased to function. Rodgers and Kirke subsequently formed Bad Company.

Albums: *Tons Of Sobs* (1968), *Free* (1969), *Fire And Water* (1970), *Highway* (1971), *Free Live* (1971), *Free At Last* (1972), *Heartbreaker* (1973). Compilations: *The Free Story* (1974), *Completely Free* (1982), *All Right Now* (1991).

Frehley, Ace

b. Paul Frehley, 27 April 1951, Bronx, New York, USA, Ace Frehley was the lead guitarist for the major USA hard rock band Kiss during its prime years. Often nicknamed 'Space Ace' by fans, Frehley, like all the band members, wore make-up onstage and in all group photos intended to resemble an extra-terrestrial being. Frehley released his first solo album, self-titled, in September 1978, simultaneously with solo albums by the other three members of Kiss. Released on Casablanca Records, the album, which found the guitarist attempting more diverse musical styles than he was allowed to follow within the context of Kiss, reached the Top 30 and spawned a number 13 single, the Russ Ballard-penned 'New York Groove'. Frehley left Kiss in 1983, following a near-fatal car accident, and tried to free himself of a drug habit for the next four years. He formed his own band, Frehley's Comet, in 1987, and recorded three albums. In 1989 he recorded a second solo album, *Trouble Walkin'.*

Albums: *Ace Frehley* (1978), *Trouble Walkin'* (1989).

Ace Frehley Comet

Albums: *Frehley's Comet* (1987), *Live + 1* (1988), *Second Sighting* (1988).

Friedman, Marty

This new-age, technically brilliant guitarist had a long and impressive pedigree. Stints with Vixen, Hawaii and Cacophony helped formulate and define his characteristic quick-fire style, before embarking on a solo career. *Dragon's Kiss* was an impressive instrumental debut, combining heavy-duty riffs and intricate solos with Far Eastern influences and undertones. Friedman later went on to produce speed-metallers Apocrypha, before commencing work on a second solo project. This has been put on permanent hold since he accepted the invitation to join Megadeth in February 1990. Album: *Dragon's Kiss* (1988).

Ace Frehley

Frehley's Comet

Following drug and alcohol-related problems, US guitarist Ace Frehley left Kiss in 1981. After a four-year period of rehabilitation, he began writing and playing again, signing to the Megaforce label in 1987. Recruiting Tod Howarth (vocals/guitar), John Regan (bass) and Anton Fig (drums), Frehley's Comet was born. With an emphasis on Americanized hard-rock, with a commercial edge, their self-titled debut was given a favourable reception from critics and Kiss fans alike. In time, Tod Howarth's creative input began to change the band's sound, pushing them in a more lightweight, AOR direction. This was clearly illustrated on *Second Sighting*. Ace, concerned that this new direction might alienate his loyal fan base, relieved Tod Howarth of vocal duties on *Trouble Walkin'* (issued as an Ace Frehley solo album), drafting in guitarist Richie Scarlet as replacement. This album was a backward step musically, and an attempt to appeal to the same market as Kiss; employing former Kiss drummer Peter Criss as guest vocalist and covering Paul Stanley's (Kiss guitarist) 'Hide Your Heart'. The rest of the band became frustrated by Frehley's control and quit halfway through the tour to support the album. Ace hit rock bottom and has not surfaced since.

G

Galactic Cowboys

This US metallic art-rock quartet was formed in 1990 by vocalist Ben Huggins and guitarist Dane Sonnier. With the addition of bassist Monty Colvin and drummer Alan Doss, they specialized in complex and densely melodic song structures that typically exceed the six-minute mark. They combined elements of Kings X, Metallica and Neil Young, with state-of-the-art technology to produce one of 1991's most impressive debut albums. Defying simple categorization, they surprise the listener, with what initially seems the *ad hoc* juxtaposition of incompatible styles. Somehow, the strange fusion works; manic thrashing gives way to harmonica solos, which in turn are followed by four-part vocal harmonies. The Galactic Cowboys are true innovators and are at the forefront of experimental hard-rock.
Albums: *Galactic Cowboys* (1991).

Gamma Ray

After leaving Helloween in 1989, the band he founded, guitarist Kai Hansen teamed up with ex-Tyran Pace vocalist Ralf Scheepers. Their intention was to record a project album of material that Hansen had previously written that had been deemed unsuitable for use by his previous band. Joining them for this proposed project album were Uwe Wessel (bass), Mathias Burchardt (drums) and a host of various guest musicians. Signing to Noise Records they entered the Horus Sound Studios in Germany with producer Tommy Newton. The resulting recordings were released under the monicker of Gamma Ray and the album *Heading For Tomorrow* was released in 1990. The album was an excellent blend of powerful melodic heavy metal with song structures reminiscent of the band Queen. The album was a success and proved a favourite with both press and public. Realizing its potential Hanson decided to form a working band unit out of the musicians who had worked on the project that could tour in support of the album. The now fully assembled Gamma Ray consisted of Ralf Scheepers (vocals), Hansen (guitar/vocals), Dirk Schlacter (guiter), Wessel (bass) and Uli Kusch (drums). The band toured extensively throughout Europe and Japan where they had gained quite a following. As a stop-gap between albums the band released an EP of new material *Heaven Can Wait*. Come the next album, *Sigh No More*, the band were in fine form; extensive touring had definitely made them into a tight cohesive unit. Though heavier than its predecessor the album was full of quality heavy metal with melody and power, a more than worthy follow-up to their impressive debut.
Albums: *Heading For Tomorrow* (1990), *Sigh No More* (1991).

Gang Green

This Boston, Massachusetts, USA quartet specializing in a fusion of hardcore and thrash was put together by guitarist/vocalist Chris Doherty. Although formed originally in 1982, it was the 1985 re-incarnation that inked a deal with Taang Records. After numerous line-up changes, a degree of stability was achieved with Doherty, plus Brian Bertzger (drums), Fritz (guitar), and Joe Gittleman (bass), the latter eventually replaced by ex-DRI member Josh Papp. Extolling the virtues of alcohol and ridiculing the PMRC at every given moment, their music is fast, aggressive and occasionally abusive. The highlight of their career is the mini-album *I81B4U*, which has an irreverent sense of fun and puts 'two fingers up' at Van Halen's OU812. Unable to progress on the songwriting front, they quickly became stuck in a musical rut. Roadrunner Records lost faith, dropping them from their roster in 1990.
Albums: *Another Wasted Night* (1986), *You Got It* (1987), *I81B4U* (1988), *Older, Budweiser* (1989).

Gaye Bykers On Acid

This UK rock group employed an image which combined traditional biker attire with elements of psychedelia and hippie camp. They were led by the colourful figure of Mary Millington (male; vocals), alongside Kevin (drums), Robber (bass) and Tony (guitar). They were later complemented by disc jockey William Samuel Ronald Monroe ('Rocket Ronnie'). Mary, who had once come second in Leicester's Alternative Miss Universe competition, was often to be seen in platform shoes and dresses, which fuelled the critics' confusion with regard to the band's name and gender orientation. After leaving Virgin they set up their own label Naked Brain, quite conceivably because nobody else would have them. Subsequent to the band's demise, which may or may not prove permanent, Kevin instigated a new band G.R.O.W.T.H. with Jeff (ex-Janitors). Tony has joined Brad Bradbury in Camp Collision, and Mary has joined ex-members of Killing Joke, Ministry and PiL in the multi-member outfit Pigface.
Albums: *Drill Your Own Hole* (1987), *Stewed To The Gills* (1989), *GrooveDiveSoapDish* (1989), *Cancer Planet Mission* (1990).

Gene Loves Jezebel

Gene Loves Jezebel

Identical twins Jay (John) and Mike Aston, ostensibly Gene Loves Jezebel, enjoyed cult appeal, largely within the UK gothic rock community, but achieved greater success in America. The pair grew up in the South Wales town of Porthcawl, together with guitarist Ian Hudson. After moving to London, they made their debut in late 1981 supporting the Higsons. A recording deal with Situation 2 resulted in 'Shavin' My Neck' (a collection of demos) the following May. The dense, experimental sound was matched by live performances, featuring bassist Julianne Regan and drummer Dick Hawkins, where they mixed almost tribal rhythms with furious guitar work. Hawkins was replaced by a succession of drummers, including John Murphy (ex-Associates and SPK) and Steve Goulding, while Regan left to front All About Eve. Her space was filled by Hudson, allowing Albio De Luca (later of Furyo) to work the guitar, in time for the tragic 'Screaming (For Emmalene)' in 1983. Following Luca's and Goulding's departure, Hudson reverted to guitar and Hawkins/Murphy offered a two-pronged drum attack. Murphy then left before a third single, the strong, commercial sound of 'Bruises' (1983). Hot on its heels came the Jezebels' powerful debut album, *Promise*, promoted by a John Peel BBC radio session. A trip to the USA in 1984 to work with John Cale ensued, before returning for two quick-fire singles 'Influenza (Relapse)' and 'Shame (Whole Heart Howl)'. Marshall then left, Mike Aston briefly switching from rhythm guitar to play bass, before Peter Rizzo was recruited. Ex-Spear Of Destiny drummer Chris Bell arrived in place of Hawkins, but it was a year before 'The Cow' hit the UK independent charts, preceding the in-demand album *Immigrant* in June 1985. After 'Desire' in November, the band left for a north American tour, a traumatic time that led to Hudson's departure, ex-Gen X guitarist James Stevenson taking his place. The group skirted the Top 75 with 'Sweetest Thing' and *Discover* (with a free live album) while 'Heartache' hinted at a passing interest in dance. They subsequently concentrated their efforts on the US market. However, all was not well in the Jezebels camp, and the future of the band has been uncertain since Mike left the group in mid-1989. Despite rumours that they will continue, no recorded product has surfaced.

Albums: *Promise* (1983), *Immigrant* (1985), *Discover*

(1986), *House Of Dolls* (1987).

G-Force

G-Force was the brainchild of ex-Skid Row, Colosseum II, and Thin Lizzy, guitarist Gary Moore. After leaving Thin Lizzy shortly after playing on the band's *Black Rose* in 1979, Moore headed for Los Angeles with the intention of forming a band there. he teamed up with some reputable local musicians and not wanting at that time to be known as the Gary Moore Band, they chose to go under the monicker of G-Force. Joining Moore in this project were Tony Newton (vocals), Willie Dee (bass) and Mark Nausseef (drums). The band played some low-key gigs in and around the Los Angeles area and signed to Jet Records where they released their debut album in 1980. Even though the album was a strong slice of melodic hard rock with more than a hint of commerciality, it flopped. Not surprisingly the band folded soon after its release.
Album: *G-Force* (1980).

Giant

Giant

Hailing from Nashville USA, Giant developed in the mid-80s when seasoned session guitarist Dann Huff met on various projects with keyboard player Alan Pasqua. However it was not until 1988 when Giant evolved into a fully-fledged unit with Huff's younger brother joining as drummer and Mike Brignardello on bass. By this time Dann Huff had taken on the lead vocal duties after an unsuccessful search for a suitable singer. Candidates for this job had included the highly successful songwriter and backing vocalist Tom Kelly. Giant signed to A&M Records in 1988 and released their debut album *Last Of The Runaways*, a potent brew of hard rock, strong on melody, in the USA in 1989. This included the Top 10 hit single 'I'll See You In My Dreams'. The success of the album and single in the USA and impressive sales on import in the UK prompted A&M to give *Last Of The Runaways* a European release in 1990 to a moderate degree of success. This was followed by a series of highly acclaimed club dates around the UK. In 1991, Huff, Pasque, and Brignardello played together on Amy Grant's *Heart In Motion*, and prepared material for a new album.
Album: *Last Of The Runaways* (1989).

Gillan

Within just a few months of dissolving the Ian Gillan Band, Ian Gillan was back in the studio with a new band, inspired by a Colin Towns song 'Fighting Man'. New members Leon Genocky (drums), Steve Byrd (guitar) and John McCoy (bass), joined Ian Gillan and Colin Towns to record *Gillan* in summer 1978. The lack of a record deal meant that this excellent album was never released in the UK, although several of the tracks did appear on the next album, *Mr. Universe*, recorded early in 1979 with Pete Barnacle on drums. The title track was based on a song of the same name which Ian Gillan had recorded with Episode Six. The album as a whole marked the return of the imposing former Deep Purple frontman, Gillan, to solid rock music. In doing so, this album was instrumental in developing the New Wave Of British Heavy Metal, a label even more applicable to Gillan's next album, *Glory Road*.
Now with Bernie Torme on guitar and former Episode Six drummer Mick Underwood, Gillan produced one of his finest albums, the first copies of which contained a second, free album, *For Gillan Fans Only*. After the slightly disappointing *Future Shock*, Torme left to be replaced by guitarist Janick Gers of White Spirit, who featured on *Double Trouble*, a double album comprising one studio and one live album, recorded mainly at the 1981 Reading rock festival, at which the band were appearing for the third consecutive year, a testimony to their popularity. Summer 1982 saw the release of *Magic*, another album of quality though sadly also the group's last. After many years of speculation and rumour, a Deep Purple

reformation seemed imminent and Gillan wound up his band amid a certain amount of acrimony and uncertainty, early in 1983.

Albums: *Gillan* (1978), *Mr. Universe* (1979), *Glory Road* (1980), *Future Shock* (1981), *Double Trouble* (1982), *Magic* (1982), *What I Did On My Vacation* (1986), *Live At Reading 1980* (1990).

Ian Gillan Band

Gillan, Ian

b. 19 August 1945, Hounslow, Middlesex, England. Heavily influenced by Elvis Presley, vocalist Gillan formed his first band at the age of 16. In 1962 he was invited to join local semi-professional R&B band the Javelins, who eventually split up in March 1964. Gillan formed the Hickies, but abandoned the project to join established soulband Wainwright's Gentlemen. Soon he was unhappy with this group and he readily accepted an invitation to join the fully professional outfit Episode Six in May 1965. A succession of tours and singles failed to produce any domestic chart placings, however, and by early 1969 the band was beginning to disintegrate. In May of the same year Gillan, and Roger Glover (b. 30 November 1945, Brecon, South Wales; bass) were recruited to join Deep Purple, forming the legendary 'MK II' line-up with Ritchie Blackmore Jon Lord and Ian Paice.

Deep Purple gradually established themselves as a major rock band, helped by their dynamic live show and an aggressive sound characterized by a mix of long instrumentals and Gillan's powerful vocals. The latter part of 1972 saw Deep Purple enter the *Guinness Book Of Records* as the loudest pop group of the time and acknowledged as the biggest selling rock band in the world, a position they consolidated with the release of the live album *Made In Japan*. In August 1972 Gillan decided to leave the band, but was persuaded to remain with them until June 1973. By the time of his last show with Deep Purple on 28 June, he had already purchased the De Lane Lea studio in London, and it was on this venture that he concentrated on leaving the band, forming Kingsway Studios. He recorded a solo album in 1974 for the Purple label, to which he was still signed, but it was apparently rejected as too radical a departure musically, and has never been released. After a brief attempt to launch Ian Gillan's Shand Grenade, which included Glover, in late 1975, it was the Ian Gillan Band which began recording *Child In Time* over New Year 1975/6. The line-up was Gillan, Ray Fenwick (guitar), Mike Moran (keyboards), Mark Nauseef (drums) and John Gustafson (bass). This first album was much lighter in tone than Deep Purple, but included some excellent songs.

The next two albums, now with Colin Towns on keyboards, demonstrated a notable jazz-rock influence, particularly on *Clear Air Turbulence*, also noted for its striking Chris Foss-designed cover. None of these albums was particularly commercially successful, and after a disappointing tour in spring 1978, Gillan disbanded the group. Between late 1978 and 1983 Gillan fronted his own band called simply Gillan. Finding that he had ended Gillan somewhat prematurely, having thought a Deep Purple reunion was imminent, Ian Gillan joined Black Sabbath, a move he claims was motivated by financial necessity. Artistically, the time he spent with this band is deplored by both Gillan and Sabbath fans. After one album and a tour with Sabbath, the much talked about Deep Purple reunion took off and Gillan had his opportunity to escape. After eleven years apart, and all with successful, if turbulent careers during that time, the essential question remained whether or not the various members of the band would be able to get on with each other. A successful tour and a sell-out British concert at the 1985 Knebworth Festival seemed to suggest the reunion had worked, but by the time of the second album, *House Of The Blue Light*, it was clear that the latent tensions within the band were beginning to prove too much. Between Deep Purple tours, and adding to the speculation about a break-up, Gillan and Glover recorded an album together; a curious but thoroughly enjoyable collection of material, it seemed to fulfil a need in both musicians to escape from the confines of the parent band. The 1988/9 Deep Purple tour revealed the true extent of the rift between the members, and Gillan's departure was formally announced in May 1989. It was effectively over from January, when he was informed that he need not attend rehearsals for the next album. Gillan's response was to perform a short tour as his alter ego, Garth Rockett, in spring 1989, before recording vocals for the Rock Aid Armenia version of 'Smoke On The Water', in July. By the end of 1989, Gillan had assembled a band to record a solo album, which he would finance himself to escape record company pressures, and record under his own name to avoid the politics of group decisions. The line-up was Steve Morris (guitar), from the Garth Rockett tour; Chris Glen (bass) and Ted McKenna (drums), both formerly of the Michael Schenker Group; Tommy Eyre (keyboards); Mick O'Donoghue (rhythm guitar) and Dave Lloyd (backing vocals/percussion). The album, *Naked Thunder*, released in July 1990 was labelled middle-of-the-road by some critics but is generally held to be true to Ian Gillan's rock traditions, described by Gillan himself as a 'hard rock band with a funky blues feel.' After touring in support of album, Gillan returned to the studio to prepare a second solo album. Now formulating a highly productive partnership with Steve Morris, they recruited Brett Bloomfield on bass and Leonard Haze on drums and produced an excellent album as a four-piece rock band, blending straightforward music with Gillan's often bizarre sense of humour and off-beat lyrics. *Toolbox* was released in October 1991 to critical acclaim, demonstrating Gillan's durability and deserved status as a central figure of British rock music.

Albums: with Episode Six *Put Yourself In My Place* (compilation, 1987); with Deep Purple *Concerto For Group And Orchestra* (1970), *In Rock* (1970), *Fireball* (1971), *Machine Head* (1972), *Made In Japan* (1972), *Who Do We Think We Are?* (1973), *Powerhouse* (1977), *In Concert 1970/72* (1980), *Scandinavian Nights - Live 1970* (1988), *Perfect Strangers* (1984), *House Of The Blue Light* (1987), *Nobody's Perfect* (1988), *Knebworth '85* (1990); with the Ian Gillan Band *Child In Time* (1976), *Clear Air Turbulence* (1977), *Scarabus* (1977), *I.G.B. Live At The Budokan* (1983); with Gillan *Mr. Universe* (1979), *Glory Road* (1980), *Future Shock* (1981), *Double Trouble* (1981), *Magic* (1982), *What I Did On My Vacation* (1986), *Live At Reading 1980* (1990); with Black Sabbath *Born Again* (1983); with Gillan/Glover *Accidentally On Purpose* (1988);

as Ian Gillan *Naked Thunder* (1990), *Toolbox* (1991); also appears on *The Garth Rockett And The Moonshiners Story* (1990).

Girlschool

The all-female heavy metal band had its origins in Painted Lady, founded by teenagers Enid Williams (bass/vocals) and Kim McAuliffe (guitar/vocals). After Kelly Johnson (guitar/vocals), and Denise Dufort (drums) had joined in 1978 the name became Girlschool and the independently-produced single 'Take It All Away' led to a tour with Motorhead. In 1980, the band signed to the Bronze label where Vic Maile produced the first two albums. There was a minor hit with a revival of Adrian Gurvitz' 'Race With The Devil', a 1968 success for Gun, before the group combined with Motorhead to reach the UK Top 10 as Headgirl with an EP called *St Valentine's Day Massacre*. The lead track was a frentic version of Johnny Kidd's 'Please Don't Touch'. Girlschool had smaller hits later in 1981 with 'Hit And Run' and 'C'mon Let's Go' but soon afterwards Williams was replaced by Gill Weston. Slade singer Noddy Holder produced *Play Dirty*, which found the group opting for a more mainstream rock sound. In 1984, Johnson left the band for a solo career and Girlschool added guitarist Chris Bonacci and lead singer Jacqui Bodimead from Canis Major. The group also switched visual style towards a more glittery look as they recorded 'I'm The Leader Of The Gang' with Gary Glitter in 1986. After the departure of Weston in 1987, McAuliffe left to work with punk singer Beki Bondage and *Take A Bite* turned out to be their last.

Albums: *Demolition* (1980), *Hit 'N' Run* (1981), *Screaming Blue Murder* (1982), *Play Dirty* (1983), *Race With The Devil* (1986), *Nightmare At Maple Cross* (1986), *Take A Bite* (1988), *Cheers You Lot* (1989).

Giuffria

This US band was formed in 1981 by Greg Giuffria (keyboards) when his previous band Angel split up. His first step was to secure a good rhythm section; Chuck Wright (bass) and Alan Krigger (drums). Rough Cutt guitarist Craig Goldy joined after that group fell apart. In 1984 Giuffria's self-titled debut album, released on MCA, demonstrated a melodic rock band which sounded symphonic in places and could have been mistaken for Angel on some tracks. Greg Giuffria refers to their music as 'cinema rock'. After the promotion tour for the album, Goldy left to join Driver and subsequently with Ronnie James Dio, and Wright returned to session work. They were replaced by Lanny Cordola (guitar) and David Sikes (bass).

Because of the personnel changes, the follow-up album, *Silk And Steel*, was not released until August 1986. This was a very much a continuation of their first album and in 1987 MCA dropped Giuffria because of poor sales.

Giuffria, Cordola, Wright, Ken Mary (drums) and David Glen Eisley (vocals) tried to start again. They gained some support from Gene Simmons of Kiss, who had just set up his own record label. However, Simmons insisted that the name be changed to House Of Lords, and that James Christian replace Eisley on vocals. *House Of Lords* in 1988 was the same symphonic AOR rock as Giuffria, but there seemed to be something extra which brought the tracks alive; probably the production of Andy Johns and Simmons or Christian's singing, or both. Before the recording of the follow-up, *Sahara*, Cordola was replaced by Mike Guy. Again Johns was the producer with Giuffria. On this album the keyboards had taken on a lesser role and the guitar had become more prominent, and a number of artists guested, including Eisley. The album went platinum.

Albums: As Giuffria *Giuffria* (1984), *Silk And Steel* (1986). As House Of Lords *House Of Lords* (1988), *Sahara* (1990).

Glover, Roger

b. 30 November 1945, Brecon, Powys, Wales. Bassist Glover's professional musical career began when his group, the Madisons, amalgamated with fellow aspirants the Lightnings to form Episode Six. This popular act released nine singles between 1966 and 1969, but eclectic interests - including harmony pop, MOR and progressive rock-styled instrumentals - engendered a commercial impasse. Frustrated, both Glover and vocalist Ian Gillan then accepted an offer to join Deep Purple, where they enjoyed considerable international acclaim. However, clashes with guitarist Ritchie Blackmore led to Glover's sacking in 1973, although he remained nominal head of A&R at Purple Records, the group's custom-created label. Roger later embarked on a successful career in production with Nazareth, Status Quo, Judas Priest and Rory Gallagher. In 1974 Glover was commissioned to write the music to *The Butterfly Ball*, which in turn inspired a book, illustrated by Alan Aldridge, and film. The album included the services of David Coverdale, Glenn Hughes and Ronnie James Dio. He recorded a solo album, *Elements*, which again included the assistance of vocalist Dio, but Glover surprised several commentators in 1979 by rejoining Blackmore in Rainbow. Any lingering animosity was further undermined in 1984 when both musicians were active in a rekindled Deep Purple which, although

unable to recreate the halcyon days of the early 70s, remains a much in-demand attraction.

Albums: *The Butterfly Ball* (1974), *Elements* (1978), *Mask* (1984), with Ian Gillan *Accidentally On Purpose* (1988).

Godz.

Originating from Cleveland, Ohio, the Godz were a heavy metal band with a strong 'biker' image. Formed in 1977 they featured vocalist/bassist Eric Moore, guitarist Mark Chatfield, drummer Glen Cataline and guitarist/keyboard player Bob Hill. Their first album, produced by Grand Funk's Don Brewer was intensely powerful with raw gutsy vocals, and remains a classic of the metal genre. *Nothing Is Sacred* was self-produced and featured Cataline on vocals. The album was a disappointment on every level and the band split up soon after its release. In 1985 Moore and Chatfield resurrected the name and a new partnership was forged with former Outlaws guitarist Freddie Salem and drummer Keith Valentine. *I'll Get You Rockin'* materialized, but met a lacklustre reception. In 1987 most of the album was re-mixed and re-recorded, with three new tracks added and re-released as *Mongolians*. However hard they have tried, Godz have never recaptured the brutal energy and excitement generated by their debut release.

Albums: *The Godz* (1987), *Nothing Is Sacred* (1979), *I'll Get You Rockin'* (1985), *Mongolians* (1987).

Gogmagog

This group was formed in London, England in 1985 by Jonathan King, who wanted to create some sort of heavy metal theatre. At first he had Cozy Powell and John Entwhistle interested, but they had other projects taking off. So the line-up was finalized as Paul Dianno (vocals), Clive Burr (drums), Pete Willis (guitar), Janick Gers (guitar) and Neil Murray (bass); a line-up that had Gogmagog being called a New Wave Of British Heavy Metal 'supergroup'. To test the water to see if anybody was interested in the project, King put Gogmagog into a studio to record three songs that he had written with Russ Ballard. With these tracks King went round to various major record companies to see if there was any support. All of the companies showed a real interest in the project. The only stumbling block was King's insistence on a substantial advance. Every company turned him down. The project subsequently fell apart, and the members of Gogmagog went their own way. After the groups demise a three-track single appeared on the Music For Nations label called 'I Will Be There'. The group's music was nowhere near the heavy metal tag it was given. but closer to pop with a slight nod towards the musicians' rock roots.

Albums: *I Will Be There* (1985, mini-album).

Goodwin, Myles

When Canadian hard-rockers April Wine disintegrated in 1985, lead vocalist Goodwin embarked on a solo career. He immediately divorced himself from the style to which he was accustomed. Forsaking his blues-rock roots, he concentrated on MOR pop/rock with understated guitar and lightweight harmonies. Utilizing the services of session musicians, he recorded a self-titled debut on the Atlantic label in 1988. This failed to win a new audience, and at the same time alienated his former fan base. The album sank without trace and little has been heard of him since.

Album: *Myles Goodwin* (1988).

Grand Funk Railroad

Formed in 1968, Grand Funk Railroad was the first American heavy-rock 'power trio' to reach massive fame, while alienating another large segment of the rock audience and critics at the same time. The group consisted of guitarist Mark Farner (b. 28 September 1948, Flint, Michigan, USA), bassist Mel Schacher (b. 3 April 1951, Owosso, Michigan, USA) and drummer Don Brewer (3 September 1948, Flint, Michigan, USA). The group was a spin-off of Terry Knight And The Pack, a popular soul-rock group in the Michigan area in the mid-60s. Farner and Brewer had both been members of that band (Brewer had also belonged to the Jazz Masters prior to the Pack). Following a single release on the small Lucky Eleven label with, 'I (Who Have Nothin)', which reached number 46 in the US, the Pack were joined by Schacher, formerly of ? And The Mysterians. At this point Knight stopped performing to become the band's manager, renaming it Grand Funk Railroad (the name was taken from the Michigan landmark the Grand Trunk Railroad).

The new trio signed with Capitol Records in 1969 and immediately began making its name by performing at several large pop festivals. Their first singles made the charts but Grand Funk soon proved its strength in the albums market. Their first, *On Time*, reached number 27 in 1969, followed by the number 11 *Grand Funk* in 1970. By the summer of 1970 they had become a major concert attraction, and their albums routinely reached the Top 10 for the next four years. Of those, 1973's *We're An American Band* was the biggest seller, reaching number 2. The group's

huge success is largely attributed to the public relations expertise of manager Knight. In 1970, for example, Knight reportedly paid $100,000 for a huge billboard in New York City's Times Square to promote the group's *Closer To Home*, which subsequently became their first Top 10 album, reaching number 6 and spawning the FM radio staple title track. That promotional campaign backfired with the press, however, which dismissed the band's efforts despite spiralling success with the public. In June 1971, for example, Grand Funk became only the second group (after the Beatles) to sell out New York's Shea Stadium. Their recordings sold in greater quantity even as many radio stations ignored their releases. The 1970 *Live Album* reached number 5 and included another concert and radio favourite in Farner's 'Mean Mistreater'. The next year saw the release of *Survival* and *E Pluribus Funk*, most notable for its round album cover.

In 1972 the group fired Knight, resulting in a series of lawsuits involving millions of dollars. (The group hired John Eastman, father of Linda McCartney, as its new manager.) In 1973 the group shortened its name officially to Grand Funk, and added a fourth member, keyboardist Craig Frost (b. 20 April 1948, Flint, Michigan, USA). Now produced by Todd Rundgren, they finally cracked the singles market, reaching number 1 with the title track 'We're An American Band', a celebration of its times on the road. In 1974 a heavy remake of Little Eva's 'Loco-motion' also reached number 1, the first time in US chart history that a cover of a song that had previously reached number 1 also ascended to that position. In 1975, with their popularity considerably diminished, the group reverted to its original name of Grand Funk Railroad. The following year they signed with MCA Records and recorded *Good Singin', Good Playin'*, produced by Frank Zappa. When it failed to reach the Top 50, Farner left for a solo career; the others stayed together, adding guitarist Billy Elworthy and changing their name to Flint, a group which did not see any commercial success with its one album. Grand Funk, this time consisting of Farner, Brewer and bassist Dennis Bellinger, reformed for two years in 1981-83 and recorded *Grand Funk Lives* and *What's Funk?* for the Full Moon label. Failing to recapture former glories, they split again. Farner returned to his solo career and Brewer and Frost joining Bob Seger's Silver Bullet Band.

Albums: *On Time* (1969), *Grand Funk* (1970), *Closer To Home* (1970), *Live Album* (1970), *Survival* (1971), *E Pluribus Funk* (1971), *Phoenix* (1972), *We're An American Band* (1973), *Shinin' On* (1974), *All The Girls In The World Beware!!!* (1974), *Caught*

Great White

In The Act (1975), *Born To Die* (1976), *Good Singin' Good Playin'* (1976), *Grand Funk Lives* (1981), *What's Funk?* (1983). Selected Compilations: *Mark, Don & Mel 1969-71* (1972), *Grand Funk Hits* (1976), *The Best Of Grand Funk Railroad* (1990), *More Of The Best of Grand Funk Railroad* (1991).

Great White

This Los Angeles-based outfit was formed in 1981 and comprised Jack Russell (vocals), Mark Kendall (guitar), Lorne Black (bass) and Gary Holland (drums). They adopted a no-frills approach from the start, relying on the music rather than on any gimmicks to impress; earthy, honest blues-rock delivered with stunning precision. The band attracted the attention of EMI Records with their self-financed mini-album *Out Of The Night*, produced by their good friend Don Dokken. Unfortunately, the momentum was not maintained and *Stick It*, their EMI debut, was erratic and sold poorly; the band was subsequently dropped by the label as a result. Far from disillusioned, they funded the recording of *Shot In The Dark*, which eventually opened the door to a new deal with Capitol Records. Lorne Black and

Gary Holland broke ranks at this stage and were replaced by Tony Montana and Audie Desbrow, respectively. Michael Lardie was also added on keyboards to expand the group to a five-piece and add an extra dimension to their sound. Enjoying the benefits of a larger budget, *Once Bitten* was recorded and received considerable critical acclaim, with its more melodic, accessible sound. Sales of this have now surpassed the million mark. *Recovery . . . Live* pays homage to their roots, being an inspired selection of bluesy cover versions from the Who, Led Zeppelin, Humble Pie and Jimi Hendrix. *Twice Shy* and *Hooked* have consolidated their success with further platinum awards. The band are highly respected by fellow musicians the world over.
Albums: *Out Of The Night* (1982), *Stick It* (1984), *Shot In The Dark* (1986), *Once Bitten* (1987), *Recovery . . . Live* (1988), *Twice Shy* (1989), *Hooked* (1991).

GTR

This short-lived mid-80s UK supergroup was assembled from ex-members of Yes, Genesis, Bronz and Marillion. Featuring guitarists Steve Hackett and Steve Howe, alongside vocalist Max

Guns N' Roses; Axl Rose

Bacon, bassist Phil Spalding and drummer Jonathon Mover, the line-up on paper was impressive. Considering the band's pedigree, it was no surprise to find them purveying sophisticated pomp-rock, with their roots firmly embedded in the early 70s progressive scene. 'When The Heart Rules The Mind' was a minor US hit, but the band split up soon after, following Steve Hackett's desire to re-vamp his solo career.
Album: *GTR* (1986).

Guns N'Roses

The founder members of the most controversial heavy rock band of the late 80s included W. Axl Rose (b. William Bailey, 7 February 1962, Lafayette, Indiana, USA) and Izzy Stradlin (b. Jeffrey Isbell, 1967). Vocalist Rose, who had first sung at five in a church choir, met guitarist Stradlin in Los Angeles in 1984. With Tracii Guns (guitar) and Rob Gardner (drums), they formed a rock band called in turn Rose, Hollywood Rose and LA Guns. Soon afterwards, Guns and Gardner left, to be replaced by two members of local band Road Crew, drummer Steven Adler (b. 1965 Ohio) and guitarist Slash (b. Saul Hudson, 23 July 1965, Stoke-on-Trent, Staffordshire, England), the

son of a clothes designer and album cover artist. With bass player Duff Rose McKagan (b. Michael McKagan, Seattle, Washington, USA), the band was renamed Guns N' Roses. Following a national US 'Hell Tour '85', Guns N' Roses released an EP, *Live?!*@ Like A Suicide* on the independent Uzi/Suicide label. This brought intense interest from critics and record companies and in 1986 the group signed to Geffen which reissued the EP the following year. During 1987, they toured intensively before releasing their first album, produced by Mike Clink. *Appetite For Destruction* went on to sell nearly 20 million copies worldwide and reached number 1 in America a year after its release date. The track 'Welcome To The Jungle' was used on the soundtrack of the Clint Eastwood film, *Dead Pool* and reached the Top 30 in the UK.

The group's regular live shows in the US and Europe brought frequent controversy, notably when two fans died during crowd disturbances at the Monsters Of Rock show in England in 1988. In 1989, the eight-song album *G N' R Lies* was issued, becoming a big hit on both sides of the Atlantic, as were the singles 'Paradise City', 'Sweet Child O' Mine' and 'Patience' However, Rose's

Guns N' Roses; Slash

G.W.A.R.

lyrics for 'One In A Million' was widely criticised for their anti-gay sentiments. Although Guns N' Roses appeared at the *Farm Aid IV* charity concert, their career was littered with incidents involving drugs, drunkenness and public disturbance offences in 1989-90. At times their excesses made the band seem like a caricature of a 60s supergroup. During this period, Adler was replaced by Matt Sorum from the Cult while Slash's growing reputation brought guest appearances on recordings by Bob Dylan and Michael Jackson. He also contributed to a tribute album to Les Paul. In 1991, the group released the highly-publicised pair of albums, *Use Your Illusion I* and *II*. These were preceded by a version of Bob Dylan's 'Knockin' On Heaven's Door' from the soundtrack of *Days Of Thunder* and the hit singles , 'You Could Be Mine' (featured in the film *Terminator II*) and 'Don't Cry'. Apparently more restrained in their private life, Guns N' Roses added Dizzy Reed (keyboards) for a 1991-2 world tour where their exciting and unpredictable performances brought favourable comparisons with the heyday of the Rolling Stones. Their appearance at the 1992 Freddie Mercury Aids Benefit concert prompted the reissue of 'Knockin' On Heaven's Door' and

while Dylan fans groaned with disbelief the band's vast following were happy to see their heroes scale the charts shortly after its release.
Albums: *Appetite For Destruction* (1987), *G N' R Lies* (1989), *Use Your Illusion I* (1991), *Use Your Illusion II* (1991).

GWAR

This theatrical shock-rock quintet emerged from Richmond, Virginia, USA. Assuming bizarre pseudonyms, they comprised Oderus Urungus (vocals), Balsac, The Jaws Of Death (guitar), Flattus Maximus (guitar), Beefcake The Mighty (bass) and Nippleus Erectus (drums). Renowned for an outrageous live show which involves the band adorned in hideous papier mâché masks and blood spattered torture implements, the music takes second place to the visuals. This is no more than amateurish thrash, complete with unintelligible vocals. Without the visual back-up, their albums are anti-climactic.
Albums: *Hell-O* (1988), *Scumdogs Of The Universe* (1990).

Gypsy Queen

This US heavy metal group was fronted by twin

sisters Pam and Paula Mattiola. Their debut album featured guitarists Pedro Riera and Bryan Le Mar, bassist Mars Cowling and drummer Keith Daniel Cronin and was produced by Aerosmith supremo Jack Douglas. Mid-paced pop-metal anthems and the occasional power-ballad were the order of the day, penned within a very limited musical framework. The album sold poorly and the Mattiola twins fired the entire band, recruiting Scott Migone (guitar), Joey O'Jeda (bass/keyboards) and Kenny Wendland (drums) in their place. A second album recorded in 1989 remained unreleased.

Album: *Gypsy Queen* (1987).

H

Sammy Hagar

Hagar, Sammy

b. 13 October 1947, Monterey, California, USA. Hagar was a singer, guitarist and songwriter whose father was a professional boxer. Legend has it that Elvis Presley persuaded him not to follow in his father's footsteps, and instead he started out in 60s San Bernardino bands the Fabulous Castillas, Skinny, Justice Brothers and rock band Dust Cloud. He joined Montrose in 1973 (formed by ex-Edgar Winter guitarist Ronnie Montrose) and became a minor rock hero in the Bay Area of San Francisco, in particular acquiring a reputation as a potent live performer. After two albums with Montrose he left to go solo, providing a string of semi-successful albums and singles. He took with him Bill Church (bass), and added Alan Fitzgerald (keyboards), and later Denny Carmassi (also ex-Montrose; drums). The band picked up good press on support tours with Kiss, Boston and Kansas, but by 1979 created a radically altered line-up with Gary Pihl (guitar), Chuck Ruff (drums) and Geoff Workman (keyboards) backing Hagar and Church. 1983's *Three Lock Box* became their first Top 20

entry, including 'Your Love Is Driving Me Crazy', which made number 13 in the singles chart. Hagar then took time out to tour with Journey guitarist Neal Schon, Kenny Aaronson (bass) and Mike Shrieve (ex-Santana; drums), recording a live album under the band's initials HGAS. Under this title they also cut a studio version of Procol Harum's 'Whiter Shade Of Pale'. Returning to solo work Hagar scored his biggest hit to date with *Voice Of America* out-take 'I Can't Drive 55'. However, in 1985 he surprised many by joining Van Halen from whom Dave Lee Roth had recently departed. However, he has continued to pursue a parallel, if intermittent solo career. 1987's *Sammy Hagar* had its title changed to *I Never Said Goodbye* after an MTV competition, though no copies were pressed with the new motif. His solo work continues to be characterized by a refreshing lack of bombast which is unusual for the genre.

Albums: *Nine On A Scale Of Ten* (1976), *Sammy Hagar Two* (1977), *Musical Chairs* (1978), *All Night Long - Live* (1978), *Street Machine* (1979), *Danger Zone* (1979), *Loud And Clear* (1980), *Standing Hampton* (1982), *Rematch* (1982), *Three Lock Box* (1983), *Live From London To Long Beach* (1983), *VOA* (1983), as Hagar, Schon, Aaronson and Shrieve *Through The Fire* (1984), *Voice Of America* (1984), *Looking Back* (1987), *Sammy Hagar* (1987).

Hallows Eve

The first incarnation of the heavy metal band Hallows Eve dates back to 1984, when the nucleus of Stacy Anderson (vocals), Tommy Stewart (bass) and David Stuart (guitar) plus second guitarist Skellator and drummer Tym Helton recorded a demo which was included on the *Metal Massacre IV* compilation. Their music from the outset has been extreme. They represent one of the far outposts in the rock spectrum, unleashing a high-speed, turbulent wall-of-noise. Lyrics deal with death, reincarnation, torture and mutilation, but the sentiments are usually indecipherable through frantic background thrashing. *Tales Of Terror* was recorded on a low budget, with a dreadful production, but does feature the band's strongest material. *Death And Insanity* and *Monument*, although sonically more satisfying, are cliched and formularized. Stacy Anderson quit in 1988, and the band have been inactive ever since.

Albums: *Tales Of Terror* (1985), *Death And Insanity* (1986), *Monument* (1988).

Hanoi Rocks

This Finnish heavy rock band had a leaning towards 70s glam rock. Initially the brainchild of Andy McCoy (b. Antti Hulkko) and Michael Monroe (b. Matti Fagerholm) back in 1976, they

were not formed until 1980 when singer Monroe gathered up Nasty Suicide (b. Jan Stenfors; guitar), Stefan Piesmack (guitar), Pasi Sti (bass) and Peki Senola (drums). By September, when they cut their debut album, *Bangkok Shocks, Saigon Shakes, Hanoi Rocks* (initially only released in Scandinavia) - the line-up was Monroe, Suicide, McCoy (guitar), Sam Yaffa (b. Sami Takamaki; bass) and Gyp Casino (b. Jesper Sporre; drums). McCoy had previously played with two Finnish punk bands, Briard and Pelle Miljoona Oy. In addition Suicide had played in Briard, and Yaffa in Pelle Miljoona Oy at various times. Hanoi Rocks debut single - 'I Want You', was released on the Finnish Johanna label in 1980 and preceded the album. The band then went to London where they began recording their *Oriental Beat*. Soon after it was finished Casino was sacked (and joined the Road Rats) and replaced by Razzle (b. Nicholas Dingley, Isle Of Wight, England) who had previously played with Demon Preacher, and also the Dark. In 1983 they were signed to CBS and started to attract attention in the British music press. They hit the UK charts for the one and only time in 1984 with a cover version of Creedence Clearwater Revival's 'Up Around The Bend', but the year ended in tragedy. The band were in the US when Razzle was killed in a car crash on 7 December. The car driver - Vince Neil of Mötley Crüe - was later found guilty of Vehicular Manslaughter. Former Clash drummer Terry Chimes was brought in as a replacement and when Yaffa left (to form Chain Gang then join Jetboy) Rene Berg (ex-Idle Flowers) also joined the group. However, Monroe never really accepted the loss of Razzle and in early 1985 he told the band he intended to quit. Hanoi Rocks played their final gig in May 1985. Monroe has since embarked on a solo career. Piesmack joined Pelle Miljoona Oy then quit music, Sti and Senola also left the music scene, and McCoy (who had already formed a side project in 1983 - the Urban Dogs with Charlie Harper, Alvin Gibbs (UK Subs) and Knox (Vibrators) went on to form the Cherry Bombz with Suicide, Chimes and ex-Toto Coelo vocalist Anita Chellemah. The Cherry Bombz barely lasted a year and the members went on to play in various short-lived outfits, most notably Suicide (with Gibbs once more) in Cheap 'n' Nasty.
Albums: *Bangkok Shocks, Saigon Shakes, Hanoi Rocks* (1981), *Oriental Beat* (1982), *Self Destruction Blues* (1982), *Back To Mystery City* (1983), *Two Steps From The Move* (1984), *All Those Wasted Years* (1985), *Rock 'N' Roll Divorce* (1985), *Best Of Hanoi Rocks* (1985), *Dead By Christmas* (1986), *Tracks From A Broken Dream* (1990).

Hansen, Randy

Raised in Seattle, Washington, USA, guitarist Hansen first attracted attention as a member of nightclub act Kid Chrysler And The Cruisers. The group's tongue-in-cheek repertoire encompassed several styles of popular music, but was marked by the musician's imperturbable pastiche of Jimi Hendrix. Having formed a trio, Machine Gun, in 1977, Hansen took his tribute on tour, but achieved a greater notoriety when he contributed Hendrix-influenced effects to the film soundtrack of *Apocalypse Now*. This in turn engendered a management deal with San Francisco-based entrepreneur David Rubinson who began promoting his client as an artist in his own right. *Randy Hansen* comprised original material which sadly paled in comparison to that of his mentor. Hendrix's songs still provided the focal point to the guitarist's live act and in 1984 he reverted completely to the role of imitator by joining drummer Buddy Miles in a revamped version of Band Of Gypsies.
Album: *Randy Hansen* (1981).

Headgirl

A project conceived by British rock bands Motorhead and Girlschool. Both bands shared the same manager and record company, Bronze. Motorhead (line-up: Lemmy, 'Fast' Eddy Clarke, 'Philthy' Phil Taylor) had had to cancel a tour following their drummer, Taylor, breaking his neck. They were at a Girlschool recording session, the line-up of which was Kim McAuliffe (vocals/guitar), Enid Williams (bass), Kelly Johnson (guitar) and Denise Dufort (drums). Producer Vic Maile suggested that they work together. The result was the EP, *St. Valentine's Day Massacre* which contained the hit, 'Please Don't Touch', a cover of a Johnny Kidd And The Pirates song from 1960. The EP was recorded in December 1980 at the Jackson studio, Rickmansworth, Hertfordshire, and its success led to Headgirl (an amalgamation of the names of the two bands) appearing no less than three times on the UK television music programme *Top Of The Pops*.

Hear 'N' Aid

The Hear 'N' Aid project came about after Jimmy Bain and Vivian Campbell had taken part in a Radiothon held over a weekend by KLOS of Los Angeles for the famine in Africa. They had noticed that there were not many rock starts taking part and that is when the whole idea was born. Initially, they got in touch with Ronnie James Dio, singer in the group Dio, to tell him of the project. While Dio was ringing round to get

support, Bain and Campbell wrote the score, and Dio produced the lyrics. 'Stars' was recorded over a four-month period in 1946. While they gained considerable support, there was also opposition. In addition to the single release, a video was planned and all the sessions were filmed. The most ambitious part was to have an album released with each act writing a track for the record, but this never occurred. Instead, bands donated tracks, most of which were live recordings. Another idea was for a session to be held in London, so all the European rock stars could be included, but this had to be aborted due to lack of participants. Those that did take part came from the following groups: Queensrÿche, Rough Cutt, Iron Maiden, Mötley Crüe, Vanilla Fudge, Dio, Blue Öyster Cult, Don Dokken, Yngwie Malmsteen, Quiet Riot, Judas Priest, King Cobra and Journey.
Album: *Hear 'N' Aid* (1986).

Heart

This US soft rock band featured the talents of sisters Ann (b. June 19 1951, San Diego, California, USA) and Nancy Wilson (b. 16 March 1954, San Francisco, California, USA). The elder sister had released two singles as Ann Wilson And The Daybreaks on a local label in 1967. After a series of unreleased demos she took her sister to Vancouver, in Canada, in search of a backing band. There they found bassist Steve Fossen and guitarist Roger Fisher (b. 1950), and Heart was born (two initial monickers the Army and White Heart were rejected). After *Dreamboat Annie* emerged on Mushroom Records in 1976, their second single 'Crazy On You' brought them to public attention. Michael Derosier became the band's first permanent drummer, and they were also joined by multi-instrumentalist Howard Leese (b. 1952). They maintained their high profile when *Little Queen* and the single, 'Barracuda', became mainstays in the US charts. By the time *Dog And Butterfly* arrived in 1978, the professional relationships within the band had escalated to ones of a more personal nature, with Nancy Wilson dating guitarist Fisher, while sister Ann was involved with his brother Mike. By this time Mike Fisher had become the band's unofficial manager. However, before *Bebe Le Strange* was issued on Epic, the relationships had soured and Fisher left the band, leaving the album bereft of the lead guitar which had previously been so prominent in the group's formula. By the time they resurfaced with *Private Audition* in 1983, Fossen and Derosier were also on the verge of departure. Their replacements were Mark Andes (ex-Spirit) and Denny Carmassi (ex-Montrose and Sammy Hagar Band), though their efforts on *Passionworks* were

not enough to inspire any kind of revival in Heart's fortunes. Their confidence was bolstered, however, when Ann's duet with Mike Dean (Loverboy) produced 'Almost Paradise . . . Love Theme From Footloose', which rose to number 7 in the US charts. When Epic allowed their contract to lapse, Heart joined Capitol in 1985, seemingly with their career in its death throes. The new label brought about a transformation in the band's image, projecting them as a more rock-orientated concern, but could hardly have expected the turnaround in Heart's fortunes which resulted. *Heart* gave them a number 1 in the US, and highly lucrative singles 'What About Love' and 'Never', before 'These Dreams' finally achieved the equivalent number 1 slot in the singles chart. The follow-up, *Bad Animals*, was almost as successful, stalling at number 2. While both Wilson sisters continued to work on soundtrack cuts, the most profitable of which was Ann's duet with Robin Zander (Cheap Trick) 'Surrender To Me', Nancy married *Rolling Stone* writer Cameron Crowe. Heart's success continued with the long-conceived *Brigade* in 1990, from which 'All I Wanna Do Is Make Love To You' became a Top 10 hit in the UK and a number 1 in the US. Both Wilson sisters are currently involved in solo projects, though they intend to keep the Heart name alive. Former companions Fossen, Fisher and Derosier, meanwhile, have embarked on a new career with Alias, which scored two big US single hits in 1990.
Albums: *Dreamboat Annie* (1976), *Little Queen* (1977), *Dog And Butterfly* (1978), *Bebe Le Strange* (1980), *Greatest Hits Live* (1981), *Private Audition* (1982), *Passionworks* (1983), *Heart* (1985), *Bad Animals* (1987), *Brigade* (1990) *Rock The House (Live)* (1991).

Heir Apparent

Formed in Seattle, Washington, USA in 1984 the band's original line-up consisted of Paul Davidson (vocals), Terry Gorle (guitar), Michael Jackson (keyboards), Derek Peace (bass) and Ray Black (drums). Due to some early demos, the band attracted the attention of the French based Black Dragon Records. This resulted in the band's debut *Graceful Inheritance*,a worthy slice of Americanized melodic rock, being released in 1986. After an uneventful European tour with Savage Grace, vocalist Paul Davidson left the band to be replaced by Steve Benito. The band also briefly lost bassist Derek Peace to Savage Grace before he realized his mistake and rejoined the band. However all this had taken its toll and the band was dropped by their record company. After several new demos the band attracted the attention of Metal Blade

Helix

Records. This resulted in *One Small Voice* being released in 1989. Shortly after, both Black and Gorle left the band to be replaced by Gary McCormick and Klaus Derendorf, respectively. However little was heard from the band after its release and they disappeared into the Seattle club scene.

Albums: *Graceful Inheritance* (1986), *One Small Voice* (1989).

Helix

Formed in Ontario, Canada in 1978 the band's original line-up consisted of Brian Vollmer (vocals), Brent Doerner (guitar), Paul Hackman (guitar), Keith Zurbrigg (bass) and Brian Doerner (drums). They released two albums *Breaking Loose* and *White Lace & Black Leather* to a less than enthusiastic reception in 1979 and 1981 respectively. The music on offer was basic hard rock. However these releases gained the attention of Capitol Records who signed the band and released their third album *No Rest For The Wicked* in 1983. Judged to be their best album to date, it was a solid collection of hard rock songs, which sold well. *Walkin' The Razors Edge,* released in 1984, had the new bassist Daryl Gray. This line-up

went on to record two more albums for Capitol *Long Way To Heaven* and *Wild In The Streets* released in 1985 and 1987, respectively, which showed the band to be taking a much more commercial direction.

Albums: *Breaking Loose* (1979), *White Lace & Black Leather* (1981), *No Rest For The Wicked* (1983), *Walkin' The Razors Edge* (1984), *Long Way To Heaven* (1985), *Wild In The Streets* (1987).

Hellanbach

Formed in Newcastle-upon-Tyne, England in 1980, Hellanbach was one of the many groups to come out of the New Wave Of British Heavy Metal. The band consisted of Jimmy Brash (vocals), Dave Patton (guitar), Kev Charlton (bass), and Steve Walker (drums). Instead of taking the usual route of making demos to get a recording contract, the band went straight ahead with recording and releasing a four-track EP at their own expense. *Out To Get You* was a heavy yet melodic debut. Hellanbach then seemed to leave the scene for a while until re-emerging on the Neat Records label and releasing their debut album *Now Hear This* in 1983. It was received by the press with mixed reaction, however the comparison to Van Halen was to dog them for the rest of their career. By the time *The Big H* was released in 1984, the band had obviously taken note of the criticisms that had been levelled against them. Again, this album was a worthy release from a dedicated band, full of melodic choruses. However, due to a lack of media interest, the band soon folded.

Albums: *Now Hear This* (1983), *The Big H* (1984).

Helloween

Helloween

Formed in Hamburg, Germany in 1984 out of the ashes of local bands Second Hell and Iron Fist, their original line-up comprised, Kai Hansen (guitar/vocals), Michael Weikath (guitar), Markus Grosskopf (bass) and Ingo Schwichenburg (drums). After having two tracks included on the compilation album *Death Metal* released by Noise Records in 1984, the label issued their self-titled debut mini-album in 1985. This was soon followed by *Walls Of Jericho* and an EP *Judas*. The band quickly gained a strong following with their unique blend of high speed power metal. Soon after its release Helloween decided to add a vocalist/frontman, namely Michael Kiske, a charismatic 18-year-old. *Keeper Of The Seven Keys Part I*, released in 1987, showed the band to be taking a much more melodic approach and Kiske proved a worthy addition. Helloween then toured Europe relentlessly, building a sizeable following in the process. *Keeper Of The Seven Keys Part II* was released in 1988, together with a successful appearance at the Donnington Monsters Of Rock Festival that year. They released an EP *Dr. Stein*, but behind the scenes all was not well. They had become increasingly unhappy with their record company and started to negotiate with several major labels who had previously shown interest in the band. As a stop gap the band released *Live In The UK*, recorded at the Hammersmith Odeon in 1989. Kai Hansen left the band to form his own outfit Gamma Ray. His replacement was Roland

Grapow in 1989. A protracted legal battle with their record company meant that it was not until 1990 that the band was back in action. They finally signed to EMI Records and gained major management in the form of the Smallwood/Taylor organization. The band's debut for their new label, *Pink Bubbles Go Ape* released in 1990 showed the band to be a shadow of their former selves and sadly missing Kai Hansen and his songwriting skills.

Albums: *Helloween* (mini-album 1985), *Walls Of Jericho* (1986), *Keeper Of The Seven Keys Part I* (1987), *Keeper Of The Seven Keys Part II* (1988), *Live In The UK* (1989), *Pink Bubbles Go Ape* (1990).

Helmet

This New York, USA- based, hardcore-metal quartet were put together by jazz-trained guitarist/vocalist Page Hamilton. With the addition of Henry Bogdan (bass), Peter Mengele (guitar) and John Stanier (drums) the band's line-up was finalized in 1990. Adopting a non-image of short haircuts and sensible clothes, they are the visual antithesis of the heavy metal/rock 'n' roll lifestyle. However, musically they deliver bone-crunching riffs of mesmeric intensity, tortured vocals and bludgeoning rhythms. Black Flag, Black Sabbath and The Henry Rollins Band are their musical signposts as they fuse metal, punk and thrash methodologies to superb effect. Signed to the independent Interscope label, they started to attract media interest in the spring of 1992 with their second album *Meantime*.

Albums: *Strap It On* (1991), *Meantime* (1992).

Helstar

Formed in Houston, Texas, USA in 1982, the band's original line-up consisted of James Rivera (vocals), Larry Barragan (guitar), Robert Trevin (guitar), Jerry Abarca (bass) and Rene Lima (drums). Due to an excellent four-track demo recorded in 1983 the band quickly became a favourite on the underground tape trading scene. Attracting the attention of Combat Records, the band released their debut album *Burning Star* in 1984. The album produced by ex-Rods drummer Carl Canedy did not have the spark of the early demo but was still a worthy slice of classy power metal. Due to internal wrangles both guitarist Robert Trevin and drummer Rene Lima left the band to be replaced by André Corbin and Frank Feræeira respectively. The band's second album *Remnants Of War* was released in 1986 and followed closely in the footsteps of its predecessor. The band had been dissatisfied with their record label for some time and after due deliberation both

Jimi Hendrix Experience, with Arthur Brown

parties parted company amicably. Helstar then relocated to Los Angeles where they signed a new recording agreement with the Metal Blade Records label. Their first release was *A Distant Thunder* in 1988. The band had now developed their own distinctive sound and were picking up many fans. They toured across America and Europe in support of the album and on their return to America moved back to Houston. The next album, entitled *Nosferatu,* released in 1989 was a concept album telling the story of Dracula. However this new approach towards their songwriting did not suit the now distinctive Helstar style and the album proved to be somewhat of a disappointment.

Albums: *Burning Star* (1984), *Remnants Of War* (1986), *A Distant Thunder* (1988), *Nosferatu* (1989).

Hendrix, Jimi

b. Johnny Allen Hendrix, 27 November 1942, Seattle, Washington, USA, d. 18 September, 1970. His father subsequently changed his son's name to James Marshall Hendrix. More superlatives have been bestowed upon Hendrix than almost any other rock star. Unquestionably one of music's most influential figures, Jimi Hendrix brought an unparalleled vision to the art of playing electric guitar. Self-taught and with the burden of being left-handed with a right-handed guitar he spent hours absorbing the recorded legacy of southern-blues practitioners, from Robert Johnson to Muddy Waters, Howlin' Wolf to B.B. King. The aspiring musician joined several local R&B bands while still at school, before enlisting as a paratrooper in the 101st Airborne Division. It was during this period that Hendrix met Billy Cox, a bass player upon whom he would call at several stages in his career. Together they formed the King Kasuals, an in-service attraction later resurrected when both men returned to civilian life. Hendrix was discharged in July 1962 after breaking his right ankle. He began working with various touring revues backing, among others, the Impressions, Sam Cooke and the Valentinos. He enjoyed lengthier spells with the Isley Brothers, Little Richard and King Curtis, recording with each of these acts, but was unable to adapt to the discipline their performances required. Despite such individuality, the experience and stagecraft gained during this formative period proved essential to the artist's subsequent development.

By 1965, Jimi was living in New York. In October he joined struggling soul singer Curtis Knight, signing a punitive contract with the latter's manager, Ed Chaplin. This ill-advised decision would return to haunt the guitarist. In June the following year Hendrix, now calling himself Jimmy James, formed a group initially dubbed the Rainflowers, then Jimmy James And The Blue Flames. The quartet, which also featured future Spirit member Randy California, was appearing at the Cafe Wha? in Greenwich Village when Chas Chandler was advised to see them. The Animals' bassist immediately recognized the guitarist's extraordinary talent and persuaded him to come to London in search of a more receptive audience. Hendrix arrived in England in September 1966. Chandler became his co-manager, in partnership with Mike Jeffries (aka Jeffreys), and immediately began auditions for a suitable backing group. Noel Redding (b. 25 December 1945, Folkstone, Kent, England) was selected on bass, having recently failed to join the New Animals, while John 'Mitch' Mitchell (b. 9 July 1947, Ealing, Middlesex, England), a veteran of the Riot Squad and Georgie Fame's Blue Flames, became the trio's drummer.

The new group, dubbed the Jimi Hendrix Experience, made its debut the following month at Evercux in France. On returning to England they began a string of club engagements which attracted pop's aristocracy, including Pete Townshend and Eric Clapton. In December the trio released its first single, the brilliantly understated 'Hey Joe', but its UK Top 10 placing encouraged a truly dynamic follow-up in 'Purple Haze'. The latter was memorable for its pyrotechic guitar work and psychedelic-influenced lyrics, such as the famous line: "Scuse me while I kiss the sky'.

His trademark Fender Stratocaster and Marshall Amplifier were punished night after night. Having fulfilled pop's requirements, the group enhanced its reputation with exceptional live appearances. Here Hendrix drew on black music's cultural heritage to produce a startling visual and audio bombardment. Framed by a halo of long, wiry hair, his slight figure was clad in colourful, *de rigueur* psychedelic garb, and although never a demonstrative vocalist, his delivery was curiously effective. Hendrix's playing technique drew its roots from the blues artists, but it encompassed an emotional palette far greater than any contemporary guitarist. Eric Clapton, Jeff Beck and Pete Townshend all tried: but Hendrix *did it*, while they stood aghast. Rapier-like runs vied with measured solos, matching energy with ingenuity, while a plethora of technical possibilities - distortion, feedback and even sheer volume - brought texture to his overall approach. His technique was so impressive it was irrational. This assault was enhanced by a flamboyant stage persona in which Hendrix used the guitar as a physical appendage. He played his instrument behind his back, between his legs or, in simulated sexual ecstasy, on the floor. Such practices brought criticism from radical quarters, who claimed the artist had become an 'Uncle Tom', employing tricks to carry favour with a white audience. These accusations had denied a similar showmanship from generations of black performers, from Charley Patton to T-Bone Walker, but Hendrix prevailed and in doing so created a climate to allow future stars such as Michael Jackson and Prince to express themselves fully.

Redding's clean, uncluttered bass lines provided the backbone to Hendrix's improvisations, while Mitchell's anarchic drumming, as unfettered as his leader's guitar work, was an innovatory foil. Their concessions to the pop world now receding, the Experience completed an astonishing debut album which ranged from the apocalyptical vision of 'I Don't Live Today', the blues of 'Red House' to the funk of 'Fire' and 'Foxy Lady'. Jimi Hendrix returned to America in June 1967 to appear, sensationally, at the Monterey Pop Festival. During one number (Dylan's 'Like A Rolling Stone') he paused and informed the crowd that he was re-tuning his guitar, later in the same song he admits forgetting the words. Such cheek, humour and unparalleled confidence endeared him to the crowd. His performance was a sensation, best remembered for his largesse in picking the guitar with his teeth and then burning it with lighter fuel.

He was now fêted in his homeland, and following an ill-advised tour supporting the Monkees, the Experience enjoyed reverential audiences in the country's nascent concert circuit. *Axis: Bold As Love*, revealed a lyrical capability, notably the title track, the jazz-influenced 'Up From The Skies', and 'Little Wing', a delicate love song bathed in emotion through the delicate tones of his guitar, which offered a gentle perspective closer to that of the artist's shy, offstage demeanour. Released in December 1967, the collection completed a triumphant year, artistically and commercially, but within months the fragile peace began to fragment. In January 1968, the Experience embarked on a gruelling American tour encompassing 54 concerts in 47 days. Hendrix was now tiring of the wild man image which had brought initial attention, but his desire for a more eloquent art was perceived as diffident by spectators anticipating gimmickry. An impulsive artist, he was unable to disguise below-par performances, while his relationship with Redding grew increasingly fraught as the bassist rebelled against the set patterns he was expected to play.

Electric Ladyland, the last official Experience album, was released in October. This extravagant double set was initially deemed 'self-indulgent', but is now recognized as a major work. It revealed the guitarist's desire to expand the increasingly limiting trio format, and contributions from members of Traffic (Chris Wood and Steve Winwood) and Jefferson Airplane (Jack Casady) embellished several selections. The collection featured a succession of classic-styled performances - 'Gypsy Eyes', 'Crosstown Traffic' - while the astonishing 'Voodoo Chile (Slight Return)', a posthumous number 1 single, showed how Hendrix had brought rhythm, purpose and mastery to the recently invented wah-wah pedal. *Electric Ladyland* included two UK hits, 'The Burning Of The Midnight Lamp' and 'All Along The Watchtower'. The former dared to tell us in the plausible lyric that 'traffic lights turn blue' before the listener realises. The latter, an urgent restatement of a Bob Dylan song, was particularly impressive, and received the ultimate accolade when the composer adopted Hendrix's interpretation when performing it live on his 1974 tour.

Despite such creativity, the guitarist's private and professional life was becoming problematic. He was arrested in Toronto for possessing heroin, but although the charges were later dismissed, the proceedings clouded much of 1969. Chas Chandler had meanwhile withdrawn from the managerial partnership and although Redding sought solace with a concurrent group, Fat Mattress, his differences with Hendrix were now irreconcilable. The Experience played its final concert on June 29 1969; Jimi subsequently formed the Gypsies Sons And Rainbows with Mitchell, Billy Cox (bass), Larry Lee (rhythm guitar), Juma Sultan and Jerry Velez (both percussion). This short-lived unit closed the Woodstock Festival, during which Hendrix performed his famed rendition of the 'Star Spangled Banner'. Perceived by some critics as a political statement, it came as the guitarist was increasingly subjected to pressures from different radical quarters. In October he formed an all-black group, Band Of Gypsies, with Cox and drummer Buddy Miles, intending to accentuate the African-American dimension in his music. The trio made its debut on 31 December 1969, but its potential was marred by Miles' comparatively flat, pedestrian drumming and unimaginative compositions. Part of the set was issued as *Band Of Gypsies*, but despite the inclusion of the exceptional 'Machine Gun', this inconsistent album was only released to appease former manager Chaplin, who acquired the rights in part-settlement of a miserly early contract.

The Band Of Gypsies broke up after a mere three concerts and initially Hendrix confined his efforts to completing his Electric Ladyland recording studio. He then started work on another double set, the unreleased *First Rays Of The New Rising Sun*, and later resumed performing with Cox and Mitchell. His final concerts were largely frustrating, as the aims of the artist and the expectations of his audience grew increasingly divergent. His final UK appearance, at the Isle Of Wight festival, encapsulated this dilemma, yet at times the music produced at this concert was truly mesmerizing.

The guitarist returned to London following a short European tour. On 18 September 1970, his girlfriend, Monika Danneman, became alarmed when she was unable to rouse him from sleep. An ambulance was called, but Hendrix was pronounced dead on arrival at a nearby hospital. The inquest recorded an open verdict, death caused by suffocation due to inhalation of vomit. Eric Burdon claimed at the time to possess a suicide note but this has never been confirmed.

Two posthumous releases, *Cry Of Love* and *Rainbow Bridge*, mixed portions of the artist's final recordings with masters from earlier sources. These were fitting tributes, but many others were tawdry cash-ins, recorded in dubious circumstances, mispackaged, mistitled and serving only to dilute his outstanding career. This imbalance has been redressed of late with the release of fitting archive recordings, but the Hendrix legacy also rests in his prevailing influence on fellow musicians. Many, notably white, guitarists, have adopted superficially his trademarks, but Jimi's influence on black performers, from Miles Davis to George Clinton and Prince, has in turn inspired new and compulsive music. Hendrix has influenced and appears likely to influence rock music more than any other individual, and remains a colossal legend.

Albums: *Are You Experienced?* (1967), *Axis: Bold As Love* (1967), *Electric Ladyland* (1968), *Band Of Gypsies* (1970). The rest of the extensive Hendrix catalogue was compiled after his death. *Cry Of Love* (1971), *Experience* (1971), *Isle Of Wight* (1971), *Rainbow Bridge* (1971), *Hendrix In The West* (1971), *More Experience* (1972), *War Heroes* (1972), *Soundtrack Recordings From The Film Jimi Hendrix* (1973), *Loose Ends* (1974), *Crash Landing* (1975), *Midnight Lightnin'* (1975), *Nine To The Universe* (1980), *The Jimi Hendrix Concerts* (1982), *Jimi Plays Monterey* (1986), *Band Of Gypsies 2* (1986), *Live At Winterland* (1987), *Radio One* (1988), *Live And Unreleased* (1989). Compilations: *Smash Hits* (1968), *The Essential Jimi Hendrix* (1978), *The Essential Jimi Hendrix Volume Two* (1979), *The Singles Album* (1983), *Kiss The Sky* (1984),

Cornerstones (1990).

Further reading: *Hendrix - A Biography*, Chris Welch. *Jimi - An Intimate Biography Of Jimi Hendrix*, Curtis Knight. *Jimi Hendrix - Voodoo Child Of The Aquarian Age*, David Henderson. *Crosstown Traffic/Jimi Hendrix And Post-War Pop*, Charles Shaar Murray. *Jimi Hendrix - Electric Gypsy*, Harry Shapiro and Caesar Glebbeek. *The Hendrix Experience*, Mitch Mitchell and John Platt. *Are You Experienced*, Noel Redding and Carol Appleby.

Heretic

Formed in Los Angeles, California, USA in 1984 the band's original line-up consisted of Julian Mendez (vocals), Brian Korban (guitar), Bobby Marquez (guitar), Dennis O'Hara (bass) and Rick Merrick (drums). Quickly gaining popularity on the club circuit in and around the Los Angeles area, the band attracted the attention of Metal Blade Records. Heretic's debut release for the label was a mini-album *Torture Knows No Boundaries* in 1987. The album was a worthy slice of hard fast power metal but was slightly marred because Julian Mendez's vocals were not really suited to the band's hard-hitting approach. Mendez realized this and left the band, to be replaced by Mike Howe later the same year. On their second and full-length *Breaking Point*, they sounded much more confident. However, when later that same year, vocalist Howe left the band to join Metal Church, a series of vocal replacements could not prevent the band folding in 1989.

Albums: *Torture Knows No Boundaries* (1987), *Breaking Point* (1988).

High Tide

Formed in 1969 this UK group comprised: Tony Hill (guitar), Simon House (violin), Peter Pavli (bass) and Roger Hadden (drums). Signed as part of Liberty Records' attempt to climb on the progressive bandwagon, *High Tide* was more than a credible debut, complete with Mervyn Peake-styled sleeve illustrations. The unique blending of guitar and violin was for many an unaccustomed taste. However, the dramatic and powerful songs laced with Hill's Jim Morrison-like vocals appealed to the UK progressive market. By the time of the second album though, the formula had worn thin and the band broke up, with House eventually joining Hawkwind.

Albums: *Sea Shanties* (1969), *High Tide* (1970), *Interesting Times* (1986), *The Flood* (c.80s), *Ancient Gates* (c.80s), *A Fierce Native* (1990). Solo album: Tony Hill *Playing For Time* (1991).

Hirax

Formed in Los Angeles, California, USA in 1984

the band's original line-up consisted of Katon W. De Pena (vocals), Scott Owen (guitar), Gary Monardo (bass) and John Tabares (drums). Their promising demos attracted the attention of the Metal Blade Records label which included one of the band's demo tracks on the *Metal Massacre VI* compilation album released in 1985. Metal Blade promptly signed the band resulting in the its debut album *Raging Violence* being released in 1985. The album was full of short sharp ultra-fast thrash metal. Shortly after its release, drummer John Tabares left the band to be replaced by ex-DRI percussionist Eric Brecht. The band's next release was a mini-album *Hate, Fear And Power* which was released in 1986. The material on offer was very much in the same vein as before but the production this time around was much better. Due to internal band wrangles vocalist Katon W. De Pena left to be replaced by ex-Exodus vocalist Paul Baloff. He, in turn, did not stay long before being replaced himself by Billy Wedgeworth. However, a stable line-up could not be maintained and the band folded after recording several further demos in 1988.
Albums: *Raging Violence* (1985), *Hate, Fear And Power* (1986).

Holocaust

Formed in Edinburgh, Scotland in 1978. The original line-up consisted of Gary Lettice (vocals), John Mortimer (guitar), Edward Dudley (guitar), Robin Begg (bass) and Paul Collins (drums). They were quickly signed by the small independent Phoenix Records label which released the band's debut single 'Heavy Metal Mania' in 1980. The band's debut *The Nightcomers* was released in 1981. The material on offer was basic hard rock fuelled by the enthusiasm that the NWOBHM inspired. This album was to be a very influential release, and thrash supergroup Metallica later covered one of the album tracks on their EP *Garage Days Revisited*. Come 1982 and the release of the Holocaust's second single, 'Coming Through', the band was falling apart. A posthumous live album appeared in 1983 again on the Phoenix Records label entitled *Live, Hot Curry & Wine*. Guitarist Edward Dudley left to form the band Hologram who recorded one album also for the Phoenix Records label entitled *Steal The Stars* which was released in 1982. Hologram was short lived as Holocaust reformed and released a third album *No Mans Land* in 1984. However, soon after its release the band folded. With the resurgence of interest in the NWOBHM bands due to Metallica cover versions the band started working together again in 1989.
Albums: *The Nightcomers* (1981), *Live, Hot Curry & Wine* (1983), *No Mans Land* (1984).

House Of Lords

This five-piece US heavy rock supergroup was put together by ex-Angel keyboardist Gregg Giuffria. Augmented by bassist Chuck Wright (ex-Quiet Riot), drummer Ken Mary (ex-Alice Cooper), vocalist James Christian (ex-Canata) and guitarist Lanny Cordola (ex-Giuffria) the line-up was impressive and promised much. With Giuffria in control, the band pursued an overstated melodic approach with swathes of keyboards, multi-phased harmonies and atmospheric arrangements redolent of mid-70s arena rock. Signing to RCA Records, their self-titled debut was recorded with the help of Andy Johns and long-time friend Gene Simmons (Kiss bassist) at the production desk. The result was well received, a state-of-the-art pomp-rock album with a powerful and sparkling sound. Apart from a few support slots on the Scorpions' European tour, the band did not commit themselves to touring in the way that was needed to stimulate album sales. Lanny Cordola quit as a result and was replaced by Michael Guy (ex-Fire) before the band entered the studio again. *Sahara* continued in the same musical vein, but the interest it generated was once again allowed to ebb away as the band was still reluctant to tour.
Albums: *House Of Lords* (1988), *Sahara* (1990).

Howe II

After recording a solo instrumental album in 1988, guitarist Greg Howe decided to expand his musical horizons and incorporate his talents within a band framework. Brother Al stepped in as vocalist, with Vern Parsons and Joe Nevolo taking on bass and drum duties respectively. Released in 1989, their debut album was a highly accomplished work that combined elements of Van Halen and Rising Force; Al Howe's vocals was reminiscent of vintage Dave Lee Roth, while Greg's guitar style was not far removed from that of the Swedish guitarist Yngwie Malmsteen. Their second album built on these solid foundations, but featured more melodic compositions.
Albums: *High Gear* (1989), *Now Hear This* (1991).

HSAS

This US group was formed in the early part of 1984 by Sammy Hagar (vocals) and Neil Schon (guitar). Both are from the San Francisco area and had planned a collaboration for some time. So when Hagar had finished promoting his latest solo record and Neil Schon had completed touring with Journey, HSAS was formed. They brought in Peter Schrieve (drums) and Kenny Aaronson (bass), because they shared the same management. They wrote approximately 15 songs in a month and then decided to go out on a small tour. It was while they were touring that they hit upon the idea to record the album live instead of going into a studio. There was only one place to record, and that was their home town of San Francisco, so they hired a mobile recording studio and two shows were recorded. A deal was struck with Sammy Hagar's label Geffen and *Through The Fire* was nearly ready for release. The only problem was that American radio does not like live records, so most of the crowd noise was taken out of the final mix, with the exception of two tracks where the audience actually participated in the songs.

Because it was a Hagan/Schon project, it was never a permanent band so after the album's release, Sammy Hagar returned to his solo career and Neil Schon went back to Journey. HSAS got their name from the first letter of the members' surnames. Aaronson-Schrieve were the obvious choices for the last two letters, but a coin was tossed for the order of the first two. Hagar won, Schon lost; so the discussion ended with the name HSAS.

Album: *Through The Fire* (1944).

Hughes/Thrall

This was a short-lived collaboration between former Deep Purple and Trapeze bassist/vocalist Glenn Hughes and guitarist Pat Thrall, who had previously played with Automatic Man and Pat Travers. With the help of various session drummers, including Frankie Banali (later of Quiet Riot) they recorded an album that fused rock and funk through the use of synthesized guitar effects. Shortly after the album was released Pat Thrall went back to session work, while Glenn Hughes had stints with Gary Moore, Black Sabbath and Phenomena. In 1987 they worked together again, on the soundtrack of the film *Dragnet* with Dan Akroyd of the Blues Brothers.

Albums: *Hughes/Thrall* (1982).

Hurricane

Formed in Los Angeles, California, USA in 1983 this heavy metal band's original line-up consisted of Kelly Hanson (vocals), Robert Sarzo (guitar), Tony Cavazo (bass) and Jay Schellen (drums). Robert Sarzo is the brother of Whitesnake bassist Rudy Sarzo and Tony Cavazo is the brother of Quiet Riot guitarist Carlos Cavazo. Their debut was a mini-album released in 1986, entitled *Take What You Want* on Roadrunner Records. It was a fine debut of hard edged melodic rockers. The band switched labels, signing to Enigma Records and released *Over The Edge* in 1988. Unfortunately it failed to sell and during 1989 Robert Sarzo left the band to be replaced by ex-Lion guitarist Doug Aldrich. This line-up went on to record the much

Hurricane

improved *Slave To The Thrill*, released in 1990 to critical acclaim.

Albums: *Take What You Want* (1986), *Over The Edge* (1988), *Slave To The Thrill* (1990).Albums: *Mouth Harp Maestro* (1988), *Fine Cuts* (1978).

I

Icon

This group was formed in Phoenix, Arizona, USA in 1981 by school friends Dan Wexler (guitar), Tracy Wallach (bass/backing vocals) and Stephen Clifford (lead vocals). Drummer Pat Dixon and John Aquilino (guitar) joined a couple of months later. Icon spent the first three years playing local bars and recording demo tapes. Mike Varney heard the band and signed them to his Shrapnel label. Icon went into the studio to record their first album with Varney and Dan Wexler producing. After the record was finished Varney realized that he had a commercial record on his hands and so sold Icon to Capitol Records. In late 1984 *Icon* was released, a dynamic record in the Don Dokken style of melodic heavy metal. Not many people acknowledged the existence of the record and it failed to sell. Brushing this aside Icon entered the studio in 1985 with producer Eddie Kramer to record the follow-up, *Night Of The Crime* which also sold poorly. Capitol subsequently dropped them from their roster and Icon went back to Phoenix. At this point, Clifford was replaced by Jerry Harrison. In 1987 Icon released a cassette album, sold locally. In 1989 Johnny Zazula heard this tape and signed them to his Megaforce label, which had just negotiated a worldwide distribution deal with Atlantic Records. In the middle of 1989 Icon were about to start recording when Aquilino left the band. His replacement was Drew Bollmann, who came from the Phoenix area. With Dan Wexler producing *Right Between The Eyes*, Icon came up with their best record in their AOR/melodic heavy rock vein - with Alice Cooper guesting on two tracks. However, this was not to be Icon's great return because after a short UK tour Dan Wexler announced their break-up.
Albums: *Icon* (19484), *Night Of The Crime* (1985), *Right Between The Eyes* (1989).

Impelliteri, Chris

Impelliteri is one of the new-age guitarists influenced by a combination of rock and classical music styles. Utilizing a high-speed fretboard technique, he attempts to cram as many notes imaginable into the shortest possible time-span. Moving to Los Angeles in 1986, he recorded a self-financed mini-album of up-tempo instrumentals. The following year he formed Impelliteri, which featured vocalist Graham Bonnet (ex-MSG and Rainbow), drummer Pat Torpey (ex-Ted Nugent), bassist Chuck Wright (ex-Quiet Riot) and keyboardist Phil Wolfe. They recorded the stunning hard rock album *Stand In Line* and although it provoked unjust accusations of plagiarism from Rainbow devotees, the music was powerful, exciting and melodic. The band disintegrated soon after the album's release; Chuck Wright joined House Of Lords and Pat Torpey teamed up with Mr. Big. Chris Impelliteri joined forces with ex-Dio keyboard player Claude Schnell and vocalist Mark Weisz in 1990.
Albums: *Impelliteri* (1986), *Stand in Line* (1988).

Iommi, Tony

b. Anthony Frank Iommi, 19 February 1948, Birmingham, England. A blues/jazz influenced guitarist, Iommi was eager to escape the mundanity of industrial Birmingham and his job repairing typewriters. A number of small-time bands including Polka Tulk and Earth gradually led to the formation of Black Sabbath in 1969 with Iommi on guitar, John 'Ozzy' Osbourne (vocals), Terence 'Geezer' Butler (bass) and Bill Ward (drums). It was with Black Sabbath that Iommi was to make his international reputation as a guitarist of skill and inventiveness. The Black Sabbath sound was built on the devastatingly powerful and heavy riffing style of Iommi, delivered with a fuzzy, distorted guitar tone that was to become his trademark. He was, and still is, the godfather of the heavy metal riff. Personal differences between Iommi and Osbourne contributed to the latter's departure from Black Sabbath in 1978, to be replaced by American Ronnie James Dio. After Dio's own departure in 1982, Black Sabbath entered a highly unstable phase, and it was Iommi who held the band together and kept the Black Sabbath name alive. Iommi has a unique soloing and rhythm style, and sports an unusual set of plastic finger extensions on his right hand as a result of an accident; (Iommi is left handed.) A tall, dark, moustachioed man, he is also famed for his lack of movement on stage. The album *Seventh Star* came out under the moniker of 'Black Sabbath Featuring Tony Iommi', according to record company wishes. Iommi, however, had intended it to be a solo album and so the songs had a slightly different emphasis than any pure Black Sabbath album.
Albums with Black Sabbath: *Black Sabbath* (1970), *Paranoid* (1971), *Master of Reality* (1971), *Volume 4* (1972), *Sabbath Bloody Sabbath* (1973), *Sabotage* (1975), *Live At Last* (1976), *Technical Ecstasy* (1977), *Never Say Die* (1978), *Heaven And Hell* (1980), *Mob Rules* (1981), *Live Evil* (1982), *Born Again* (1983), *Seventh Star* (1986), *Eternal Idol*

Iron Maiden

(1987), *Headless Cross* (1989), *Tyr* (1990).

Iron Maiden

Formed in London, England in the late 70s by bassist Steve Harris (b. 12 March 1957), Iron Maiden was from the start his brainchild. Named after a medieval torture device, the music was suitably heavy and hard on the senses. The heavy metal scene of the late 70s was regarded to be stagnant, even in decline, with only a handful of bands proving their ability to survive and produce music of long-term consistent quality. It was just at this time that a new breed of young British bands began to emerge. This movement, which really began to surge in 1979 and 1980, was known as the New Wave Of British Heavy Metal or NWOBHM. Iron Maiden were one of the foremost bands to come out of this genre. The bands of the NWOBHM were younger and meaner, dealing in faster, more energetic heavy metal than many of their forefathers. Other notable bands of the period included Saxon and Diamond Head. There were several line-up changes in the Iron Maiden ranks in the very early days, and come the release of their debut album, the members were Harris, Dave Murray (b. 23 December 1955; guitar), Dennis Stratton (guitar), Paul Dianno (vocals) and Clive Burr (b. 8 March 1957; drums). *Iron Maiden* was a roughly produced album, but did well and contained longstanding popular tracks such as 'Phantom Of The Opera' and UK hit single 'Running Free'. *Killers* was superior to the first album, and saw Dennis Stratton replaced by guitarist Adrian Smith (b. 27 February 1957). The album was a hit, and even at this stage, Iron Maiden were immensely popular among heavy metal fans, inspiring almost fanatical devotion.

The release of *Number Of The Beast* was crucial to the development of the band. Without it, Iron Maiden might never have gone on to be such a universal force in the field of heavy metal. The album was a spectacular success, the true sound of a band on the crest of a wave. It was also the debut of new vocalist Bruce Dickinson, replacing Paul Dianno. Singles such as 'The Number Of The Beast' and 'Run To The Hills' were big UK chart hits, and by this time Iron Maiden were leaving behind their NWOBHM counterparts in terms of success, just as the movement itself was beginning to fade out. *Piece Of Mind* continued their success and was a major hit in the USA (number 14).

Clive Burr was replaced by Nicko McBrain, formerly the drummer with French metal band Trust. *Piece Of Mind* was not dissimilar to the previous album; it showcased the strong twin guitar harmonic attack of Murray and Smith, coupled with memorable vocal lines while still retaining the all-important heaviness. The singles 'The Trooper' and 'Flight of Icarus' were instant hits. With *Powerslave* some critics accused Iron Maiden of conforming to a self-imposed writing formula, and playing safe with tried and tested ideas. There was no significant departure from the two previous albums, but it was accepted nonetheless, and further UK chart hits were had with the singles 'Aces High' and 'Two Minutes To Midnight'. *Live After Death* was a double live album, and was a watershed for the band. It was a good-value package of all their best-loved material from previous albums recorded live on a gargantuan world tour that saw them play to vast arenas of fans and enjoy incredible popularity. At this point, Iron Maiden had secured themselves an almost unassailable position on top of the metal scene across the world. *Somewhere In Time* was a slight departure for the band. It featured more melody than before, and heralded the use of guitar synthesizers. Their songwriting ability still shone through and the now obligatory hit singles were easily attained in the shape of 'Wasted Years' and 'Stranger In A Strange Land'. This album reached number 11 in the USA and was another million plus seller.

Since the mid-80s, Maiden had been staging increasingly spectacular live shows, with elaborate lighting effects and stage sets. The *Somewhere In Time* tour was no exception, ensuring their continuing attraction as a live band, the basis for much of their success. *Seventh Son Of A Seventh Son* was very much in the same vein as the previous album, with a slight progressive feel. A concept album, it still retained its commercial edge and yielded more hit singles including 'Can I Play With Madness' and 'The Clairvoyant'. After another exhausting mammoth world tour, the band announced their intention to take a well-earned break of at least a year. Speculation abounded that this meant the dissolution of the band, but it was not to be. After a considerable hiatus, news of the band surfaced again. Steve Harris felt that the direction pursued with the last two albums had been taken as far as was possible, and a return to the style of old was planned. Not wishing to pursue this heavier direction, Adrian Smith left to be replaced by Janick Gers, once guitarist with Gillan. The live show was also to be scaled down in a return to much smaller venues. *No Prayer For The Dying* was indeed much more like mid-period Iron Maiden, and was predictably well received, with enormous UK hit singles with 'Holy Smoke' and 'Bring Your Daughter To The Slaughter' which went straight to number 1. With an accompanying world tour, Iron Maiden remain one of the major attractions of the past decade.

Albums: *Iron Maiden* (1980), *Killers* (1981), *Number Of The Beast* (1982), *Piece Of Mind* (1983), *Powerslave* (1984), *Live After Death* (1985), *Somewhere In Time* (1986), *Seventh Son Of A Seventh Son* (1988), *No Prayer For The Dying* (1990).

Ironhorse

This US group was founded by Randy Bachman, formerly the leader of the Canadian rock group Bachman Turner Overdrive. The initial line-up comprised Bachman (guitar/vocals), John Pierce (bass), Tom Sparks (guitar/vocals) and Mike Baird (drums). They scored a US Top 40 hit in 1979 with 'Sweet Lui-Louise' and by the time the second album was recorded, the line-up had undergone a few alterations with Ron Foos and Chris Leighton replacing Pierce and Baird respectively. This largely undistinguished outfit were to record one further album, the title of which summed up the attitude of their critics.

Albums: *Ironhorse* (1979), *Everything Is Grey* (1980).

J

Jade

The first working unit of Jade was formed in Winnipeg, Canada in 1982. The original line-up consisted of Roxy Lyons (vocals), Pat Belrose (guitar), Terry Rudd (bass) and Dave Samson (drums). The band played on the local club circuit realizing soon a lack of any real rock scene. They decided to relocate to Ottawa where they quickly struck a one-off album deal with the small independent Zaphia Records label. Their debut *Teasing Eyes* released in 1984 was a mediocre release of jaded pop rock. Realizing their mistake in choice of locale they relocated once again, this time to Toronto where the rock scene was much livelier. Owing to disagreements on personal and professional matters Lyons left the band to be replaced by ex-Agressor vocalist Sweet Marie Black. The band worked hard on their songwriting, taking a more rocky approach and subsequent demos led to the band being signed by the Roadrunner Records label which released *If You're Man Enough* in 1985. With more rock and less pop, the album nevertheless failed to attract any real attention and the band sank in 1986.
Albums: *Teasing Eyes* (1984), *If You're Man Enough* (1985).

Jag Panzer

Formed in Colorado, USA in 1981 the band's original line-up consisted of the curiously-named The Tyrant (vocals), Mark Briody (guitar), John Tetley (bass) and Butch Carlson (drums). Quickly signing to the small independent Azra Records label their debut mini-album *Jag Panzer* was released in 1983. Basically a collection of demo tracks, it was a rough and ready affair of straight ahead power-metal inspired rock. The band decided to add an additional guitarist to give them an extra dimension, and with this in mind they decided to relocate to Los Angeles to seek young hopefuls. The band auditioned countless guitarists until Joey Tafolla was recruited. They headed straight back to Colorado to record their first full-length *Ample Destruction*, released in 1984. (This was later re-released in 1990 on Metalcore Records label). The album was an improvement on their debut, with Tafolla contributing guitar to the more memorable power-metal orientated material. Unfortunately, the album still only established the band as a strong underground act with minimal cult status. Dissatisfied with this lack of success, Tafolla left the outfit for a solo career and later went on to play in Alice Cooper's touring band. Shortly after his departure both The Tyrant and Carlson also left the band. The Tyrant joined Riot, albeit briefly, before forming his own band Titan Force. This left Briody and Tetley to pick up the pieces and reform the band. Joining them in this new incarnation of Jag Panzer were Bob Parduba (vocals), Christian Lasage (guitar) and Rikard Stjernqvist (drums). This line-up went on to record an impressive demo that secured them a new recording agreement with Auburn Records in 1987, resulting in *Chain Of Command* being released the same year.
Albums: *Jag Panzer* (mini-album 1983), *Ample Destruction* (1984), *Chain Of Command* (1987), *Ample Destruction* (reissue 1990).

Jagged Edge

This UK based quartet was formed in 1986 by guitarist Myke Gray. A series of personnel changes ensued before Andy Robbins (guitar), Fabio Del Rio (drums) and Matti Alfonzetti (vocals) arrived to cement the current line-up into place. Picked up by Polydor Records, their debut five-track mini-album was rushed out, and although it featured some fine guitar work, complemented by Gray and Alfonzetti's spine-tingling vocals, the songs were weak. *Fuel For Your Soul*, released later the same year was in a different class. Intricate solos, power-ballads and hard driving rock 'n' roll combined with a dynamic production by Jeff Glixman, indicating that the band had come of age.
Albums: *Trouble* (1990), *Fuel For Your Soul* (1990).

Jaguar

This band was formed in Bristol, England in 1979 and the original line-up comprised Rob Reiss (vocals), Garry Pepperd (guitar), Jeff Cox (bass) and Chris Lovell (drums). Early demos led to the band having a track included on the *Heavy Metal Heroes* compilation album. The unit attracted the attention of Neat Records which released two singles, 'Back Street Woman' and 'Axe Crazy' in 1981 and 1982 respectively. The band quickly gained popularity with their New Wave Of British Heavy Metal rooted speed metal. The single 'Axe Crazy' was the first release to feature new vocalist Paul Merrell who replaced Reiss. Merrell's powerful melodic voice was in fine form for the band's debut album *Powergames* released on the Neat Records label in 1983. The album was well received with its excellent vocal and guitar work over the high speed power-metal rhythms. The band quickly gained a strong following in Europe especially in The Netherlands where they toured extensively. However, this all changed with the band's drastic shift in musical style on their next album. After switching labels to Roadrunner Records, *This Time* was released in 1984. On this album the band had mellowed and slowed down considerably, playing melodic rock accompanied by the guest keyboard player Larry Dawson. The album was a failure and lost the band a lot of fans. Shortly after its release drummer Lovell was replaced by Gary Davies. However, owing to adverse press reaction the album received, the band folded in 1985.

Albums: *Powergames* (1983), *This Time* (1984).

Jetboy

This UK glam/sleaze rock quintet featured ex-Hanoi Rocks bassist Sam Yaffa, with Mickey Finn (vocals), Fernie Rod (guitar), Billy Rowe (guitar) and Ron Tostenson (drums) completing the line-up. Applying cosmetic surgery to the riffs of AC/DC, Poison and Aerosmith, they leaned towards the bluesier end of this genre. However, Jetboy failed to add the necessary sparkle to their material to make it memorable or commercially successful. Yaffa quit in 1990 to join forces with former Hanoi Rocks vocalist Michael Monroe, and Jetboy have been inactive since.

Albums: *Feel The Shake* (1988), *Damned Nation* (1990).

Jethro Tull

Jethro Tull

Jethro Tull was formed in Luton, England in 1967 when Ian Anderson (b. 10 August 1947, Edinburgh, Scotland; vocals/flute) and Glenn Cornick (b. 24 April 1947, Barrow-in-Furness, Cumbria, England; bass), members of a visiting Blackpool blues group, John Evan's Smash, became acquainted with Mick Abrahams (b. 7 April 1973, Luton, Bedfordshire, England; guitar/vocals) and Clive Bunker (b. 12 December 1946, Blackpool, Lancashire, England; drums), Abrahams' colleague in local attraction,

McGregor's Engine, completed the original line-up which made its debut in March the following year with 'Sunshine Day'. This commerically-minded single, erroneously credited to Jethro Toe, merely hinted at developments about to unfold. A residency at London's famed Marquee club and a sensational appearance at that summer's Sunbury Blues Festival confirmed a growing reputation, while 'Song For Jeffrey', the quartet's first release for the Island label, introduced a more representative sound. Abrahams' rolling blues licks and Anderson's distinctive, stylized voice combined expertly on *This Was* - for many Tull's finest collection. Although the material itself was derivative, the group's approach was highly exciting, with Anderson's propulsive flute playing, modelled on jazzman Raahsan Roland Kirk, particularly effective. The album reached the UK Top 10, largely on the strength of Tull's live reputation in which the singer played an ever-increasing role. His exaggerated gestures, long, wiry hair, ragged coat and distinctive, one-legged stance cultivated a compulsive stage personality to the extent that, for many spectators, Jethro Tull was the name of this extrovert frontman and the other musicians merely his underlings. This impression gained credence through the group's internal ructions. Mick Abrahams left in November 1968 and formed Blodwyn Pig. When future Black Sabbath guitarist Tony Iommi proved incompatible, Martin Barre (b. 17 November 1946) joined Tull for *Stand Up*, their excellent, chart-topping, second album. The group was then augmented by John Evan (b. 28 March 1948; keyboards), the first of Anderson's Blackpool associates to be invited into the line-up. *Benefit*, the last outwardly blues-based album, duly followed and this period was also marked by the group's three UK Top 10 singles, 'Living In The Past', 'Sweet Dream' (both 1969) and 'The Witch's Promise' (1970). Cornick then quit to form Wild Turkey and Jeffrey Hammond-Hammond (b. 30 July 1946), already a legend in Tull's lexicon through their debut single, 'Jeffrey Goes To Leicester Square' and 'For Michael Collins, Jeffrey And Me', was brought in for *Aqualung*. Possibly the group's best-known work, this ambitious concept album featured Anderson's musings on organized religion and contained several tracks which remained long-standing favourites, including 'My God' and 'Locomotive Breath'.

Clive Bunker, the last original member, bar Anderson, left in May 1971. A further John Evan-era acolyte, Barriemore Barlow (b. 10 September 1949), replaced him as Jethro Tull entered its most controversial period. Although *Thick As A Brick* topped the US chart and reached number 5 in the UK, critics began questioning Anderson's reliance on obtuse concepts. However, if muted for this release, the press reviled *A Passion Play*, damning it as pretentious, impenetrable and the product of an egotist and his neophytes. Such rancour obviously hurt. Anderson retorted by announcing an indefinite retirement, but continued success in America, where the album became Tull's second chart-topper, doubtlessly appeased his anger. *War Child*, a US number 2, failed to chart in the UK, although *Minstrel In The Gallery* proved more popular. *Too Old To Rock 'N' Roll, Too Young To Die* marked the departure of Hammond-Hammond in favour of John Glascock (b. 1953, London, England, d. 17 November 1979), formerly of the Gods, Toe Fat and Chicken Shack. Subsequent releases, *Songs From The Wood* and *Heavy Horses*, reflected a more pastoral sound as Anderson abandoned the gauche approach marking many of their predecessors. David Palmer, who orchestrated each Tull album, bar their debut, was added as a second keyboards player as the group embarked on another highly-successful phase culminating in November 1978 when a concert at New York's Madison Square Garden was simultaneously broadcast around the world by satellite. However, Glascock's premature death in 1979 during heart surgery ushered in a period of uncertainty, culminating in an internal re-alignment. In 1980 Anderson began a projected solo album, retaining Barre and new bassist Dave Pegg (ex-Fairport Convention), but adding Eddie Jobson (ex-Curved Air and Roxy Music; keyboards) and Marc Craney (drums). Longtime cohorts Barlow, Evan and Palmer were left to pursue their individual paths. The finished product, *A*, was ultimately issued under the Jethro Tull banner and introduced a productive period which saw two more group selections, plus Anderson's solo effort, *Walk Into Light*, issued within a two-year period. Since then Jethro Tull has continued to record and perform live, albeit on a lesser scale, using a nucleus of Anderson, Barre and Pegg. *Catfish Rising* in 1991, although a disappointing album was a return to their blues roots. The singer has also become a renowned entrepreneur, owning tracts of land on the west coast of Scotland and the highly-successful Strathaird Salmon processing plant.

Albums: *This Was* (1968), *Stand Up* (1969), *Benefit* (1970), *Aqualung* (1971), *Thick As A Brick* (1972), *A Passion Play* (1973), *War Child* (1974), *Minstrel In The Gallery* (1975), *Too Old To Rock 'N' Roll Too Young To Die* (1976), *Songs From The Wood* (1977), *Heavy Horses* (1978), *Live - Bursting Out* (1978), *Storm Watch* (1979), *A* (1980), *The Broadsword And The Beast* (1982), *Under Wraps* (1984), *Crest Of A Knave* (1987), *Rock Island* (1989), *Live At Hammersmith* (1991), *Catfish Rising* (1991). Compilations: *Living In The Past* (1972), *M.U.: Best Of Jethro Tull* (1976), *Repeat, The Best Of Jethro Tull - Volume II* (1977), *Original Masters* (1985), *20 Years Of Jethro Tull* (1988, box set). Ian Anderson solo: *Walk Into The Light* (1983).

Johnny Crash

Following the break up of Tokyo Blade, vocalist Vicki James Wright became disillusioned with the British rock scene and moved to Los Angeles in the search for compatible musicians. After a series of false starts, he finally stabilized a line-up of August Worchell and Christopher Stewart (guitars), Andy Rogers (bass) and Stephen Adamo (drums) under the name Johnny Crash. Blatantly parading influences such as Mötley Crüe, AC/DC and Kiss, they delivered a high-energy blast of streetwise, blues-based rock 'n' roll on their Tony Platt produced debut.

Albums: *Neighbourhood Threat* (1990).

Jojo

This Toto-style, German rock quartet was put together by former Tokyo guitarist Robby Musenbilcher and vocalist/guitarist Roko Kohlmeyer after working together as session musicians. Recruiting ex-Tokyo keyboard player Lothar Krell, vocalist George Liszt and ex-Saga drummer Curt Cress, they selected 11 tracks from the 40 they had written for inclusion on their debut album. Produced by Yes supremo Eddie Offord, the album was produced to high standards, it was sophisticated but ultimately rather clinical. It somehow lacked the necessary heart and soul to give the band real identity.

Album: *Jojo* (1988).

Josefus

This band was formed in Houston, Texas, USA, in 1969, and comprised of Pete Bailey (vocals/harmonica), Dave Mitchell (guitar), Ray Turner (bass) and Doug Tull (drums). They had previously worked together as United Gas and were also briefly known as Come, under which name they recorded 'Crazy Man'/'Country Boy', before adopting the above appellation. The self-financed *Dead Man* featured a hard-rock version of the Rolling Stones 'Gimme Shelter', but is also notable for its lengthy title track. The heavy-styled follow-up, *Josefus*, was a comparative disappointment, and despite an undoubted popularity in Texas, the group was unable to reach a wider audience. They split up in December 1970, although Bailey and Turner were reunited in Stone Axe. In 1978 the vocalist rejoined Mitchell in a reformed Josefus which completed two singles – 'Hard Luck' and 'Let Me Move You' – on their recativated Hookah label before disbanding again.

Albums: *Dead Man* (1969), *Josefus* (1970).

Joshua

This American band was formed by Joshua Pehahia (guitar/vocals) in 1981 after he had left Blind Alley. In the early days there was never a constant line-up except for singer Stephen Fontaine, who possessed a vocal range of four octaves. It was Perahia and Fontaine, plus two more acquaintances, who recorded the mini-album, *The Hand Is Quicker Than The Eye* released in 1982 by Olympic Records. The title was suggested by one of the studio engineers who saw Perahia's dexterity on the fret board. After the album's release, Joshua attempted to tour, but found it impractical due to frequent personnel changes and no more than four dates were done with the same line-up. In 1984 Joshua were signed to the Polydor label in America with Perahia (guitar/vocals), Kenneth Tamplin (guitar/vocals), Patrick Bradley (keyboards/vocals), Loren Robinson (bass/vocals), Jo Galletta (drums) and Jeff Fenholt (lead vocals). Perahia produced the album and all the song arrangements. *Surrender* was released in 1985 and contained classy American hard rock, but the European arm of Polydor was not interested and the album ended up being released in Europe by FM Revolver Records. Fenholt was not a permanent member of the band and left after the album was finished. Gregory Valesco joined them as vocalist for touring. Tamplin went to form his own unit Shout. Joshua then signed to RCA Records with completely different personnel: Perahia (guitar/vocals), Bob Rock (lead vocals), Greg Schultz (keyboards/vocals), Emil Lech (bass) and Tim Gehrt (drums). These members recorded *Intense Defence*, which was slightly more restrained. Bob Rock helped to raise the level of the songwriting and their future looked good. However, Rock, Schultz and Lech left the band after the recording was finished, and formed their own band, Driver.

Albums: *The Hand Is Quicker Than The Eye* (1982), *Surrender* (1985), *Intense Defense* (1988).

Journey

This US rock group was formed in 1973 by ex-Santana members Neil Schon (guitar) and Greg Rolie (keyboards) plus Ross Valory (ex-Steve Miller band; bass) and Aynsley Dunbar (drums). George Tickner was added later as rhythm guitarist and lead vocalist. On New Year's Eve the same year, they made their live debut in front of 10,000 people at San Fransisco's Winterland. The following day they played to 10 times as many at an open-air festival in Hawaii. Initially they specialized in jazz-rock, complete with extended and improvised solo spots. This style can clearly be heard on their first three albums. The switch to highly sophisticated pomp-rock occurred with the recording of *Infinity*. At this juncture, Tickner left and was replaced by ex-Alien Project vocalist Steve Perry. In addition, Roy Thomas Baker was brought in as producer to give the band's sound a punchy and dynamic edge. The album was a huge success reaching number 21 on the Billboard album charts. Dunbar was unhappy with this new style and quit, to be replaced by Steve Smith. *Evolution* followed and brought the band their first Top 20 hit, 'Lovin', Touchin', Squeezin''. *Captured* was a double live album that surprised many of the critics, being far removed from their technically excellent and clinically produced studio releases; instead, it featured cranked-up guitars and raucous hard rock, eventually peaking at number 9 in the US album chart. Founder member Rolie departed after its release, to be replaced by Jonathan Cain, who had previously played with the Babys. Cain's arrival was an important landmark in Journey's career, as his input on the writing side added a new dimension to the bands sound. *Escape* was the pinnacle of the band's success, reaching number 1 and staying in the chart for over a year. It also spawned three US Top 10 hit singles in the form of 'Who's Crying Now', 'Don't Stop Believin'', and 'Open Arms'. The follow-up *Frontiers* was also successful, staying for nine weeks at the number 2 position on the Billboard album chart; 'Separate Ways', culled as a single from it climbed to number 8 in the US singles chart.

After a series of internal disputes the band reduced to a three-man nucleus of Schon, Cain and Perry to record *Raised On Radio*. This was to become Journey's last album, before Schon and Cain joined forces with John Waite's Bad English in 1988. A Greatest Hits compilation was posthumously released to commemorate the band's demise.

Albums: *Journey* (1975), *Look Into The Future* (1976), *Next* (1977), *Infinity* (1978), *Evolution* (1979), *In The Beginning* (1979), *Departure* (1980), *Dream After Dream* (1980), *Captured* (1981), *Escape* (1981), *Frontiers* (1983), *Raised On Radio* (1986). Compilation: *Greatest Hits* (1988).

Judas Priest

This group was formed in Birmingham, England, in 1970 by guitarist K.K. Downing and close

Judas Priest

friend, bassist Ian Hill. As another hopeful, struggling young rock band, they played their first gig in Essington in 1971 with a line-up completed by Alan Atkins (vocals) and John Ellis (drums). The name Judas Priest came from Atkins's previous band before he joined up with Hill and Downing, but it was retained as the best choice. Consistent gigging continued with Alan Moore taking over on drums only to be replaced at the end of 1971 by Chris Campbell. 1972 was spent mostly on the road in the UK, and in 1973 both Atkins and Campbell departed leaving the nucleus of Hill and Downing once more. At this point, their fortunes took a turn for the better. Vocalist Rob Halford and drummer John Hinch from the band Hiroshima joined the unit. More UK shows followed as the bands following grew steadily. In 1974 the they toured abroad for the first time in Germany and the Netherlands, and returned home to a record deal with the small UK label, Gull. The band recruited second guitarist Glenn Tipton and then in September 1974, *Rocka Rolla* was released. They were very disappointed with the recording, and the album failed to make any impact.

In 1975, the bands appearance at the Reading Festival went down well. Hinch left at this point to be replaced by the returning Alan Moore. *Sad Wings Of Destiny*, was an improvement on the debut, having been produced by the band. The album received good reviews, but their financial situation was desperate.

A worldwide contract with CBS saved the day, and *Sin After Sin* was a strong and positive album, with Simon Philips sitting in for the departed Moore. The band then visited America for the first time with drummer Les Binks, who appears on *Stained Class*, an album which showed Priest going from strength to strength. *Killing Machine* yielded the first UK hit single 'Take On The World', and featured shorter, punchier, but still extremely heavy songs. *Unleashed In The East* was recorded on the 1979 Japanese tour, and in that year, Les Binks was replaced on drums by Dave Holland of Trapeze. After major tours with both Kiss and AC/DC, Priest's popularity was beginning to gather momentum. *British Steel* smashed into the UK album charts at number 3, and contained the hit singles 'Breaking The Law' and 'Living After Midnight'. After appearing at the 1980 Castle Donington Monsters of Rock festival, they began recording *Point Of Entry*. It provided the hit single 'Hot Rockin', and was followed by sell-out UK and US tours. The period surrounding *Screaming For Vengeance* was phenomenally successful for the band. The hit single 'You've Got Another Thing Comin'' was followed by a lucrative six month US

tour with the album going platinum in the USA. *Screaming For Vengeance* was Priest's heaviest album, and *Defenders Of The Faith* did well to match it. *Turbo* was slightly more commercial and not particularly well received. *Ram It Down* was pure heavy metal by comparison, but by this time their popularity had begun to wane. Dave Holland was replaced by Scott Travis for *Painkiller* which was a *bone fide* return to form. Although not as universally popular as before, Priest were still a big live attraction and a top class metal band. Judas Priest are in many ways the epitome of heavy metal; screaming guitars and screaming vocalist, all clad in studs and leather. They laid the groundwork for much of the metal genre, and it is their enduring talent and popularity that has made them known worldwide as one of the ultimate metal bands.

Albums: *Rocka Rolla* (1974), *Sad Wings Of Destiny* (1976), *Sin After Sin* (1977), *Stained Class* (1978), *Killing Machine* (1978), *Unleashed In The East* (1979), *British Steel* (1980), *Point Of Entry* (1981), *Screaming For Vengeance* (1982), *Defenders Of The Faith* (1984), *Turbo* (1986), *Priest Live* (1987), *Ram It Down* (1988), *Painkiller* (1990).

Juggernaut

Formed in Texas, California, USA in 1985, the band's original line-up consisted of Harlan Glenn (vocals), Eddie Katilius (guitar), Scott Womack (bass) and Bobby Jarzombek (drums). They signed to the Metal Blade Records label and had an early demo track included on the *Metal Massacre VII* compilation album, their debut *Baptism Under Fire* was released in 1986. Their music was as the band name suggests, very heavy. The outfit received little attention from the media and Glen soon left the band to be replaced by Steve Cooper in time for *Trouble Within* was released in 1987 and also made little impact. Owing to this lack of success the band folded early in 1988.

Albums: *Baptism Under Fire* (1986), *Trouble Within* (1987).

Junkyard

This five-piece USA combo was made up of seasoned Los Angeles club circuit musicians. Formed in 1988 they comprised of David Roach (vocals), Chris Gates and Brian Baker (guitars), Clay Anthony (bass) and Patrick Muzingo (drums). Signing to Geffen Records, their debut offering featured 'trashy metallic boogie'. Two years later, *Sixes Sevens And Nines* emerged and the songwriting partnership of Roach and Gates had matured considerably, with the emphasis now on the music rather than the image. Musically, Junkyard slide in somewhere between Great

White, Dokken and Z.Z. Top, dealing in abrasive raunch 'n' roll. Producer Ed Stasium achieved a harder and bluesier sound, without pushing them in a blatantly commercial direction.

Albums: *Junkyard* (1989), *Sixes, Sevens And Nines* (1991).

K

Kat

The self-proclaimed 'Great Kat' began her musical career as a classically trained violinist. After six years of solid practising and performing on the instrument, she switched to the guitar and began experimenting with a fusion of classical and rock music. Adopting a high-speed technique, she concentrated on short instrumentals. *Worship Me Or Die* was poorly received. Undaunted she released *Beethoven On Speed*, which marked a considerable improvement in both musical and production terms. Promoting herself as a grotesque parody of a 'wild woman of rock' fell flat with UK audiences and, despite her potential to produce an innovative metal/classical crossover album, little has been heard from the artist since.
Albums: *Worship Me Or Die* (1987), *Beethoven On Speed* (1990).

Kik Tracee

This US hard-rock quintet was formed in 1990 by Stephen Shareux (vocals) and Michael Marquis (guitar). The line-up was completed by the addition of Rob Grad (bass), Gregory Hex (rhythm guitar) and Johnny Douglas (drums). Picked up by RCA Records, they debuted in 1991 with *No Rules*, a varied and uncompromising collection of mature rock numbers which, in an unusual choice of cover material, included a version of Simon And Garfunkel's 'Mrs. Robinson'.
Album: *No Rules* (1991).

Kill For Thrills

Hailing from Los Angeles, California, USA, this group delivered a familiar trademark sound best described as 'sleaze rock'. Featuring the talents of Gilby Clarke (vocals/guitar), Jason Nesmith (guitar), Todd Muscat (bass) and David Scott (drums) their 1990 debut, *Dynamite From Nightmare Land* was a prime example of no-nonsense standard chord hard-rock. The album was produced by Vic Maile and Ric Browde who are renowned, respectively, for their work with Motorhead and Poison.
Album: *Dynamite From Nightmare Land* (1990).

Killers

This UK quintet were put founded in 1991 by former Iron Maiden vocalist Paul Di'Anno. Recruiting Steve Hopgood (drums), Cliff Evans (guitar), Gavin Cooper (bass) and Nick Burr (guitar) their approach is firmly rooted in the New Wave Of British Heavy Metal movement of the early 80s. Murder One, released in early 1992 was rather anachronistic, sounding virtually identical to early Iron Maiden, Judas Priest and at times shades of Accept crept in.
Album: Murder One (1992).

King Diamond

The group Mercyful Fate split into two separate factions in March 1985. Vocalist King Diamond, Michael Denner (guitar) and Timi Hansen (bass) wanted to pursue their obsession with satanic heavy metal and the occult, while the others sought a more mainstream and commercial direction. King Diamond's music was characterized by supernatural storylines, high-pitched, banshee-like vocals and meandering guitar work. On live performances, he specialized in cheap and amateurish theatrics to bring the songs to life. This included face make-up, not dissimilar to Alice Cooper. Since 1985, there have been numerous line-up changes, but the most successful and long-lived have included Andy La Roque (guitar), Pete Blakk (guitar), Hal Patino (bass) and Snowey Shaw (drums). Each successive album has had even more complex plots and sub-themes, resulting in them being the musical equivalent of a sinister version of Dungeons and Dragons.
Albums: *Fatal Portrait* (1986), *Abigail* (1987), *Them* (1988), *The Dark Sides* (1988), *Conspiracy* (1989), *The Eye* (1990).

King Kobra

After departing as drummer in Ozzy Osbourne's band in 1984, Carmen Appice decided to form his own outfit, under the King Kobra monicker. Enlisting the services of four relative unknowns, Mark Free (vocals), David Michael-Phillips (guitar), Mike Sweda (guitar) and Johnny Rod (bass), he negotiated a deal with EMI Records, which eventually resulted in *Ready To Strike* in 1985. This hard-rock album was full of infectious hooks and pyrotechnic guitar breaks. On the strength of this release they were offered the chance to write the theme music for the film, *Iron Eagle*. They changed styles at this juncture, switching to a more sophisticated and lightweight AOR approach. As a consequence of this, album sales dried up and they were dropped by their label. Johnny Rod left to join W.A.S.P. and the band fell apart. A few months later, the nucleus of Appice and Michael-Phillips rebuilt the band with the addition of ex-Montrose vocalist Johnny Edwards, Jeff Northrup (guitar) and Larry Hart (bass). They returned to their former hard-rock

King Kobra

origins and released *King Kobra III* on the independent MFN label, but it was again poorly received. The band finally became obsolete when Appice left to join John Sykes's Blue Murder project in 1989.

Albums: *Ready To Strike* (1985), *Thrill Of A Lifetime* (1987), *King Kobra III* (1988).

Kings X

Initially known as the Edge and specializing in Top 40 cover versions, Doug Pinnick (bass/vocals), Ty Tabor (guitar) and Jerry Gaskell (drums) relocated to Houston, Texas, USA in 1985 and were taken under the wing of Z.Z. Top video producer, Sam Taylor. Under Taylor's guidance, they concentrated on their own material and changed their name to Kings X. After recording several demos and being turned down by several major record companies in the USA, they finally secured a deal with the independent Megaforce label. Out Of The Silent Planet, with its unique sound and off-beat approach, emerged in 1988 to widespread critical acclaim. Fusing Beatles' style harmonies with hard-rock and blues riffs, they encompassed a variety of genres that defied simple pigeon-holing. Gretchen Goes To Nebraska was an even greater triumph, building on previous strengths, but adding depth in both a

technical and lyrical sense. Faith, Hope, Love, released in 1990, scaled even greater heights with its state-of-the-art production and inspired compositions.

Albums: Out Of The Silent Planet (1987), Gretchen Goes To Nebraska (1989), Faith, Hope, Love (1990).

Kiss

Kiss

Following the demise of Wicked Lester, Kiss was formed in 1972 by Paul Stanley (b. Stanley Eisen, 20 January 1950, New York, USA; rhythm guitar/vocals) and Gene Simmons, (b. Gene Klein, 25 August 1949, New York, USA; bass/vocals) who went on to recruit Peter Criss (b. Peter Crisscoula, 20 December 1945, New York, USA; drums/vocals) and Ace Frehley (b. Paul Frehley, 27 April 1950, New York, USA; lead guitar/vocals) At their second show at the Hotel Diplomat, Manhattan, 1973, Flipside producer, Bill Aucoin offered the band a management deal, and within two weeks they were signed to Neil Bogart's recently established Casablanca Records. In just over a year, Kiss had released their first three albums with a modicum of success. In the summer of 1975 their fortunes changed with the release of *Alive* which spawned their first US hit single 'Rock 'N' Roll All Nite'. The appeal of Kiss has always been based on their live shows: the garish greasepaint make-up, outrageous costumes, and over-the-top pyrotechnic stage effects, along with their hard-rocking anthems, combined to create what was billed as 'The Greatest Rock 'n' Roll Show On Earth'. The live success caused a dramatic upswing in record sales, and *Alive* became their first certified platinum album in the USA. *Destroyer* proved just as successful, and also gave them their first US Top 10 single, earning Peter Criss a major songwriting award for the uncharacteristic ballad 'Beth'. Subsequent releases *Rock And Roll Over*, *Love Gun* (their first album to attain platinum status in the USA), and *Alive II* confirmed Kiss as major recording artists.

By 1977 Kiss had topped the prestigious Gallup poll as the most popular act in the USA. They had become a marketer's dream. Kiss merchandise included: make-up kits, masks, board games, and pinball machines. *Marvel Comics* produced two super-hero cartoon books, and even a full length science-fiction film, *Kiss Meet The Phantom Of The Park* was produced. The ranks of their fan club, the Kiss Army, had swollen to a six figure number. In 1978, all four group members each produced a solo album which were released on the same day, a feat never before achieved and never since matched. This represented the biggest shipment of albums from one 'unit' to record stores in the history of music. The albums received a varying degree of success; Ace Frehley's record came out on top and included the US hit single 'New York Groove'. Gene Simmons, whose album featured an impressive line-up of guests, including Cher, Donna Summer, Bob Seger and Janis Ian, had a hit single in the UK with 'Radioactive', which reached Number 41 in 1978. After the release of *Dynasty* in 1979, which featured the worldwide hit single 'I Was Made For Lovin' You', cracks appeared in the ranks. Peter Criss left to be replaced by session player Anton Fig, who had previously appeared on Ace Frehley's solo album. Fig played drums on the 1980 release *Unmasked* until a permanent replacement was found in the form of New York born, Eric Carr, who made his first appearance during the world tour of 1980. Carr's debut appearance came on *Music From The Elder*, an album that represented a radical departure from traditional Kiss music and included several ballads, an orchestra and a choir. It was a brave attempt to break new ground but failed to capture the imagination of the record-buying public. Frehley, increasingly disenchanted with the musical direction of the band finally left in 1983. The two albums prior to his departure had featured outside musicians. Bob Kulick, who had contributed to the studio side of *Alive II* and played on Stanley's solo album, supported the lead work to the four previously unreleased tracks on the *Killers* compilation of 1982 and Vincent Cusano (later to become Vinnie Vincent) was responsible for the lead guitar on the 1982 release, *Creatures Of The Night*. By 1983, the popularity of the band was waning and drastic measures were called for.

The legendary make-up which had concealed their true identities for almost 10 years was removed on MTV in the USA. Vinnie Vincent made his first official appearance on *Lick It Up*, an album which saw Kiss with their first Top 10 hit in the UK. The resurgence of the band continued with *Animalize*. Vincent had been replaced by Mark St. John (b. Mark Norton) who was a seasoned session player and guitar tutor. His association with the band was short lived for he was tragically struck down by Reiters Syndrome. Bruce Kulick, the brother of long-time Kiss cohort Bob, was drafted in as a temporary replacement on the 1984 European Tour and subsequently became a permanent member when it became apparent that St. John would not be able to continue as a band member. Further commercial success was achieved with *Asylum* and *Crazy Nights*, the latter featuring their biggest UK hit single 'Crazy, Crazy Nights' which peaked at number 4 in 1987 and this was followed by a further two Top 40 hit singles 'Reason To Live' and 'Turn On The Night'. *Hot In The Shade* succeeded their third compilation album, *Smashes, Thrashes And Hits,* and included their highest charting hit single in the US, 'Forever', which reached number 4 in 1990. Work on a new Kiss album with producer Bob Ezrin was delayed following Eric Carr's illness due to complications from cancer. He died in 1991, in New York at the age of 41. Despite this setback, Kiss contributed a cover of Argent's classic 'God Gave Rock 'N' Roll To You' to the soundtrack of the film, *Bill And Ted's Bogus Journey*. With a history spanning three decades, Kiss have been one of the most influential groups in hard-rock history.

Albums: *Kiss* (1974), *Hotter Than Hell* (1974), *Dressed to Kill* (1975), *Alive* (1975), *Destroyer* (1976), *Rock And Roll Over* (1976), *Love Gun* (1977), *Alive II* (1977), *Dynasty* (1979), *Unmasked* (1980), *Music From The Elder* (1981), *Creatures Of The Night* (1982), *Lick It Up* (1983), *Animalize* (1984), *Asylum* (1985), *Crazy Nights* (1987), *Hot In The Shade* (1989), *Revenge* (1992). Compilations: *Double Platinum* (1978), *Killers* (1982), *Smashes, Thrashes And Hits* (1988), *Revenge* (1992).

Kiss Of The Gypsy

This UK, melodic hard-rock quintet (formerly known as Fantasia) was formed in Blackpool, Lancashire in 1990, by Tony Mitchell (vocals/guitar) and Martin Talbot (bass). With the addition of Darren Rice (guitar), George Williams (keyboards) and Scott Ellliot (drums) they signed to Atlantic the following year. The band's music is blues-rock based, with a sense of energy similar to that of Bad Company or Whitesnake. Following successful support slots to Winger, Magnum and Great White, the band released their self-titled debut album on the WEA/East West label in 1992. The band are widely regarded as being one of the most promising British outfits to emerge since Def Leppard.

Album: *Kiss Of The Gypsy* (1992).

Kix

Kix

This US group was formed by Donnie Purnell (bass) and Ronnie Younkins (guitar) in 1980. After experimenting with a number of line-ups, Steve Whiteman (vocals), Brian Forsythe (guitar) and Jimmy Chalfant (drums) were drafted in on a permanent basis. Their style was typically American east coast, being a brash amalgam of influences that included Mötley Crüe, AC/DC and Kiss. Securing a contract with Atlantic Records in 1981, their first two albums were a touch derivative and poorly promoted. Midnight Dynamite however, produced by Beau Hill (who had previously worked with Ratt) attracted some attention, and the band were given the support slot on Aerosmith's 1985 USA tour. Blow My Fuse and Hot Wire received a good reception on both sides of the Atlantic, with the band maturing as songwriters and starting to develop an identity of their own.

Albums: Atomic Bomb (1981), Cool Kids (1983), Midnight Dynamite (1985), Blow My Fuse (1988), Hot Wire (1991).

Kotzen, Richie

This highly gifted, new-age rock guitar god was very much in the Joe Satriani mould. By the time Kotzen had reached his seventh birthday, he had moved from piano to guitar lessons, and was playing live with his own band, Arthur's Museum, when he entered his teens. Taken under the wing of Mike Varney, he was introduced to bassist Stuart Hamm and ex-Journey drummer Steve Smith, to record a solo instrumental album. This showcased Kotzen's inherent ability and feel for the electric guitar, but also highlighted the limitations of rock music without vocals. Realizing this, he formed Fever Dream, a power-trio comprising Danny Thompson (bass), Atma Anur (drums) and himself on guitar and vocals.

Although the guitar breaks were excellent, there was a paucity of hooks to latch onto and a scarcity of real tunes.

Albums: *Richie Kotzen* (1989), *Fever Dream* (1990).

Kreator

Formed in Essen, Germany in 1984, under the name of Tormentor, this heavy metal band comprised Mille Petroza (guitar/vocals), Rob (bass) and Ventor (drums). Their vicious thrash style was fired by the filth and industrial pollution problem that Essen, on the River Ruhr, was experiencing. After changing their name to Kreator, they signed with Germany-based label Noise, and their debut album *Endless Pain* appeared in 1985. Despite roughshod production, it was eagerly received by fans of the then fast-growing thrash-metal scene. After the release of *Pleasure To Kill*, Kreator became one of the most popular bands of the genre, especially in Europe. Lyrically, Kreator have always dealt with the darker side of life and have never wavered from their musical path, endearing them to fans who have helped maintain their place in the crowded and highly competitive field of thrash and death metal. They have gone through a number of second guitarists, settling on Frank Blackfire, once with fellow German thrash metallers Sodom.

Albums: *Endless Pain* (1985), *Pleasure to Kill* (1986), *Terrible Certainty* (1988), *Out Of The Dark Into The Light* (1989), *Extreme Aggression* (1989), *Coma Of Souls* (1990).

Krokus

Hailing from Soluthurn, Switzerland, Krokus appeared in 1974 playing symphonic rock similar to Yes, Genesis and Emerson, Lake And Palmer. After four years and two rather lacklustre albums they switched to a hard-rock style and dropped all the frills, in favour of a back-to-basics approach in the mode of AC/DC. The group comprised Chris Von Rohr (vocals), Fernando Von Arb (guitar), Jurg Naegeli (bass), Tommy Kiefer (guitar) and Freddy Steady (drums). The songs were formula numbers based on simple riffs and predictable choruses that were chanted repeatedly. With Von Rohr's voice lacking the necesary vocal range, he stepped down to became the bass player, in favour of the new arrival Maltezer Marc. Naegeli occasionally played keyboards and took over the technical side of the band. *Metal Rendez-vous* was the turning point in the band's career; released in 1980, it was heavier than anything they had done before and coincided with resurgence of heavy metal in Britain. They played the Reading Festival in 1980 and were well received. Their next two albums continued the aggressive approach, but

Krokus

they streamlined their sound to make it more radio-friendly. *Hardware* and *One Vice At A Time* made the UK album charts at numbers 44 and 28, respectively. Before *Headhunter* materialized, a series of personnel changes took place. The most important of these was the addition of Mark Storace (lead vocals), Mark Kohler (guitar) and Steve Pace (drums). Produced by Tom Allom, *Headhunter*'s high-speed, heavy-duty approach propelled it to number 25 in the *Billboard* album charts. Further line-up changes delayed the release of *The Blitz*, an erratic album, which reached number 31 on the US chart mainly on the strength of its predecessor. Since 1985, there has been a continuing downward trend in the band's fortunes, as their personnel has been in a constant state of flux. Their music has progressed little during the last decade and relies heavily, even today, on the legacy of AC/DC and the Scorpions.

Albums: *Krokus* (1975), *To You All* (1977), *Painkiller* (1978), *Metal Rendez-vous* (1980), *Hardware* (1981), *One Vice At A Time* (1982), *Headhunter* (1983), *The Blitz* (1984), *Change Of Address* (1985), *Alive And Screamin'* (1986), *Heart Attack* (1987), *Stampede* (1990).

L

(1989), *Hollywood Vampires* (1991).

Last Crack

This Wisconsin, US band specialized in schizophrenic 'acid-metal', a truly unique experience that desecrates all musical boundaries from thrash to blues, then back through funk, psychedelia and rock 'n' roll. Lead vocalist, Buddo caterwauls with a mixture of gut-wrenching passion, over-the-top flamboyance and deranged eccentricity. The backbeat is equally unpredictable, with guitarists Pablo Schuter and Don Bakken switching and blending styles with consummate ease. Phil Buerstate (drums) and Todd Winger (bass) provided the necessary power in the rhythm section. The latter was replaced by Dave Truehardt in 1990.
Albums: *Sinister Funkhouse #17* (1989), *Burning Time* (1991).

Leatherwolf

The origins of this Californian quintet date back to 1983 when Michael Olivieri (vocals/guitar), Geoff Gayer (guitar), Carey Howe (guitar), Matt Hurich (bass) and Dean Roberts (drums) were at high school together. Influenced by a range of styles from hard rock to jazz, they recorded a self-titled, five-track mini-album that attracted the attention of Island Records. Matt Hurich was replaced by Paul Carman before they left to record their second album in the Bahamas, under the guidance of REO Speedwagon producer Kevin Beamish. *Street Ready* avoided the pitfalls of their previous release. Developing their own identity, they ventured into the pop-metal crossover market. Beamish achieved a harder and more powerful sound this time, but with an added dimension of accessibility and the potential for commercial success.
Albums: *Leatherwolf* i (1986), *Leatherwolf* ii (1987), *Street Ready* (1989).

Led Zeppelin

This pivotal quartet was formed in October 1968 by British guitarist Jimmy Page (b. 9 January 1944, Heston, Middlesex, England) on the demise of his former band, the Yardbirds. John Paul Jones (b. John Baldwin, 31 January 1946, London, England; bass/keyboards), a respected arranger and session musician, replaced original member Chris Dreja, but hopes to incorporate vocalist Terry Reid floundered on a contractual impasse. The singer unselfishly recommended Robert Plant (b. 26 August 1947, Birmingham, England), then frontman of struggling Midlands act Hobbstweedle, who in turn introduced drummer, John Bonham (b. 31 May 1947, Birmingham,

L.A. Guns

L.A. Guns

This US group was formed by ex-Guns N' Roses guitarist Tracii Guns and ex-Girl vocalist Phil Lewis in Los Angeles, 1987. Working on material that was a hybrid of glam-rock, sleaze and blues-based rock 'n' roll, they signed with PolyGram Records in the USA the following year. With the addition of Mick Cripps (guitar), Kelly Nickels (bass) and Steve Riley, (drums, ex-W.A.S.P.) the line-up was complete. However, with Riley arriving too late to appear on their self-titled debut, the group used the services of Nickey Alexander. *Cocked And Loaded* was a marked improvement over its predecessor; the band had matured as songwriters and Lewis's vocals were stronger and more convincing. *Hollywood Vampires* saw the band diversifying musically, but retaining the essential energy and rough edges for which they had become renowned. Initially labelled as Guns N' Roses clones, they have evolved considerably since their inception and now have a style of their own.
Albums: *L.A. Guns* (1988), *Cocked And Loaded*

Leatherwolf

England, d. 25 September 1980) when first choice B.J. Wilson opted to remain with Procol Harum. The quartet gelled immediately and having completed outstanding commitments under the name 'New Yardbirds', became Led Zeppelin following an off-the-cuff quip by the Who's Keith Moon, who remarked when rating their prospects that they would probably go down like a lead Zeppelin.

Armed with a prestigious contract with Atlantic Records, the group toured the USA supporting Vanilla Fudge prior to the release of their explosive debut *Led Zeppelin*, which included several exceptional original songs, including; 'Good Times, Bad Times', 'Communication Breakdown', 'Dazed And Confused' - a hold-over from the Yardbirds' era, and skilled interpretations of R&B standards 'How Many More Times?' and 'You Shook Me'. The set vied with Jeff Beck's *Truth* as the definitive statement of English heavy blues/rock, but Page's meticulous production showed a greater grasp of basic pop dynamics, resulting in a clarity redolent of 50s rock 'n' roll. His staggering dexterity was matched by Plant's expressive, beseeching voice, a combination that flourished on *Led Zeppelin II*. The group was

already a headline act, drawing sell-out crowds across the USA, when this propulsive collection confirmed an almost peerless position. The introductory track, 'Whole Lotta Love', a thinly-veiled rewrite of Willie Dixon's 'You Need Love', has since become a classic, while 'Livin' Lovin' Maid' and 'Moby Dick', Bonham's exhibition piece, were a staple part of the quartet's early repertoire. Elsewhere, 'Thank You' and 'What Is And What Should Never Be' revealed a greater subtlety, a factor emphasized more fully on *Led Zeppelin III*. Preparation for this set had been undertaken at Bron-Y-Aur cottage in Snowdonia (immortalized in 'Bron-Y-Aur Stomp') and a resultant pastoral atmosphere permeated the acoustic-based selections, 'That's The Way' and 'Tangerine'. 'The Immigrant Song' and 'Gallow's Pole' reasserted the group's traditional fire and the album's release confirmed Led Zeppelin's position as one of the world's leading attractions. In concert, Plant's sexuality and Adonis-like persona provided the perfect foil to Page's more mercurial character, yet both individuals took full command of the stage, the guitarist's versatility matched only by the singer's unfettered roar.

Confirmation of the group's ever-burgeoning

Led Zepplin

strengths appeared on *Led Zeppelin IV*, also known as 'Four Symbols', the 'Runes Album' or 'Zoso', in deference to the fact the set bore no official title. It included the anthemic 'Stairway To Heaven', a *tour de force*, viewed as the unit's finest performance and which became their in-concert finale in 1975. The latter song is arguably the definitive heavy-rock song, it continues to win polls and the memorable inroduction remains every guitar novice's first hurdle. The approbation granted this ambitious piece initially obscured other contents, but the propulsive 'When The Levee Breaks' is now lauded as a masterpiece, particularly for Bonham's drumming, which later became the subject of widespread sampling. 'Black Dog' and 'Rock 'N' Roll' were Zeppelin at their immediate energetic best, while 'The Battle Of Evermore' was marked by a contribution by singer Sandy Denny. However, the effusive praise this album generated was notably more muted for *Houses Of The Holy*. Critics queried its musically diverse selection - the set embraced folksy ballads, reggae and soul - yet when the accustomed power was unleashed, notably on 'No Quarter', the effect was inspiring.

A concurrent US tour broke all previous attendance records, the proceeds from which helped finance an in-concert film, issued in 1976 as *The Song Remains The Same*, and the formation of the group's own record label, Swan Song, allowed Led Zeppelin total artistic freedom. Bad Company, the Pretty Things and Maggie Bell were also signed to the company. *Physical Graffiti*, a double set, gave full rein to the quartet's diverse interests with material ranging from compulsive hard-rock ('Custard Pie' and 'Sick Again') to pseudo-mystical experimentation ('Kashmir'). The irrepressible 'Trampled Underfoot' joined an ever-growing lexicon of peerless performances while 'In My Time Of Dying' showed an undiminished grasp of progressive blues. Sell-out appearances in the UK followed the release, but rehearsals for a projected world tour were abandoned in August 1975 when Plant sustained multiple injuries in a car crash. A new album was prepared during his period of convalescence, although problems over artwork delayed its release. Advance orders alone assured *Presence* platinum status, yet the set was regarded as a disappointment and UK sales were noticeably weaker. The 10-minute maelstrom, 'Achilles Last Stand', was indeed a remarkable performance, but the remaining tracks were competent rather than fiery and lacked the accustomed sense of grandeur. In 1977, Led Zeppelin began its rescheduled US tour, but on 26 July news reached Robert Plant that his six-year-old son, Karac, had died of a viral infection. The remaining dates were cancelled amid speculation that the group would break up.

They remained largely inactive for over a year, but late in 1978 flew to Abba's Polar recording complex in Stockholm. Although lacking the definition of earlier work, *In Through The Out Door* was a strong collection on which John Paul Jones emerged as the unifying factor. Two concerts at Britain's Knebworth Festival were the prelude to a short European tour on which the group unveiled a stripped-down act, inspired, in part, by the punk explosion. Rehearsals were then undertaken for another US tour, but in September 1980, Bonham was found dead following a lengthy drinking bout. On 4 December, Swansong announced that the group had officially retired, although a collection of archive material, *Coda*, was subsequently issued. Jones later became a successful producer, notably with the Mission, while Plant embarked on a highly-successful solo career, launched with *Pictures At Eleven*. Page scored the film *Death Wish 2* and, after a brief reunion with Plant and the Honeydrippers project in 1984, he inaugurated the short-lived Firm with Paul Rogers. He then formed the Jimmy Page Band with John Bonham's son, Jason, who in turn drummed with Led Zeppelin on their appearance at Atlantic's 25th Anniversary Concert in 1988. Despite renewed interest in the group's career, particularly in the wake of the retrospective *Remasters*, entreaties to make this a permanent reunion have been resisted. Although their commercial success is unquestionable, Led Zeppelin is now rightly recognized as one of the most influential bands of the rock era and their catalogue continues to provide inspiration to successive generations of musicians.

Albums: *Led Zeppelin* (1969), *Led Zeppelin II* (1969), *Led Zeppelin III* (1970), *Led Zeppelin IV* (1971), *Houses Of The Holy* (1973), *Physical Graffiti* (1975), *Presence* (1976), *The Song Remains The Same* (1976, film soundtrack), *In Through The Out Door* (1979), *Coda* (1982). Compilation: *Remasters* (1990).

Further reading: *Hammer Of The Gods*, Stephen Davis. *Led Zeppelin: A Celebration*, Dave Lewis.

Le Griffe

Although using the French moniker Le Griffe (meaning 'The Claw') the band was formed in Stoke-On-Trent, Staffordshire, England in 1980. Le Griffe's original line-up consisted of Chris Hatton (vocals/guitar), Paul Wood (guitar), Tim Blackwood (guitar), Kevin Collier (bass) and Martin Allen (drums). Quickly becoming popular on their local live circuit, the band signed to the (now defunct) Bullet Records label, who released a three-track EP entitled *Fast Bikes* (1981). The EP was a worthy debut of melodic rockers reminiscent of early Def Leppard coupled with 12-bar Status Quo-style boogie. The band gigged extensively throughout the UK and released a mini-album again on the Bullet Records label, *Breaking Strain* in 1984. The album was simlar to previous releases but more melodic. At the time of its release, guitarist Tim Blackwood left the band to be replaced by Amos Sanfillipo but due to a lack of any substantial success the band dissolved early in 1985. Bassist Kevin Collier went on to join Rogue Male.

Album: *Breaking Strain* (1984).

Legs Diamond

Legs Diamond

Deriving their name from an infamous 1920s gangster, Legs Diamond were formed by Michael Diamond (bass) and Jeff Poole (drums) in San Francisco, California during 1977. Moving to Los Angeles, they recruited Rick Sanford (vocals), Michael Prince (guitar/keyboards) and Roger Romeo (guitar) to consolidate the line-up. Picked up by Mercury Records, their debut release was a classy hard rock album that paid respect to Led Zeppelin, Deep Purple and Wishbone Ash. The songs were all strong, but the album was let down by a weak production. The follow-up was every bit as strong, with the band alternating between brooding and intense power ballads and unabashed rockers. They toured as support to Ted Nugent, Kiss and Styx, but to their surprise, were dropped by their label shortly afterwards. They negotiated a deal with the independent Cream label, releasing *Fire Power* in 1978. This marked a change in style to a more AOR oriented approach, but it was poorly received. The band, disillusioned, decided to go their separate ways. Six years later, Rick Sanford resurrected the band, and after several personnel changes, stabilized the line-up with Romeo and Prince and new members Dusty Watson (drums) and Mike Christie (bass). Signing

to the independent metal specialist label MFN (Music For Nations), they have delivered three albums of sophisticated hard-rock and captured the excitement and promise that they never fulfilled the first time around.

Albums: *Legs Diamond* (1977), *A Diamond Is A Hard Rock* (1977), *Fire Power* (1978), *Out On Bail* (1984), *Land Of The Gun* (1986), *Town Bad Girl* (1990).

Life, Sex & Death

This trio were formed in Los Angeles, USA during 1991 by demented vocalist and ex-Chicago street hobo Stanley. LSD, as they are often known are completed by drummer Brian Michael Horak and ex-Enuff Z'Nuff guitarist Alex Kane. Signing to Warner Brothers, they debuted in July 1992 with The Silent Majority, which met with a mixed reception. Influences as diverse as Cheap Trick, the Sex Pistols, the Beatles and Guns N'Roses manifested themselves clearly, but Stanley's rasping, yet inherently melodic vocal style gave the band some identity. LSD are certain to earn some notoriety with their provocative album cover and Stanley's outrageous claim to having not washed for over a year!

Albums: The Silent Majority (1992).

Lillian Axe

This melodic rock quintet originally from Michigan USA, comprised Ron Taylor (vocals), Steve Blaze (guitar), Jon Ster (guitar/keyboards), Rob Stratton (bass) and Danny King (drums). Initially known as Stiff, the band were taken under the wing of Ratt guitarist Robbin Crosby and changed their name to Lillian Axe. Produced by Crosby, their debut was a fine amalgam of infectious rockers and hard-edged pop tunes. *Love And War* was even more impressive, featuring extended atmospheric compositions, that were both anthemic and memorable. The record sold poorly and MCA dropped the band from their roster. In 1990, Danny King and Rob Stratton were replaced by Gene Barnett and Darren DeLatta respectively. A third album remained unreleased.

Albums: *Lillian Axe* (1988), *Love And War* (1989).

Limelight

This UK heavy metal trio, based in Mansfield, Nottinghamshire, was put together by the Scrimshaw brothers; Glen (guitar/keyboards), Mike (bass/vocals), plus Pat Coleman (drums). Limelight specialized in extended melodic compositions of a progressive nature, featuring complex time changes and individual virtuoso sections (similar to that of Yes, while incorporating

Lillian Axe

the contemporary style of the New Wave Of British Heavy Metal). Their one and only album contained very strong material, but was let down by a small budget production and weak vocals. The Scrimshaw brothers returned to the pub rock scene, playing mainly pop-rock covers.
Album: *Limelight* (1980).

Lion

After the demise of the highly-underrated and largely overlooked UK hard-rock band Tytan, vocalist Kal Swan left England for Los Angeles to put together his own band. Formed 1983, Lion consisted of Kal Swan (vocals), Doug Aldrich (guitar), Jerry Best (bass) and ex-Steeler drummer Mark Edwards. The band quickly put out a self-financed EP *Powerlove* (only available as a Japanese release) which gained the band a strong following in the Far East. Due to the immense amount of positive interest being shown towards them and the fact that they contributed songs to the soundtracks of the films *The Wraith* and *Transformers,* they attracted the attention of the Scotti Brothers Records label who promptly signed them. This resulted in the band's debut *Dangerous Attraction* being released in 1987. The

album proved to be a strong, melodic hard rock release on which Kal Swans' soaring vocals came to the fore. However, Scotti Brothers refused to promote the release and, as a result, album sales suffered. Subsequently dropped by their previous label, the band signed a new recording agreement with the Grand Slamm Records label, resulting in *Trouble At Angel City* being released in 1989. Unfortunately, soon after its release, the band folded due to drummer Mark Edwards experiencing a debilitating accident and guitarist Doug Aldrich leaving to join Hurricane.
Albums: *Dangerous Attraction* (1987), *Trouble At Angel City* (1989).

Liquid Jesus

This experimental, Los Angeles-based quintet were formed in 1990 by bassist Johnny Lonely and guitarist Scott Tracey. Adding Todd Rigione (guitar), Buck Murphy (vocals) and John Molo (drums), they gigged incessantly on the LA bar and club circuit. Fusing psychedelic, blues, jazz and metal influences to bizarre extremes, they debuted with an independently released live album. Tipped as the next possible Jane's Addiction, they were signed by Geffen Records in 1991 and delivered

Lion

Pour In The Sky. This paid respect to Jimi Hendrix, Led Zeppelin, the Red Hot Chili Peppers and Queen, but carefully sidestepped accusations of plagiarism by virtue of their totally deranged and unpredictable delivery.
Albums: *Liquid Jesus Live* (1990), *Pour In The Sky* (1992).

Little Angels

This UK heavy rock quintet were formed in Scarborough, Yorkshire, during the late 80s. Comprising Toby Jepson (vocals), Bruce John Dickinson (guitar), Mark Plunkett (bass), Jimmy Dickinson (keyboards) and Michael Lee (drums) they are a youthful outfit, whose energy and enthusiasm in the live setting won them a loyal fan base in their native north east. Following a series of independent releases, they attracted the attention of Polydor Records, which signed them immediately. *Don't Prey For Me* included a dozen gems of melodic, but rough-shod rock 'n' roll, characterized by Jepson's raucous and charismatic vocals. The big budget follow-up, mixed by the Steve Thompson/Michael Barbiero partnership, was a disappointment. Abandoning their roots, they made a concerted attempt to break into the American FM radio market, with a faceless amalgam of Foreigner, Def Leppard, Styx and even Elton John influences. Internal disputes began to manifest themselves in 1991, drummer Michael Lee secretly auditioned for the Cult, and was ejected from the band as a result.
Albums: *Too Posh To Mosh* (1987), *Don't Prey For Me* (1989), *Young Gods* (1991).

Lizzy Borden

This theatrical rock outfit, formed in Los Angeles in 1983. The group took their name from the infamous axe murderess. Utilizing strong sexual, leather and horror images, their visual image owed much to Alice Cooper. The group featured Lizzy Borden (vocals), his brother Joey Scott Harges (drums), Mike Kenny (bass) and Tony Matuzak (guitar). Their contribution to the *Metal Massacre IV* compilation impressed Metal Blade boss Brian Slagel enough, to offer them a contract. The mini-album, *Give 'Em The Axe* emerged in the summer of 1984, followed a year later by *Love You To Pieces*, their official full-length debut. Both were highly derivative of Rainbow/Iron Maiden, with Lizzy's vocals sounding very similar to Geoff Tate's of Queensryche. Alex Nelson replaced Tony Matuzak on guitar at this juncture before the recording of *The Murderess Metal Roadshow*. This was a double live set that did not show the band at their best, with low-tech recording and poor production. Two more studio albums followed, Gene Allen was added as a second guitarist and Jesse Holmes and Mychal Davis replaced Nelson and Kenny respectively, before the recording of, what is arguably, the band's finest and most commercial set, *Visual Lies*. Loosely based around a central theme of visual illusions, the album was varied, hard-hitting and full of infectious hooks, anthemic choruses and smouldering guitar breaks. They played the Reading Festival in 1987, to an indifferent reaction and Lizzy disbanded the group shortly afterwards. Concentrating on a solo career he released *Master Of Disguise*, an ambitious concept album, that consisted of a few good ideas spread over a dozen songs.
Albums: *Give 'Em The Axe* (1984), *Love You To Pieces* (1985), *The Muderess Metal Roadshow* (1986), *Menace To Society* (1986), *Terror Rising* (1987), *Visual Lies* (1987). Lizzy Borden solo album: *Master Of Disguise* (1989).

Lone Star

This traditional, hard-rock quintet was formed in 1975 by Kenny Driscoll (lead vocals), Tony Smith (guitar), Paul 'Tonka' Chapman (guitar), Pete Hurley (bass) and Dixie Lee (drums). Specializing in dynamic heavy rock, they attracted considerable attention with their Roy Thomas Baker-produced debut, having an approach and sound that was a synthesis of Queen, Led Zeppelin and UFO. Driscoll was replaced by John Sloman in 1977, before the release of *Firing On All Six*. This album pushed the dual guitars of Chapman and Smith to the forefront and concentrated on heavier material by dropping the delicate touches and finishes that appeared on their debut. Shortly after its release, the band disintegrated, with Sloman joining Uriah Heep, Chapman replacing Michael Schenker in UFO and Dixie Lee teaming up with Wild Horses.
Albums: *Lone Star* (1976), *Firing On All Six* (1977).

Love/Hate

Love/Hate

This US, Los Angeles, California-based quartet, comprised Jizzy Pearl (lead vocals), Jon E. Love (guitar), Skid Rose (bass) and Joey Gold (drums). With a streetwise attitude and a highly talented frontman, their debut album, produced by Tom Werman, was released to widespread critical acclaim. Seeming like a hybrid of Guns N' Roses and Mötley Crüe, their songs dealt with the well-worn themes of sex, drugs, drink and rock 'n' roll. In the live setting the band are awesome, playing with total commitment and generating incredible intensity with their inimitable brand of funk-infused, jitterbug rock. *Wasted In America* confirmed many people's faith in the band and recruited many converts.

Albums: *Blackout In The Red Room* (1990), *Wasted In America* (1992).

Loverboy

Formed in Toronto, Canada in 1980 by Mike Reno (vocals), Paul Dean (guitar), Doug Johnston (keyboards), Scott Smith (bass) and Matthew Frenette (drums). Reno was formerly with Moxy, and Dean and Frenette had been members of Sweetheart, a melodic AOR/heavy rock band. Loverboy were signed by CBS Records as soon as they were formed. They went into the studio with producer Bruce Fairbairn and recorded a self-titled album that was to be Loverboy's trademark for years to come. It was American-style, melodic hard rock, that also contained reggae and jazz styles. With the hit singles 'Turn Me Loose' and 'The Kid Is Hot Tonite' the album went platinum. After touring, Loverboy entered the studio in 1981, again with Fairbairn producing, to record the follow-up, *Get Lucky*. The album lived up to its name, as it entered the charts and sold over two million copies, helped by the success in the singles charts of 'Working For The Weekend'. The only territory where the band failed was Europe. After more touring Fairbairn produced *Keep It Up* in 1983, from which 'Hot Girls In Love' charted. *Keep It Up* was a multi-platinum success. Loverboy's form of melodic AOR rock had now become a fine art. However, the success of this album had kept the band on the road for nearly two years, but still with little recognition in Europe. On *Lovin' Every Minute Of It* they were joined by Tom Allom, known for his work with Judas Priest. The result was a harder-edged album which was the band's least successful, though it still sold well over a million copies. The title track, released as a single, was written by the producer of Def Leppard, Robert John 'Mutt' Lange.

Fairbairn had by now made his name as the producer of Bon Jovi, but again produced Loverboy's *Wildside*, released in 1987, their most complete album to date. Bryan Adams, Richie Sambora and Jon Bon Jovi all co-wrote some tracks. 'Notorious' was the band's most successful single, and went platinum three times over. Loverboy went on a marathon two-year tour, their longest yet. They did, however, take a break for two months to record some tracks with producer Bob Rock before they came over to support Def Leppard on their European tour in the spring of 1988. After this, Loverboy returned home to Canada and an uncertain future. Dean and Reno announced plans to record as soloists and this left the rest of the band in limbo. In 1989, a compilation album was released by CBS, *Big Ones*, which also contained three new tracks that had been recorded with Bob Rock. Later that year Dean released the solo *Hard Core*, assisted by Loverboy drummer Frenette and also Jon Bon Jovi on harmonica. Since the release of the compilation album in 1989, Loverboy has been inactive.

Albums: *Loverboy* (1980), *Get Lucky* (1981), *Keep It Up* (19483), *Lovin' Every Minute Of It* (1985), *Wildside* (1987). Compilation: *Big Ones* (1989). Solo album: Paul Dean *Hard Core* (1989).

Lynott, Phil

b. 20 August 1951, Dublin, Eire, d. 4 January

1986. Having enjoyed considerable success in Thin Lizzy, Lynott recorded solo in 1980, the same year that he married Caroline Crowther, daughter of the television celebrity Leslie Crowther. Lynott's first single 'Dear Miss Lonely Hearts' reached number 32 in the UK charts and was followed by the album *Solo In Soho*. A tribute to Elvis Presley, 'King's Call' also reached number 35. Lynott had to wait until 1982 for his next hit 'Yellow Peril', which reached the UK Top 20 after being used as a theme tune for the television show *Top Of The Pops*. In the summer of 1983, Thin Lizzy split up and it was expected that Lynott would achieve solo fame. A new group Grand Slam failed to develop and Lynott's subsequent solo single 'Nineteen' did not sell. In 1986, he suffered a drug overdose and, following a week in a coma, died of heart failure, exacerbated by pneumonia.

Album: *Solo In Soho* (1980).

M

Macalpine, Tony

Initially trained as a classical pianist, Tony Macalpine graduated to the electric guitar with an ambition to fuse rock and classical influences into a musical form that would have widespread appeal. Teaming up with ex-Journey drummer Steve Smith and ex-David Lee Roth bassist Billy Sheehan, he recorded *Edge Of Insanity*, which featured a set of classical-jazz-rock fusion instrumental numbers. The album was characterized by Macalpine's ability to improvise and imbue feeling and emotion even at break-neck speed. Following this, he experimented with the idea of forming a straightforward rock band. He signed up Tommy Aldridge (drums), Rudi Sarzo (bass) and Robert Rock (vocals) to record Project Driver under the M.A.R.S. monicker; a disappointing Rainbow-style collection of hard-rock numbers. The band split up soon after the release and Macalpine returned to former solo status, forming his own Squawk label. He released another all-instrumental album, but realized afterwards that he had taken the format as far as it could go. On *Eyes Of The World*, he added Alan Schorn on lead vocals, Mark Robertson (keyboards), Billy Carmassi (drums) and Mike Jacques (drums) to form Macalpine, the band. They specialized in highly polished and melodic rock, punctuated by fluid but economical guitar breaks.
Albums: *Edge Of Insanity* (1986), *Maximum Security* (1987), *Eyes Of The World* (1990).

McDonald, Brian, Group

This melodic, pop-rock outfit was put together in 1987 by keyboard wizard Brian McDonald. Enlisting the services of Will Hodges (guitar), Andrew G.Wilkes (bass), and D.W. Adams (drums), they signed to Capitol Records and released Desperate Business the same year. Influenced by Nightranger, Bryan Adams and Jeff Paris, the album was a solid musical statement, marred only by McDonald's vocals, which lacked both power and range.
Album: Desperate Business (1987).

Magnum

The Birmingham, UK based pomp rockers were formed in 1972 by Tony Clarkin (guitar), Bob Catley (vocals), Kex Gorin (drums) and Dave Morgan (bass). They remained unsigned until

Magnum

1978, when they were picked up by Jet Records. By this time, Morgan had departed, to be replaced by Colin 'Wally' Lowe, and Richard Baily had joined as keyboard player. Between 1978 and 1980, Magnum released three albums to a moderate degree of success, and toured relentlessly with Judas Priest, Blue Oyster Cult, and Def Leppard. *Chase The Dragon* was released in 1982, with new keyboard player Mark Stanway, and gave them their first Top 20 album; it featured the grandiose pomp of 'Sacred Hour' and 'The Spirit', both of which still appear in their current live set. Following the release of *Eleventh Hour* problems beset the band: Clarkin became ill, and there was a dispute with Jet Records. These combined to cause the band to fragment. The troubles were soon resolved, and a number of low-key club dates persuaded them to continue. FM Records signed the band in 1985 for *On A Story-teller's Night*. Its Top 40 success, along with a highly successful tour of the UK, prompted Polydor Records to offer a long-term contract. *Vigilante*, which featured new drummer Mickey Barker, was the first release under a new deal, and was produced by Queen's Roger Taylor. The backing of a major label paid immediate dividends with a Top 30 album and a sold-out UK tour. This success was taken one step further with *Wings Of Heaven* (1988), their first gold album and UK Top 10 hit. Top 40 single success came with 'Days Of No Trust', 'Start Talkin' Love', and 'It Must Have Been Love'. Numerous compilation albums including *Mirador* and *Anthology* were released along with re-issues of their back-catalogue from Jet Records. A two-year gap between official releases resulted in the Keith Olsen-produced *Goodnight L.A.* and again Top 40 success was achieved by the single 'Rocking Chair', with Top 10 status for the album. Extensive touring backed-up *Goodnight L.A.* and several shows were recorded for the double live *The Spirit*. After years of struggling and set-backs,

Magnum built up their popularity by constant touring, and through the release of high quality albums, they became one of the UK's most popular rock bands.

Albums: *Kingdom Of Madness* (1978), *Magnum II* (1979), *Marauder* (1980), *Chase The Dragon* (1982), *The Eleventh Hour* (1983), *On A Story - Teller's Night* (1985), *Vigilante* (1986), *Wings Of Heaven* (1988), *Goodnight L.A.* (1990), *The Spirit* (1991).

Mahogany Rush

Recovering in hospital from a bad drugs experience, Frank Marino claimed he was visited by an apparition of Jimi Hendrix. After leaving hospital he picked up a guitar for the first time and was able to play Hendrix riffs. The group was formed in Montreal during 1970 when Marino recruited bassist Paul Harwood and drummer Jim Ayoub to fulfil his desire to work in a power trio format. Their first three albums were derivative in the extreme; every component of Hendrix's unique style had been dismantled, adapted, then re-built under their own song titles. Nevertheless, they were not condemned as copyists, but instead, were revered for paying tribute to the great man in such an honest and sincere fashion. By 1976, Marino had started to develop his own style, based on the extension of the Hendrix tricks he had already acquired. This is clearly evident on *Mahogany Rush IV* and *World Anthem*, released in 1976 and 1977, respectively. Eventually he outgrew the Hendrix comparisons as his own style began to dominate the band's material. The name was amended to Frank Marino and Mahogany Rush, then to Frank Marino, following the release of *What's Next* and the departure of Ayoub.

Albums: *Maxoom* (1971), *Child Of The Novelty* (1974), *Strange Universe* (1975), *Mahogany Rush IV* (1976), *World Anthem* (1977), *Live* (1978), *Tales Of The Unexpected* (1979), *What's Next* (1980).

Malmsteen, Yngwie

This Swedish-born guitar virtuoso was the originator of the high-speed, technically precise, neo-classical style that developed during the 80s. Influenced by Jimi Hendrix, Ritchie Blackmore and David Lee Roth, Malmsteen first picked up a guitar at the age of eight and had formed his first band, Powerhouse, by the time he had entered his teens. At the age of 14, he formed Rising, named after Rainbow's second album and recorded a series of demo tapes. One of the tapes was picked up by producer and guitar specialist Mike Varney. Malmsteen was persuaded by Varney to relocate to Los Angeles and join Ron Keel's Steeler as lead guitarist. They went straight into the studio to record their debut album. Following this, he was

approached by Kiss, UFO and Ozzy Osbourne, but declined their offers in favour of teaming up with Graham Bonnet in a new group called Alcatrazz. This association lasted for one studio album and a live set, recorded in Japan.

Leaving Alcatrazz, Malmsteen was immediately offered a solo deal by Polydor Records, as his reputation and stature was beginning to escalate. He released the self-produced *Rising Force*, utilizing ex-Jethro Tull drummer Barriemore Barlow, vocalist Jeff Scott Soto and keyboardist Jens Johansson. This comprised a mixture of new songs and re-worked demo material that had been available for several years. Deciding to work within a band framework, but exercising tight control, Malmsteen formed Rising Force with Soto and Johansson, plus bassist Marcel Jacob and drummer Anders Johansson. This basic line-up recorded two albums that showcased Malmsteen's amazing virtuosity and penchant for combining speed with melody. (Although *Trilogy* saw Soto replaced by ex-Ted Nugent vocalist Mark Boals) Following an 18-month break after a serious road accident involving Malmsteen, Rising Force was resurrected again with ex-Rainbow vocalist Joe Lynn Turner. Produced by Jeff Glixman and mixed by the Thompson/Barbiero team, *Odyssey* was released in 1988 to widespread acclaim. At last, Malmsteen's guitar pyrotechnics had been incorporated within commercial hard-rock numbers. For once, the guitar solos, for once were economical and did not detract from the songs. The album reached number 40 on the USA *Billboard* album chart. Eager to capitalize on this success, Malmsteen issued a disappointing and self-indulgent live album recorded in Leningrad. The momentum was lost and Joe Lynn Turner was dismissed, to be replaced with a Swedish vocalist, Goran Edman. *Eclipse* emerged in 1990 with weak vocals and a very restrained Malsteen on guitar. It appeared that he was suppressing his real desires and ability in the search for commercial success. He switched back to his old flamboyant style on *No Mercy*, which featured classical material and a string orchestra.

Albums: *Yngwie Malmsteen's Rising Force* (1984), *Marching Out* (1985), *Trilogy* (1986), *Odyssey* (1988), *Live In Leningrad* (1989), *Eclipse* (1990), *No Mercy* (1992).

Mama's Boys

The three McManus brothers began their musical careers as folk musicians, playing the local dance hall and club circuit in their native Northern Ireland. After experiencing the Irish electric folk-rock outfit Horslips in concert in 1978, they decided to abandon their acoustic guitars and

Yngwie Malmsteen

tambourines and become a hard-rock power trio. John took on vocals and bass, Pat picked up lead guitar and Tommy occupied the drumstool. Merging traditional Irish influences with blues and heavy rock, they quickly developed a unique style that also incorporated elements of Thin Lizzy, UFO, Status Quo and Wishbone Ash. Their first two albums contained high-energy boogie and driving blues, but from Turn It Up onwards, they began to show a greater awareness of melody and veered towards AOR. Realizing the limitations of John on vocals, they expanded to a quartet in 1987, adding ex-Airrace vocalist Keith Murrell. Growing Up The Hard Way followed and was undoubtedly the band's most accomplished album to-date, with its sophisticated Foreigner meets Styx approach. After four years of recording inactivity, Live Tonite emerged. Recorded on their 1990 European tour, it featured the latest vocalist, Mike Wilson, plus four brand new songs. Albums: Official Bootleg (1980), Plug It In (1982), Turn It Up (1983), Mama's Boys (1984), Power And The Passion (1985), Growing Up The Hard Way (1987), Live Tonite (1991).

Mammoth

The prerequisite for joining this outfit was to weigh in excess of 20 stone! Consequently, potential members were few and far between. Nevertheless, vocalist Nicky Moore (ex-Samson) and bassist John McCoy (ex-Gillan) eventually found guitarist Big Mac Baker and drummer 'Tubby' Vinnie Reid large enough for their requirements. The idea behind Mammoth was to present the musical antithesis of Poison, Bon Jovi and Mötley Crüe, where the music, rather than the image, was most important. Unfortunately, due to contractual problems with their record company Jive, their debut album was delayed for 10 months and the interest they generated had evaporated by the time it was released. It comprised a poorly produced but workmanlike selection of hard-rock and R&B numbers, with guitarists Bernie Torme and Kenny Cox guesting on a couple of tracks. The single 'Can't Take The Hurt Anymore' was included on the soundtrack to Nightmare On Elm Street 5, The Dream Child. The band collapsed shortly after the album's release. Album: Mammoth (1988).

Manowar

This 'macho' heavy-metal quartet from the USA was formed in 1981 by bassist Joey Demaio and ex-Shakin Street and Dictators' guitarist Ross The Boss. Recruiting vocalist Eric Adams and drummer Donnie Hamzik, they decided on an approach that was to be the total antithesis of

Man O' War

melodic AOR. Dressed in animal skins, they delivered a brutal series of riffs that were characterized by Adam's barbaric vocals and the dense bass-work of Demaio. They debuted in 1982 with Battle Hymns, a milestone in the metal genre. With subject material firmly centred on fighting, bloodshed, death and carnage, they came over as a turbo-charged hybrid of Ted Nugent and Black Sabbath. The album was notable for an amazing version of the 'William Tell Overture', played as an electric bass solo. Battle Hymns failed to sell, and with the press treating the band as an absurd joke, they were dropped by Liberty Records in 1982.

Signing to MFN, Scott Columbus took over the drumstool on Into Glory Ride. This was another intensely heavy, chest-beating collection of metal epics. They built up a small yet loyal cult following, but were generally panned by the rock mainstream. Their UK tours in 1983 and 1984 attracted poor audiences, but they had more success in Europe. With each subsequent release, the band tried to become more extreme; consequently they had to seek a new record company after the release of each album. Sign Of The Hammer, released in 1985, featured some excellent guitar work from Ross The Boss and contained the band's most accessible compositions to date. Once again it flopped, and after a serious re-think, they returned two years later with *Fighting The World*. On this album the band incorporated elements of Kiss and Judas Priest into their songwriting, but although it was aimed at the rock mainstream, it failed to win many new fans. *Kings Of Metal* was released the following year and met with a similar fate. Disillusioned, Ross The Boss quit in 1988, with Scott Columbus following suit two years later. The future of the group is still uncertain. Manowar are colourful, flamboyant and rather kitsch, but nevertheless an essential component in the music industry; the perfect antidote to the sometimes conservative rock fraternity.

Albums: *Battle Hymns* (1982), *Into Glory Ride* (1983), *Hail To England* (1984), *Sign Of The Hammer* (1985), *Fighting The World* (1987), *Kings Of Metal* (1988).

Mantas

This short-lived hard-rock quartet was formed by Mantas after quitting the demonic thrash metallers Venom. Enlisting the help of vocalist Pete Harrison, second guitarist Al Barnes and Keith Nichol on keyboards, their debut and only release comprised nine new originals penned by Mantas. Moving away from the one-dimensional approach of Venom, they straddled the ground between AOR and the more commercial rock of Rainbow, Saxon and Dio. *Winds Of Change* featured computerized drums and extensive use of keyboards; Harrison's vocals lacked distinction and the material was dull. The album was ignored by mainstream record purchasers. After a careful re-think, Mantas disbanded the group and re-joined Venom in 1989.

Album: *Winds Of Change* (1988).

Marino, Frank

This Canadian guitarist initially based his style obsessively on Jimi Hendrix. Forming Mahogany Rush in 1970 (later known as Frank Marino And Mahogany Rush), he decided to work solely under his own name from 1980 onwards. Playing the Heavy Metal Holocaust Festival in Port Vale during 1981, he was the surprise success of the day, upstaging headliners Triumph by a truly dazzling display of guitar pyrotechnics and showmanship. *The Power Of Rock 'N' Roll* was the first release under Marino's own name and featured a more aggressive style, coupled with acute lyrical references to sensitive social and political issues of the time. *Juggernaut* built on this success, but increased the tempo and introduced a greater degree of melody in the material. A four-year break from recording ensued, owing to business

and management setbacks, before *Full Circle* appeared in 1986. A stunning double live album was issued two years later, but nothing appeared until a single track contribution to the *Guitar Speak Vol.2* album was released in 1990.

Albums: *The Power Of Rock 'N' Roll* (1981), *Juggernaut* (1982), *Full Circle* (1986), *Double Live* (1988).

M.A.R.S

This short-lived supergroup project was assembled in 1987. Featuring Tony Macalpine (guitar), Tommy Aldridge (drums), Robert Rock (vocals) and Rudi Sarzo (bass), their collective pedigrees promised more than what was delivered. Produced by Mike Varney, their debut album would have been indistinguishable from Vinnie Moore's, Tony Macalpine's, Marty Friedman's, Jason Becker's or Greg Howe's instrumental albums, were it not for the additional vocals of Rock. *Project Driver* seriously lacked identity, being influenced by Yngwie Malmsteen and Rainbow. The band dissolved itself soon after the release, with Sarzo and Aldridge joining Whitesnake, Rock taking over vocals in Joshua and Macalpine picking up his solo career once more.

Album: *Project Driver* (1987).

Marsden, Bernie

This masterly UK guitarist came to prominence in the 70s during his stints with Babe Ruth, UFO and Whitesnake. At the turn of the 70s, Marsden took time out between Whitesnake projects, to record solo material. He was assisted by noteworthy musicians who included Ian Paice, Cozy Powell and Simon Phillips (drums), Don Airey (keyboards), Neil Murray and Jack Bruce (bass). The albums featured melodic hard rock, with Marsden successfully handling the vocals as well as some extended guitar workouts. He subsequently formed Bernie Marsden's S.O.S. which later became known as Alaska. Marsden is an accomplished musician able to give enormous variety and depth to his heavy-rock based music.

Albums: *And About Time Too* (1979), *Look At Me Now* (1981).

Marseille

This band was formed in London, England, in 1976, and the original line-up consisted of Paul Dale (vocals), Neil Buchanan (guitar), Andy Charters (guitar), Steve Dinwoodie (bass) and Keith Knowles (drums). Signing to the now-defunct Mountain Records label, the band released their debut album in 1978. *Red, White And Slighty Blue* was a subtle blend of melodic rock and pop. A couple of tours followed, supporting, among others UFO who the band were later to model themselves on. This was most noticeable on the band's second album *Marseille* where the band had a more traditional hard rock sound. The group then ran into difficulties as Mountain Records went bankrupt. This left Marseille in limbo but they resufaced in 1983 with new personnel and a record deal. The new line-up consisted of ex-Savage Lucy vocalist Sav Pearse, Mark Hays (guitar), Neil Buchanan (guitar), Steve Dinwoodie (bass) and Keith Knowles (drums). They went on to record the band's third and final album, *Touch The Night*, which appeared on the Ultra Noise Records label in 1984. Still failing to make any real impact with either press or public, the band soon folded.

Albums: *Red, White And Slightly Blue* (1978), *Marseille* (1979), *Touch The Night* (1984).

Marshall Law

This Birmingham, England-based heavy-metal quintet comprises Andy Pike (vocals), Dave Martin (guitar), Andy Southwell (guitar), Rog Davis (bass) and Mick Donovan (drums). Following in the tradition of UK rockers such as Judas Priest, Saxon and Iron Maiden, they transpose melody onto infectious, circular power-riffs, cleverly avoiding any monotony by the injection of twin lead guitar solos between rousing choruses. Signing to the Heavy Metal Records label, they released their self-titled debut in 1989 to considerable critical acclaim. They may yet be the spearhead of a new revival in British heavy rock.

Album: *Marshall Law* (1989).

Massacre

Massacre

Formed in the US in the mid-80s, Massacre were one of the earliest extreme 'thrash metal' bands now known as death metal. They were pioneers of the style which was a hugely popular underground phenomenon before ever attained public attention

and widespread success. The early death-metal bands spread their name and their music by recording demo tapes which were sent around the world and traded with various contacts. This succeeded in spreading the music without the use of conventional commercial means. In the late 80s, death metal and extreme thrash were becoming increasingly popular, and bands were much more widespread than when Massacre began. After a period of non-activity, this new attention provided an opportunity for Massacre to begin work again, and they succeeded in gaining a record deal with UK label Earache, specialists in extreme music. Their debut album featured Kam Lee (vocals), Rick Rozz (guitar), Terry Butler (bass) and Bill Andrews (drums). Rozz, Butler and Andrews had also been part of extreme metal innovators Death.

Album: *From Beyond* (1991).

Masters Of Reality

This short-lived, New York, USA-based quartet featured Chris Goss (vocals/guitar), Tim Harrington (guitar), Googe (bass) and Vinnie Ludovico (drums). Deriving their name from the title of Black Sabbath's third album, they fused a diverse array of rock styles into a form that refused to be easily pigeon-holed. Influences such as the Doors, Vanilla Fudge, Love and Deep Purple were apparent. With the aid of producer Rick Rubin, they distilled these into a potent and powerful sound which had its roots in the 70s but was delivered with the technology of today. Their self-titled debut was released to widespread critical acclaim in 1989, but Chris Goss quit during the promotional USA tour, and subsequently the band folded.

Album: Masters Of Reality (1989).

May, Brian

b. 19 July 1947, Twickenham, Middlesex, England. Best known as the flamboyant and highly original guitarist in Queen, May has also recorded in his own right. In the summer of 1983, he teamed-up with Eddie Van Halen (guitar), REO Speedwagon's Alan Gratzer (drums), Fred Mandel (keybords) and Phil Chen (bass) for a super session, which was released under the title *Star Fleet Project*. He subsequently produced the spoof heavy metal group Bad News and as well as the recording of 'Anyone Can Fall In Love' by his actress/lover Anita Dobson. He also worked with Steve Hackett, completed a solo album and, in 1991, wrote and recorded the score for a production of Shakespeare's *Macbeth*. Following a commission for an advertisement by the Ford Motor Company in 1991, May released 'Driven By You' as a single which became a sizeable hit at the end of 1991.

He was one of the prime organiser's of the Freddy Mercury Aid Benefit in 1992.

Album: *Star Fleet Project* (1983).

Meanstreak

Hailing from New York, Meanstreak were formed in 1985 by guitarists Marlene Apuzzo and Rena Sands. Recruiting vocalist Bettina France, bassist Martens Pace and drummer Diane Keyser, they were the first all-female thrash metal band to record an album. Signing to the independent MFN label, they released *Roadkill*, produced by Alex Perialas and ex-Raven drummer Rob Hunter. Recorded within a week, it was amateurish and even shambolic at times. The songs were rigidly formularized, lacked identity and featured weak vocals. The album is only of interest to thrash aficionados, even then, on an historical, rather than musical level.

Album: *Roadkill* (1988).

Meatloaf

b. Marvin Lee Aday, 27 September 1947, Dallas, Texas, USA. The name Meatloaf originated at school, when aged 13, he was christened 'Meatloaf' by his football coach, owing to his enormous size and ungainly manner. He moved to Los Angeles in 1967 and formed Popcorn Blizzard, a psychedelic rock outfit which toured the club circuit, opening for acts which included the Who, Ted Nugent and the Stooges. In 1969 Meatloaf successfully auditioned for a role in *Hair*, where he met soul vocalist Stoney. Stoney and Meatloaf recorded a self-titled album in 1971, which spawned the minor *Billboard* chart hit 'What You See Is What You Get'. *Hair* closed in New York, 1974, and Meatloaf found new work in *More Than You Deserve*, a musical written by Jim Steinman, then took the part of Eddie in the film version of *The Rocky Horror Picture Show*. In 1976, he was recruited by Ted Nugent to sing lead vocals on his *Free For All*, after which he joined up with Jim Steinman again in the famous US satirical comedy oufit, the National Lampoon Roadshow. Meatloaf and Steinman struck up a working musical relationship and started composing a grandiose rock opera. After a long search, they found Epic Records and producer Todd Rundgren sympathetic to their ideas and demo tapes. Enlisting the services of Bruce Springsteen's E Street Band and vocalist Ellen Foley, they recorded *Bat Out Of Hell* in 1978. The album was ignored for the first six months after release, although Meatloaf toured extensively, supporting Cheap Trick, among others. Eventually the breakthrough came, and the album rocketed towards the top of the charts in country after country. It stayed in the UK and US album charts for 395 and 88 weeks, respectively, and sold in excess of five million copies.

After a three-year gap, the eagerly anticipated follow-up, *Dead Ringer* was released. Once again, mainly written by Steinman, it continued where *Bat Out Of Hell* had left off, comprising grandiose arrangements, anthemic choruses and scintillating rock 'n' roll. The title song made the Top 5 in the UK and the album hit number 1, but it only dented the lower end Top 50 *Billboard* album chart. Meatloaf and Jim Steinman went their separate ways from this point, and consequently the standard of songwriting on future releases weakened. Concentrating on Europe, relentless touring helped both *Midnight At The Lost And Found* and *Bad Attitude* to creep into the Top 10 UK album charts. Nevertheless, this represented a significant decline in popularity compared with his Steinman penned albums.

Blind Before I Stop saw Meatloaf teaming up with John Parr for the single 'Rock'n'Roll Mercenaries', which, surprisingly, was not a hit. The album was his strongest, post-Steinman release and featured a fine selection of accessible, blues-based, hard-rock numbers. With live performances, things had never been better; Meatloaf's band included Bob Kulick (brother of Kiss guitarist Bruce Kulick, and now of Skull), and ex-Rainbow drummer Chuck Burgi. They delivered an electrifying show which ran for nearly three hours. Recorded at London's Wembley Stadium, *Meatloaf Live* emerged in 1987, and featured raw and exciting versions of his finest songs. Apart from re-releases and compilations, he has maintained vinyl silence ever since. However, he signed a new deal with Virgin Records in 1990, and has apparently been working on new material with Jim Steinman again.

Albums: *Bat Out Of Hell* (1978), *Dead Ringer* (1981), *Midnight At The Lost And Found* (1983), *Hits Out Of Hell* (1984), *Bad Attitude* (1984), *Blind Before I Stop* (1986), *Meatloaf Live* (1987).

Megadeth

This uncompromising and intense thrash metal quartet was founded in San Francisco, California, USA by guitarist Dave Mustaine after leaving Metallica in 1983. Recruiting bassist Dave Ellefson, guitarist Chris Poland and drummer Gars Samuelson, Mustaine negotiated a deal with the independent Combat label. Working on a tight budget, Megadeth produced *Killing Is My Business . . . And Business Is Good* in 1985. This was a ferocious blast of high-energy thrash metal, weakened by a thin production. Nevertheless, Capitol Records, realizing the band's potential,

Meatloaf

Megadeth

immediately signed them up, even though Mustaine was beginning to acquire a reputation for his outspoken and provocative manner. *Peace Sells. . . But Who's Buying?* was a marked improvement over their debut, both technically and musically. It was characterized by incessant, heavy duty riffing, bursts of screaming guitar and lyrics which reflected Mustaine's outspoken perception of contemporary social and political issues. In 1988, Mustaine fired Poland and Samuelson, bringing in Jeff Young and Chuck Behler as replacements before the recording of *So Far, So Good, So What!* This built on their aggressive and vitriolic style, and included a cover of 'Anarchy In The UK', with Sex Pistols' guitarist Steve Jones making a guest appearance. Following two years of heroin-related problems, and the enforced departure of Poland and Behler, Mustaine re-appeared in 1990 with guitar virtuoso Marty Friedman and drummer Nick Menza. *Rust In Peace* was released to widespread critical acclaim, with its anti-nuclear message and the explosive guitar pyrotechnics of Friedman. Along with Slayer, Metallica and Anthrax, Megadeth are still at the forefront of the thrash metal genre.
Albums: *Killing Is My Business. . . And Business Is Good* (1985), *Peace Sells. . . But Who's Buying?* (1986), *So Far, So Good, So What!* (1988), *Rust In Peace* (1990).

Messiah Force

Formed in Jonquire, Canada, in 1984, the band consisted of Lynn Renaud (vocals), Bastien Deschênes (guitar), Jean Tremblay (guitar), Eric Parisé (bass) and Jean-Francois Boucher (drums). Basically the band was formed out of the ashes of two local power metal bands, Exode and Frozen. Utilizing a sound that was reminiscent of early Warlock, the band released their debut, *The Last Day,* on the small, independent Haissem Records label in 1987. Though a powerful power metal

release, the album went largely unnoticed resulting in the band's demise soon after its release.
Album: *The Last Day* (1987).

Metal Church

Formed in the USA in 1984, this group consisted of David Wayne (vocals), Kurt Vanderhoof (guitar), Craig Wells (guitar), Duke Erickson (bass) and Kirk Arrington (drums). Their first album was a phenomenal work, brimming with energy and promise. The style was the then-evolving thrash metal sound, and Metal Church executed their own brand with awesome precision and power. *The Dark* was a strong follow-up, but failed to top the debut, and Wayne left at this point to be replaced by Mike Howe for the recording of *Blessing In Disguise*, which was a commendable album. Kurt Vanderhoof left,owing to his dislike of touring, and was replaced by John Marshall, previously guitar technician for Metallica. Metal Church have proved to be a consistently excellent band, but have failed to rise to the level of success suggested by their first album.
Albums: *Metal Church* (1985), *The Dark* (1987), *Blessing In Disguise* (1989).

Metallica

Formed during 1981, in California, USA by Lars Ulrich (b. 26 December 1963, Copenhagen, Denmark; drums) and James Alan Hetfield (b. 3 August 1963, USA; guitar/vocals) after each separately advertised for fellow musicians in the classified advertisements of the American publication *The Recycler*. They recorded their first demo with Lloyd Grand (guitar) who was replaced in January 1982 by David Mustaine, a guitarist whose relationship with Ulrich and Hetfield proved unsatisfactory. Jef Warner (guitar) and Ron McGovney (bass) each had a brief involvement with the group, and at the end of 1982, Clifford Lee Burton (b. 10 February 1962, USA; bass), formerly of Trauma, joined the band, playing his first live performance on 5 March 1983. Mustaine departed to form Megadeth and was replaced by Kirk Hammett (b. 18 November 1962; guitar). Hammett, who came to the attention of Ulrich and Hetfield while playing with the rock band Exodus, played his first concert with Metallica on 16 April 1983. The Ulrich, Hetfield, Burton and Hammett combination lasted until disaster struck the band in the small hours of 27 September 1987, when Metallica's tour bus overturned in Sweden, killing Cliff Burton.
After deciding that to stop playing would be an insult to their bassist's memory, the remaining three members chose to recruit Jason Newsted (b. 4 March 1963; bass) of Flotsam And Jetsam.

Metal Church

Newsted never imitated Burton, but complemented the band with his own musical style, as he demonstrated at his first concert with the band on 8 November 1986. The original partnership of Ulrich and Hetfield is responsible for Metallica's lyrics and musical direction. Having worked with the likes of Johnny Zazula and, most recently, producer Bob Rock, they have retained all the aggression and exuberance of their debut, *Kill 'Em All*, the album sleeve of which bore the legend 'Bang that head that doesn't bang', while maturing musically, as subsequent albums demonstrated. Their songs deal with large themes – justice and retribution, insanity, war, religion and relationships. Their music has grown from iconoclastic chaos to thoughtful harmony, and is hallmarked by sudden and unexpected changes of mood and tempo. Classed by some as being a 'thrash metal' band, Metallica are more than that, and Ulrich's early preoccupations with British heavy metal bands like Black Sabbath and Motörhead, offer a better clue as to the nature of their music. Indeed, the band gained much experience by touring with Ozzy Osbourne, Twisted Sister and Motörhead. Metallica thus draw,, on many musical sources, and have created their own unique style. They shun fashion and dare to put out music which ranges from fast songs to gentle ballads. To quote from 'Nothing Else Matters' on *Metallica*: '. . . Trust I seek and I find in you/Every day for us something new/Open mind for a different view . . .'. This band who have a musically 'open mind' played their third Donington Monsters of Rock festival in 1991, and the rapturous acclaim they received there is a fitting tribute to their experimental originality and daring.

Albums: *Kill 'Em All* (1983), *Ride The Lightning* (1984), *Master Of Puppets* (1986), *. . . And Justice For All* (1988), *Metallica* (1991). Mini Album: *The $5.98 Garage Days Re-Revisited* (1987). Videos: *Cliff 'Em All* (1987), *One The Video* (1988).

Miller, Donnie

This American guitarist and singer/songwriter was renowned for his leather-clad biker image. Influenced by Steve Earle, Bruce Springsteen and the old blues masters, he specialised in a laid-back, understated approach, with fluid but economical lead guitar breaks. Signed to Epic Records, he released One Of The Boys, ably assisted by Vince Kirk (second guitar), Norman Dahlor (bass), Kurt

Metallica

Zodiac Mindwarp

Carow (keyboards) and Tim 'Kix' Kelly (drums). The album also featured guest appearances from Cyndi Lauper and Tommy Shaw (of Damn Yankees). 'The Devil Wears Lingerie' attracted some attention as a single, with its provocative and sordid promotional video.
Album: One Of The Boys (1989).

Mindfunk

This intense, American, thrash-funk quintet were formed in 1990 by vocalist Patrick R. Dubar and rhythm guitarist Jason Coppola. Adding John Monte (bass), Reed St. Mark (ex-Celtic Frost drummer) and Louis J. Suitek (guitar), they signed to Epic and debuted with a self-titled album the same year. Faith No More, Slayer, Red Hot Chili Peppers and Anthrax are obvious reference points, but the band perform with such aggression and conviction that these comparisons can become rather superfluous.
Album: Mindfunk (1991).

Mindstorm

Mindstorm is the rock vision of vocalist Travis Mitchell. Relying heavily on the Led Zeppelin legacy, the group is in essence the Canadian equivalent of Kingdom Come or Katmandu. Employing Al Rodgers (guitar), Bruce Moffet (drums), Russ Boswell (bass) and Gary Moffet (keyboards) the songs are immaculately constructed and delivered with raucous aplomb. However, their credibility and creativity remains questionable because of the overwhelming feeling of *deja-vu*. With monstrously aching riffs and thunderous drumming, Mindstorm careers along a well-worn rock 'n' roll highway, but takes the occasional musical detour to inject an air of unpredictability into the proceedings. These include Eastern influences, simple acoustic bridges and brooding power ballads. Combining 70s ideology with 90s technology, Mindstorm should impress all but the most fervent Zeppelin worshippers.
Albums: *Mindstorm* (1987), *Back To Reality* (1991).

Mindwarp, Zodiac, And The Love Reaction

Formed in 1985, Zodiac Mindwarp And The Love Reaction projected an image of sex maniacs, party animals and leather-clad bikers all rolled into one. Put together by Zodiac (real name Mark Manning), a former graphic designer, their image and attitude was always more interesting than their music. With twin guitarists Cobalt Stargazer and Flash Bastard, plus Trash D. Garbage and Slam Thunderhide on bass and drums, respectively, they were the ultimate science-fiction garage band, influenced by Alice Cooper, Motorhead and the Stooges. After releasing the mini-album *High Priest Of Love* on the independent Food label, they were picked up by Mercury Records, which funded the recording of *Tattoed Beat Messiah*. Although rigidly formularized, it did spawn the hits 'Prime Mover' and 'Back Seat Education', which were accompanied by expensive and saucy videos. The creative juices soon ran dry, however. Zodiac's backing band disintegrated and Mercury dropped him from its roster in 1989. In 1991, he reformed the band with Stargazer, Thunderhide and new bassist Suzy X, and released the single 'Elvis Died For You'.

Albums: *High Priest Of Love* (1986), *Tattooed Beat Messiah* (1988).

Mr. Big

Mr. Big (not to be confused with the 70s group of the same name) are a supergroup project, featuring bassist Billy Sheehan (ex-David Lee Roth), guitarist Paul Gilbert (ex-Racer X), drummer Pat Torpey (ex-Impellitteri and Robert Plant) and vocalist Eric Martin (ex-Eric Martin Band). Signing to Atlantic Records, their self-titled debut was a high-energy blast of sophisticated hard-rock. *Lean Into It*, released two years later, marked a considerable progression; the band had evolved their own style and sounded more comfortable together. Drawing on influences from a wider musical spectrum, the album was well received by the critics and charted on both sides of the Atlantic.

Albums: *Mr. Big* (1989), *Lean Into It* (1991).

Molly Hatchett

Molly Hatchet

This Lynyrd Skynyrd-style, blues-rock boogie outfit emerged from the USA's deep south. The name is taken from a lady who beheaded her lovers with an axe after sleeping with them, back in 17th-century Salem! The initial line-up comprised guitarists Dave Hlubek, Steve Holland and Duane Roland plus bassist Bonner Thomas, vocalist Danny Joe Brown and drummer Bruce Crump. Their debut album, produced by Tom Werman (of Cheap Trick and Ted Nugent fame), was an instant success, with its three- pronged guitar onslaught and gut-wrenching vocals. Brown was replaced by Jimmy Farrar in 1980, before the recording of *Beatin' The Odds*. Farrar's vocals were less distinctive than Brown's, and an element of their identity was lost while the former fronted the band. Nevertheless, commercial success ensued, with both *Beatin' The Odds* and *Take No Prisoners* peaking on the *Billboard* album chart at number 25 and 36, respectively. In 1982, Danny Joe Brown rejoined the band, while Thomas was replaced by Riff West on bass. *No Guts...No Glory* emerged and marked a return to their roots: explosive guitar duels, blood-stained vocals and exhilarating rock 'n' roll. Amazingly, the album flopped and Hlubek insisted on a radical change in direction. Steve Holden quit and keyboardist John Galvin was recruited for the recording of *The Deed Is Done*. This was a lightweight pop-rock album, largely devoid of the band's former trademarks. Following its release, the band retired temporarily to lick their wounds and re-assess their future. In 1985, *Double Trouble Live* was unleashed, a real triumph that marked a return to former glories. It included stunning versions of their best-known songs plus a superb Skynyrd tribute in the form of 'Freebird'. Founder member Dave Hlubek departed, to be replaced by Bobby Ingram in 1989. They signed a new deal with Capitol Records and released *Lightning Strikes Twice*. This leaned away from their southern roots towards highly polished AOR. It featured covers of Paul Stanley's 'Hide Your Heart' and Miller/Burnette's 'There Goes The Neighbourhood', but was poorly received by fans and critics alike.

Albums: *Molly Hatchet* (1978), *Flirtin' With Disaster* (1979), *Beatin' The Odds* (1980), *Take No Prisoners* (1981), *No Guts...No Glory* (1983), *The Deed Is Done* (1984), *Double Trouble Live* (1985), *Lightning Strikes Twice* (1989).

Monroe, Michael

When Hanoi Rocks folded, following the death of drummer Razzle in 1984, Monroe took several years off before deciding to start again and build a solo career. In 1988, *Nights Are So Long* emerged on the independent Yahoo label, featuring a mixture of originals and covers of songs by the Heavy Metal Kids, Johnny Thunders, MC5 and

Michael Monroe

the Flamin' Groovies. This low-key comeback was a soul-cleansing process for Monroe, before he signed to Mercury Records, and threw himself back into the spotlight with all guns blazing. Recruiting Phil Grande (guitar), Tommy Price (drums), Kenny Aaronson (bass) and Ed Roynesdal (keyboards), he recorded *Not Fakin' It*, a streetwise selection of sleazy rock 'n' roll numbers, delivered in Monroe's inimitable, gutter-cat style. The album was well received and the tour to support it was a triumph. It also suggested that Monroe had been the lynchpin in Hanoi Rocks, as all the other Hanoi spin-offs had met with little success.
Albums: *Nights Are So Long* (1988), *Not Fakin' It* (1989).

Montrose

After working with Van Morrison, Boz Scaggs and Edgar Winter, guitarist Ronnie Montrose formed Montrose in the autumn of 1973. Comprising vocalist Sammy Hagar, bassist Bill Church and drummer Denny Carmassi, they signed to Warner Brothers and released their self-titled debut the following year. Produced by Ted Templeman, Montrose was an album that set new standards; the combination of Hagar's raucous vocals with Montrose's abrasive guitar sound was to become the new blueprint, against which new bands judged themselves for years to come. Including the classic recordings 'Bad Motor Scooter', 'Space Station No. 5' and 'Rock The Nation', the album still ranks today as one of the cornerstones of the hard-rock genre. Alan Fitzgerald replaced Bill Church on bass before the recording of the follow-up, Paper Money. Hagar was fired shortly after the tour to support it was completed. Bob James and Jim Alcivar were drafted in on vocals and keyboards, but they never recaptured the magic of the debut release. Following two commercially disappointing albums, Montrose collapsed and leader Ronnie embarked on a solo career.
Albums: Montrose (1974), Paper Money (1975), Warner Brothers Presents Montrose (1975), Jump On It (1976).

Montrose, Ronnie

After rock guitarist Ronnie Montrose (b. Colorado, USA) dissolved his own band Montrose in 1976, he decided to pursue a solo career. Switching styles from hard-rock to jazz-rock, he released *Open Fire*, an instrumental album that was unpopular with the fans and critics alike. Disillusioned by this, he formed Gamma, who recorded three albums between 1979 and 1982. When Gamma ground to a halt in 1983, Ronnie recorded *Territory*, another low-key solo album. In 1987 he teamed up with vocalist Johnny Edwards (now of Foreigner), drummer James Kottak (later of Kingdom Come) and ex-Gamma bassist Glen Letsch. *Mean* was the result, an uncompromising hard rock record that had the guts and musical firepower of Montrose's debut, released 13 years earlier. This line-up was short-lived, with Johnny Bee Bedanjek replacing Edwards and the addition of synthesizer player Pat Feehan, before *The Speed Of Sound* was recorded. Adopting a more sophisticated, melody conscious approach, it lost the ground that had been recaptured by the previous album. Ronnie decided to go solo again, producing *The Diva Station* in 1990. This was a semi-instrumental affair and incorporated rock, metal, jazz and soul influences, including an amazing version of the old Walker Brothers' hit 'Stay With Me Baby'. Ronnie Montrose is an extremely talented guitarist, but as yet he has found it difficult to channel his energies in a direction that is successful in a commercial sense.
Albums: *Open Fire* (1978), *Territory* (1986), *Mean* (1987), *The Speed Of Sound* (1988), *The Diva Station* (1990).

Moore, Gary

b. 4 April 1952, Belfast, Northern Ireland. This talented, blues-influenced singer and guitarist

Gary Moore

After The War had a strong celtic influence, and also featured guest artists such as Ozzy Osbourne and Andrew Eldritch (Sisters Of Mercy). But his breakthrough to mainstream commercial acceptance came in 1990 with the superb, confident guitarwork and vocals of *Still Got The Blues*. Mixing blues standards and originals, Moore was acclaimed as the UK's foremost blues artist, a stature which the subsequent release of *After Hours* - featuring cameo appearances from B.B. King and Albert Collins - has confirmed.

Albums: *Back On The Streets* (1979), *Corridors Of Power* (1982), *Live At The Marquee* (1983), *Rockin' Every Night - Live In Japan* (1983), *Life* (1984, live), *Run For Cover* (1985), *Wild Frontier* (1988), *After The War* (1989), *Still Got The Blues* (1990), *After Hours* (1992). With Skid Row *Skid Row* (1970), *Thirty Four Hours* (1971). With Gary Moore Band *Grinding Stone* (1973). With Colosseum II *Strange New Flesh Bronze* (1976), *Electric Savage* (1977), *War Dance* (1977). With Thin Lizzy *Black Rose* (1979). With G-Force *G-Force* (1979). With Greg Lake Band *Greg Lake* (1981), *Manoeuvers* (1983).

formed his first major band, Skid Row, when he was 16 years old - initially with Phil Lynott, who left after a few months for form Thin Lizzy. Skid Row continued as a three-piece, with Brendan Shields (bass) and Noel Bridgeman (drums). They relocated from Belfast to London in 1970 and signed a deal with CBS. After just two albums, they disbanded, leaving Moore to form the Gary Moore Band. Their debut, *Grinding Stone*, appeared in 1973, but their progress was halted the following year while Moore assisted Thin Lizzy after guitarist Eric Bell had left the band. This liaison lasted just four months before Moore was replaced by Scott Gorham and Brian Robertson.

Moore subsequently moved into session work before joining Colosseum II in 1976. He made three albums with them, and also rejoined Thin Lizzy for a 10-week American tour in 1977 after guitarist Brian Robertson suffered a severed artery in his hand. Moore finally became a full-time member of Thin Lizzy, but he subsequently left midway through a US tour and formed a new band called G-Force, though this outfit soon foundered. Moore then resumed his solo career, cutting a series of commercially ignored albums until he scored hit singles in 1985 with 'Empty Rooms' and another collaboration with Phil Lynott, 'Out In The Fields'. Moore's 1989 album

Vinnie Moore

Moore, Vinnie

b. 1965. This jazz-trained virtuoso guitarist was playing the guitar competently by the age of 12. Picked up by guitar talent scout Mike Varney, he was introduced to the techno-thrash band Vicious

Rumours, with whom he recorded *Soldiers Of The Night* in 1985. He left the band as soon as the album was released to concentrate on a solo career. *Mind's Eye* emerged in 1986, a self-written guitar instrumental album. This combined a fusion of classical jazz, blues and hard rock that was both heavily melodic and technically brilliant, ranking alongside Joe Satriani's finest work. The following two albums followed a similar pattern but were mellower. He was employed by Alice Cooper as lead guitarist on his 1991 Hey Stoopid tour.

Albums: *Mind's Eye* (1986), *Time Odyssey* (1988), *Meltdown* (1991).

Morbid Angel

Morbid Angel

Formed in Florida, USA in 1984, the band's original line-up consisted of Stering Von Scarborough (bass/vocals), Trey Azagthoth (guitar), Richard Brunelle (guitar) and Pete Sandoval (drums). The band quickly gained a following on the underground death metal scene because of their extreme ultra-fast musical approach. The band recorded a self-financed *Abominations Of Desolation* in 1986. However, unhappy with the resulting recordings, they decided not to release them, as had originally been intended, on their own, now defunct Gorque Records label. The band then underwent a personnel change replacing the recently departed

bass/vocalist Scarborough with David Vincent, who gave the band much more of an identity due to his strong charismatic image. The band continued to gain momentum and eventually attracted the attention of the Earache Records label resulting in the band's official debut *Altars Of Madness* being released in 1989. This was a relentless wall of noise made up of complex guitar riffs and ultra-fast drums. Death metal fans loved it and the band soon became one of the leaders of the death metal genre. By the release of the band's next album, *Blessed Are The Sick* they had toured Europe extensively, building a strong following as a result. The album was a marked improvement on their previous effort and strengthened their position as one of death metal's leading lights. Owing to furious bootlegging and the band's burgeoning popularity, Earache Records released the original recordings of *Abominations Of Desolation* in 1991.

Albums: *Altars Of Madness* (1989), *Blessed Are The Sick* (1991), *Abominations Of Desolation* (1991).

Mordred

Formed in San Fransisco, USA, in 1985, Mordred were one of the first of a new breed of thrash metal bands that incorporated elements of funk into their high-speed onslaught. Comprising Scott Holderby (vocals), Danny White (guitar), James Sanguinetti (guitar), Art Liboon (bass) and Gannon Hall (drums) they signed to Noise Records and released *Fool's Game* in 1989. On their next album they recruited Aaron (Pause) Vaughn, a scratching disc jockey to give their sound a new dimension. This new approach had enormous crossover potential, and the band combine mix elements of Faith No More, PiL, Megadeth and Parliament.

Albums: *Fool's Game* (1989), *In This Life* (1991).

Mother Love Bone

This short-lived, Seattle based quintet comprised Andrew Wood (vocals), Greg Gilmore (drums), Bruce Fairweather (guitar), Stone Gossard (guitar) and Jeff Ament (bass). Drawing influences from the Doors, the Stooges, MC5 and the Velvet Underground they specialized in heavy-duty garage rock laced with psychotic overtones. Signing to Polydor, they debuted with Apple in 1990 to widespread critical acclaim. Their promising career was curtailed abruptly by the untimely death of vocalist Andrew Wood shortly after the album was released. Gossard and Ament went on to further success with Temple Of The Dog and later Pearl Jam.

Album: Apple (1990).

Mother's Finest

Despite the 90s fixation with funk rock, Mother's Finest have long been considered as the world's finest in this musical field. Led by vocalist Baby Jean and hailing from Atlanta, Georgia, USA the band boasts the talents of Moses Mo (guitar), Glen Murdock (guitar), Mike (keyboards), Wizzard (bass) and B.B. Queen (drums). Formed in 1974, their music was basically funk with a metal edge and Baby Jean's vocals ranged from the sensual to all-out attack. The band never quite made the big league in their home-land and only gained a cult following in Europe, although they were successfull in Holland. In 1983 the band split-up. B.B. Queen played with southern boogie merchants, Molly Hatchet and then teamed up with former colleague Moses Mo in Illusion. The original line-up reformed in 1989 but their new album did not capture the fire and soul of earlier releases. Undaunted, they soldiered on and released a live recording, *Subluxation* to critical acclaim.

Albums: *Mother's Finest* (1974), *Mother's Finest* (1976), *Another Mother Further* (1977), *Mother Factor* (1978), *Live Mutha* (1979), *Iron Age* (1982), *One Mother To Another* (1983), *Looks Could Kill* (1989), *Subluxation* (1990).

Mötley Crüe

This heavy rock band were formed in 1980 by Nikki Sixx (b. Frank Faranno, 11 December 1958, California, USA; bass) and consisted of former members of other Los Angeles-based groups. Tommy Lee (b. 3 October 1962, Athens, Greece; drums) was recruited from Suite 19; Vince Neil (b. Vince Neil Wharton, 8 February 1961, Hollywood, California, USA; vocals) from Rocky Candy; while Nikki himself had recently left London. Mick Mars (b. Bob Deal, 3 April 1956, USA; guitar) was added to the line-up after Sixx and Lee answered an advertisement claiming 'Loud, rude, aggressive guitarist available'. Their first single, 'Stick To Your Guns', was issued in 1981 on their own Ledathür label, followed by their self-produced debut, *Too Fast For Love*. The band signed to Elektra in 1982, and the album was remixed and reissued that August. The following year, they recorded a new album, *Shout At The Devil*, with producer Tom Werman. He stayed at the helm for the two albums which broke them to a much wider audience in the USA, *Theatre Of Pain* (which sold more than two million copies) and *Girls, Girls, Girls*, which achieved the highest entry for a heavy metal album on *Billboard*'s album chart since *The Song Remains The Same* by Led Zeppelin in 1976. These albums refined the raw sound of earlier releases, without hiding the

Mötley Crüe

influence which Kiss and Aerosmith have had on their work. This change in style, which saw Mötley Crüe experimenting with organs, pianos and harmonicas in addition to their traditional instruments, has been described as a move from 'club-level metal glam' to 'stadium-size rock 'n' roll'.

The band have not been without their problems: in 1984, Vince Neil was involved in a major car crash in which Hanoi Rocks drummer Razzle was killed, while three years later, Nikki Sixx came close to death after a heroin overdose. But the band survived to appear at the Moscow Peace Festival in 1989 before more than 200,000 people, and then in 1991 to issue *Decade Of Decadence*, a compilation of their classic material plus some new material.

Albums: *Too Fast For Love* (1981), *Shout At The Devil* (1983), *Theatre Of Pain* (1985), *Girls, Girls, Girls* (1987), *Raw Tracks* (1988), *Dr. Feelgood* (1989). Compilation: *Decade Of Decadence* (1991).

Motorhead

In 1975 Lemmy (b. Ian Kilminster, 24 December 1945, Stoke, England; vocals/bass) was sacked from Hawkwind. The last song he wrote for them was called 'Motorhead', and this became the name of the band he formed with Larry Wallis of the

Motorhead

Pink Fairies on guitar and Lucas Fox on drums. Fox left Motorhead to join Warsaw Pact, being replaced by Phil Taylor (b. 21 September 1954, Chesterfield, England; drums). Taylor, in fact, had no professional musical experience, but was a casual friend of Lemmy. Motorhead was a four-piece band for less than a month, with Eddie Clark of Continuous Performance as second guitarist, when Wallis departed. The Lemmy/Taylor/Clarke combination lasted six years, until 1982. In May of that year Clarke was replaced by Brian Robertson, who had played with Thin Lizzy and Wild Horses. This combination released *Another Perfect Day*. Robertson stayed with Motorhead for two years before being replaced by Wurzel (b. Michael Burston, 23 October 1949, Cheltenham, England; guitar) - so-called on account of his scarecrow-like hair. In 1984 Philip Campbell (b. 7 May 1961, Pontypridd, Wales; guitar) left Persian Risk, thereby swelling the Motorhead ranks to four. In February of the same year, Pete Gill left Saxon to play the drums in Motorhead instead of Phil Taylor, who with Brian Robertson formed the band Operator. Three years later, Phil Taylor rejoined Motorhead. The most recent line-up has Lemmy on bass and vocals, Wurzel and Phil Campbell as guitarists and Phil Taylor playing the drums. Motorhead are perhaps the archetypal British heavy metal band. They are loud and brash, projecting an indomitable and fearless image. They do not lack a sense of fun, as was proven by the Headgirl project in 1980 when they teamed up with Girlschool. In recent years Lemmy's lyrics have been less concerned with motorbikes and fast living, and have shown a surprising sensitivity, in particular the title track of *1916* which shocked many with its ballad-like qualities. This was quite a change for Lemmy, whose idiosyncratic singing style, usually half-growl, half-shout, and with his neck craned up at 45 degrees to the microphone, seemed to sacrifice nothing in power, while taking on a new dimension in intensity.

Albums: *Motorhead* (1977), *Overkill* (1979), *Bomber* (1979), *Ace Of Spades* (1980), *No Sleep Till Hammersmith* (1981), *Iron Fist* (1982), *Another Perfect Day* (1983), *No Remorse* (1984), *Orgasmatron* (1986), *Rock'N'Roll* (1987), *No Sleep At All* (1988), *1916* (1991).

Mountain

Mountain were one of the first generation heavy

metal bands, formed by ex-Vagrants guitarist Leslie West (b. Leslie Weinstein, 22 October 1945, Queens, New York, USA) and bassist Felix Pappalardi (b. 1939, Bronx, New York, USA, d. 17 April 1983) in New York 1968. Augmented by drummer Corky Laing and Steve Knight on keyboards they played the Woodstock festival in 1970, releasing *Mountain Climbing* shortly afterwards. Featuring dense guitar lines from West and the delicate melodies of Pappalardi, they quickly established their own sound, although Cream influences were noticeable in places. The album was an unqualified success, peaking at number 17 in the *Billboard* album chart in November 1970. Their next two albums built on this foundation, and the band refined their style into an amalgam of heavy riffs, blues-based rock and extended guitar and keyboard solos. *Nantucket Sleighride* and *Flowers Of Evil* made the *Billboard* charts at numbers 16 and 35, respectively. A live album followed, which included interminably long solos and was poorly received. The group temporarily disbanded to follow separate projects. Pappalardi returned to producing, while West and Laing teamed up with Cream's Jack Bruce to record as the trio (West, Bruce And Laing). In the autumn of 1974, Mountain rose again with Alan Schwartzberg and Bob Mann replacing Laing and Knight to record *Twin Peaks*, live in Japan. This line-up was shortlived as Laing rejoined for the recording of the disappointing studio album *Avalanche*. The band collapsed once more and West concentrated on his solo career again. Pappalardi was shot and killed by his wife in 1983. Two years later, West and Laing resurrected the band with Mark Clarke (former Rainbow and Uriah Heep bassist) and released *Go For Your Life*. They toured with Deep Purple throughout Europe in 1985, but split up again soon afterwards. Albums: *Mountain Climbing* (1970), *Nantucket Sleighride* (1971), *Flowers Of Evil* (1971), *The Road Goes On Forever-Mountain Live* (1972), *Best Of* (1973), *Twin Peaks* (1974), *Avalanche* (1974), *Go For Your Life* (1985).

MSG

After stints with UFO and the Scorpions, guitarist Michael Schenker, (b. 10 January 1955, Savstedt, Germany) decided to step out into the spotlight on his own in 1980. Enlisting the services of Gary Barden (vocals), Simon Phillips (drums), Mo Foster (bass) and Don Airey (keyboards), the Michael Schenker Group (later shortened to MSG) was born. Their approach, characterized by Schenker's screaming guitar work, had much in common with both his previous bands. Schenker, now in complete control, hired and fired

musicians at will, so the line-up of MSG has rarely been stable. Only Barden survived to record their second album; Cozy Powell (drums), Chris Glen (bassist, ex-Sensational Alex Harvey Band) and Paul Raymond (keyboard player, ex-UFO) were the replacements. They enjoyed great success in the Far East, where they recorded a double live set at the Budokan Hall, Tokyo. This album finally helped to establish the band in Europe. Graham Bonnet replaced Barden on *Assault Attack* and ex-Rory Gallagher drummer Ted McKenna was also recruited. Bonnet insisted on making a significant contribution to the compositions and his influence can clearly be heard on the album, which is far more blues-orientated than previous releases. Schenker fired Bonnet shortly after the album's launch and welcomed back former vocalist Gary Barden. The next two album releases were rigidly formularized. Old ideas were simply re-hashed and the band were stuck in a creative rut. Even the contribution of Derek St. Holmes (ex-Ted Nugent vocalist) could not elevate the very ordinary material. Barden left to form Statetrooper and MSG disintegrated. Schenker moved back to Germany and teamed up with singer Robin McCauley (ex-Grand Prix) to form the McCauley Schenker Group, still retaining the acronym MSG. They completed the new-look band, with Steve Mann, Rocky Newton and Bobo Schopf on keyboards, bass and drums, respectively. They also concentrated on a more melodic direction, as McCauley's proliferant writing skills were accepted by Schenker. With the release of *Perfect Timing* and *Save Yourself*, they have begun to re-establish a solid fan base once more. Schenker took time between MSG albums in 1991 to collaborate on the Contraband supergroup project, with members of Vixen, Ratt, L.A. Guns and Shark Island. Albums: *The Michael Schenker Group* (1980), *MSG* (1981), *One Night At Budokan* (1982), *Assault Attack* (1982), *Built To Destroy* (1983), *Rock Will Never Die* (1984), *Perfect Timing* (1987), *Save Yourself* (1989).

Murder Inc.

This Avant-garde/industrial metal band were formed in London during 1992 by ex-Killing Joke members and ex-Revolting Cocks vocalist Chris Connelly. Utilizing two drummers in Martin Atkins and Paul Ferguson, their style is dominated by a strong rhythmic percussive element. Geordie Walker (guitar), Paul Raven (bass) and John Bechdel (guitar/keyboards) complete the line-up. Contracted to Music For Nations Records, the band debuted with a self-titled album in June 1992. This built on the brutal rhythms of Killing

Joke's material, but added a more experimental
approach to the proceedings.
Album: Murder Inc. (1992).

N

Napalm Death

This quartet from Birmingham, England, was formed in 1982. They combined punk and thrash metal influences in the new sub-genre of grindcore, the most extreme of all musical forms. Comprising Lee Dorrian (vocals), Bill Steer (guitar), Shane Embury (bass) and Mick Harris (drums), they specialized in sub-two minute blasts of metallic white noise, over-ridden by Dorrian's unintelligible vocal tirade. The lyrics deal with social and political injustices, but actually sound like somebody coughing up blood. They originally attracted a small but loyal cult following on the underground heavy metal scene. Since then, grindcore has developed considerably and found mass acceptance among the rank and file of the metal world. They remain, however, the antithesis of style, melody and taste and represent the punk concept taken to its ultimate extreme. The band members also have side projects; Bill Steer is a member of Carcass, Shane Embury plays with Unseen Terror and Mick Harris drums in Extreme Noise Terror.

Albums: *Scum* (1987), *From Enslavement To Obliteration* (1988), *The Peel Sessions* (1989), *Harmony Corruption* (1990), *Utopia Banished* (1992).

Nasty Idols

This Swedish glam-metal quintet were formed in 1988 by vocalist Andy Pierce and guitarist Jonnie Wee, with Dick Qwarfort (bass), George Swanson (drums) and Roger White (keyboards) completing the line-up. They initially pursued a hard-rock direction in the style of Bon Jovi and Whitesnake. They debuted with *Gigolos On Parole* to widespread indifference. Wee was soon replaced by Peter Espinoza on guitar, and his arrival marked a move towards a more glam-metal image, with Mötley Crüe, Hanoi Rocks and Guns N' Roses influences taking over. *Cruel Intention* was the result, released in 1991, and marked an improvement on their debut.

Albums: *Gigolos On Parole* (1989), *Cruel Intention* (1991).

Nasty Savage

This heavy metal/thrash quintet was formed in Brandigan, Florida, USA during 1983 by vocalist

Napalm Death

Nasty Ronnie and guitarist Ben Meyer. Assisted by David Austin (guitar), Fred Dregischan (bass) and Curtis Beeson (drums), they made their debut with demo tracks that appeared on the *Metal Massacre IV* and *Iron Tyrants* compilations in 1984. This led to a contract with Metal Blade Records, producing four albums over the next five years. From an initial hard-rock base of Iron Maiden and Judas Priest-styles, they gradually incorporated more thrash elements into their music, drawing inspiration and ideas from Metallica, Anthrax and Slayer. They have been through four bass players in as many years, with the current guitarist Richard Bateman having taken up duties in 1988. Rob Proctor replaced Beeson on drums the following year. The band are renowned for their crazy live show, which features the wildman vocalist smashing television sets on stage.

Albums: *Nasty Savage* (1985), *Indulgence* (1987), *Abstract Reality* (1988), *Penetration Point* (1989).

Nazareth

Nazareth

Formed in 1968 in Dunfermline, Fife, Scotland, Nazareth evolved out of local attraction, the Shadettes. Dan McCafferty (vocals), Manny Charlton (guitar), Pete Agnew (bass) and Darrell Sweet (drums) took their new name from the opening line in 'The Weight', a contemporary hit for the Band. After completing a gruelling Scottish tour, Nazareth opted to move to London. Nazareth and Exercises showed undoubted promise, while a third set, Razamanaz, spawned two UK Top 10 singles in 'Broken Down Angel' and 'Bad Bad Boy' (both 1973). New producer Roger Glover helped focus the quartet's brand of melodic hard-rock, and such skills were equally prevalent on Loud 'N' Proud. An unlikely rendition of Joni Mitchell's 'This Flight Tonight' gave the group another major chart entry, while the Charlton-produced Hair Of The Dog confirmed Nazareth as an international attraction. Another cover version, this time of Tomorrow's

'My White Bicycle', was a Top 20 entry and although Rampant did not yield a single, the custom-recorded 'Love Hurts', originally a hit for the Everly Brothers, proved highly successful in the US and Canada. Nazareth's popularity remained undiminished throughout the 70s but, having tired of a four-piece line-up, they added guitarist Zal Cleminson, formerly of the Sensational Alex Harvey Band, for No Mean City. Still desirous for change, the group invited Jeff 'Skunk' Baxter, late of Steely Dan and the Doobie Brothers, to produce Malice In Wonderland. While stylistically different from previous albums, the result was artistically satisfying. Contrasting ambitions then led to Cleminson's amicable departure, but the line-up was subsequently augmented by former Spirit keyboard player, John Locke. Baxter also produced the experimental The Fool Circle, while the group's desire to capture their in-concert fire resulted in 'Snaz. Glasgow guitarist Billy Rankin had now joined the group, but dissatisfaction with touring led to Locke's departure following 2XS. Rankin then switched to keyboards, but although Nazareth continued to enjoy popularity in the US and Europe, their stature in the UK was receding. Bereft of a major recording deal, Nazareth suspended their career during the late 80s, leaving McCafferty free to pursue solo ambitions. A comeback album in 1992 with the addition of Billy Rankin produced the outstanding No Jive, yet Nazareth's past low profile in the UK will demand a lot of live work to capitalize on this success.

Albums: Nazareth (1971), Exercises (1972), Razamanaz (1973), Loud 'N' Proud (1974), Rampant (1974), Hair Of The Dog (1975), Close Enough For Rock 'N' Roll (1976), Play 'N' The Game (1976), Expect No Mercy (1977), No Mean City (1978), Malice In Wonderland (1980), The Fool Circle (1981), 'Snaz (1981), 2XS (1982), Sound Elixir (1983), The Catch (1984), Play The Game (1985), No Jive (1992). Compilations: Greatest Hits (1975), Hot Tracks (1976), 20 Greatest Hits: (1985), Nazareth (1988).

Nelson

The twin sons of early rock 'n' roll star Rick Nelson and wife Kris, Matthew and Gunnar Nelson were born on 20 September 1967, Los Angeles, California, USA. Musically-inclined as children, the boys learned to play bass and drums and sang. Their father booked recording studio time for them for their 12th birthday, and they recorded a self-penned song with vocal backings by the Pointer Sisters. By the early 80s the twins had joined a heavy metal band called Strange Agents, which later changed its name to the

Nelson

Nelsons. In 1990, now simply called Nelson, the twins, both sporting waist-length blond hair, signed with David Geffen's new DGC record label and recorded a self-titled pop-rock album. The first single release, '(Can't Live Without Your) Love And Affection', reached number 1 in the US charts, while the album made the US Top 20.
Album: *Nelson* (1990).

Neon Cross

This Californian 'white metal' quartet was formed in 1984 by David Raymond Reeves (lead vocals) and Don Webster (guitar). Enlisting the services of Ed Ott (bass) and Michael Betts (drums), it took a further four years, before the band made their debut with a track on 1988's *California Metal* compilation. A deal with Regency Records ensued and their self-titled first album emerged as a competent amalgam of Stryper, Barren Cross and Bloodgood. It was however, discredited somewhat by Reeves' limited vocal ability.
Album: *Neon Cross* (1988).

Neon Rose

This progressive rock group was formed in Sweden 1973 by vocalist Roger Holegard and guitarist Gunnar Hallin. Augmented by Piero Mengarelli (guitar), Beno Mengarelli (bass/vocals) and Thomas Wilkund (drums), they signed to Vertigo the following year. Inspired by Iron Butterfly, Emerson, Lake And Palmer and Deep Purple, Neon Rose were an experimental quintet that indulged in long, esoteric and frequently blues-based workouts. They debuted with A Dream Of Glory And Pride in 1974, which showcased the band's instrumental capabilities, but also highlighted their vocal shortcomings. Two further albums were released, but the quality of material declined significantly. They disappeared from the scene in 1976, having only made an impact in their native Sweden.

Albums: A Dream Of Glory And Pride (1974), Neon Rose Two (1974), Reload (1975).

New England (UK)

This British hard-rock quartet were formed in 1990 by Paul McKenna (lead vocals) and Dave Cook (guitar). Enlisting the services of Chris Huxter (bass) and Ian Winters (drums) they secured a deal with the independent Street Link label. *You Can't Keep Living This Way* emerged in 1991 and confused the critics, because the music was awkward to tie down and not easily pigeonholed. It fused influences as diverse as Led Zeppelin, Faith No More, the Doors and Van Halen, yet the songs were stamped with New England's unique persona. Given time to develop and adequate backing from a major label, they have the potential to make a significant impact on the 90s heavy rock scene.
Albums: *You Can't Keep Living This Way* (1991).

New England (US)

This American quartet comprised John Fannon (guitar/vocals), Jimmy Waldo (keyboards), Gary Shea (bass) and Hirsh Gardener (drums). Taken under the wing of Kiss's manager, Bill Aucoin, they purveyed sophisticated, melodic rock in a vein similar to Styx and Journey. In 1979, they were given the chance to impress on a big stage, landing the support slot on the American leg of the Kiss tour. Although competent, their music lacked individuality and the band themselves had a nondescript image. After a third album, produced by Todd Rundgren, the band disintegrated in 1981, with Waldo and Shea eventually going on to join Alcatrazz.
Albums: *New England* (1979), *Explorer Suite* (1980), *Walking Wild* (1981).

New Frontier

This melodic US pop-rock group was formed in 1988 by ex-Billy Satellite vocalist Monty Byron and ex-Gamma bassist Glen Letsch. Adding David Neuhauser (keyboards) and Marc Nelson (drums), they successfully negotiated a deal with the newly-formed Mika label. Their debut album was produced by Ritchie Zito (of Heart and Cheap Trick fame) and featured a collection of hi-tech AOR numbers that were targeted at the Billboard charts. Failing to generate media interest, the band disintegrated shortly after the album's release. Letsch went on to play with Robin Trower.
Album: New Frontier (1988).

New Wave Of British Heavy Metal

This phrase was coined by rock journalist Geoff Barton while he was working for the English weekly music paper *Sounds*. It was used to promote all the heavy metal and hard-rock bands that came out in the years 1979-80. Their names would speak for them, such as Venom, Sledgehammer, Rage, Prowler, Weapon and Vardis, and these only gained some national recognition. More famous were Iron Maiden, Saxon, Def Leppard, Girlschool, Samson, Diamond Head and Praying Mantis. Most of the bands would lend one another equipment or band members if they were in a make-or-break situation. Even though they were influenced by Thin Lizzy, Led Zeppelin, Black Sabbath and Judas Priest, they played with more of an urgency and hunger for success. For the fans, the movement proved to be an alternative to the punk music and an opportunity to retain their long hair. Lyrically, many groups stayed faithful to the formula of Sex (the heavy metal fantasy of 'rock 'n' roll women' in leather), Teenage Confusion and Frustration (usually brought on by thoughts of the former) and of course, the perennial satanic references, whether they were proclaiming they were indeed the Beast incarnate, or that they alone were about to do battle with the horned one on the Astral Plane. Diamond Head sang 'Am I evil . . . Yes I am . . .' Def Leppard sang 'Well we were gettin' ready just the other night, when a knock on the dressing room door gave way to a leather jacketed little girl who we'd never seen before. In her red satin dress and her high-heeled shoes she took us all by surprise, and when she asked what we wanted to do, she said it with her eyes . . . Just getcha rocks off'. Samson were 'Riding with the angels . . . I'm riding with the angels'. Just like the punk scene, there were many albums brought out by the record companies to cash in on the explosion of bands, but, similarly, most of them were uninspired and in time all that remained were the worthwhile few.

Compilations: *Brute Force* (1980), *Metal For Muthas, Vols. 1 & 2* (1980), *N.W.O.B.H.M-Revisited* (1990).

New York Dolls

One of the most influential rock bands of the last 20 years, the New York Dolls pre-dated the punk and sleaze-metal movements which followed long after their own demise. Formed in 1972, the line-up stabilized with David Johansen (vocals), Johnny Thunders (guitar), Arthur Harold Kane (bass), Sylvain Sylvain (guitar/piano) and Jerry Nolan (drums), the last two having replaced Rick Rivets and Billy Murcia (who died in November 1972). The band sported an outrageous, glam-rock image: lipstick, high-heels and tacky leather outfits being the norm. Underneath, they were a first rate

rock 'n' roll band, dragged up on the music of Stooges, Rolling Stones and MC5. Their self-titled debut, released in 1973, is a minor landmark in rock history, oozing attitude, vitality and controversy from every note. It was met with widespread critical acclaim, but this never transferred to commercial success. The follow-up, Too Much Too Soon, was an appropriate title and indicated that alcohol and drugs were beginning to take their toll. The album is a charismatic collection of punk/glam-rock anthems, delivered with a chaotic coolness, that has yet to be equalled. It received a unanimous thumbs down from the music press and the band began to implode shortly afterwards. Johansen embarked on a solo career and Thunders formed Heartbreakers. The Dolls continued for a short time with Blackie Lawless (now W.A.S.P.'s vocalist) on guitar, before eventually grinding to a halt in 1975. Jerry Nolan died as a result of a stroke on 14 January 1992 whilst undergoing treatment for pneumonia and meningitis. Red Patent Leather is a poor quality and posthumously-released live recording from May 1975.

Albums: New York Dolls (1973), Too Much Too Soon (1974), Red Patent Leather (1984). Compilation: Lipstick Killers (1983).

Niagara

This melodic rock group was formed in Madrid, Spain during 1987 by Angel Arias (bass) and V. M. Arias (guitar). The line-up was completed with the addition of Tony Cuevas (lead vocals), Joey Martos (drums) and Ricky Castaneda (keyboards). Using English lyrics and concentrating on a style that embodied elements of Europe and Whitesnake, they have built up a sizeable following on the European heavy rock scene. Produced by Baron Rojo guitarist Carlos de Castro, Now Or Never was an impressive debut that featured abrasive guitar work, coupled with razor-sharp arrangements.

Album: Now Or Never (1988).

Night Ranger

This talented and sophisticated American pomp-rock group released a string of first class albums between 1981 and 1988. Featuring Jack Blades (vocals/bass), Brad Gillis (guitar, ex-Ozzy Osbourne), Alan Fitzgerald (keyboards, ex-Montrose), Kelly Keagy (drums) and Jeff Watson (guitar), they gigged in and around their Californian hometown, San Francisco. They soon attracted the attention of promoter Bill Graham, who secured them the support slots to Santana, Judas Priest and the Doobie Brothers. Their first four albums made the *Billboard* Top 40 album

Night Ranger

Kansas and Journey. Percival quit shortly after the album's release and the band continued as a four-piece to record *Black Summer*. This moved towards a more metallic style, in keeping with the New Wave Of British Heavy Metal, that was in full swing at the time. The band expanded to a five-piece, with the arrival of vocalist Max Bacon for the more raw *Stand Up And Be Counted*. Bacon's stay was short-lived as he soon moved on to Bronz, with Johnson also breaking ranks soon afterwards. Dave Evans and Glynn Porrino were swiftly recruited to fill in on vocals and guitar, but their compositional abilities could not match those of Johnson. Consequently, *My Kingdom Come* represented the nadir of the band's creative capabilities. The band were in their death throes; they finally gave up the proverbial ghost after the disappointing *Night Of Mystery, Alive!, Alive!*

Albums: *Something In The Air* (1980), *Black Summer* (1982), *Stand Up And Be Counted* (1983), *My Kingdom Come* (1984), *Night Of Mystery, Alive!, Alive!* (1985).

1994

This US melodic-rock quartet was formed in 1977 by ex-L.A. Jets duo Karen Lawrence (vocals) and John Desautels (drums). With the addition of Steve Schiff (guitar) and Bill Rhodes (bass), they signed to A&M Records and released a self-titled debut the following year. This was characterized by Lawrence's powerful vocals and a style that incorporated elements of Heart, Aerosmith and Foreigner. Guitarist Steve Schiff was replaced by Rick Armand on *Please Stand By*, which lacked the rough edges of their debut, and moved towards mainstream AOR. Success eluded the band and Lawrence quit in 1980. After a decade of less than successful projects, which have included collaborations with Cheap Trick, Jeff Beck and Rod Stewart, it is has often been rumoured that she may reform 1994.

Albums: *1994* (1978), *Please Stand By* (1979).

Nirvana

Formed in Aberdeen, Washington, USA in 1988, Nirvana originally comprised Kurt Cobain, 20 February 1967; guitar/vocals), Chris Novoselic (b. 16 May 1965; bass) and Dave Grohl (b. 14 January 1969; drums). Grohl was 'something like our sixth drummer', explained Cobain, and had been recruited from east coast band Dave Brammage, having previously played with Scream, who recorded for Minor Threat's influential Dischord label. Their original drummer was Chad Channing; at one point Dinosaur Jr's J. Mascis had been touted as a permanent fixture, along with Dan Peters from Mudhoney. Having been signed

charts, with *Seven Wishes* reaching the Top 10 in June 1985. They also scored two Top 10 single hits in the USA with 'Sister Christian' and 'Sentimental Street' peaking at number 5 and 8, respectively. *Man In Motion* saw the departure of Fitzgerald and the band adopting a more hard-rock direction. Produced by Keith Olsen, the album was their first commercial failure. The band split up shortly afterwards, with *Live In Japan* emerging two years later, featuring one of their 1988 concerts. Jack Blades joined Damn Yankees with Ted Nugent, Tommy Shaw and Michael Cartelone. Night Ranger were an impressive outfit in the Journey/ Kansas/Styx mould; however, despite their success in the USA, they did not make any real impression in Europe.

Albums: *Dawn Patrol* (1982), *Midnight Madness* (1983), *Seven Wishes* (1985), *Big Life* (1987), *Man In Motion* (1988), *Live In Japan* (1990). Compilation: *Greatest Hits* (1989).

Nightwing

After the demise of Strife in 1978, bassist/vocalist Gordon Rowley formed Nightwing, with Alec Johnson (guitar), Eric Percival (guitar), Kenny Newton (keyboards) and Steve Bartley (drums). They debuted in 1980 with *Something In The Air*, a grandiose AOR-rock album in the style of Styx,

by the Seattle-based Sub Pop label, the trio completed their debut single, 'Love Buzz'/'Big Cheese', the former a song written and first recorded by 60s Dutch group, Shocking Blue. Second guitarist Jason Everman was then added prior to *Bleach*, which cost a meagre $600 to record. The set confirmed Nirvana's ability to match heavy riffs with melody and it quickly attracted a cult following. However, Channing left the group following a European tour, and as a likely replacement proved hard to find, Dan Peters from labelmates Mudhoney stepped in on a temporary basis. He was featured on the single 'Sliver', Nirvana's sole 1990 release. Everman also dropped out of the line-up, but new drummer David Grohl reaffirmed a sense of stability. The revamped trio secured a prestigious deal with Geffen Records whose faith was rewarded with *Nevermind*, which broke them commercially. This was a startling collection of songs which transcended structural boundaries. It topped the US charts early in 1992, eclipsing much-vaunted competition from Michael Jackson and Dire Straits. and topped many polls for the Album of the Year. The opening track, 'Smells Like Teen Spirit', echoed the crossover appeal of the Pixies and by reaching the UK Top 10, the single confirmed that Nirvana now combined critical and popular acclaim. In early 1992 the romance of Cobain and Courtney Love of Hole was sealed when the couple married.
Albums: *Bleach* (1989), *Nevermind* (1991).

Nitzinger, John
b. Texas, USA. This energetic and highly talented guitarist/vocalist specialized in blues-based hard-rock and boogie. He has worked with Bloodrock, Alice Cooper and Carl Palmer's P.M., supplying ferocious Ted Nugent-like guitar chords. His three solo albums are highly varied and explore a wider range of styles than might at first be imagined. Psychedelia, jazz, rock, blues and metal nuances have been integrated within his own inimitable and extrovert approach.
Albums: Nitzinger (1971), One Foot In History (1972), Live Better . . . Electrically (1976).

No Exqze
This melodic rock quartet was formed by ex-Vandenberg bassist Dick Kemper in 1987. Recruiting Geert Scheigrond (guitar), Leen Barbier (vocals) and Nico Groen (drums), they signed to Phonogram and debuted with *Too Hard Too Handle* in 1988. No Exqze allowed Kemper to develop his writing talents, which had previously been suppressed and ignored in Vandenberg. Produced by Tony Platt, the album was dominated by Barbier's soulful vocals, which added depth and character to Kemper's rather average AOR-style compositions.
Album: *Too Hard Too Handle* (1988).

No Sweat
This Dublin-based, six-piece melodic rock group comprised Paul Quinn (lead vocals), Dave Gooding (guitar), Jim Phillips (guitar), P.J. Smith (keyboards), Jon Angel (bass) and Ray Fearn (drums). They impressed Def Leppard vocalist Joe Elliot, who took over the production on their debut album and helped them secure a deal with London Records. They supported Thunder on their 'Backstreet Symphony' tour in 1990 and were generally well received. Paul Quinn's voice oozes emotion, but their material has yet to stamp its own identity.
Album: *No Sweat* (1990).

Nokemono
This Japanese hard-rock quintet was formed in 1978. Inspired by fellow countrymen Bow Wow, Yukihiro 'Ace' Nakaya (vocals) and Shigeo 'Rolla' Nakano (guitar) decided to put a band together along similar lines. Recruiting Bunzo 'Bunchan' Satoh (guitar), Masaaki 'Cherry' Chikura (bass) and Tadashi 'Popeye' Hirota (drums), they were picked up by the local SMS label. *From The Black World* combined Van Halen, Deep Purple and UFO influences. It was an impressive debut, but was let down by an inferior production. The band have remained virtually unknown outside Japan.
Albums: *From The Black World* (1979).

Norum, John
Norum was formerly the guitarist in Europe but quit just as the band were on the verge of worldwide recognition with 'The Final Countdown'. After completing the recording of the *Countdown* album, he decided to break ranks because he was unhappy with the pop-metal direction that vocalist Joey Tempest was intent on pursuing. He enlisted the help of Marcel Jacob (bass, ex-Yngwie Malmsteen), Peter Hermansson (drums, ex-220 Volts) and Goran Edman (vocals, ex-Madison) to record *Total Control* in 1987. Musically this followed a similar path to Europe, Whitesnake and Foreigner, but featured more up-front guitar and less polished vocals. He later moved to Los Angeles to work on material with Glenn Hughes, and later collaborated with Don Dokken.
Albums: *Total Control* (1987), *Live In Stockholm* (1988).

Nuclear Assault

Norum, Tone

Tone is the younger sister of former Europe guitarist, John Norum. She debuted in 1986 with One Of A Kind, an album written, arranged and played on by Joey Tempest and her brother John. Predictably, the musical direction was very similar to that of Europe; melodic pop-metal, with the occasional power ballad. This Time followed a similar pattern, but used session musicians and the Billy Steinberg/Tom Kelly writing team, that had previously penned hits for Madonna and Whitney Houston. The result was a highly polished melodic rock album in the style of Heart and Starship. Red saw Tone move away from AOR towards folk-rock.

Albums: One Of A Kind (1986), This Time (1988), Red (1989).

Nova, Aldo

b. Aldo Caparucio. Nova is a virtuoso guitarist of Italian descent. He arrived onto the rock scene in 1981 with a self-titled debut of melodic AOR/pomp-rock that incorporated elements of Boston and Styx. Momentum was lost however, with Subject, a disjointed and ultimately disappointing concept album. Twitch made amends somewhat, with a return to smooth, sophisticated and melody-conscious symphonic rock. Disillusioned by the lack of media response and complex legal wrangles contractual commitments, he left the music business in 1985. After almost a six-year break, he was lured back into the studio by his good friend Jon Bon Jovi. Together they wrote the material for Blood On The Bricks, a stunning collection of hard-rock songs, saturated with infectious hooks and inspired guitar breaks. The album was well received in the music press and drew comparisons with Bryan Adams, Europe and, naturally enough, Bon Jovi. It may prove the launching pad for the second phase of Aldo Nova's career.

Albums: *Aldo Nova* (1981), *Subject: Aldo Nova* (1983), *Twitch* (1985), *Blood On The Bricks* (1991).

Nowherefast

This Californian melodic rock quartet was formed in 1981 by Steve Bock (vocals/bass) and Jeff Naideau (guitar/keyboards). Enlisting the services of Bob Frederickson (guitar) and Jimmy Hansen (drums), they soon struck a contract with the WEA/Scotti Brothers label. Incorporating elements of blues and funk into Kansas and

Journey-like AOR, they delivered a self-titled debut in 1982. The album was unsuccessful and the band's name unfortunately was a fair summation of the impact they had made.
Album: *Nowherefast* (1982).

Nuclear Assault

Formed in New York, USA in 1985 this group consisted of John Conelly (guitar/vocals), Anthony Bramante (guitar), Dan Lilker (bass) and Glenn Evans (drums). Lilker formed Nuclear Assault after his departure from Anthrax, one of the earliest thrash metal bands. The sound of Nuclear Assault is much more aggressive, merging the styles of hardcore and thrash with socially aware lyrics. They have become immensely popular due to constant touring and a refusal to compromise in their recorded work. After five albums however, their individual tendencies to indulge in solo projects has put the future of the band in question.
Albums: *Game Over* (1986), *The Plague* (1987), *Survive* (1988), *Handle With Care* (1989), *Out Of Order* (1991).

Ted Nugent

Nugent, Ted

b. 13 December 1949, Detroit, Michigan, USA. Excited by 50s rock 'n' roll, Nugent taught himself the rudiments of guitar playing at the age of 8. As a teenager he played in the Royal Highboys and

Lourds, but this formative period ended in 1964 upon his family's move to Chicago. Here, Nugent assembled the Amboy Dukes, which evolved from garage-band status into a popular, hard-rock attraction. He led the group throughout its various permutations, assuming increasing control as original members dropped out of the line-up. In 1974 a revitalized unit - dubbed Ted Nugent And The Amboy Dukes - completed the first of two albums for Frank Zappa's Discreet label, but in 1976 the guitarist abandoned the now-anachronistic suffix and embarked on a fully-fledged solo career. Derek St. Holmes (guitar), Rob Grange (bass) and Cliff Davies (drums) joined him for *Ted Nugent* and *Free For All*, both of which maintained the high-energy rock of previous incarnations. However, it was as a live attraction that Nugent made his mark - he often claimed to have played more gigs per annum than any other artist or group. Ear-piecing guitar work and vocals - 'If it's too loud you're too old' ran one tour motto - were accompanied by a cultivated 'wild man' image, where the artist would appear in loin-cloth and headband, brandishing the bow and arrow with which he claimed to hunt food for his family. The aggression of a Nugent concert was captured on the platinum selling *Double Live Gonzo*, which featured many of his best-loved stage numbers, including 'Cat Scratch Fever', 'Motor City Madness' and the enduring 'Baby Please Don't Go'. Charlie Huhn (guitar) and John Sauter (bass) replaced St. Holmes and Grange for *Weekend Warriors*, and the same line-up remained intact for *State Of Shock* and *Scream Dream*. In 1981 Nugent undertook a worldwide tour fronting a new backing group, previously known as the D.C. Hawks, comprising Mike Gardner (bass), Mark Gerhardt (drums) and three guitarists; Kurt, Rick and Verne Wagoner. The following year the artist left Epic for Atlantic Records, and in the process established a new unit which included erstwhile sidemen Derek St. Holmes (vocals) and Carmine Appice (drums; ex-Vanilla Fudge). Despite such changes, Nugent was either unwilling, or unable, to alter the formula which had served him so well in the 70s. Successive solo releases offered little new and the artist drew greater publicity for appearances on talk shows and celebrity events. In 1989 Nugent teamed up with Tommy Shaw (vocals/guitar, ex-Styx), Jack Blades (bass, ex-Night Ranger) and Michael Cartellone (drums) to form the successful 'supergroup', Damn Yankees.
Albums: with the Amboy Dukes *Call Of The Wild* (1973), *Tooth, Fang And Claw* (1974), solo *Ted Nugent* (1975), *Free For All* (1976), *Cat Scratch Fever* (1977), *Double Live Gonzo* (1978), *Weekend*

Warriors (1978), *State Of Shock* (1979), *Scream Dream* (1980), *Intensities In Ten Cities* (1981), *Nugent* (1982), *Penetrator* (1984), *Little Miss Dangerous* (1986), *If You Can't Lick 'Em...Lick 'Em* (1988). Compilations: *Great Gonzos: The Best Of Ted Nugent* (1981), *Anthology: Ted Nugent* (1986).

Nutz

This UK hard-rock quintet was formed in 1973 by Dave Lloyd (vocals) and Mick Devonport (guitar). With the addition of Keith Mulholland (bass), Kenny Newton (keyboards) and John Mylett (drums), they gained a reputation as the ubiquitous support act. Playing competent, blues-based rock and boogie, their exuberant and high-energy live shows always overshadowed the drab and lifeless studio recordings. Their sexist album covers were typical of the genre. Newton left to join Nightwing in 1978 and the band changed their name to Rage. This was a deliberate attempt to jump the N.W.O.B.H.M. bandwagon, that was starting to roll at this time.
Albums: *Nutz* (1974), *Nutz Two* (1975), *Hard Nutz* (1976), *Live Cutz* (1977).

N.W.O.B.H.M (see New Wave Of British Heavy Metal)

O

Obituary

Obituary

This intense and disturbingly extreme death-metal group hailed from Florida USA. After recording a single and contributing two tracks to *Metal Massacre* compilations as Xecutioner, they changes their name to Obituary. This was initiated by the appearance of another inferior act, who also went under the Xecutioner banner. Signed to Roadrunner Records, the band comprised John Tardy (vocals), Allen West (guitar), Trevor Peres (guitar), David Tucker (bass) and Donald Tardy (drums). *Slowly We Rot*, unleashed in 1989, was characterized by Tardy's gurgling sewer-like vocals over a maelstrom of crashing powerchords and demonic drumming. *Cause Of Death* saw the band refine their unique style with ex-Death guitarist James Murphy and bassist Frank Watkins in place of West and Tucker respectively. Obituary specialize in a hideous and brutal musical carnage and represent the death-metal concept, taken to its ultimate conclusion.
Albums: *Slowly We Rot* (1989), *Cause Of Death* (1990).

Obsession

This US, Connecticut-based outfit was formed in 1983 by vocalist Mike Vescara and guitarist Bruce Vitale. Adding Art Maco (guitar), Matt Karugas (bass) and Jay Mezias (drums), they made their debut with a track on a *Metal Massacre* compilation album in 1983. Combining Judas Priest, Venom and Anvil influences, they recorded the *Marshall Law* mini-album; a high-speed, dual guitar onslaught, punctuated by Vescara's banshee-like howl. A contract with Enigma ensued and the two albums that followed showed the band diversifying into more melodic territory. In mid-88, Maco and Mezias quit, but the band finally folded when Vescara accepted the position of frontman with Japanese rockers Loudness.
Albums: *Marshall Law* (1984), *Scarred For Life* (1986), *Methods Of Madness* (1987).

Obsession

Obus

This Spanish melodic metal band was formed in 1980 by vocalist Fortu and guitarist Francisco Laguna. Recruiting Fernando Sanches (drums) and Juan Luis Serrano, they restricted their potential audience by insisting on singing in their native tongue. Signing to the local Chapa Discos label, they recorded three amateurish albums lacking in fresh ideas.
Albums: *Preparato* (1981), *Podoroso Como El Trueno* (1982), *El Que Mas* (1984).

Offenbach

This progressive rock outfit originating from Quebec, Canada. The band were assembled in 1975 by Gerard Boulet (vocals/keyboards) and Breen Laboeuf (vocals/bass). Following the addition of Jean Gravel (guitar), John McGale (guitar) and Pierre Ringuet (drums), they signed to A&M Records in 1976. Debuting with Never Too Tender, they initially opted for English lyrics, which sounded rather wooden in their extended psychedelic, blues-based workouts. Realizing this, they switched to singing in French from Offenbach onwards. Changing labels to RCA in 1979, saw a swing towards an earthy R&B style, not that dissimilar to Joe Cocker. Failing to find an audience with this new direction, they started to incorporate wind instruments, extend the length of compositions and move into the domain of symphonic folk-rock.

Albums: Never Too Tender (1976), Offenbach (1977), Victoire D'Armour (1978), Traversion (1979), Encore (1980), Coup De Foudu (1981).

Omen

This Los Angeles, USA-based, melodic power-metal outfit formed in 1984. Comprising J.D. Kimball (vocals), Kenny Powell (guitar), Jody Henry (bass) and Steve Wittig (drums), they debuted with a track on the Metal Massacre V compilation. This led to a contract with Metal Blade and the release of Battle Cry the same year. This was a competent, if uninspired, collection of Iron Maiden-style rockers, which lacked distinction due to Kimball's weak vocals. Three more albums followed a similar pattern, with 1987's mini-opus Nightmares being the most interesting, as it featured a strong cover of AC/DC's 'Whole Lotta Rosie'. Coburn Pharr replaced Kimball in 1988 and the band produced Escape From Nowhere, their finest recorded work. Adding Rush and Led Zeppelin elements to the basic metal framework, it was characterized by Pharr's powerful and high-pitched vocals. Surprisingly, it did not sell and Pharr left to join Annihilator in 1990.

Albums: Battle Cry (1984), Warning Of Danger (1985), The Curse (1986), Nightmares (1987), Escape From Nowhere (1988).

Only Child

This heavy metal group was put together by the multi-talented Paul Sabu (guitar/vocals/songwriter/producer) in 1988. Featuring Tommy Rude (keyboards), Murril Maglio (bass) and Charles Esposito (drums), their self-titled debut was critically acclaimed melodic rock. The praise heaped upon the album by Kerrang magazine, in particular, was rather premature, as the overtly commercial riffs and obvious hooks soon wore thin. This was borne out by the fact that the album failed to sell anywhere near the numbers anticipated. Esposito was replaced by Tommy Amato in 1989 and they were signed by Geffen Records to start work on new material.

Album: Only Child (1988).

Onslaught

This UK thrash metal quintet was formed in Bristol 1983 by guitarist Nige Rockett and drummer Steve Grice. With the addition of vocalist Paul Mahoney and bassist Jason Stallord, they recorded Power From Hell on the independent Cor label in 1985. This opened the doors to a contract with Under One Flag, the thrash subsidiary of MFN. The Force saw the band expand to a quintet, with the arrival of new vocalist Sy Keeler; Mahoney was relegated to bass and Stallord switched to rhythm guitar. The album was heavily reliant on the styles of Slayer, Metallica and Anthrax, with little original input of their own. Mahoney was replaced by James Hinder on bass shortly after the album was released. Moving to London Records, In Search Of Sanity was their make or break album. Before it was completed Steve Grimmett (ex-Grim Reaper) and Rob Trottman replaced Keeler and Stallord respectively. After a series of delays, the album finally surfaced in early 1989. Producer Stephan Galfas had watered down their aggressive sound in an attempt to court commercial success. The cover of AC/DC's 'Let There Be Rock' less strong than expected, and the material generally lacked excellence. They had moved away from hard-line thrash towards mainstream metal with negative results. The album was slated in the music media and Grimmett quit in 1990. A replacement was found in the form of Tony O'Hara, but the band were dropped by their label soon after. Disillusioned, they went their separate ways in 1991.

Albums: Power From Hell (1985), The Force (1986), In Search Of Sanity (1989).

Orange

This Yugoslavian hard-rock quintet was formed in 1981 by vocalist Zlato Magdalenic and guitarist Nijo Popovic. With the addition of Tomaz Zontar (keyboards), Marko Herak (bass) and Franc Teropic (drums), they secured a contract with the local RTB label. Musically, they incorporated elements of AC/DC, Deep Purple and Accept, but added little creative input of their own. The band were known as Pomeranca in Yugoslavia and attracted a small but loyal cult following after the release of their debut album in 1982. This featured Yugoslav lyrics and consequently closed down a large section of their potential audience. Madbringer saw the band using English lyrics, but their crude enunciation failed to enhance their appeal.

Albums: Peklenska Pomeranca (1982), Madbringer (1983).

Ozzy Osborne

Orphan

This Canadian melodic rock quartet was formed in 1982 by ex-Pimps duo Chris Burke Gaffney (vocals/bass) and Brent Diamond (keyboards). Enlisting the services of guitarist Steve McGovern and drummer Ron Boivenue, they negotiated a contract with the Portrait label the following year. Drawing inspiration from Bryan Adams, Bon Jovi and Queen, they debuted with *Lonely At Night*, a sophisticated collection of easily accessible AOR anthems. *Salute* saw Boivenue succeeded by Terry Norman Taylor and the guest appearance of guitarist Aldo Nova, but the songs lacked the impact of those on their debut release.
Albums: *Lonely At Night* (1983), *Salute* (1985).

Osbourne, Ozzy

b. John Osbourne, 3 December 1948, Birmingham, England. In 1979 this highly individual and infamous vocalist/song-writer left Black Sabbath, a band whose image and original musical direction he was central in creating. He set up a band, with Lee Kerslake, formerly of Uriah Heep, on drums, Rainbow's Bob Daisley (bass), and Randy Rhoads, who had been a member of Quiet Riot, on guitar. Rhoads' innovative playing ability is much in evidence on the debut, *Blizzard Of Oz*. By the time of the second album, Daisley and Kerslake had left to be replaced by Pat Travers Band drummer Tommy Aldridge, and Rudy Sarzo (bass). Throughout his post-Black Sabbath career, Osbourne has courted outrageous publicity, and in 1982 he had to undergo treatment for rabies following an on-stage accident whereby he bit the head off a bat. In the same year his immensely talented young guitarist, Rhoads, was killed in an air crash. In came Brad Gillis, former guitarist in Night Ranger, but the general feeling was that Rhoads could never be replaced, so unique was his talent, and so close his friendship to Osbourne. *Speak Of The Devil* was released later in 1982, a live album consisting of Sabbath songs. Following a tour during which Sarzo and Gillis decided to leave, Osbourne re-thought the line-up of his band in 1983 and Daisley rejoined, along with guitarist Jake E. Lee of Ratt. Aldridge left following the release of *Bark At The Moon*, being replaced by the renowned virtuoso drummer Carmine Appice. This combination was to be short-lived, however, Randy Castillo replacing Appice, and Phil Soussan taking on the bass guitar. Daisley appears on *No Rest For The Wicked*, although Sabbath bassist Geezer Butler played on the subsequent live dates, leaving Ozzy in 1990. The 80s were a trying time for Osbourne. He went on trial in America for allegedly using his lyrics about the devil and satanism to incite some youngsters to commit suicide; he was eventually cleared of these charges. His manager is his wife, Sharon (daughter of Don Arden), who has helped Osbourne to overcome the alcoholism which was the subject of much of his work. His lyrics deal with subjects such as the agony of insanity, and *The Ultimate Sin* is concerned almost exclusively with the issue of nuclear armaments. In later years Osbourne has kept to more contemporary issues, rejecting to a certain extent the satanic, werewolf image he constructed around himself in the early 80s.

Albums: with Black Sabbath *Black Sabbath* (1970), *Paranoid* (1970), *Master Of Reality* (1971), *Black Sabbath Vol. IV* (1972), *Sabbath Bloody Sabbath* (1974), *Sabotage* (1975), *Technical Ecstasy* (1976), *We Sold Our Soul For Rock And Roll* (1976), *Never Say Die* (1978); solo: *Blizzard Of Oz* (1981), *Diary Of A Madman* (1981), *Speak Of The Devil* (1982), *Bark At The Moon* (1983), *The Ultimate Sin* (1986), *Tribute* (1987), *No Rest For The Wicked* (1989), *Just Say Ozzy* (1990), *No More Tears* (1991).

Ostrogoth

This Belgian hard-rock outfit was formed in Gent, Belguim during 1983, by guitarist Rudy Vercruysse and drummer Mario Pauwels. After a series of false starts, the line-up stabilized with the addition of Marc Debrauwer (vocals), Marnix Vandekauter (bass) and Hans Vandekerckhove (guitar). They debuted with the mini-album *Full Moon's Eyes*, a competent if predictable re-hash of Iron Maiden and Judas Priest riffs. This line-up recorded two further albums in the same direction, which received no recognition outside their native Belgium. The band splintered in 1985, with only the nucleus of Vercruysse and Pauwels remaining. They re-built Ostrogoth with Peter de Wint (vocals), Juno Martins (guitar), Sylvain Cherotti (bass) and Kris Taerwe (keyboards). In 1987 they produced *Feelings Of Fury*, which featured a more melodic direction. The group subsequently disbanded and Pauwels later went on to Shellshock and Hermetic Brotherhood.

Albums: *Full Moon's Eyes* (1983), *Ecstasy And Danger* (1983), *Too Hot* (1985), *Feelings Of Fury* (1987).

Outside Edge

Formerly known as Blackfoot Sue and Liner, this band switched to the name of Outside Edge in 1984, to pursue a melodic AOR direction. Comprising Tom Farmer (vocals/bass), Eddie Golga (guitar), Pete Giles (keyboards) and Dave Farmer (drums), they signed to WEA Records and released a self-titled debut in 1985. This was Americanized melodic rock, but featured rough and ragged vocals from Farmer, instead of the style that might have been expected. Running Hot followed in 1986 and was produced by Terry Manning (of Z.Z. Top fame), but they were still unable to break through on a commercial level. The Farmer brothers left in 1989 and the remaining duo recruited new members to become Little Wing.

Albums: *Outside Edge* (1985), *Running Hot* (1986).

Overkill

This New York thrash metal quartet was formed in 1984 by vocalist Bobby Ellsworth and guitarist Bobby Gustafson. Enlisting the services of bassist D.D. Vernie and drummer Sid Falck, they self-financed the recording of a mini-album. Desperately short of cash and exposure, they sold the rights to the small Azra label and made a net loss. They were soon picked up by Megaforce and released their full debut album in 1985; *Feel The Fire* was a brutal speed-metal riff assault, but lacked the variation in light and shade to compete with groups such as Metallica and Anthrax. Three more albums followed a similar pattern, with *Under The Influence* elevating the band's profile and courting comparisons with Testament. Following *The Years Of Decay*, Gustafson quit and was replaced by Rob Cannavino and Merrit Gant (ex-Faith Or Fear). Now expanded to a quintet, the band recorded *Horrorscope,* their finest work to-date. Unlike their earlier releases, they varied their approach and only switched to hyperspeed mode at crucial moments, in order to maximize the impact of their delivery. The album features an incredible cover of Edgar Winter's 'Frankenstein'. Their reputation has continued to increase, following successful support slots on Helloween and Slayer tours.

Albums: *Feel The Fire* (1985), *Taking Over* (1987), *Under The Influence* (1988), *The Years Of Decay* (1989), *Horrorscope* (1991).

Oz

This Finnish heavy metal outfit was formed by The Oz (vocals) and Eero Hamalainen (guitar) in 1977. Complemented by Kari Elo (bass) and Tauno Vajavaara (drums), they adopted an approach that fused elements of Black Sabbath and Motorhead into a violent power chord frenzy. It took five years before the band made their debut with *The Oz,* a heavy rock album, which suffered from a budget production and weak vocals. Elo

and Hamalainen were fired shortly after the album's release, with bassist Jay C. Blade and guitarists Speedy Foxx and Spooky Wolff recruited as replacements. The band relocated to Sweden and produced *Fire In The Brain*; tough and uncompromising power-metal that acknowledged the work of Judas Priest and Iron Maiden. This brought them to the attention of RCA Records who offered them a European deal. The two albums that followed were disappointing. The band had moved away from their metallic roots and experimented with a greater use of melody. This approach did not suit them, and they subsequently lost their contract. Disillusioned, the band split up in 1987. In 1989, the band re-formed with no original members in the line-up. Comprising Ape De Martini (vocals), Mark Ruffneck (drums), T.B. Muen (bass), Michael Loreda (guitar) and Mike Paul (guitar) they entered the studio to start work on new material.
Albums: *The Oz* (1982), *Fire In The Brain* (1983), *III Warning* (1984), *Decibel Storm* (1986).

Ozz

This American hard-rock project was formed by vocalist Alexis T. Angel and guitarist Gregg Parker. Using session musicians to complete the band, they debuted with *Prisoners* in 1980. Produced by Andy Johns, it combined Led Zeppelin and Jimi Hendrix influences, without ever verging on the imitative. Parker's guitar work was exemplary and provided the perfect foil for Angel's vocal acrobatics. Parker relocated to London in 1982 to form the short-lived Ninja. *Exploited* is a compilation of live material and studio out-takes.
Albums: *Prisoners* (1980), *Exploited* (1983).

P

Page, Jimmy

b. James Patrick Page, 9 January 1944, Heston, London, England. One of rock's most gifted and distinctive guitarists, Page began his professional career during the pre-beat era of the early 60s. He was a member of several groups, including Neil Christian's Crusaders and Carter Lewis And The Southerners, the latter of which was led by the popular songwriting team, Carter And Lewis. Page played rousing solos on several releases by Carter/Lewis proteges, notably the McKinleys' 'Sweet And Tender Romance' and the guitarist quickly became a respected session musician. He appeared on releases by Lulu, Them, Tom Jones and Dave Berry, as well as scores of less-renowned acts, but his best-known work was undertaken for producer Shel Talmy. Page appeared on sessions for the Kinks and the Who, joining an elite band of young studio musicians which included Nicky Hopkins, John Paul Jones and Bobby Graham. The guitarist completed a solo single, 'She Just Satisfies', in 1965 and although it suggested a frustration with his journeyman role, he later took up an A&R role with Immediate Records, where he produced singles for Nico and John Mayall. Having refused initial entreaties, Page finally agreed to join the Yardbirds in 1966 and he remained with this groundbreaking attraction until its demise two years later. The guitarist then formed Led Zeppelin, with which he forged his reputation. His propulsive riffs established the framework for a myriad of tracks - 'Whole Lotta Love', 'Rock 'N' Roll', 'Black Dog', 'When The Levee Breaks' and 'Achilles Last Stand' - now established as rock classics, while his solos have set benchmarks for a new generation of guitarists. His acoustic technique, featured on 'Black Mountain Side' and 'Tangerine', is also notable, while such work with Roy Harper, in particular on *Stormcock* (1971), is among the finest of his career. Page's work since Led Zeppelin's dissolution has been ill-focused. He contributed the soundtrack to Michael Winner's film *Death Wish II*, while the Firm, a collaboration with Paul Rodgers, formerly of Free and Bad Company, was equally disappointing. However, a 1988 release, *Outrider*, did much to re-establish his reputation with contributions by Robert Plant, Chris Farlowe and Jason Bonham, the son of Zeppelin's late drummer, John. The guitarist then put considerable effort into remastering that group's revered back catalogue.
Album: *Death Wish II* (1982, film soundtrack), with Roy Harper *Whatever Happened To Jugula* (1985), *Outrider* (1988). Compilations and archive collections: *Jam Session* (1982), *No Introduction Necessary* (1984), *Smoke And Fire* (1985).

Pallas

This UK progressive rock outfit was formed in Aberdeen, Scotland in 1975, by Evan Lawson (vocals) and Neil Mathewson (guitar). Recruiting the services of Ronnie Brown (keyboards), Graeme Murray (bass) and Derek Forman (drums) they toured the British club circuit for many years, being constantly rejected by the record company A&R representatives. Undeterred, they decided to self-finance the recording of a demo album. This materialized in 1981 as *Arrive Alive*, a quality collection of melodic and grandiose songs. The sets modest success led to a deal with EMI, the services of Yes producer, Eddie Offord and a large budget to record *The Sentinel* in the USA. This was an ambitious and intricate concept album and betrayed influences of Marillion, Magnum and Yes. Lawson split at this juncture, to be replaced by Alan Reed. *The Wedge* followed and represented the pinnacle of the group's creativity. However, the albums commercial failure led to EMI severing links with Pallas. Despite this, the band remained together, but have yet to find a new label sympathetic to their cause.
Albums: *Arrive Alive* (1991), *The Sentinel* (1984), *The Wedge* (1986).

Pandemonium

This Alaskan heavy metal band was formed by Chris (vocals), Eric (bass) and David (guitar) Resch in 1981. They relocated to Los Angeles, California and teamed up with Chris Latham (guitar) and Dave Graybill (drums) in 1982. Making their debut on the first *Metal Massacre* compilation with 'Fighting Backwards', it opened the door to a full contract with Metal Blade Records. Three albums followed over the next five years, with each successive release becoming more and more formularized and displaying strong influences of Van Halen.
Albums: *Heavy Metal Soldiers* (1984), *Hole In The Sky* (1985), *The Kill* (1988).

Pandora's Box

This one-off project was put together by US producer Jim Steinman to record his rock opera Original Sin. The band featured Roy Bittan (piano), Jeff Bova (synthesizers), Jim Bralower (drums), Eddie Martinez (guitar) and Steve Buslowe (bass). Utilizing a series of guest vocalists,

Paradise Lost

which included Elaine Caswell, Ellen Foley, Gina Taylor, Deliria Wild, Holly Sherwood and Laura Theodore, Original Sin was a grandiose concept album on the theme of sex. Featuring classical interludes, spoken introductions, atmospheric ballads and breathtaking rock 'n' roll, it was almost too ambitious. Complete with a state-of-the-art production (courtesy of Steinman) it never received recognition and disappeared without trace, a short time after it was released.

Album: Original Sin (1989).

Pantera

This Texan heavy metal quartet was formed in 1981. They initially comprised Terry Glaze (guitar/vocals), Darrell Abbott (guitar), Vince Abbott (drums) and Rex Rocker (bass). Drawing musical inspiration from Kiss, Aerosmith and Deep Purple, they debuted with *Metal Magic* in 1983. This was well received and led to prestigious support slots to Dokken, Stryper, and Quiet Riot. *Projects In The Jungle* indicated that the band were evolving quickly and starting to build a sound of their own. The Kiss nuances had disappeared and the band sounded, at times, similar to early Def Leppard. The band members altered their names at

this juncture with Glaze becoming Terence Lee, Darrell Abbott switching to Diamond Darrell and brother Vince emerging as Vinnie Paul. *Power Metal* saw Phil Anselmo take over on vocals, but the album lacked the depth and polish of previous efforts. Diamond Darrell turned down the offer to join Megadeth at this point in order to concentrate on new Pantera material. The decision proved crucial, as a return to form was made with 1990's *Cowboys From Hell*. This was an inspired collection of infectious hard-rock anthems, which were infused with melody and showed a keen sense of dynamics.

Albums: *Metal Magic* (1983), *Projects In The Jungle* (1984), *I Am The Night* (1985), *Power Metal* (1988), *Cowboys From Hell* (1990).

Paradise Lost

This UK, death-metal quintet, from Yorkshire was formed in 1989. Comprising Nick Holmes (vocals), Gregor Mackintosh (guitar), Aaron Aedy (guitar), Stephen Edmondson (bass) and Matthew Archer (drums), they were signed to the independent Peaceville label on the strength of two impressive demos. They debuted in 1990 with Lost Paradise, which was heavily influenced by

Napalm Death, Obituary and Death. This featured indecipherable grunting from Holmes, over a barrage of metallic white noise. *Gothic* saw a major innovation in the 'grindcore' genre; it included female vocals, keyboards and guitar lines that for once, were not lost in the mix. With indications in the early 90s of the metal sub-genres becoming accepted within the mainstream, it is a distinct possibility that Paradise Lost could find a wider audience.

Albums: *Lost Paradise* (1990), *Gothic* (1991).

Paradox

This German thrash-metal outfit was formed in 1986 by ex-Warhead duo Charly Steinhauer (vocals/guitar) and Axel Blaha (drums). After a series of false starts and a track included on the *Teutonic Invasion Part 1* compilation, the line-up stabilized with the addition of Markus Spyth (guitar) and Roland Stahl (bass). Signing to the UK Roadrunner label, they delivered *Product Of Imagination* in 1987, which contained standard speed-metal material. *Heresy* saw a major personnel reshuffle and a marked improvement in their style of Metallica meets Anthrax, neck-snapping metal. Stahl and Spyth had been replaced by Dieter Roth (guitar), Manfred Springer (guitar) and Armin Donderer (bass), with the expanded line-up showing a greater degree of flexibility in the live setting and in the studio.

Albums: *Product Of Imagination* (1987), *Heresy* (1989).

Pariah (UK)

Formerly known as Satan, they became Pariah in 1988, feeling that their original name may have led to misconceptions concerning their style. They were never a true black metal outfit as the name Satan suggested, but merely part of the New Wave Of British Heavy Metal scene, along with Def Leppard, Iron Maiden and Saxon. The band comprised Michael Jackson (vocals), Steve Ramsey (guitar), Russ Tippins (guitar), Graeme English (bass) and Sean Taylor (drums). They debuted with *The Kindred* in 1988, a hard, fast metal album, that was characterized by the dual guitar onslaught of Ramsey and Tippins. Following *Blaze Of Obscurity*, Jackson quit and was replaced by Mark Allen. Along with Demon, Pariah were one of the most talented, yet unfairly ignored metal acts of the last decade. Originality and commitment is obviously no guarantee of success in the music business.

Albums: *The Kindred* (1988), *Blaze Of Obscurity* (1989).

Pariah (USA)

This Florida, USA-based speed-metal quartet formed in 1987 by the Egger brothers. The band comprised Garth Egger (vocals), Shaun Egger (guitar), Chris Egger (drums) and Wayne Derrick (guitar). Unable to find secure a record deal in the US, they were finally signed to the Dutch Moshroom label in 1988. They debuted with *Take A Walk*, a mixture of styles that alternated between amateurish Anthrax/Metallica-style thrash and the characterless pop-metal of Europe and Bon Jovi. The album failed commercially and little has been heard from the group since.

Album: *Take A Walk* (1988).

Paris

This US power-trio was put together in 1975 by former Fleetwood Mac guitarist Bob Welch and ex-Jethro Tull bassist Glenn Cornick. Adding Thom Mooney on drums, they signed to Capitol Records in 1976 and released their self-titled debut album. Weaving mystical lyrical tapestries, within psychedelic, blues-based progressive rock, their strange and tormented style was ignored at the time of release, and remains an odd curio even today. Hunt Sales replaced Mooney on Big Towne 2061 and the band adopted a more mainstream approach, with the lyrics taking on a religious emphasis. This also failed to find an audience and the band went their separate ways soon after its release. Welch embarked on what was to become a highly successful solo career.

Albums: Paris (1975), Big Towne 2061 (1976).

Paris, Jeff

This American vocalist/guitarist started his career in the jazz-rock group Pieces. He subsequently played with a number of similar bands on a short-term basis, and built up a reputation as a quality backing vocalist and talented songwriter. He worked with Cinderella, Y&T, Vixen and Lita Ford in this capacity and was offered a solo recording deal by Polygram in 1986. He debuted with *Race To Paradise* the same year, a highly polished and melodic collection of AOR anthems, similar in style to Michael Bolton and Eric Martin. *Wired Up* saw Paris toughen up his approach. The album was typical North American rock and drew comparisons with Bruce Springsteen and Bryan Adams. Both albums failed commercially and Polygram terminated his contract in 1988.

Albums: *Race To Paradise* (1986), *Wired Up* (1987).

Parr, John

This British vocalist/guitarist/composer/producer specialized in highly melodic AOR. He has worked mainly in the USA on the Atlantic label

John Parr

Pearl Jam

of other acts offering the same kind of material. The band split not long after the album was released.

Album: *Organised Crime* (1985).

and has been compared to Rick Springfield and Eddie Money. Parr composed the themes for the movies American Anthem and St. Elmo's Fire, the latter of which made the UK Top 10 singles chart in 1985. He duetted with Meatloaf on the single 'Rock 'N' Roll Mercenaries', which finished up as a musical white elephant. Producing two solo albums, his self-titled debut in 1984 made only number 60 in the UK album charts, but Running The Endless Mile in 1986 did not fare as well. His finest moment remains the energetic 'St. Elmo's Fire'.

Albums: John Parr (1984), Running The Endless Mile (1986).

Partners In Crime

This short-lived supergroup was put together by ex-Status Quo drummer John Coghlan. Enlisting the services of Noel McCalla (vocals, ex-Moon), Mark de Vanchque (keyboards, ex-Wildfire), Ray Major (guitar, ex-Mott) and Mac Mcaffrey (bass), they specialized in Americanized melodic rock. Debuting with *Organised Crime* in 1985, it was obvious that this set of seasoned musicians gelled together very well. Produced by John Eden (Status Quo) and James Guthrie (Pink Floyd, Queensryche) it was a strong album in most respects, yet it failed to stand out fom the plethora

Pearl Jam

This grunge-rock quintet were formed in Seattle, USA in the early 90s, and were put together by former Mother Love Bone members Jeff Ament (bass) and Stone Gossard (rhythm guitar). With former Temple Of The Dog guitarist Mike McCready, drummer Dave Krusen and vocalist Eddie Vedder completing the line-up, the band signed to Epic in 1991. Debuting the following year with *Ten*, they successfully incorporated elements of Soundgarden, Mother Love Bone, Nirvana and Temple Of The Dog with older influences such as the Doors, Velvet Underground, the Stooges and the MC5. Dynamic live performances and a subtle commercial edge to their material has catapulted them from total obscurity to virtual superstars in a very short time.

Album: *Ten* (1992).

Pell, Axel Rudi

This German heavy metal guitar virtuoso left Steeler in 1988 to concentrate on a solo career. Influenced by Deep Purple, Rainbow, Scorpions, Yngwie Malmsteen and Tony Macalpine, he combined explosive guitar pyrotechnics within a traditional metal framework. *Wild Obsession* featured vocalist Charlie Huhn (vocals), Bonfire member Joerg Deisinger (bass) and Jorg Michael (drums, ex-Rage). It was well received by the music press, but this was not translated into healthy sales figures, partly due to Pell's reluctance to take the band out on the road. *Nasty Reputation* represented a quantum leap forward in songwriting terms. The heart of the music was still in the early 70s, but the guitar work and the sheer energy of the delivery was nothing short of

stunning. Bob Rock, now on vocals, gave the music great authority, with the expanded five-man line-up also including two more new faces, Volker Krawczak (bass) and Kai Raglewski (keyboards).
Albums: *Wild Obsession* (1989), *Nasty Reputation* (1991).

Perry, Joe, Project

b. 10 September 1950, Boston, Massachusetts, USA. Having severed an apprenticeship in the aspiring Jam Band, guitarist Perry became a founder member of Aerosmith. This durable hard-rock act became one of USA's leading attractions during the 70s, principally through the artist's exciting, riffing style and vocalist Steve Tyler's charismatic appearance. Tension between the group's leading figures led to former's departure in 1979. He formed the Joe Perry Project with Ralph Mormon (vocals), David Hull (bass) and Ronnie Stewart (drums) but neither *Let The Music Do The Talking* nor *I've Got The Rocks 'N' Rolls Again*, which featured new singer Charlie Farren, captured the fire of the guitarist's previous group. Perry then established a new line-up around Mach Bell (vocals), Danny Hargrove (bass) and Joe Pet (drums) for *Once A Rocker, Always A Rocker*, but once again the combination failed to generate commercial approbation. Former Aerosmith colleague Brad Whitford (guitar) was then added to the group, but it was disbanded in 1984 when a full-scale reunion of the former act was undertaken. The ensuing *Done With Mirrors* featured the title song of the Project's debut album, but Aerosmith's subsequent successful rebirth brought Perry's external aspirations to a premature close.
Albums: *Let The Music Do The Talking* (1980), *I've Got The Rocks 'N' Rolls Again* (1981), *Once A Rocker, Always A Rocker* (1984).

Persian Risk

This heavy metal outfit was based in the North of England. Their line-up was in a constant state of flux during their formative period in the early 80s. At one time Phil Campbell and Jon Deverill, later of Motorhead and the Tygers Of Pan Tang respectively, were involved. They debuted with a track on the *Heavy Metal Heroes, Vol. 2* compilation, and later recorded a single for Neat Records. It took a further three years to record an album, because of the regular line-up shuffles. *Rise Up* finally saw the light of day in 1986 and the band comprised Carl Sentance (vocals), Phil Vokins (guitar), Graham Bath (guitar), Nick Hughes (bass), and Steve Hopgood (drums). Formularized and rather out-dated, the songs were rooted in the early phase of the New Wave Of British Heavy Metal, which, unlike Persian Risk, had matured and progressed considerably since its inception. The album was unsuccessful and the band disintegrated when Bath and Hopgood left to join Paul DiAnno's Battlezone.
Album: *Rise Up* (1986).

Pestilence

This German speed/thrash metal quartet was put together by guitarists Randy Meinhard and Patrick Mameli in 1986. Enlisting the services of Marco Foddis (drums) and Martin van Drunen (vocals/bass), they debuted with a track on the compilation *Teutonic Invasion II* (1987) on the Rock Hard label. A deal with Roadrunner ensued and they cut *Mallevs Maleficarum*, a high speed metallic blur reminiscent of Slayer and Testament. Meinhard quit soon after the album was released to form Sacrosanct. Ex-Theriac guitarist Patrick Uterwijk stepped in as replacement and the band entered the studio to record *Consuming Impulse*. This marked a distinct technical and musical improvement over their enthusiastic, but slightly amateurish debut. Produced by Harris Johns, the album took off in the USA and Pestilence toured extensively with Death and Autopsy during 1990.
Albums: *Mallevs Maleficarum* (1988), *Consuming Impulse* (1989).

Peterik, Jim

This US keyboardist/composer started his career as a session musician. His first taste of success came with 'Ides Of March' at the end of the 60s. It was 1977 before he actually got round to recording a solo album; Don't Fight The Feeling was a mature, melodic rock album, that drew comparisons with Bob Seger, Bruce Springsteen and Michael Bolton. However, the album made little impact and Peterik went back to session work, guesting on Sammy Hagar and .38 Special albums. In 1978 he formed Survivor with guitarist Frankie Sullivan and went on to multi-platinum success.
Album: Don't Fight The Feeling (1977).

Petra

One of the first US Christian hard rock bands, Petra were formed in 1972, by vocalist Greg Volz and guitarist Bob Hartman. They recruited Mark Kelly (bass), John Slick (keyboards) and Louie Weaver (drums) to their cause. The group specialized in a varied musical approach that incorporated elements of the Eagles, Joe Walsh, Kansas and Deep Purple. Petra have released 14 quality albums to date, with their popularity having gradually waned from its peak in 1984. At this time, they appeared in the US Top 12 best-attended bands list in *Performance* magazine. *Not Of This World* sold in excess of quarter of a million units. John Schlitt (ex-Head East) replaced Volz after 1986's *Back To The Street* and the band adopted a heavier direction thereafter. John Lawry and Ronnie Cates replaced Slick and Kelly on keyboards and bass respectively in 1988. Their two most current releases owe much to Kiss and Stryper and are much more aggressive than their earlier material. This excellent outfit have never been swayed by passing trends and have stuck to their own musical ideals and beliefs.

Albums: *Petra* (1974), *Come And Join Us* (1977), *Washes Whiter Than* (1979), *Never Say Die* (1981), *More Power To Ya* (1982), *Not Of This World* (1983), *Beat The System* (1985), *Captured In Time And Place* (1986), *Back To The Street* (1986), *This Means War* (1987), *On Fire* (1988), *Petra Means Rock* (1989), *Petra Praise - The Rock Cries Out* (1989), *Beyond Belief* (1990).

Pez Band

This US melodic pop-rock outfit was formed in 1976 by vocalist Mimi Betinis and guitarist Tommy Gawenda. Enlisting the services of Mike Gorman (bass) and Mick Rain (drums), they debuted with a self-titled album on the Passport label. This was overtly commercial, featuring paper-thin melodies and lightweight guitar work. The album flopped and the band changed direction to hard-driving, blues-based rock. Laughing In The Dark was a remarkable improvement and featured up-front lead guitar, reminiscent of Gary Moore and Pat Travers. This failed to find favour, as the band were already labelled as an unsuccessful pop act. Disillusioned by the lack of media response, they bowed out with the live mini-album 30 Seconds Over Schaumberg. They reformed temporarily in 1981, releasing Cover To Cover, but soon disbanded again.

Albums: Pezband (1977), Laughing In The Dark (1978), 30 Seconds Over Schaumberg (1978), Cover To Cover (1981).

Phantom Blue

This guitar-oriented melodic rock outfit came from Los Angeles, California, USA. The all-female line-up, comprising vocalist Gigi Hangach (vocals), guitarists Nicole Couch (guitar), Michelle Meldrum (guitar), Kim Nielsen (bass) and Linda McDonald (drums) was impressive on a technical, visual and musical level. Under the guiding hand of Shrapnel Records' guitar supremo Mike Varney, the girls were introduced to Steve Fontano and Marty Friedman, (later of Megadeth) who became responsible for producing and arranging their debut album. Comprising nine originals, it was a much needed shot in the arm for the credibility of female rock. The guitars screamed and the album displayed their individual style. In 1990, they were signed by Geffen Records, who hoped to tap their enormous potential.

Album: *Phantom Blue* (1989).

Phenomena

This ambitious video and musical project was co-ordinated by Tom Galley (brother of former Whitesnake guitarist Mel Galley). The albums are concept affairs, centred on the theme of supernatural phenomena. Utilizing an impressive list of guest musicians has not always guaranteed a good result and Phenomena went some way towards proving this. With Neil Murray (bass), Cozy Powell (drums), Mel Galley (guitar) and Glenn Hughes (vocals) among the starting line-up, great things were obviously expected. However, the songs were often over complex and lacked a central melody line. *Dream Runner* released two years later suffered from similar problems, but the music was less of a disappointment. It featured an impeccable array of guests once more, with Ray Gillen, Max Bacon, Scott Gorham, Kyoji Yamamoto and John Wetton contributing in one form or another. The album received good reviews in the music media, but sold poorly. As a result, the plans to make the Phenomena projects into films were aborted.

Albums: *Phenomena* (1985), *Phenomena II - Dream Runner* (1987).

Phoenix

This UK group rose up from the ashes of Argent in 1975. The band comprised John Verity (vocals/guitar), Robert Henrit (drums) and Jim Rodford (keyboards/bass). The trio continued in much the same vein as before; hard-rock infused with melody and a keen sense of dynamics. They debuted with a self-titled album in 1976 and landed the support slot to Ted Nugent's UK tour. The band went down a storm live, but this was never translated into album sales. They split up after just 12 months together. In 1979 Verity and Henrit re-formed Phoenix with Russ Ballard (keyboards/vocals), Bruce Turgon (bass), Ray Minnhinnett (guitar) and Michael Des Barres (vocals). This short-lived collaboration produced In Full View, a non-descript melodic rock album that sold poorly. The band disintegrated shortly afterwards, with Verity and Henrit joining Charlie and then later forming Verity, under the vocalists own surname.

Albums: Phoenix (1976), In Full View (1979).

Picture

This Dutch heavy metal quartet was formed in 1979 by Ronald van Prooyen (lead vocals) and Jan Bechtum (guitar). With the addition of bassist Rinus Vreugdenhil and drummer Laurens 'Bakkie' Bakker, they modelled themselves on British bands, with noticeably influenced by Uriah Heep, Deep Purple and Motorhead. They went through numerous line-up changes during their seven-year, seven-album career, but produced consistently high quality material throughout. Vocalists included Pete Lovell, Shmoulik Avigal and Bert Heerink (ex-Vandenberg) while Chris van Jaarsueld, Henry van Manen and Rob van Enhuizen were responsible for six-string duties at one time or another. The band folded in 1987, but played a one-off reunion concert the following year.
Albums: *Picture* (1980), *Heavy Metal Ears* (1981), *Diamond Dreamer* (1982), *Eternal Dark* (1984), *Traitor* (1985), *Every Story Needs Another Picture* (1986), *Marathon* (1987)

Plant, Robert

b. 20 August 1948, Birmingham, West Midlands, England. Plant's early career was spent in several Midlands-based R&B bands, including the New Memphis Bluesbreakers and Crawling King Snakes, the latter of which featured drummer, and future colleague, John Bonham. In 1965 Robert joined Lee John Crutchley, Geoff Thompson and Roger Beamer in Listen, a Motown-influenced act later signed to CBS Records. A cover version of 'You Better Run', originally recorded by the (Young) Rascals made little headway, and Plant was then groomed for a solo career with two 1967 singles, 'Laughing, Crying, Laughing' and 'Long Time Coming'. Having returned to Birmingham, the singer formed Band Of Joy in which his growing interest in US 'west coast' music flourished. This promising group broke up in 1968 and following a brief association with blues veteran Alexis Korner, Robert then joined another local act, Hobstweedle. It was during this tenure that guitarist Jimmy Page invited the singer to join Led Zeppelin. Plant's reputation as a dynamic vocalist and frontman was forged as a member of this highly-influential unit, but he began plans for a renewed solo career following the death of John Bonham in 1980. *Pictures At Eleven* unveiled a new partnership with Robbie Blunt (guitar), Paul Martinez (bass) and Jezz Woodruffe (keyboards) and while invoking the singer's past, also showed him open to new musical directions. *The Principle Of Moments* contained the restrained UK/US Top 20 hit, 'Big Log' (1983), and inspired an ambitious world tour. Plant then acknowledged vintage R&B in the Honeydrippers, an *ad hoc* group which featured Page, Jeff Beck and Nile Rodgers, whose mini-album spawned a US Top 3 hit in 'Sea Of Love'. Having expressed a desire to record less conventional music, Robert unveiled *Shaken 'N' Stirred*, which divided critics who either lauded its ambition or declared it too obtuse. The singer then disbanded his group, but resumed recording in 1987 on becoming acquainted with a younger pool of musicians, including Phil Johnstone, Dave Barrett, Chris Blackwell and Phil Scragg. *Now And Zen* was hailed as a dramatic return to form and a regenerated Plant now felt confident enough to include Zeppelin material in live shows. Indeed one of the album's standout tracks, 'Tall Cool One', featured a cameo from Jimmy Page and incorporated samples of 'Black Dog', 'Whole Lotta Love' and 'The Ocean', drawn from their former group's extensive catalogue. The singer's artistic rejuvenation continued on the acclaimed *Maniac Nirvana*.
Albums: *Pictures At Eleven* (1982), *The Principle Of Moments* (1983), *Skaken 'N' Stirred* (1985), *Now And Zen* (1989), *Maniac Nirvana* (1990).

Point Blank

Essentially from the same mould as Texan Blues Boogie supremos, Z.Z. Top, Point Blank's first two releases were produced by Bill Ham who had masterminded the Top's rise to fame. Point Blank's line-up has been somewhat fluid but in the main featured John O'Daniel (vocals), Rusty Burns (guitar), Kim Davis (guitar), Bill Randolph (bass), Mike Hamilton (keyboards) and Buzzy Gren (drums). Their third venture into the recording studio resulted in *Airplay* which saw a slightly less intensive boogie stance, but this was rectified on 'The Hard Way' a part-live release which saw the band in blistering form. Bobby Keith replaced John O'Daniel in 1981 and their last two albums boasted a more radio-friendly approach to their sound.
Albums: *Point Blank* (1976), *Second Season* (1977), *Airplay* (1980), *American Excess* (1981), *On A Roll* (1982).

Poison

This heavy metal band was formed in Pennsylvania, USA in the spring of 1983 by Bret Michaels (b. Bret Sychalk, 15 March 1962, Harrisburg, Pennsylvania, USA; vocals) and Rikki Rockett (b. Richard Ream, 8 August 1959, Pennsylvania, USA; drums). They were soon joined by Bobby Dall (b. Kuy Kendall, 2 November 1958, Miami, Florida, USA; bass) and Matt Smith (guitar). The quartet played local clubs under the name Paris, before moving to Los

Poison

Possessed

Angeles and changing their name. It was at this point that Smith left the band and was replaced by C.C. Deville (b. 14 May 1963, Brooklyn, New York, USA; guitar). They were signed by Enigma Records in 1985 and released their first album in 1986, which went double platinum in America and produced three hits. *Open Up And Say . . . Ahh!* gave them their first US number 1, 'Every Rose Has Its Thorn'. Four other singles were also released, including a cover of 'Your Mama Don't Dance' which was a major US hit for Loggins And Messina in 1972. Poison were originally considered a 'glam band' because of the make-up they wore, but by the release of *Flesh And Blood*, in 1990, this image had been toned down dramatically. That year they also played their first UK shows, and fans showed their love for songs like 'Unskinny Bop' and 'Talk Dirty To Me' when the band made their official UK debut in front of 72,500 people at the Donnington Monsters of Rock Festival on 18 August 1990.

Albums: *Look What The Cat Dragged In* (1986), *Open Up And Say . . . Ahh!* (1988), *Flesh And Blood* (1990).

Possessed

Formed in San Francisco, California in 1983, this heavy metal band consisted of Jeff Beccarra (bass/vocals), Mike Tarrao (guitar), Larry Lalonde (guitar) and Mike Sus (drums). Due to some early demos and the fact that the band had a track included on the *Metal Massacre VI* compilation album released on the Metal Blade Records label in 1984, the band attracted the attention of the Combat Records label who promptly signed the band. This resulted in the band's debut *Seven Churches* being released in 1985. Growling vocals and ultra-fast Slayer-influenced riffs were the order of the day and the band quickly made their mark on the 'death metal' scene. The next album produced by ex-Rods drummer Carl Canedy entitled 'Beyond The Gates' released in 1986 the band had toured throughout Europe building a strong following. On their return to America the band recorded and released a mini-album entitled *The Eyes Of Terror*. Produced by guitar maestro Joe Satriani, the album was, as expected, heavily guitar-oriented but due to internal band wrangles the band folded soon after its release.

Albums: *Seven Churches* (1985), *Beyond The Gates* (1986), *The Eyes Of Terror* (1987, mini-album).

Powell, Cozy

b. 29 December 1947, England. Powell is a virtuoso drummer who has played with the likes of Jeff Beck, Rainbow, and Emerson, Lake And Powell. Powell's musical career began in 1965 when he was a member of the Sorcerers. He worked with Casey Jones And The Engineers for a couple of months before returning to the Sorcerers. Following this band changing its name first to Youngblood and then to Ace Kefford Stand, Powell moved on to Big Bertha. In 1971, Jeff Beck founded a group consisting of Robert Tench (vocals), Max Middleton (keyboards), Clive Chaman (bass), and Powell. The Jeff Beck group was one of the premier exponents of R&B jazz-rock, and Powell appears on two of its albums. It was after his work with Bedlam, the band he formed in 1972 with Frank Aiello (vocals), Dennis Ball (bass) and Dave Ball (guitar), that Powell came to the attention of producer Micky Most. This gave Powell the opportunity to release hit singles such as 'Dance With The Devil' and 'The Man In Black'. This latter single was recorded whilst Powell was in Cozy Powell's Hammer, a group with Bedlam's Aiello as vocalist, along with newcomers Don Airey (keyboards), Clive Chaman (bass) and Bernie Marsden (guitar). This project came to an end in April 1975 when Powell decided to take a break and spend three months motor racing. Strange Brew was formed in July 1975, with Powell on drums, but this project then lasted for little more than a month. He then joined Ritchie Blackmore's Rainbow, with whom he played until 1980, his farewell concert with them being at the first Donnington rock festival. He released three solo albums in the early 80s, working with Gary Moore. In 1981 Powell appeared on the Michael Schenker Group's *MSG*, and in the mid-80s he replaced Carl Palmer, becoming the third member of Emerson, Lake And Powell. The album he recorded with them had little chart success and Powell subsequently left. He also played briefly in Whitesnake. In 1987 Cozy appeared on and produced Black Sabbath's *Headless Cross*.

Albums: with Jeff Beck *Rough And Ready* (1971), *The Jeff Beck Group* (1972); with Bedlam *Bedlam* (1973); with Rainbow *Rising* (1976), *On Stage* (1977), *Long Live Rock 'N' Roll* (1978), *Down To Earth* (1979); with the Michael Schenker Group *MSG* (1981); with Emerson, Lake And Powell *Emerson, Lake And Powell* (1985), with Black Sabbath *Headless Cross* (1987); solo *Over The Top* (1979), *Tilt* (1981), *Octopus* (1983).

Praying Mantis

Formed in London, England in 1977 the band were at the forefront of the New Wave Of British Heavy Metal. The original line-up consisted of Tino Troy (guitar/vocals), Roberto Angelo (guitar), Tino's brother Chris Troy (bass/vocals) and Mick Ransome (drums). Owing to some early demo recordings the band attracted the attention of the heavy metal club disc jockey Neal Kay, who helped them release an independent three-track EP *The Soundhouse Tapes*, a title also used by Iron Maiden for their first release. The band's career can be closely linked with Iron Maiden during those early years as not only did both bands appear on the *Metal For Muthas* compilation released by EMI Records in 1980, they also toured England together. Signing to Arista Records and replacing Roberto Angelo and Mick Ransome with guitarist/vocalist Steve Carroll and ex-Ten

Years After drummer Dave Potts, the band's debut *Time Tells No Lies* was released in 1981. It was not well received due to its lacklustre production and basic melodic rock sound. The band decided a line-up change was needed, replacing the departed Steve Carroll with ex-Grand Prix vocalist Bernie Shaw, and they also recruited keyboard player Jon Bavin. This line-up went on to record 'Turn The Tables' for a compilation album released on the Yet Records label in the mid-80s. Due to a lack of any real media interest the band metamorphosed into the band Stratus, who released two standard melodic rock albums which also featured ex-Iron Maiden drummer Clive Burr. To celebrate the 10th anniversary of the NWOBHM the band re-formed early in 1990 to tour Japan. This new line-up consisted of founder members Tino and Chris Troy, ex-Iron Maiden vocalist Paul Di'anno, ex-Iron Maiden guitarist Dennis Stratton and Bruce Bisland on drums.

Album: *Time Tells No Lies* (1981).

Precious Metal

This US glam-metal rock group were formed in Los Angeles, California in the mid-80s. They came to the public's attention via their 1985 debut, *Right Here, Right Now*, which was produced by AOR producer and guitar-hero, Paul Sabu. Springing from Los Angeles this all-female outfit featured Leslie Wasser (vocals), Janet Robin (guitar), Mara Fox (guitar), Alex Rylance (bass) and Carol Control (drums). Unfairly compared with 70s all-girl outfit the Runaways, Precious Metal set about proving that not only did they have the looks but that they could play and write competently. Their second and third album releases ably demonstrated these points.

Albums: *Right Here, Right Now* (1985), *That Kind Of Girl* (1988), *Precious Metal* (1990).

Pretty Maids

This Danish heavy metal quintet was formed in 1981 by vocalist Ronnie Atkins and guitarist Ken Hammer. Taking their musical brief from British acts such as Deep Purple, Judas Priest and UFO, their style is such, that enthusiasm always outweighs originality. The band have gone through numerous line-up changes, with the current outfit comprising Atkins and Hammer along with Ricky Marx (guitar), Allan Delong (bass) and Phil Moorhead (drums). Although they are competent musicians, at times their delivery, image, attitude and song titles verge on Spinal Tap-like parody. *Future World* from 1987 is the band's strongest release to date, whilst the more recent Roger Glover (Deep Purple bassist)-produced *Jump The Gun* failed to offer anything

new.
Albums: *Pretty Maids* (1983), *Red, Hot And Heavy* (1984), *Future World* (1987), *Jump The Gun* (1990).

Princess Pang

This New York-based rock quintet was formed in 1986 around the nucleus of Jeni Foster (vocals), Ronnie Roze (bass) and Brian Keats (drums). The line-up was finally completed a year later, by the addition of guitarists Jay Lewis and Andy Tyernon. Signing to Metal Blade Records, they were introduced to Ron St. Germain, (of Bad Brains fame) who eventually handled the production of their debut album. Released in 1989, it was a gutsy hard-rock album, full of tales of New York's low-life. Foster, with her aggressive sublimate delivery, drew comparisons to Guns N' Roses' W. Axl Rose.
Album: *Princess Pang* (1989).

Prism

This Canadian rock group has always proved difficult to categorize in terms of musical style, and major commercial success has proven elusive. Their most stable line-up comprised Ron Tabak (vocals - replaced by Henry Small in 1981), Lindsay Mitchell (guitar), Al Harlow (bass) and Rocket Norton (drums). Their first two releases on the Ariola label were lightweight pop rock with layers of keyboards while *Armageddon* saw the band, now signed to the Capitol label, move towards a more heavy, grandiose style with several lengthy compositions. However, further line-up changes resulted in a typical AOR American rock sound, ideal for radio play on their next two recordings and they found considerable success as a live act on the American circuit.
Albums: *Prism* (1977), *See Forever Eyes* (1978), *Armageddon* (1979), *Young And Restless* (1980), *Small Change* (1981), *Beat Street* (1983).
Compilation: *The Best Of Prism* (1988).

Prong

This US trash-hardcore rock trio was formed in the mid-80s. Hailing from New York's Manhattan lower east side, the band comprised Tommy Victor (vocals/guitar), Mike Kirkland (vocals/bass) and Ted Parsons (drums), caused an immediate stir with their first release on the independent Spigot label. Emotionally angry, lyrically brutal, Prong produce a relentless assault and fierce guitar-riffing. Their second album for the major Epic label *Prove You Wrong* in 1991 was their most significant work to date.
Albums: *Primitive Origins* (1987), *Force Fed* (1988), *Third From The Sun* (1989), *Beg To Differ* (1990), *Prove You Wrong* (1991).

Q

Q5

This US group was formed in Seattle, Washington, USA in 1983 by the innovative guitarist Floyd Rose. He is best known for being the inventor of the locking tremelo system, the now indispensable device that ensures the guitar stays in tune even after the heaviest of tremelo use. Joining Floyd Rose in Q5 were Jonathan K (vocals), Rick Pierce (guitar), Evan Sheeley (bass/keyboards) and Gary Thompson (drums), all previously with the band TKO. Signing to the small independent Albatross Records label the band released their debut *Steel The Light* in 1984. It was later released in Europe on the Roadrunner Records label in 1985. The album was typically Americanized melodic hard rock and in a sea of such releases went largely unnoticed. Floyd Rose built his own recording studio at his home which the band decided to use for the recording of their next album. With virtually unlimited studio time available the band were under no pressure recording their second album. *When The Mirror Cracks* was released on the Music For Nations Records label in 1986. Full of melody it did, however, tend to sound slightly over-produced. The band fell apart in 1987, with only these two albums to their credit, and Floyd Rose will be remembered for his contribution to guitar technology rather than for his recordings with Q5. Albums: *Steel The Light* (1985), *When The Mirror Cracks* (1986).

Quartz

Formed in Birmingham, England, the band's first venture came in 1977 with *Quartz*. This should have been the first stage to major stardom as it was produced by legendary Black Sabbath guitarist, Tony Iommi, who took an early interest in the group's fortunes. Indeed, Quartz supported both Black Sabbath and AC/DC on UK tours. Mick Taylor (vocals), Mike Hopkins (guitar), Dek Arnold (bass/vocals) and Malcom Cope (drums) found themselves moving from label to label in search of commercial success. They had a crack at the singles market with their version of Mountain's classic, 'Nantucket Sleighride' which

Queensryche

was used as the theme to UK television's *Weekend World* current affairs programme. Released on the independent Reddington's Rare Records label, it disappeared without trace. Undaunted, the band soldiered on, releasing a 12-inch red vinyl single, 'Satan's Serenade' also on Reddingtons and had a track featured on EMI's *Mutha's Pride* EP showcase. Quartz recorded a further three fine examples of basic British heavy rock, the title of the last being particularly apt.

Albums: *Quartz* (1977), *Live Songs* (1979), *Stand Up And Fight* (1980), *Against All Odds* (1983).

Queensryche

Queensryche were formed in Seattle, USA by Geoff Tate (vocals), Chris DeGarmo (guitars), Michael Wilton (guitars), Eddie Jackson (bass), and Scott Rockenfield (drums). Their self-financed *Queen Of The Ryche* EP (1983) caused quite a stir in rock circles and led to EMI offering them a major deal. 'Queen Of The Ryche' was quickly re-released and grazed the UK Top 75. Their first full album for EMI *The Warning* was comparatively disappointing, failing to live up to the promise shown on the EP, with only 'Road To Madness' and 'Take Hold Of The Flame' still both current live favourites meeting expectations. *Rage For Order* followed in 1986 and saw the band creating a more distinctive style, making full use of modern technology to give a unique ground-breaking album. This showed both Tate's incredible vocal range and the twin guitar sound of DeGarmo and Wilton. 1988 saw the Peter Collins produced *Operation Mindcrime*, a George Orwell-inspired concept album which was greeted with highly enthusiastic critical acclaim on its release. Despite their popularity and support from the rock press, they could still only manage a cult following, but this all changed with the release of *Empire*. This went into the Top 10 on both sides of the Atlantic, and the single 'Silent Lucidity' was a Top 5 hit in the US and was their first Top 20 hit in the UK. This was followed by 'Best I Can' and 'Jet City Woman' which became Top 40 hits in 1991. Throughout their career Queensryche have created their own instantly distinguishable style which has gained both critical acclaim and commercial success.

Albums: *The Warning* (1984), *Rage For Order* (1986), *Operation Mindcrime* (1988), *Empire* (1990).

Quiet Riot

Heavy metal band Quiet Riot had its shining moment in 1983 with a remake of a Slade song, 'Cum On Feel The Noize' and a US number 1 album, *Metal Health* - the first metal album to reach that position in the US charts - but was

Quiet Riot

unable to maintain that momentum with subsequent releases. The band formed in 1975 with lanky vocalist Kevin DuBrow (b. 1955), Randy Rhoads (guitar), Drew Forsyth (drums) and Kelly Garni (bass). They recorded two albums with that line-up, released only in Japan. Rudy Sarzo then replaced Garni. Rhoads left in 1979 to join Ozzy Osbourne and was later tragically killed in a plane crash in March 1982. At that point the band briefly split up, with some members joining the vocalist in a band called DuBrow. Quiet Riot regrouped around DuBrow, Sarzo, guitarist Carlos Cavazo and drummer Frankie Banali and signed to the Pasha label for the breakthrough album and single, their musical and fashion style fashioned after the harder rocking glam acts of the 70s, particularly Slade. Friction within the group followed their quick success and resultant publicity affected sales of the follow-up *Condition Critical*, which reached number 15 in the USA but was considered disappointing. After several personnel changes, Quiet Riot recorded another album in 1986, which reached number 31 but showed a marked decline in the group's creativity. DuBrow was subsequently ejected from the band and a self-titled 1988 album barely made the charts. The group then disbanded.

Albums: *Quiet Riot* (1977), *Quiet Riot II* (1978),

Metal Health (1983), *Condition Critical* (1984), *QRIII* (1986), *Quiet Riot* (1988). Compilation: *Wild Young And Crazee* (1987).

Quireboys

After violent incidents at some early live shows, the UK band altered their name from the Queerboys to the Quireboys, to avoid further trouble. Comprising Spike (vocals), Nigel Mogg (bass, and brother of Phil in UFO), Chris Johnstone (keyboards), Guy Bailey (guitar), Ginger (guitar) and Coze (drums) they were originally all drinking buddies in London pubs. Drawing musical inspiration from the Faces, Rolling Stones and Mott The Hoople, they specialized in bar-room boogie, beer-soaked blues and infectious raunch 'n' roll. Spike's rough-as-a-gravel-path vocal style, closely resembling Rod Stewart's, added fuel to the accusations of the band being no more than Faces imitators. After releasing two independent singles, they signed to EMI and immediately underwent a line-up re-shuffle. Coze and Ginger were removed and replaced by Ian Wallace and Guy Griffin. They recorded A Bit Of What You Fancy in Los Angeles, under the production eye of Jim Cregan (former Rod Stewart and Family guitarist). It was an immediate success, entering the UK album charts at number 2. 'Hey You' lifted as a single also met with similar success, peaking at number 14 in January 1990. An eight-track live album followed, which duplicated most of the numbers from their first album. This was released as a stop-gap measure to bridge the long period between successive studio releases.
Albums: A Bit Of What You Fancy (1990), Live Around The World (1990).

R

Rabin, Trevor

b. 1955, South Africa. Trevor Rabin learned classical piano and guitar from an early age, forming his first band, Rabbitt when he was aged only 14. They were a short-lived teenybop sensation in South Africa during the early 70s, releasing two albums which reached gold status. Moving to England in 1977, he signed to Chrysalis Records and polished up some demos he had previously recorded in South Africa for release as his first solo album. This featured a mixture of styles, and included jazz, rock, blues and AOR numbers. Future releases pursued a more mainstream melodic rock approach, with Wolf, released in 1981 being his tour-de-force. He also ventured into production with Wild Horses and Manfred Mann. He accepted the invitation to join Yes in 1983, and it was not until there was a major conflict in this camp, that he managed to find enough time to record another solo effort. Can't Look Away, surfacing in 1989, had more in common with Yes, than with his previous solo work.
Albums: Trevor Rabin (1978), Face To Face (1979), Wolf (1981), Can't Look Away (1989).

Racer X

This Los Angeles band earned a reputation for guitar-orientated melodic rock, delivered with hyperspeed precision. Featuring Jeff Martin (ex-Surgical Steel vocalist), Paul Gilbert (guitar), John Alderete (bass) and Harry Gschoesser (ex-Nobros drummer) they released Street Lethal, a high-tech fusion of relentless guitar work and memorable songs. Scott Travis (ex-Hawk) took over the drum stool and Bruce Bouillet was added as a second guitarist in 1986. Second Heat was issued the following year; the band had matured and the music was more accomplished and exciting on every level. Paul Gilbert left in 1988 to join Mr. Big, and was replaced by Chris Arvan. Jeff Martin broke ranks shortly afterwards and Scott Travis accepted the offer to join Judas Priest. The band ground to a halt in 1990.
Albums: Street Lethal (1986), Second Heat (1987), Extreme Volume...Live (1988).

Rage

Formerly known as Avenger, this German power trio changed their name to Rage in 1985, to avoid confusion with the British Avenger. A series of line-up changes ensued before the combination of vocalist Peavey Wagner, guitarist Manni Schmidt and drummer Chris Efthimiadis gelled. Their first two albums were rather one-dimensional, being competent, but uninspiring techno-thrash affairs. With the recording of Perfect Man, they experimented more with song structures and had improved considerably as musicians. Future releases combined the technical prowess and subtle melodies of Rush, with the unbridled aggression of Megadeth. Their reputation in Germany has grown rapidly, but they have yet to make any significant impression outside their homeland.
Albums: Reign Of Fear (1986), Execution Guaranteed (1987), Perfect Man (1988), Secrets In A Weird World (1989), Reflections Of A Shadow (1990).

Rainbow

Rainbow

In 1974, guitarist Ritchie Blackmore (b. 14 April 1945, Weston-Super-Mare, England; guitar) left Deep Purple, forming Rainbow the following year. His earlier involvement with American band Elf, led to his recruitment of Elf's Ronnie James Dio (vocals), Mickey Lee Soule, (keyboards), Craig Gruber on bass and Gary Driscoll as drummer. Their debut, Ritchie Blackmore's Rainbow, was released in 1975, and was undeservedly seen by some as a poor imitation of Deep Purple. Rainbow was intended to go in a different musical direction to Deep Purple. The constant turnover of personnel was representative of Blackmore's quest for the ultimate line-up and sound. Dissatisfaction with the debut album led to a new line-up being assembled. Jimmy Bain took over from Gruber, and Cozy Powell replaced Driscoll. With Tony Carey on keyboards, Rainbow Rising was released, an album far more confident than its predecessor. Shortly after this, Bain and Carey left, being replaced by Bob Daisley and David Stone respectively. It was when Rainbow moved to America that difficulties between Dio and Blackmore came to a head, resulting in Dio's departure from the band in 1978. His replacement was Graham Bonnet, whose only album with Rainbow, *Down To Earth*, saw the return as bassist of Roger Glover, the man Blackmore had forced out of Deep Purple in 1973. The album was a marked departure from the Dio days, and while it is often considered one of the weaker Rainbow albums, it did provide an enduring single, 'Since You've Been Gone', written and originally recorded by Russ Ballard. Bonnet and Powell soon became victims of another reorganization of Rainbow's line-up. New vocalist Joe Lynn Turner brought a much more American feel to the band, introducing a commercial sound to *Difficult To Cure*, the album which produced the big hit, 'I Surrender'. Thereafter the band went into decline as their increasingly middle-of-the-road albums were ignored by the fans. In 1984 the Rainbow project was ended following the highly popular Deep Purple reunion. The compilation *Finyl Vinyl* appeared in 1986, and featured several different incarnations of Rainbow and some unreleased recordings.

Albums: *Ritchie Blackmore's Rainbow* (1975), *Rainbow Rising* (1976), *Live On Stage* (1977), *Long Live Rock And Roll* (1978), *Live In Germany* (1976, 1990), *Down To Earth* (1979), *Difficult To Cure* (1981), *Straight Between The Eyes* (1982), *Bent Out Of Shape* (1983). Compilation: *Finyl Vinyl* (1986).

Ratcat

Emerging in 1986 from Australia's thrash metal scene and based in Sydney, Ratcat relocated to the UK to promote their Ramones tinged pop rock. The trio comprises Simon Day (vocals, guitar), Amr Zaid (bass and occasional vocals) and Andrew Polin (drums). If UK audiences were surprised to see them occupy support slots for INXS, it was less of a shock in their homeland, where they regularly top the charts and appear on the covers of teenage magazines. Despite the obvious commercial validity of the band, their music remains rooted in pure garage group aesthetics: 'We've always said that, at heart, we're basically scuzz rats. We're at our best when we're at our scuzziest'.

Albums: *Tingles* (1991), *Blind Love* (1991).

Ratt

This heavy metal group formed in Los Angeles, USA, and featured Stephen Pearcy (vocals), Robbin Crosby (guitar), Warren D. Martini (guitar), Juan Groucier (bass) and Bobby 'The Blotz' Blotzer (drums). They evolved out of 70s band Mickey Ratt, transmuting into their present form in 1983, with a hint of pop about their brand of metal similar to Cheap Trick or Aerosmith.

Ratt; Stephen Pearcy

They released a self-titled mini album in 1983 on a local label, and struck up a close personal friendship with members of Mötley Crüe which no doubt helped them to sign to Atlantic the following year. They made their breakthrough with their first full album *Out Of The Cellar* which stayed in the *Billboard* Top 20 for six months. They toured with Ozzy Osbourne before joining a Billy Squier jaunt where they were apparently 'thrown off' because they were more popular than the headline act. Their subsequent output has seen them follow a familiar heavy metal route with accusations over sexist videos contrasting with their ability to sell out concert halls and produce recordings that receive platinum discs. *Decimater* featured several songs co-written with Desmond Childs and is their most adventurous recording to date.

Albums: *Ratt* (1983), *Out Of The Cellar* (1984), *Invasion Of Your Privacy* (1985), *Dancing Undercover* (1986), *Reach For The Sky* (1988), *Decimater* (1990).

Rattlesnake Kiss

This Birmingham, UK-based heavy metal quintet, formed in 1990 by vocalist Sean Love and guitarists Ralph Cardall and Bill Carroll. Influenced by American bands such as Foreigner,

Queensryche, Van Halen and Rush, they specialize in highly sophisticated and technically accomplished hard rock. Their songs infuse melody, power and dynamics to startling effect, but come over far more powerfully in the live setting, than in the studio. Picked up by the independent Sovereign label, they released a self-titled debut album in early 1992. This does not fully reflect the band's musical prowess and energy as the production was thin. Rattlesnake Kiss have undoubted potential, and with a larger budget next time, their second album should make a greater and much more significant impact.
Album: *Rattlesnake Kiss* (1992).

Raven

Formed in 1980, Raven was one of the first bands to be associated with the New Wave Of British Heavy Metal movement. Hailing from Newcastle, it comprised the Gallagher brothers, John (vocals/bass) and Mark (guitar) plus drummer Rob Hunter. Unleashing a three-man wall of noise punctuated by searing guitar work and high-pitched vocals, they signed to the local independent label, Neat Records. Their reputation grew with the release of the single 'Don't Need Your Money' and the ensuing live shows to promote it. After four albums on Neat Records, including the excellent *Live At The Inferno*, they relocated to America and secured a deal with Atlantic Records. Adopting a more melodic approach, *Stay Hard* emerged in 1985 and sold well, but only in the USA. Since then, the band has reverted back to its former blitzkrieg style, releasing a string of competent, but rather dated and pedestrian albums. Drummer Rob Hunter moved into production work in 1988, to be replaced by Joe Hasselvander.
Albums: *Rock Until You Drop* (1981), *Wiped Out* (1982), *All For One* (1983), *Live At The Inferno* (1984), *Stay Hard* (1985), *The Devil's Carrion* (1985), *The Pack Is Back* (1986), *Mad* (1986), *Life's A Bitch* (1987), *Nothing Exceeds Like Excess* (1988).

Real Kids

This American quartet gained recognition amid the punk-rock explosion in New York during the late 70s. Formed by vocalist/guitarist John Felice in 1975, they pre-dated the punk movement, but jumped on the bandwagon as soon as it started to roll. With bassist Allen 'Alpo' Paulino, Billy Borgioli (guitar) and Howard Ferguson (drums) completing the line-up, they were a talented outfit and competent musicians to boot. Delivering a varied and classy selection of predominantly high-energy rockers, they infused reggae, rock 'n' roll and pop influences into their songs, making them

instantly memorable. Their self-titled debut, released in 1977, is one of the great unheralded classics of this genre. Borgioli and Ferguson departed to be replaced by Billy Cole and Robby 'Morocco' Morin before the recording of their second album. Outta Place was a disappointment, for Felice's new compositions lacked the infectious sparkle that made their debut so special. A shambolic live album, recorded in Paris, 1983 was their final offering, before disbanding.
Albums: The Real Kids (1977), Outta Place (1982), All Kindsa Jerks Live (1983).

Realm

This Milwaukee, USA based, hi-tech thrash metal quintet was formed by guitarists Takis Kinis and Paul Laganowski in 1985. By a process of trial and error, they finally completed the line-up with Mark Antoni (vocals), Steve Post (bass) and Mike Olson (drums). Following a string of successful club shows, they landed the support slots on the Wendy O. Williams and Megadeth tours in 1986. Signing to Roadracer Records they released *Endless War* in 1988. This was a complex fusion of hard-rock, thrash and jazz influences and included a remarkable cover of the Beatles' 'Eleanor Rigby'. Their second album saw them becoming too complex with a multitude of unnecessary time-changes, rendering much of the material incoherent and unmelodic.
Albums: *Endless War* (1988), *Suiciety* (1990).

Re-Animator

Formed in Hull, England in 1987, the band consists of Kevin Ingleson (guitar/vocals), Mike Abel (guitar), John Wilson (bass) and Mark Mitchell (drums). Strongly influenced by the legacy of the New Wave Of British Heavy Metal and armed with the new thrash metal attitude, the band signed to the Music For Nations subsidiary label, Under One Flag. The band released their debut mini-album, *Deny Reality*, in 1989, a harsh frustration of thrash that stood them in good stead for their next release *Condemned To Eternity* which appeared in 1990. It was not a great departure in musical style but was regarded as a very solid thrash album. The release of *Laughing* in 1991 saw a major change in musical direction for the band. The album incorporated funk elements with some rather quirky musical styles. Albeit making for a very varied release it also made the album sound jumbled and patchy.
Albums: *Deny Reality* (1989), *Condemned To Eternity* (1990), *Laughing* (1991).

Red Dogs

This UK, blues-based rock 'n' roll quintet was

Raven

formed in 1989, by Mickey 'The Vicar' Ripley (vocals) and Chris John (guitar). Enlisting the services of Mick Young (bass), Paul Guerin (guitar) and Stow (drums), they signed to Episode Records the following year. They debuted with Wrong Side Of Town, a six-track offering that paid respect to the Georgia Satellites, Rolling Stones and Quireboys. The Red Dogs raised their profile by supporting Cheap And Nasty and UFO on their 1991 UK tours. Taking their infectious brand of bar-room boogie to a larger stage proved highly successful. They are currently working on material for a new album.

Album: Wrong Side Of Town (1989).

Redd Kross

This Los Angeles, USA band was formed in 1979, Redd Kross melded elements of 70s glam-rock, 60s psychedelia and 80s heavy metal to become a popular 'alternative' act in the 80s. Originally called the Tourists, the band changed its name to Red Cross. (They were later forced to change the spelling after the International Red Cross organization threatened to sue.) At the beginning, the band consisted of 15-year-old Jeff McDonald as singer, his 11-year-old brother Steve on bass, Greg Hetson on guitar and Ron Reyes on drums. After gaining local recognition opening for such punk outfits as Black Flag, Red Cross made its first recordings in 1980 for a compilation album on the punk Posh Boy label. Shortly afterwards Hetson left to form the Circle Jerks and Reyes joined Black Flag. Other musicians came and went throughout the band's history, the McDonald brothers being the only mainstay. The group's popularity grew steadily, particularly among those who listened to college radio stations, and by the end of the 80s they had recorded three albums in addition to the debut. Some featured covers of songs by such influences as the Rolling Stones and Kiss, while some of the group's originals seemed to cross 70s punk with the bubblegum hits of the 60s. The group resurfaced in the autumn of 1990 with Third Eye, their first album for a major label, Atlantic Records.

Albums: Red Cross (1981), Born Innocent (1982), Teen Babes From Monsanto (1984), Neurotica (1987), Third Eye (1990).

Reed, Dan, Network

Towards the end of the 80s a funk metal phenomenon was beginning to rise to prominence, building upon the foundations laid down by Mother's Finest, Parliament, and Funkadelic in the 70s, with bands such as Living Colour, Faith No More, the Electra Boys, and Dan Reed Network leading the way. Hailing from

Dan Reed Network

Oregon, USA, the Network featured Dan Reed (vocals), Melvin Brannon II (bass), Brion James (lead guitar), Daniel Pred (drums), and Blake Sakamoto (keyboards). The band was signed to Mercury Records and released their first, self-titled album in 1988 which combined the commercial rock element of artists such as Bon Jovi with the funk edge of Prince. The album was enthusiastically received by those people craving rock music with a difference. Tracks such as 'Get To You' and 'Ritual' soon became dance floor hits at rock clubs. The debut was followed by Slam produced by Nile Rodgers of Chic fame, who gave the album a slightly rockier feel while still retaining the funk element of its predecessor. The single 'Rainbow Child' provided the band with its first minor UK hit single, briefly entering the Top 40 in 1989. Prestigious support slots were gained in 1990 in Europe with Bon Jovi and the Rolling Stones, which helped to raise their profile and bring their music to much larger audiences. In 1991 The Heat was released which saw them reunited with Bruce Fairburn - the producer of their first album. This included a unique version of Pink Floyd's 'Money' as well as the singles 'Mix It Up' and 'Baby Now I', both of which failed to make an impression in the charts. Despite critical acclaim, support slots on major tours and a fair degree of radio exposure, Dan Reed Network have yet to achieve their big commercial break and have had to watch their contemporaries such as Living Colour and Faith No More achieve platinum status. Even though major success has eluded them, Dan Reed Network are still regarded as one of the main instigators of the funk metal scene.

Albums: Dan Reed Network (1988), Slam (1989), The Heat (1991).

REO Speedwagon

Formed in Champaign, Illinois, USA in 1970

REO Speedwagon

when pianist Neil Doughty (b. 29 July 1946, Evanston, Illinois, USA) and drummer Alan Gratzer (b. 9 November 1948, Syracuse, New York, USA) were joined by guitarist and songwriter Gary Richrath (b. 10 October 1949, Peoria, Illinois, USA). Although still in its embryonic stage, the group already had its unusual name which was derived from an early American fire-engine, designed by one Ransom E. Olds. Barry Luttnell (vocals) and Greg Philbin (bass) completed the line-up featured on *REO Speedwagon*, but the former was quickly replaced by Kevin Cronin (b. 6 October 1951, Evanston, Illinois, USA). The quintet then began the perilous climb from local to national prominence, but despite their growing popularity, particularly in America's mid-west, REO was initially unable to complete a consistent album. Although *REO Two* and *Ridin' The Storm Out* eventually achieved gold status, disputes regarding direction culminated in the departure of their second vocalist. Michael Murphy took his place in 1974, but when ensuing albums failed to generate new interest, Cronin rejoined his former colleagues. Bassist Bruce Hall (b. 3 May 1953, Champaign, Illinois, USA) was also brought into a line-up acutely aware that previous releases failed to reflect their in-concert prowess. The live *You Get What You Play For* overcame this problem to become the group's first platinum disc, a distinction shared by its successor, *You Can Tune A Piano, But You Can't Tuna Fish*. However, sales for *Nine Lives* proved disappointing, inspiring the misjudged view that REO had peaked. Such impressions were banished in 1980 with the release of *Hi Infidelity*, a crafted, self-confident collection which topped the US album charts and spawned a series of highly-successful singles. An emotive ballad, 'Keep On Lovin' You', reached number 1 in the US and number 7 in the UK, while its follow-up, 'Take It On The Run' also hit the US Top 5. However, a lengthy tour in support of the album proved creatively draining and *Good Trouble* is generally accepted as one of REO's least worthy efforts. Aware of its faults, the quintet withdrew from the stadium circuit and having rented a Los Angeles warehouse, enjoyed six months of informal rehearsals during which time they regained a creative empathy. *Wheels Are Turning* recaptured the zest apparent on *Hi Infidelity* and engendered a second US number 1 in 'Can't Fight This Feeling'. *Life As We Know It* emphasized the group's now accustomed professionalism, and while too often dubbed 'faceless', or conveniently bracketed with other in-concert 70s favourites Styx and Kansas, REO Speedwagon have proved the importance of a massive, secure, grass roots following.

Albums: *REO Speedwagon* (1971), *REO Two* (1972), *Ridin' The Storm Out* (1973), *Lost In A Dream* (1974), *This Time We Mean It* (1975), *REO* (1976), *REO Speedwagon Live/You Get What You Play For* (1977), *You Can Tune A Piano But You Can't Tuna Fish* (1978), *Nine Lives* (1979), *Hi Infidelity* (1980), *Good Trouble* (1982), *Wheels Are Turning* (1984), *Life As We Know It* (1987). Compilations: *A Decade Of Rock 'N' Roll 1970-1980* (1980), *A Second Decade Of Rock 'N' Roll 1981-1991* (1991).

Riff Raff

Featuring Doug Lubahn (vocals/bass), Ned Lubahn (guitar/keyboards), Werner Fritzching (guitar) and Mark Kaufman (drums), this group from New York, USA released just one album of superb melodic heavy rock. *Vinyl Futures* is a mixture of styles in the vein of early Rush and Foreigner.
Album: *Vinyl Futures* (1981).

Riggs

This Californian quartet was founded by vocalist/guitarist Jerry Riggs in 1981. With Jeremy Graf (guitar), David Riderick (bass) and Stephen Roy Carlisle (drums) completing the line-up, they specialized in hard-edged, metallic pop, with considerable crossover potential. Riggs on vocals was particularly distinctive, sounding rather like a hybrid of Bryan Adams and Jon Bon Jovi. Their debut and only release, still remains today an undiscovered gem of infectious and classy AOR. They were unfortunate, in that they lacked a strong visual image and did not receive a strong, promotional push. Disillusioned, they disbanded, with Jerry Riggs later going on to play with Pat Travers.
Album: *Riggs* (1982).

Roadhouse

This melodic UK hard rock quintet was assembled in 1991 around former Def Leppard guitarist Pete Willis. Utilizing the talents of Wayne Grant (bass), Richard Day (guitar), Paul Jackson (vocals) and Trevor Brewis (drums), the band were signed by Phonogram. Their self-titled debut album was a major disappointment, featuring an average collection of commercial AOR-style songs. The band lack identity and have so far been unable to inject drive or spontaneity into their uptempo numbers, while the ballads seem to lack sincerity, emotion and real class.
Album: *Roadhouse* (1991).

Roberts, Kane

Kane Roberts first came to prominence as the Rambo-style lead guitarist in Alice Cooper's band, during his mid-80s comeback. He was lured from Lone Justice to add musical and visual muscle to Cooper's theatrical live show. With the help of Cooper's management, he secured a solo deal with MCA Records in 1987. His debut release was somewhat at odds with his tough-guy image, featuring a collection of AOR and ballads. He quit Cooper's band the following year to concentrate

fully on his solo career. Playing down the muscleman image, he teamed up with Desmond Child to write material for *Saints And Sinners*. This was a highly polished melodic rock album in a Bon Jovi meet Kiss vein, with John McCurry (guitar), Steven Steele (bass), Myron Grombacher (drums) and Chuck Kentis (keyboards) being recruited as permanent band members.
Albums: *Kane Roberts* (1987), *Saints And Sinners* (1991).

Rock City Angels

This USA blues-based hard rock quintet, were formed by vocalist Bobby Durango and bassist Andy Panik in 1982. After a series of false-starts under the names the Abusers and the Delta Rebels, they settled on the name of Rock City Angels, with the addition of guitarists Doug Banx and Mike Barnes and drummer Jackie D. Jukes completing the line-up. *Young Man's Blues* was an impressive debut album. Utilizing full digital technology, it was a double album that featured a superb amalgam of earthy rockers and honest blues numbers. Durango's vocals have a southern twang to them, while the songs themselves combine elements of Lynyrd Skynyrd, Little Feat and the

Georgia Satellites. The album failed commercially and disillusioned, the band broke-up in 1989, with Durango immediately starting a new outfit under his own name.

Album: *Young Man's Blues* (1989).

Rods

This New York power-trio exploded onto the heavy metal scene in 1980. Formed by ex-Elf guitarist David Feinstein, the line-up was completed by drummer Carl Canedy and bassist Stephen Farmer. Although heavily influenced by Kiss, Ted Nugent and Deep Purple, they transformed these influences into a unique sound that was aggressive, powerful and uncompromising. *Rock Hard*, released on the independent Primal label, was a terse and heavily anthemic debut, which eventually led to the inking of a deal with Arista. Gary Bordonaro replaced Farmer before their first major-label release, a re-mixed version of *Rock Hard*, with three additional tracks. *Wild Dogs* was a disappointing follow-up and the album sold poorly, consequently the band were dropped by their label. Now consigned to the independent labels, *In The Raw* was a poorly produced collection of demos, while the live album suffered from muddy sound and uninspired performances. By this stage the band had largely alienated their original fan base. *Let Them Eat Metal*, although a marked improvement still failed to sell and they branched into more melodic rock, recruiting Andy McDonald (guitar), Rick Caudle (vocals), and Emma Zale (keyboards) to produce the FM radio-oriented *Hollywood*. In 1987 the band were back to a three-piece again, with Craig Gruber replacing Bordonaro, but Ex-Picture vocalist Shmoulic Avigal was added to record *Heavier Than Thou*. This was the third successive release that failed to make any impact. Subsequently the band imploded and went their separate ways.

Albums: *Rock Hard* (1980), *The Rods* (1981), *Wild Dogs* (1982), *In The Raw* (1983), *Live* (1983), *Let Them Eat Metal* (1984), *Hollywood*, (1986), *Heavier Than Thou* (1987).

Rogue Male

Formed in London, England in 1984 the band's original line-up consisted of Jim Lyttle (vocals/guitar), John Fraser Binnie (guitar), Kevin Collier (bass) and Steve Kingsley (drums). Quickly signing to the Music For Nations Record label their debut *First Visit* was released in 1985. The album was full of fast, tough, punk-influenced metal. With live gigs showing mainman Jim Lyttle to be a charismatic bandleader they embarked on an ill-fated American tour. Blaming their American label Elecktra Records for a lack of promotion the band returned to England to begin work on their second album. At this point Steve Kingsley left the band to be replaced by session drummer Charlie Morgan who played on the album recordings, but he was replaced soon after by Danny Fury. *Animal Man* was released in 1986 but due to a lack of public interest the band dissolved soon after its release.

Albums: *First Visit* (1985), *Animal Man* (1986).

Rossington Collins

This US rock band was formed in 1979 by the four surviving members of the 1977 Lynyrd Skynyrd plane crash; Gary Rossington (guitars), Allen Collins (guitars), Billy Powell (keyboards) and Leon Wilkerson (bass), who joined with Dale Krantz (vocals), Barry Harwood (guitars) and Derek Hess (drums). They continued in the best traditions of Skynyrd, though the female lead vocals gave them a different sound. They broke up in 1983 after just two albums. Powell later joined the Christian rock band Vision, while Collins was paralysed from the waist down in a car accident in the mid-80s, and died of pneumonia on 23 January 1990. Krantz married Rossington and both they and Powell took their place in the Lynyrd Skynyrd reunion tour of 1987.

Albums: *Anytime, Anyplace, Anywhere* (1980), *This Is The Way* (1982).

Roth, David Lee

David Lee Roth was the former lead vocalist with Van Halen. His first desire to go solo was initiated by a period of band inactivity during 1985. He recorded the mini-album *Crazy From The Heat*, featuring a varied selection of material that was a departure from the techno-metal approach of Van Halen. The album was favourably received and after much speculation, he finally broke ranks in the autumn of 1985. Roth soon found himself in the Us Top 3 with an unlikely version of the Beach Boys' 'California Girls' (complete with a suitably tacky video) and an even more unlikely cover of 'I Ain't Got Nobody'. This bizarre change must have baffled and bemused his fans. He soon assembled an impressive array of musicians, notably guitar virtuoso Steve Vai (ex-Zappa and Alcatrazz), bassist Billy Sheehan (ex-Talas) and drummer Greg Bissonette to record *Eat 'Em And Smile*. This featured an amazing selection of blistering rockers and offbeat, big production numbers. It proved that Roth was still a great showman; the album was technically superb and infused with an irreverent sense of Yankee humour. *Skyscraper*, released two years later, built on this foundation, but focused more on an

David Lee Roth

elaborately produced hard rock direction. Billy Sheehan departed shortly after its release to be replaced by Matt Bissonette. Brett Tuggle on keyboards was also recruited to expand the line-up to a five piece and add an extra dimension to their sound. Steve Vai left in 1989 to pursue a solo career, but was only temporarily missed as Jason Becker stepped in, a new six-string whizz kid of the Malmsteen school of guitar histrionics. *A Little Ain't Enough* emerged in 1991 and, although technically faultless, it tended to duplicate ideas from his previous two albums. His ego continues to expand, but whether he can continue to match it in creative terms now remains questionable.

Albums: *Crazy From The Heat* (1985), *Eat 'Em And Smile* (1986), *Skyscraper* (1988), *A Little Ain't Enough* (1991).

Rough Diamond

This highly-touted supergroup was formed to considerable fanfare in 1976. Dave Clempson (ex-Bakerloo, Colosseum, Humble Pie; guitar), Damon Butcher (keyboards), Willie Bath (bass) and Geoff Britton (ex-Wings; drums) joined former Uriah Heep singer David Byron, but their launch was undermined by a court case brought by another group claiming the same name. The delay undermined the quintet's confidence and an ensuing album was highly disappointing. Its appearance during the punk explosion exacerbated problems and although the band looked to the USA for solace, friction between Byron and his colleagues proved insurmountable. The singer embarked on a solo career in October 1977 while the remaining members added Garry Bell and adopted a new name, Champion.

Album: *Rough Diamond* (1977).

Rudd, Mike

b New Zealand. Rudd relocated to Australia with the Chants R'N'B in 1966. In 1968 he joined another similar combo Party Machine, containing future members of Daddy Cool. This band evolved into an 'underground' experimental band - the short-lived Sons Of The Vegetal Mother in 1969. Forming his own band Spectrum that same year, Rudd teamed up with long-term collaborator bassist Bill Putt and wrote most of the material. Rudd led the band (and their alter-ego, Murtceps), through the blues orientated heavy rock music period in Australia during 1971-73. Next came Ariel (1973-74), a band which was a more exotic spectacle consisting of weird and wonderful costumes, exotic light shows and smoke bombs. Instant Reply followed (1978-79) which later changed their name to the Heaters. As trends changed, the Heaters become Rudd's post punk,

new wave band, touring frequently during 1979-1982 but not achieving any commercial success with *Unrealist*. Rudd briefly returned to his roots with the Living Legend Blues Band, subsequently forming W.H.Y. in 1983, which toured and recorded in Germany, and was a more experimental outfit, as was the similar Mike Rudd's No. 9. He now performs in the Suburban Blues Band, a good-time cover band. He later briefly reformed Spectrum in early 1990. His song, 'I'll Be Gone', recorded by Spectrum, remains one of the most recognizable Australian hits of the early 70s.

Running Wild

This quartet from Hamburg, Germany were strongly influenced by the New Wave Of British Heavy Metal Movement of the early 80s. Formed in 1983, by guitarist/vocalist Rock'n'Rolf, a plethora of personnel changes occurred before Majik Moti (guitar), Jens Becker (bass) and Iain Finlay (drums) were recruited, and a degree of stability was achieved. They initially pushed a black-metal image, but made little impact with their rigidly formularized, one-paced rantings. They changed course musically, with their third album and tried to emulate the style of Iron Maiden. They also adopted a swashbuckling pirates image. However, Rolf's weak vocals and the repetitiveness of their material will always hinder their chances of promotion to the first division of hard-rock.

Albums: *Gates Of Purgatory* (1984), *Branded And Exiled* (1985), *Under Jolly Roger* (1987), *Ready For Boarding* (1988), *Port Royal* (1988), *Death Or Glory* (1990).

Rush

Rush

This Canadian heavy rock band comprised of Geddy Lee (b. 29 July 1953, Willowdale, Toronto, Canada; keyboards/bass/vocals), Alex Lifeson (b. 27 August 1953, British Columbia,

Canada; guitar) and John Rutsey (drums). From 1969-72 they performed in Toronto playing a brand of Cream inspired material. but they gained more recognition when they supported the New York Dolls in 1973. In 1974 they took the name Rush and released *Rush* on Mercury Records following its success on the independent Moon Records. The same year, Neil Peart (b. 12 September 1952, Hamilton, Ontario, Canada; drums), who was to be the main songwriter of the band, replaced Rutsey, and Rush undertook their first full tour of the USA. Rush's music is typified by Lee's oddly high-pitched voice, a tremendously powerful guitar sound, especially in the early years, and a great interest in science fiction and fantasy. This is most notable in the now classic 1976 concept album, *2112*, based on the work of novelist/philosopher Ayn Rand, which has as its central theme the idea of freewill and individualism. By 1979 Rush were immensely successful worldwide, and the Canadian Government gave them the title of official Ambassadors of Music. As the 80s progressed Rush altered their image from the science fiction dominated tracks to become more sophisticated, clean-cut and undoubtedly intellectual music-makers. Some early fans criticised the band's seeming determination to progress musically with each new album, while others lauded their very iconoclasm. Now major artists worldwide, they still sell large numbers of records despite rarely playing outside their native Canada. Often criticized for being lyrically pretentious, Rush have weathered the storm and remain Canada's leading rock band.

Albums: *Rush* (1974), *Fly By Night* (1975), *Caress Of Steel* (1975), *2112* (1976), *All The World's A Stage* (1976), *A Farewell To Kings* (1977), *Archives* (1978), *Hemispheres* (1978), *Permanent Waves* (1980), *Rush Through Time* (1980), *Moving Pictures* (1981), *Exit: Stage Left* (1981), *Signals* (1982), *Grace Under Pressure* (1984), *Power Windows* (1985), *Hold Your Fire* (1987), *Presto* (1989), *Roll The Bones* (1991).

S

S.A.D.O.

This German group specialized in hard-rock. They achieved a degree of notoriety during the mid-80s, with their Tubes-like stage show, that incorporated a selection of scantily clad females in sado-masochistic uniform. Vocalist Andre Cook has been the only permanent member since the band's inception in 1983. They made an attempt to jump on the thrash-metal bandwagon with *Dirty Fantasy*, but attracted minimal attention. They adopted a more melodic FM-radio approach with *Sensitive*. Their most recent line-up included Cook, plus Matthias Moser (guitar), Duncan O'Neill (bass) and Danny (drums).
Albums: *Shout* (1984), *Circle Of Friends* (1987), *Dirty Fantasy* (1988), *Another Kind Of . . .* (1989), *Sensitive* (1990).

St. Paradise

This short-lived, US hard-rock group was formed in 1978, by ex-Ted Nugent band duo Derek St. Holmes (vocals/guitar) and Rob Grange (bass/vocals). Recruiting ex-Montrose drummer Denny Carmassi, the line-up looked very promising. Signed by Warner Brothers, they released a self-titled debut in 1979. Comprising Americanized power-metal, the album lacked both drive and individuality and compared unfavourably with everything that the band's members had been associated with before. Following a European tour supporting Van Halen, which failed to win new fans for St. Paradise, the band disintegrated. Carmassi joined Gamma and St. Holmes worked with Aerosmith's Brad Whitford for a short time, before rejoining Nugent once more.
Album: *St. Paradise* (1979).

Samson

This UK heavy metal group were formed in 1979 by guitarist Paul Samson, and have since been dogged by line-up changes, management disputes and record company problems. These have occurred at critical points in their career, just as major success seemed imminent. The first incarnation of the band comprised Paul Samson (guitar), Chris Aylmer (bass), Bruce Bruce (vocals) and Clive Burr (drums), the latter soon moving on to Iron Maiden and replaced by the masked Thunderstick. They specialized in high energy blues-based rock, with melodic undercurrents. In

Samson

1981, they were among the leading lights of the New Wave Of British Heavy Metal movement, with each of their first four albums being minor classics of the genre. In 1981, Bruce Bruce and Thunderstick departed, the former assumed his real name, Bruce Dickinson and joined Iron Maiden as lead vocalist. Thunderstick formed a new group under his own name. Nicky Moore (ex-Tiger) and Mel Gaynor (ex-Light Of The World) stepped in on vocals and drums respectively, but Gaynor soon moved on to Simple Minds, with Pete Jupp filling in as replacement. Both *Before The Storm* and *Don't Get Mad, Get Even* are Samson's most accomplished works, with Moore's gritty and impassioned vocals giving the band a sound that was both earthy and honest. Chris Aylmer left in 1984 and was replaced by ex-Diamond Head bassist, Merv Goldsworthy before the recording of the excellent live album *Thank You And Goodnight*. The band split soon after, with *Head Tactics* being a posthumous release comprising remixes of tracks from the *Head On* and *Shock Tactics*. Nicky Moore went on to form Mammoth, while Paul Samson released the solo *Joint Forces* in 1986. The band reformed in 1988 and released *Refugee* in 1990, a classy, if slightly dated collection of bluesy hard-rock numbers.

Albums: *Survivors* (1979), *Head On* (1980), *Shock Tactics* (1981), *Before The Storm* (1982), *Don't Get Mad, Get Even* (1984), *Thank You And Goodnight* (1984), *Pillars Of Rock* (1990), *Refugee* (1990), *Live At Reading* (1991).

Sanctuary

Sanctuary

Formed in Seattle, Washington, USA in 1985 the band consisted of Warrel Dane (vocals), Lenny Rutledge (guitar/vocals), Sean Blosl (guitar/vocals), Jim Sheppard (bass) and Dave Budbill (drums/vocals). Due to having a couple of early demo tracks included on a low budget compilation *Northwest Metal Fest*, the band attracted the attention of Megadeth's guitarist Dave Mustaine who offered to produce their next recording. The band signed to CBS/Epic Records and Mustaine was duly drafted as producer. *Refuge Denied* was a mixture of Megadeth influenced riffs and Sanctuary's basic thrash metal sound. After extensive touring with Megadeth, Sanctuary released *Into The Mirror Black*. The band broke up shortly afterwards.
Albums: *Refuge Denied* (1987), *Into The Mirror Black* (1990).

Saraya

Formed in the USA by vocalist Sandi Saraya and keyboard player Gregg Munier in 1987 they originally went under the name Alsace Lorraine. With the addition of Tony Rey (guitar), Gary Taylor (bass) and Chuck Bonfarte (drums), they changed their name to Saraya. Fusing influences such as Heart, the Pretenders and Pat Benatar, they recorded their self-titled debut; a melodic and highly polished collection of AOR numbers, characterized by Sandi's raunchy and infectious vocal style. Following internal disputes, Rey and Taylor quit in 1990 and replaced respectively by Tony Bruno and Barry Dunaway. They released *When The Blackbird Sings* in 1991, which built on their former style.
Albums: *Saraya* (1989), *When The Blackbird Sings* (1991).

Satan

Formed in Newcastle-upon-Tyne, England in 1981 , the original line up comprised Trev Robinson (vocals), Russ Tippins (guitar), Steve Ramsey (guitar), Graeme English (bass) and Andy Reed (drums). In 1981 the band recorded two tracks for a compilation *Roxcalibur* and released a self-financed single entitled 'Kiss Of Death'. Soon after its release vocalist Robinson left the band to be replaced by Ian Swift who himself was soon supplanted by Brian Ross. Due to numerous demos and the fact that the band were building a name for themselves via the underground tape-trading scene, they attracted the attention of Roadrunner Records. Their debut *Court In The Act* was released in 1983. The album was well received for its speed-metal power riffs and excellent lead guitar work. However, the name of the band did not suit the music. The band felt the monicker was typecasting them and holding them back. Not only did they alter the name to Blind Fury but also once again changed vocalists, replacing the departed Ross with Lou Taylor. This line-up actually recorded an album using the Blind Fury appellation. *Out Of Reach* was released on the Roadrunner Records label in 1984. The band changed vocalists yet again replacing Taylor with Michael Jackson and reverted to the name Satan. A new demo attracted the interest of the German-based Steamhammer Records and *Into The Future* was released in 1986. The album's poor production was saved by the power and quiality of the material. This was quickly followed up with *Suspended Sentence* released in 1987. However, once again the name Satan was causing problems and because of record company and managerial pressure they changed their name to Pariah (UK). The band released two albums *The Kindred* and *Blaze Of Obscurity*. The band in all its guises folded in 1990.
Albums: *Court In The Act* (1983), *Into The Future*

(1986), *Suspended Sentence* (1987).

Satriani, Joe

Joe Satriani grew up in Long Island, New York, USA and is a skilled guitarist responsible for teaching the instrument to, among others, Kirk Hammett of Metallica, and Steve Vai. After travelling abroad extensively he returned to the USA to form the Squares. Due to a lack of commercial success, this project folded in 1984, giving Satriani the opportunity to concentrate on his experimental guitar playing. The outcome of this was the release of an EP, *Joe Satriani*. Following a spell with the Greg Kihn band, appearing on *Love And Rock 'N' Roll*, Satriani released *Not Of This Earth*, an album which was less polished than its successor, *Surfing With The Alien*. In 1988 he was joined by Stu Hamm (bass) and Jonathan Mover (drums). Satriani also worked for a while on Mick Jagger's late-80s tour. Never afraid to push his considerable musical skills to the limit, Satriani has played the banjo and the harmonica on various of his albums, as well as successfully attempting the vocals on *Flying In A Blue Dream*.
Albums: *Not Of This Earth* (1986), *Surfing With The Alien* (1987), *Dreaming 11* (1988), *Flying In A Blue Dream* (1990).

Savage

Formed in Mansfield, England in 1978 the band's line-up consisted of Chris Bradley (bass/vocals), Andy Dawson (guitar), Wayne Redshaw (guitar) and Mark Brown (drums). Their debut *Loose 'N' Lethal* in 1983. won critical acclaim for its ultra-heavy riffs being firmly rooted in the New Wave Of British Heavy Metal. The band then toured Europe where they quickly gained popularity, especially in Holland. Similar success in their homeland was not so forthcoming. In 1984, the band signed a new recording agreement with the Zebra Records label which released an EP *We Got The Edge*. This showed Savage to be taking a slightly different approach with a mellower, more laid-back sound. The band's *Hyperactive*, released in 1985, saw them continuing this musical approach. After this, Savage seemed to lose both momentum and direction and they disbanded in 1986.
Albums: *Loose 'N' Lethal* (1983), *Hyperactive* (1985).

Savage Grace

This power-metal rock group were formed in Los Angeles, California in 1981, since when the band have had a chequered career of unstable line-ups. Originally using the monicker of Marquis De Sade

they soon changed their name to Savage Grace (no relation to the early 70s group who recorded on Reprise Records). The original line-up consisted of Mike Smith (vocals), Chris Logue (guitar/vocals), Brian East (bass) and Dan Finch (drums). The band soon attracted the attention of the French-based Black Dragon Records label, which signed them on the strength of a previous track included on the *Metal Massacre* series of compilations and the self-financed EP *The Dominatress* which the band had released in 1983. After the band's debut *Master Of Disguise* was released in 1985, the line-up underwent changes; ex-Agent Steel guitarist Mark Marshall was added, while vocalist Mike Smith's departure left Chris Logue to handle the lead vocals. Drummer Dan Finch quit to be replaced by Mark Markum. This incarnation of the band managed to stay together long enough to record *After The Fall From Grace*, in 1986. The band then toured Europe with Heir Apparent and even replaced bassist Brian East for Heir Apparent's bassist Derek Peace before they began to work on recordings for the projected third album. However, continual line-up changes had taken their toll; bassist Derek Peace rejoined Heir Apparent and Savage Grace seemingly disappeared late in 1988.
Albums: *Master Of Disguise* (1985), *After The Fall From Grace* (1986).

Savatage

Previously known as Metropolis and Avatar, Savatage, a melodic, heavy rock quintet, were formed in Florida, USA in 1983 by the Oliva brothers. The band comprised Jon Oliva (vocals/keyboards), Chris Oliva (guitar), Steve 'Doc' Wacholz (drums) and Keith Collins (bass), the latter being eventually replaced by Johnny Lee Middleton. Their initial approach was strongly influenced by Judas Priest, Black Sabbath and Iron Maiden. Savatage's first three albums clearly reflect this, with a high-energy fusion of intense power-riffs and high-pitched vocals. *Fight For The Rock* marked a detour towards more melodic AOR, which was poorly received by their fans. Consequently, they returned to basics again for the next album. Chris Caffery was added as a second guitarist in 1989, before the recording of *Gutter Ballet*. This, and the more recent *Streets*, represent the band's finest work to date. Both are elaborate rock operas, featuring a superb mixture of dynamic hard-rock and atmospheric ballads. Utilizing an orchestra and state-of-the-art production techniques, Savatage have become one of the front-runners of their genre.
Albums: *Sirens* (1983), *The Dungeons Are Calling* (1985), *Power Of The Night* (1985), *Fight For The*

Savatage

Rock (1986), *Hall Of The Mountain King* (1987), *Gutter Ballet* (1990), *Streets* (1991).

Saxon

Formed in the north of England in the late 70s, Saxon were originally known as Son Of A Bitch and spent time paying their dues in the clubs and small venues up and down the UK. After a name change to Saxon, they signed a deal with French label Carrere, better known for its disco productions than its work with heavy metal bands. Saxon comprised, Peter 'Biff' Byford (vocals), Graham Oliver (guitar), Paul Quinn (guitar), Steve Dawson (bass) and Pete Gill (drums). During the late 70s, many young metal bands were emerging in the UK, and this became known as the New Wave Of British Heavy Metal. These bands were challenging the supremacy of the old guard of heavy metal bands, and Saxon were part of this movement along with other notable names such as Iron Maiden and Diamond Head. The first album was a solid, if basic heavy rock outing, but the release of *Wheels Of Steel* turned the tide. Saxon's popularity soared, earning themselves two UK Top 20 hits with 'Wheels Of Steel' and '747 (Strangers In The Night)'. They capitalized on this success with the release in the same year of *Strong Arm Of The Law*, another very heavy, very articulate, metal album. This set spawned another Top 20 in 'And The Bands Played On' as did the following year's *Demin And Leather* with 'Never Surrender'. They toured the USA to much acclaim and appeared at the Castle Donington 'Monsters Of Rock' festival. By the time of 1982's *The Eagle Has Landed*, which gave Saxon their most successful album, reaching the UK Top 5, the group were at their peak. That same year, Pete Gill was replaced by drummer Nigel Glockler, who had previously worked with Toyah. At this time, Saxon even rivalled the immensely popular Iron Maiden. The release of *Power And The Glory* enforced their credentials as a major heavy metal band. The follow-up, *Innocence Is No Excuse*, was a more polished and radio-friendly production but it stalled just inside the Top 40. It heralded an uncertain time for the band with the result of a slide in their popularity. The departure of Steve Dawson at this point contributed to their further decline. *Rock The Nations* was heavier, but it was too little, too late. In 1990 Saxon returned to the public eye with a UK tour that featured a set of their popular older material. *Solid Ball Of Rock* was their most accomplished album for some time, but a return to their previous status seems unlikely.
Albums: *Saxon* (1979), *Wheels Of Steel* (1980), *Strong Arm Of The Law* (1980), *Denim And Leather* (1981), *The Eagle Has Landed* (1982), *Power And The Glory* (1983), *Crusader* (1984), *Innocence Is No Excuse* (1985), *Rock The Nations* (1986), *Destiny* (1988), *Rock 'N' Roll Gypsies* (1990), *Solid Ball Of Rock* (1991). Compilation: *Anthology* (1988).

Scanner

This German rock quintet rose from the ashes of Lions Breed in 1987. Comprising Tom S. Sopha (guitar), Michael Knoblich (vocals), Wolfgang Kolorz (drums), Axel A.J. Julius (guitar) and Martin Bork (bass), their brand of metal-thrash identified them with fellow countrymen, Helloween. Signing to Noise Records in 1988, Scanner released *Hypertrace*, a science-fiction concept album. The storyline revolved around extra-terrestrial robots preventing war between the superpowers and, although far from original, it found an appreciable audience. Knoblich quit the group in 1989 and was replaced by ex-Angel Dust vocalist S.L. Coe. They recorded *Terminal Earth*, another concept album, centred this time on the aforementioned robots' concern for planet Earth, and the damage that the human race has inflicted upon it. Not surprisingly, the music bore similarities to the previous release.
Albums: *Hypertrace* (1988), *Terminal Earth* (1990).

Saxon

Schenker, Michael

b.10 January 1955, Savstedt, Germany. Schenker began his musical career at the age of 16, when, along with brother Rudolf, he formed the Scorpions in 1971. After contributing some impressive guitarwork on the band's *Lonesome Crow* debut, he was offered the chance to replace Bernie Marsden in UFO. Schenker joined the group in June 1973 with the result that their musical direction adopted an increased hard-rock stance. *Phenomenon*, released in 1974, featured the metal classics 'Doctor, Doctor' and 'Rock Bottom', with Schenker's performance on his Gibson 'Flying V', hammering home the band's new identity. A series of excellent albums followed, before Schenker eventually quit in 1978, after the recording of *Obsession*. The split had been imminent for some time as there had been personal conflict between Schenker and vocalist Phil Mogg for several years. Schenker moved back to Germany and joined the Scorpions again temporarily, contributing guitar parts to *Lovedrive*, released in 1979. Soon afterwards, he formed his own band, the Michael Schenker Group, which was later abbreviated to MSG. MSG's personnel has been in a constant state of flux, with Schenker

hiring and firing musicians, seemingly, at will. Vocalists have included Gary Barden, Graham Bonnet and more recently Robin McCauley. In 1991, Schenker took time out between MSG albums, to contribute to the Contraband project, a one-off collaboration between members of Shark Island, Vixen, Ratt and L.A.Guns. This album featured an inspired selection of covers that included Mott The Hoople's 'All The Way From Memphis' and David Bowie's 'Hang On To Yourself'. Schenker's latest album is scheduled for January 1992, with 'Never Ending Nightmare', an acoustic five-track EP preceding it as a single release.

Albums: with the Scorpions *Lonesome Crow* (1972), *Lovedrive* (1979); with UFO *Phenomenon* (1974), *Force It* (1975), *No Heavy Pettin'* (1976), *Lights Out* (1977), *Strangers In The Night* (1977), *Obsession* (1978); with MSG *The Michael Schenker Group* (1980), *MSG* (1981), *One Night At Budokan* (1982), *Assault Attack* (1982). *Built To Destroy* (1983), *Rock Will Never Die* (1984), *Perfect Timing* (1987), *Save Yourself* (1989), *Never Ending Nightmare* (1992); with Contraband *Contraband* (1991).

Michael Schenker

Schon And Hammer

This was a short lived partnership between Journey's Neal Schon (b. 1955, San Mateo, California, USA; guitar/vocals) and Jan Hammer (b. 17 April 1948, Prague, Czechoslovakia; keyboards/drums). The fusion of Schon's AOR rock and Hammer's jazz-rock produced *Untold Passion*, which largely consisted of virtuoso performances from both musicians duelling off each other. The innovative British electric jazz bassist Colin Hodgkinson, previously with Back Door, accompanied the duo in the studio on the first album. Schon's vocal contributions proved to be more satisfying than his previous efforts with his parent group. By the time of the second release, most of Schon's comrades from Journey had been enlisted, resulting in a lighter collection of songs and a departure from Schon And Hammer's *raison d'être*. The partnership was soon dissolved, with Schon returning full-time to Journey, and Hammer turning to television work, resulting in a huge success with the *Miami Vice* series.
Albums: *Untold Passion* (1981), *Here To Stay* (1982).

School Of Violence

This New York hardcore quartet was formed in 1985 by guitarist Stegmon Von Heintz. With the addition to line-up of Karl Axell (vocals), Rick Stone (bass) and M.S.Evans (drums), they debuted on *The People Are Hungry* compilation. This led to a contract with Metal Blade Records and the release of *We The People* in 1988. Assimilating Bad Brains, Dead Kennedys, Anthrax and D.O.A. influences, it featured vitriolic lyrics that commented on social and political injustices. The production was very ragged however, and the messages were swamped beneath the drum and bass-laden tumult.
Album: *We The People* (1988).

Scorpions

This German hard-rock group was formed by guitarists Rudolf and Michael Schenker in 1971. With Klaus Meine (vocals), Lothar Heinberg (bass) and Wolfgang Dziony (drums), they exploded onto the international heavy rock scene with *Lonesome Crow* in 1972. This tough and exciting record was characterized by Schenker's distinctive, fiery guitarwork on his Gibson 'Flying V' and Klaus Meine's powerful teutonic vocals. Soon after the album was released, Heinberg, Dziony and Schenker left, the latter joining UFO. Francis Buscholz and Jurgen Rosenthal stepped in on bass and drums respectively for the recording of *Fly To The Rainbow*. Ulrich Roth was recruited as Schenker's replacement in 1974 and Rudy Lenners took over the drumstool from Rosenthal the following year. The following releases, *Trance* and *Virgin Killer*, epitomized the Scorpions new-found confidence and unique style; a fusion of demonic power-riffs, wailing guitar solos and melodic vocal lines. Produced by Dieter Dierks, the improvements musically were now matched technically. Their reputation began to grow throughout Europe and the Far East, backed up by exhaustive touring. *Taken By Force* saw Herman Rarebell replace Lenners, with the band branching out into big production anthemic power-ballads for the first time. Although commercially successful, Roth was not happy with this move, and he quit to form Electric Sun following a major tour to support the album. *Tokyo Tapes* was recorded on this tour and marked the end of the first phase of the band's career. It was an electrifying live set of the band performing their strongest numbers. Mathias Jabs was recruited as Roth's replacement, but had to step down temporarily in favour of Michael Schenker, who had just left UFO under acrimonious circumstances. Schenker contributed guitar on three tracks of *Lovedrive* and toured with them afterwards. He was replaced by Jabs permanently after collapsing on stage during their European tour in 1979. The band had now achieved a stable line-up, and shared the mutual goal of breaking through in the USA. Relentless touring schedules ensued and their albums leaned more and more towards sophisticated hard-edged melodic rock. *Blackout* made the US *Billboard* Top 10, as did the following *Love At First Sting* which featured the magnificent 'Still Loving You', a fine hard-rock ballad. *World Wide Live* was released in 1985, another double live album, which only featured material from the second phase of the band's career. Superbly recorded and produced, it captured the band at their manic and melodic best, peaking at number 14 on its four-month stay on the US chart. The band took a well-earned break before releasing *Savage Amusement* in 1988, their first studio album for almost four years. This marked a slight change im emphasis again, with the band adopting a more restrained approach. The album was a huge success, reaching number five in the USA and number 1 throughout Europe.
The band switched to Phonogram Records in 1989 and ended their 20-year association with producer Dieter Dierks. *Crazy World* followed and was to become their strongest and most successful album to date. The politically poignant 'Wind Of Change', lifted as a single, became their first million-seller as it cracked the number 1 position

Scorpions

in country after country around the world. Produced by Keith Olsen, *Crazy World* transformed the band's sound, so that they had enormous crossover potential, without radically compromising their identity or alienating their original fanbase. The group now look forward into the 90s to a successful third phase of their career.

Albums: *Lonesome Crow* (1972), *Fly To The Rainbow* (1974), *In Trance* (1975), *Virgin Killer* (1976), *Taken By Force* (1978), *Tokyo Tapes* (1978), *Lovedrive* (1979), *Animal Magnetism* (1980), *Blackout* (1982), *Love At First Sting* (1984), *World Wide Live* (1985), *Savage Amusement* (1988), *Hurricane Rock* (1990), *Crazy World* (1990). Compilations: *The Best Of The Scorpions* (1979), *The Best Of The Scorpions, Volume 2* (1984), *Gold Ballads* (1987), *Best Of Rockers And Ballads* (1989).

ill-health forced him into retirement. Although he was not an exceptional performer on either instrument, Sedric fitted well into the cheerful music that Waller's accompanists offered. Thanks to this association he enjoyed a long and successful career.

Compilation: *Fats Waller And His Rhythm 1934-36 (Classic Years In Digital Stereo)* (1988).

Sea Hags

This San Franciscan glam, hard-rock outfit comprised of Ron Yocom (guitar/vocals), Frankie Wilsey (guitar), Chris Schlosshardt (bass) and Adam Maples (drums). Their first and only album was recorded for Chrysalis by the Guns N' Roses producer, Mike Clink. Largely indistinguishable from other Californian bands of their kind, they very soon expired when Ron Yocom departed.

Album: *Sea Hags* (1989).

Seducer

This hard-rock blues group was formed in Amsterdam, Netherlands, in 1980 by vocalists/guitarists Frans Phillipus and Jerry Lopies. After a series of false starts, the line-up stabilized with the recruitment of bassist Eppie Munting and drummer Rene van Leersum. Specializing in blues-based hard-rock and boogie, the band contributed tracks to the compilation *Holland Heavy Metal, Vol. 1* in 1982. A deal with the independent Universe label followed and a self-titled debut appeared in 1983. This was poorly received, and a line-up re-shuffle ensued with Van Leersum and Lopies departing in favour of ex-Hammerhead guitarist Erik Karreman, drummer

Sea Hags

Jan Koster and vocalist Thijs Hamelaers. They contributed two numbers to the *Dutch Steel* compilation in 1984, but the group disbanded shortly afterwards as Koster and Karreman formed Highway Chile, with Hamelaers went on to Germane and later the Sleez Beez.
Album: *Seducer* (1983).

Sentinel Beast

This thrash metal group was formed in Sacramento, California, USA in 1984 by bassist Mike Spencer, vocalist Debbie Gunn and drummer Scott Awes. Adding guitarists Barry Fischel and Mark Koyasako, they debuted with their theme tune 'Sentinel Beast', on the *Metal Massacre VII* compilation in 1986. This opened the door to a full contract with Metal Blade Records and the emergence of Depths Of Death the same year. This was standard Anthrax-style heavy metal, poorly produced and notable only for the high-speed cover of Iron Maiden's 'Phantom Of The Opera'. The album was a commercial flop and founder member Spencer left to join Flotsam And Jetsum soon after its release. The band subsequently disintegrated, with Debbie Gunn re-appearing later in Znowhite and Ice Age.
Albums: *Depths Of Death* (1986).

Sepultura

Sepultura

Formed in Belo Horizonte, Brazil in 1984 by brothers Igor (b. 24 September 1970, Brazil; drums) and Max Cavalera (b. 4 August 1969, Brazil; vocals/guitar), with Paulo Jnr. (b. 30 April 1969, Brazil; bass) and guitarist Jairo T, who was replaced in April 1987 by Andreas Kisser (b. 24 August 1968, Brazil; guitar). Sepultura is the Portuguese word for grave, and this is a clue as to the nature of their music which deals with the themes of death and destruction, influenced by bands such as Slayer and Venom. In 1985, Sepultura recorded an album with Brazilian band Overdose, but this debut, *Bestial Devastation*, was of poor quality and had limited circulation. Their first solo *Morbid Visions*, was released in 1986, followed a year later by *Schizophrenia*. Their music is typified by speed and aggression and anger, possibly due to the band's preoccupations with the poor social conditions in their native land. It was Monte Conner of the American record label Roadrunner who brought the band to international notice in 1989 when they released *Beneath The Remains*, which had been recorded in Rio with Scott Burns as producer. In 1990 Sepultura played at the Dynamo Festival in Holland where they met Gloria Bujnowski, manager of Sacred Reich, ; their relationship with her led to the re-release of *Schizophrenia*. Despite European and American success, Sepultura have not deserted Brazil, and they played at the Rock in Rio festival in 1990. *Arise*, released in 1991, is the best selling album in the history of the Roadrunner label.
Albums: *Morbid Visions* (1986), *Schizophrenia* (1987), *Beneath The Remains* (1989), *Arise* (1991).

Sergeant

This predominantly Swiss, six-piece group was formed from the ashes of the Steve Whitney Band. Comprising Pete Prescott (vocals), Rob Seales

(guitar), Chrigi Wiedemeier (guitar), Urs Amacher (keyboards), Rolf Schlup (bass) and Geri Steimer (drums) they specialized in Americanized hard-rock with melodic undercurrents. Signing to Mausoleum Records, they debuted in 1985 with *Sergeant*, a workman-like rock record that paid respect to Van Halen, Kiss and Foreigner. *Streetwise*, released the following year, was a major disappointment, as it merely regurgitated and reprocessed the riffs of their debut. Disillusioned by the media and public response, the band went their separate ways shortly after the album was released. In 1988 Seales and Amacher re-formed the band with new members Romy Caviezel (vocals), Harry Borner (bass) and Urs Rothenbuhler (drums), but this collaboration has yet to release any new material.
Albums: *Sergeant* (1985), *Streetwise* (1986).

707

This US melodic pomp-rock group was formed in 1979 by Kevin Russell (guitar/vocals), Jim McLarty (drums) and Phil Bryant (bass/vocals). The bands line-up was always in a constant state of flux. Tod Howarth (keyboards/guitar/vocals) and ex-Angel Felix Robinson (bass) made important contributions during the group's lifetime. 707 debuted with a radio-friendly self-titled album, characterized by strong musicianship and instantly contagious hooklines and choruses. Their next two albums adopted a more metallic approach, with *2nd Album* deservedly reaching the lower reaches of the US *Billboard* chart. *Megaforce*, produced by Keith Olsen was provided the theme tune from the film of the same name. Unfortunately, the creative ideas had started to run dry by this stage, while the songs duplicated earlier ideas and were generally less immediate. Internal disputes became more and more common, and the band finally fell apart in 1983. Howarth went on to play with Frehley's Comet.
Albums: *707* (1980), *2nd Album* (1981), *Megaforce* (1982).

Shadow King

Following Lou Gramm's departure from Foreigner in 1988, he pursued a relatively less successful solo career for three years. In 1991, his desire to be part of a band once more, led to the formation of Shadow King. Named after one of the band's songs, and based on the description of a huge, decadent and apocalyptic city; the band is completed by Vivian Campbell (guitar, ex-Ronnie James Dio and Whitesnake), Bruce Turgon (bass) and Kevin Valentine (drums). Signing to Atlantic Records, they debuted with a self-titled album in 1991. This was a strong collection of hi-tech, hard-edged AOR and characterized by Gramm's soulful vocal delivery. Campbell's guitar work is surprisingly economical and restrained, marking a distinct change from his previous flamboyant histrionics. Superbly produced by Keith Olsen, it was one of the year's most accomplished and mature rock releases.
Album: *Shadow King* (1991).

Shah

Formed in Moscow, Russia in 1985 the band comprises Antonio Garcia (vocal/guitar), Anatoly Krupnov (bass) and Andrei Sazanov (drums). The group were definitely pioneers of thrash metal in the USSR and they attracted the attention of Velerie Gaina, guitarist with fellow Soviet band Kruiz. Gaina helped Shah record their first demo, which he then took to the West to the German independent label Atom H Records. Suitably impressed the label signed the band, resulting in their debut *Beware*. The album was heavy influenced by thrash metal band Anthrax. Bearing in mind the cultural and political hurdles the band had to overcome, it was a considerable achievement. In 1990 Shah played at the Public Against Violence Festival in Ostava, Czechoslovakia along with German melodic rockers Bonfire and the UK thrash meta lband Talion and was a huge success. They continue to perform regularly and extensively in their own country.
Albums: *Beware* (1989).

Shakin' Street

This rock 'n' roll quintet was influenced by the Stooges, Rolling Stones and Blue Oyster Cult. The group took their name from a song by the MC5. Formed in Paris 1975 by Fabienne Shine (b. Tunisia; vocals) and her songwriting partner Eric Lewy (guitar/vocals), the group was completed by Mike Winter (bass), Armik Tigrane (guitar) and Jean Lou Kalinowski (drums). Signing to CBS, they debuted with the average *Vampire Rock*, a selection of predominantly uptempo rockers, notable only for Shine's unusual vocals. Ross The Boss (ex-Dictators), replaced Tigrane for the second album. This was a vast improvement, with a denser sound and more abrasive guitar work brought through in the final mix. Ross The Boss left to form Manowar with Joey De Maio in 1981, but Shakin' Street carried on for a short time with ex-Thrasher guitarist Duck McDonald (later the Rods), before finally disbanding. Their second album was an undiscovered classic of the metal genre and is much sought after by collectors.
Albums: *Vampire Rock* (1978), *Shakin' Street* (1980).

Shark Island

This five-piece, melodic hard-rock group was formed in 1986 from the ashes of LA glam rockers, the Sharks. Comprising Richard Black (vocals), Spencer Sercombe (guitar), Chris Heilman (ex-Torme bassist) and Gregg Ellis (drums) they were quickly snapped up by A&M Records in the USA. Their debut album featured an impressive collection of infectious pop-metal crossover anthems, but made little impact, mainly due to a lack of promotion. They switched to Epic in 1988 and released *Law Of The Order* the following year. This showed the band had matured considerably, both technically and musically, with the material displaying a new-found confidence. Black has developed into a very accomplished vocalist and songwriter, with a style that marries the best elements of Bryan Adams, Jon Bon Jovi and David Coverdale. He was also involved in the Contraband project in 1991, which featured Michael Schenker and members of L.A. Guns, Ratt and Vixen. Contraband was a one-off collaboration that recorded an album of cover versions inluding Shark Island's 'Bad For Each Other'.
Albums: *S'Cool Bus* (1987), *Law Of The Order* (1989).

Shaw, Tommy

After Styx broke up in 1983, former vocalist Tommy Shaw embarked on a solo career. Signing to A&M Records, he released *Girls With Guns* the following year. This was a big disappointment to Styx fans, who had high hopes for Shaw. The album comprised average melodic pop-rock anthems. The pomp and ceremony of old appeared to have vanished overnight. *What If* followed the same pattern and was another commercial disappointment. Moving to Atlantic Records, he teamed up with ex-Charlie vocalist/guitarist Terry Thomas. This produced *Ambition* and marked a real return to form. The standard of the songs and his own vocals were at last what was expected of him. Rather than build on this and develop a successful solo career, he longed to be part of a band set-up once more. Teaming up with guitarist Ted Nugent, bassist Jack Blades (ex-Night Ranger) and drummer Michael Cartellone they went on to multi-platinum success as Damn Yankees.
Albums: *Girls With Guns* (1984), *What If* (1985), *Ambition* (1987).

Sherriff

This Canadian melodic rock quintet was formed in 1981 by Arnold Lanni (vocals/keyboards) and bassist Wolf Hassel (bass). With the addition of Freddy Curci (vocals), Steve De Marchi (guitar) and Rob Elliot (drums), they signed to Capitol Records and released a self-titled debut the following year. Their approach was characterized by grandiose sweeping melodies, punctuated by fluid, yet economical guitar work. They drew inspiration from Kansas, Foreigner and Styx, but had enough ideas of their own to imbibe a high degree of originality into their songs. The album failed to attract attention and the band parted company. Lanni and Hassel later formed Frozen Ghost, while Curci and De Marchi teamed up in Alias. In 1988, quite unexpectedly, 'When I'm With You' from the debut Sherriff album became a number 1 US hit 5 years after it first charted (number 61). The album was re-released and also did well; consequently there was pressure to re-form Sherriff. Lanni and Hassel denied this as they retained rights to the name and wanted to continue with Frozen Ghost.
Album: *Sherriff* (1982).

Shire

This American hard-rock quartet was formed in 1983 by vocalist David Anthony and guitarist Alan St. Lesa. Enlisting the services of Mick Adrian (bass) and Steve Ordyke (drums), they secured a record deal with Enigma the following year. Influenced by Dokken, Kiss and Van Halen, their debut was a rigidly formularized collection of mid-paced rockers that ultimately lacked distinction. Produced by Michael Wagner, the album was eagerly anticipated, but was a major disappointment when it finally arrived. Needless to say, it failed and the band have subsequently faded.
Album: *Shire* (1984).

Shiva

This UK progressive rock trio, with metallic overtones was formed in 1981 by the multi-talented John Hall (vocals/guitar/keyboards). Teaming up with Andy Skuse (bass/keyboards) and Chris Logan (drums) they signed to Heavy Metal Records in 1982. They debuted with *Fire Dance*, a complex and inventive album that incorporated elements of Rush, Deep Purple and Uriah Heep. Instrumentally, the album was faultless, but the vocals were less impressive. Phil Williams replaced Logan in 1984, but this new line-up has yet to record.
Album: *Fire Dance* (1982).

Shok Paris

Hailing from Ohio State, USA, Shok Paris were formed in 1982 by the three- man nucleus of drummer Bill Sabo and the guitarists Eric Manderwald and Ken Erb. With vocalist Vic Hix and bassist Kel Bershire completing the line-up, they debuted with 'Go Down Fighting' on the *Cleveland Metal* compilation. This opened the door to a deal with the Auburn label and they recorded *Go For The Throat* in less than two days. Musically, with their high- energy, aggressive songs they were very much similar to Riot, Kiss and Accept. Jan Roll took over the drumstool on *Steel And Starlight*, but the album was simply a repeat formula, played under different titles with less conviction than the debut.

Albums: *Go For The Throat* (1984), *Steel And Starlight* (1987).

Shout

This US melodic rock group was put together by ex-Joshua guitarist/vocalist Ken Tamplin and ex-Idle Cure guitarist Chuck King in 1988. Recruiting bassist Loren Robinson, they entered the studio with session drummers Dennis Holt and Mark Hugenberger to record *It Won't Be Long*. This featured highly sophisticated arrangements and classy songs in the Journey, Boston and Styx mould. Joey Galletta was added as a permanent drummer for *In Your Face*, which leaned towards a significantly heavier direction. The album also featured guest appearances from guitarists Alex Masi, Marty Friedman and Lanny Cordola and was notable for some exciting six-string duels on many of the songs. The band became inactive in 1990, when Tamplin teamed up with Cordola (ex-House Of Lords) to form Magdallan.

Albums: *It Won't Be Long* (1988), *In Your Face* (1989).

Shy

This quintet were formed in Birmingham, England and specialized in Americanized, melodic heavy rock. Formed in 1982, they released their debut album the following year on the independent Ebony label. The songs were excellent and characterized by the silver-throated screams of Tony Mills, but the album was let down by a slight production. New bassist, Roy Stephen Davis joined in 1984, and along with vocalist Mills, guitarist Steve Harris, drummer Alan Kelly and keyboard player Pat McKenna they secured a new deal with RCA Records. Two quality albums of sophisticated pomp-metal followed, with 1987's *Excess All Areas* being the band's finest work to date. This included a camped up version of Cliff Richard's 'Devil Woman' and was given a live heavy metal interpretation. They gained the support slot on Meatloaf's 1987 UK tour, but the album still failed to sell in large quantities. RCA dropped the band, but they were rescued by MCA Records, which allocated a large budget to record *Misspent Youth*, with Roy Thomas Baker as producer. This album was a major disappointment as the band's naturally aggressive approach had been tempered. The songs were geared for Stateside FM-radio consumption and the group's identity had been suffocated in the clinically sterile production.

Albums: *Once Bitten, Twice...*(1983), *Brave The Storm* (1985), *Excess All Areas* (1987), *Misspent Youth* (1989).

Sieges Even

This German 'techno-thrash' quartet was put together by vocalist Franz Herde and guitarist Markus Steffen in 1986. After recording three demos they were picked up by the Steamhammer label in 1988. They debuted with *Life Cycle*, a complex and inventive speed-metal fusion of jazz, rock and classical styles. The material was characterized by a multitude of quick-fire time changes, that ultimately fragmented the songs and made them difficult to distinguish from one another. The album was generally well received, but it has made little impact outside Germany.

Album: *Life Cycle* (1988).

Silent Rage

This Californian hard-rock quartet was formed in 1986 by Mark Hawkins (vocals/guitar/synthesizer) and Timmy James Reilly (vocals/guitar). With the addition of bassist E.L. Curcio and drummer Jerry Grant they debuted with 'Make it Or Break It' on the *Pure Metal* compilation. This led to producer/guitarist Paul Sabu taking an interest in the band. He produced *Shattered Hearts* and co-wrote three numbers on the album. This followed a direction similar to Y&T, Kiss and Van Halen but featured extensive use of keyboards, which added a strong melodic base to the songs. Moving to Kiss bassist Gene Simmons' Simmons label, a subsidiary of RCA, *Don't Touch Me There* materialized in 1990. This built on the strong foundations of their debut and was immaculately produced, but blatantly geared for Stateside FM radio playlists. It appears that Sabu's influence has been the dominant control on Silent Rage product so far.

Albums: *Shattered Hearts* (1987), *Don't Touch Me There* (1990).

Silver Mountain

This melodic heavy metal group was formed in Malmo, Sweden 1978. They took their name from a song on Rainbow's debut album 'Man On The Silver Mountain'. Not surprisingly, the band's sound is an amalgam of Deep Purple, Rainbow, Judas Priest and Kiss. Silver Mountain have been

through an endless series of line-up changes, with the only constant being founder member Jonas Hansson (guitar/vocals). It took almost five years before the band secured a record deal, with Roadrunner Records. They have released four quality, if slightly old-fashioned metal albums to date and have built up strong followings in Scandinavia, Greece and Japan. The current line-up comprises Johan Dahlstrom (vocals), Jonas Hansson (guitar/vocals), Erik Bjorn Nielsen (keyboards), Per Stadin (bass) and Kjell Gustavson (drums).
Albums: *Shakin' Brains* (1983), *Universe* (1985), *Live In Japan '85* (1986), *Roses And Champagne* (1988).

Simon Chase

This Canadian melodic pop-rock partnership comprised vocalist Andy Michaels and guitarist Sil Simone. Formed in 1987, they made their debut with *Thrill Of The Chase*, which utilized session help from bassist Pete Cardinali and Greg Loates. Produced by Triumph's Rik Emmett it was an impressive debut, tailor-made for Stateside FM radio playlists. It was lightweight infectious AOR, bristling with energy and highly memorable hooklines. However, partly due to poor promotion, the album never took off and little has been heard from them since.
Album: *Thrill Of The Chase* (1988).

Sinner

This German hard-rock/thrash metal group was formed by Matthias Lasch in 1980. Lasch later became known as Mat Sinner, following the addition of guitarists Wolfgang Werner and Calo Rapallo, drummer Edgar Patrik (later of Bonfire) and keyboardist Franky Mittelbach to complete the band's initial line-up. Influenced by Accept, Judas Priest, Iron Maiden and later Metallica they released six workmanlike, but ultimately uninspiring albums between 1982-87. The personnel was in a constant state of flux, with only Sinner constant in the line-up. They began by playing New Wave Of British Heavy Metal style material, reminiscent of Angelwitch and Tygers Of Pan Tang, then moved towards a thrashier direction as Slayer and Anthrax arrived on the scene. The band have never made any impression outside Germany and the present line-up is without a record deal.
Albums: *Wild 'n' Evil* (1982), *Fast Decision* (1983), *Danger Zone* (1984), *Touch Of Sin* (1985), *Comin' Out Fighting* (1986), *Dangerous Charm* (1987).

Six Feet Under

This Swedish power-metal quintet modelled themselves on Deep Purple, Rainbow and Whitesnake. The band were formed in 1982 by vocalist Bjorn Lodin and guitarist Thomas Larsson. Recruiting Peter Ostling (keyboards), Kent Jansson (bass) and Claus Annersjo (drums), they signed to the Europa Film label the following year. They released two albums which featured few original ideas. Larsson's guitar style was based almost exclusively on Ritchie Blackmore's, which resulted in the songs having a strong feeling of *deja vu*. Marcus Kallstrum took over the drumstool on *Eruption*, which sold fewer copies than their debut. Disillusioned, the band went their separate ways in 1985.
Albums: *Six Feet Under* (1983), *Eruption* (1984).

Skagarak

This Danish melodic hard-rock quintet were formed in 1985, by vocalist Torben Schmidt and guitarist Jan Petersen. With the addition of Tommy Rasmussen (keyboards), Morten Munch (bass) and Alvin Otto (drums), they incorporated elements of Whitesnake, Night Ranger and Boston into their music. From AOR beginnings, they have gradually evolved into a heavier and more powerful group, than their self-titled debut might at first suggest. Schmidt's vocals are reminiscent of David Coverdale's; melodic, powerful and very emotional at times. Skagarak are a fine band, who have the potential for international success, but they have yet to make an impression outside Denmark.
Albums: *Skagarak* (1986), *Hungry For A Game* (1988), *A Slice Of Heaven* (1990).

Skid Row (Eire)

This blues-based rock band was put together by Gary Moore in Dublin 1968, when the guitarist was only 16 years old. Recruiting Phil Lynott (vocals/bass), Eric Bell (guitar) and Brian Downey (drums) the initial line-up only survived 12 months. Lynott, Bell and Downey left to form Thin Lizzy, with Brendan Shiels (bass/vocals) and Noel Bridgeman (drums) joining Moore as replacements in a new power-trio. The group completed two singles, 'New Places, Old Faces' and 'Saturday Morning Man' - only released in Ireland - before securing a UK deal via CBS Records. Skid Row was a popular live attraction and tours of the US and Europe, supporting Canned Heat and Savoy Brown, augered well for the future. Their albums were also well-received, but Moore's growing reputation as an inventive, and versatile, guitarist outstripped the group's musical confines. He left in 1971 to work with the folk-rock band Dr. Strangely Strange and later on to the Gary Moore Band. Although Paul

Chapman proved an able replacement, Skid Row's momentum now faltered and the trio was disbanded the following year. Sheilds has, on occasion, revived the name for various endeavours, while Chapman later found fame with UFO.

Albums: Skid Row (1970), 34 Hours (1971). Compilation: Skid Row (1987).

Skid Row

Skid Row (USA)

Hailing from New Jersey, USA, Skid Row were formed in late 1986 by Dave 'The Snake' Sabo (guitar) and Rachel Bolan (bass). Sebastian Bach (b. 3 April 1968; vocals), Scotti Hill (guitar) and Rob Affuso (drums) were soon added and the line-up was complete. Influenced by Kiss, Bon Jovi, Sex Pistols, Ratt and Motley Crüe, the band's rise to fame has been remarkably rapid. The break came when they were picked up by Bon Jovi's management and offered the support slot on their US stadium tour of 1989. Bach's wild and provocative stage antics established the band's infamous live reputation. Signed to Atlantic Records, they released their self-titled debut album to widespread critical acclaim the same year. It peaked at number 6 on the Billboard album chart and spawned two US Top 10 singles with '18 And Life' and 'I Remember You'. Slave To The Grind saw the band go from strength to

strength. Their commercial hard-rock approach had been transformed into an abrasive and uncompromising barrage of metallic rock 'n' roll, delivered with punk-like arrogance. The album surpassed all expectations and Skid Row are now on the road to world domination, alongside Guns N' Roses.

Albums: Skid Row (1989), Slave To The Grind (1991).

Skull

This hard-rock quartet was put together by ex-Meatloaf guitarist Bob Kulick in 1991. Recruiting vocalist Dennis St. James, bassist Kjell Benner and drummer Bobby Rock, they adopted an approach that bridged the musical styles of Kiss and Styx. Signing to the independent MFN label, they released No Bones About It to a mixed reception. The songs were strong and played well, but were ultimately derivative in their musical approach.

Album: No Bones About It (1991).

Skyclad

This innovative UK thrash-folk-rock crossover group were put together in 1991 by former Sabbat vocalist Martin Walkyier. Enlisting the services of Steve Ramsey (guitar), Graeme English (bass) and Keith Baxter (drums) they were signed by the Noise label. The debut Wayward Sons Of Mother Earth combined pagan lyrics, crashing powerchords and electric violin to startling effect. They are in effect, the heavy metal equivalent of Fairport Convention.

Albums: The Wayward Sons Of Mother Earth (1991), A Burnt Offering For The Bone Idol (1992).

Slaughter

When Vinnie Vincent's Invasion disintegrated in 1988, vocalist Mark Slaughter and bassist Dana Strum decided to start a new group under the name Slaughter. Recruiting guitarist Tim Kelly and drummer Blas Elias, they soon secured a deal with Chrysalis Records and recorded Stick It To Ya. With an approach that fused elements of Kiss, Motley Crüe and Bon Jovi, their style was ultimately derivative, yet distinctive due to the stratospheric-like vocals of Mark Slaughter. Three minute blasts of memorable metallic pop, complete with rousing anthemic choruses was the usual recipe. Following support slots to Kiss on their American tour, the album took off and peaked at number 18, during its six-month residency on the Billboard album chart. A live mini-album followed, which featured live versions of songs from their debut release.

Albums: Stick It To Ya (1990), Stick It To Ya Live (1990).

Slaughter; Mark Slaughter

Slayer

This intense death/thrash metal quartet was formed in Los Angeles, USA during 1982. Comprising Tom Araya (bass/vocals), Kerry King (guitar), Jeff Hanneman (guitar) and Dave Lombardo (drums) they made their debut in 1983, with a track on the compilation *Metal Massacre III*. This led to Metal Blade signing the band and releasing their first two albums. *Show No Mercy* and *Hell Awaits* were undiluted blasts of pure white metallic noise. The band played at breakneck speed with amazing technical precision, but the intricacies of detail were lost in a muddy production. Araya's lyrics dealt with death, carnage, satanism and torture, but were reduced to an indecipherable guttural howl.

Rick Rubin, producer and owner of the Def Jam label teamed up with the band in 1986 for the recording of *Reign In Blood*. Featuring 10 tracks in just 28 minutes, it took the concept of thrash to its ultimate conclusion. The song 'Angel Of Death' became notorious for its references to Joseph Mengele, the Nazi doctor who committed atrocities against humanity. Rubin achieved a breakthrough in production with a clear and inherently powerful sound, and opened the band up to a wider audience. *South Of Heaven* saw Slayer applying the brakes and introducing brain-numbing bass riffs *similar to* Black Sabbath, but delivered with the same manic aggression as before. The guitars of Hanneman and King screamed violently and Araya's vocals were clearly heard for the first time. *Seasons In The Abyss* pushed the band to the forefront of the thrash metal genre, alongside Metallica. A state-of-the-art album in every respect, and although deliberately commercial it is the band's most profound and convincing statement to date. A double live album followed, recorded in London, Lakeland and San Bernadino between October 1990 and August 1991. It captured the band at their brutal and uncompromising best and featured definitive versions of many of their most infamous numbers. Albums: *Show no Mercy* (1984), *Hell Awaits* (1985), *Reign In Blood* (1986), *South Of Heaven* (1988), *Seasons In The Abyss* (1990), *Decade Of Aggression-Live* (1991).

Sniper

This Japanese heavy metal group was formed in 1981 by guitarist Mansanori Kusakabe. Enlisting the services of Shigehisa Kitao (vocals), Romy Murase (bass) and Shunji Itoh (drums) their brand of heavy metal drew strongly on the styles of UFO and Deep Purple. Debuting with the single 'Fire' in 1983, they contributed 'Crazy Drug' to the *Heavy Metal Forces* compilation the following year. Their first album was recorded live at the Electric Ladyland Club in Nagoya 1984 and featured new recruit Ravhun Othani (ex-Frank Marino Band) as a second guitarist. The album was a limited edition of 1,000, which sold out, only to be re-pressed twice, with similar success. The band disintegrated shortly after its release, but was resurrected in 1985 by Kusakabe. The new line-up included Noboru Kaneko (vocals), Takeshi Kato (keyboards), Tsukasa Shinohara (bass) and Toshiyuki Miyata (drums). They produced *Quick And Dead*, but it made little impact outside Japan. A proposed tour of Holland to support it was cancelled and the band have been inactive since. Albums: *Open The Attack* (1984), *Quick And Dead* (1985).

Snow

This US hard-rock quartet was formed in 1980 by Carlos Cavazo (guitar) and bassist Tony Cavazo (bass). Influenced by Van Halen and Judas Priest, the line-up was stabilized with the addition of Doug Ellison (vocals) and Steve Quadros (drums). Their only release was a self-financed mini-album, released as a limited edition of 500. This featured five excellent hard-rock numbers, given distinction by Cavazo's abrasive guitar sound. Unable to attract record company interest, the

Slayer

band went their separate ways in December 1982. Carlos Cavazo went on to success with Quiet Riot, while brother Tony later joined Hurricane.
Album: *Snow* (1981).

Snowblind

This UK melodic hard-rock quintet was formed in 1982 by guitarist Andy Simmons. With Tony Mason (vocals), Ross Bingham (guitar/keyboards), Geoff Gilesoie (bass) and Kevin Baker (drums) completing the line-up, they were one of the few non-speed metal/thrash bands signed to the Belgian Mausoleum label. Using Magnum, Rush and Grand Prix as their musical blueprint, they debuted with a self-titled album in 1985. This comprised grandiose epics, punctuated by explosive guitar runs in places. The only drawback was Mason's vocals, which lacked the necessary warmth and range to give the songs real distinction. The album fared badly and little has been heard from them since.
Album: *Snowblind* (1985).

Soda, Frank

This eccentric Canadian vocalist/guitarist was known for his warped sense of humour. He appeared on stage kitted out in strange outfits and the climax of the show involved making a television set explode on his head! Backed by the Imps, a two-piece rhythm section comprising Charles Towers (bass) and John Lechausser (drums), they recorded two hard-rock albums characterized by frenzied, Frank Zappa-like guitar and Soda's shallow vocals. *Saturday Night Getaway* used session musicians instead of the Imps and featured four cuts from *In The Tube*, with the remaining new songs being second-rate in comparison. He built up a small loyal cult following in Canada, but failed to make an impression elsewhere.
Albums: *In The Tube* (1979), *Frank Soda And The Imps* (1980), *Saturday Night Getaway* (1981).

Sodom

This black metal/thrash trio was formed in 1983 by Angel Ripper (bass/vocals), Aggressor (vocals/guitar) and Witchhunter (drums). They drew inspiration from bands such as Motorhead, Anvil and Venom, making their debut with the EP *Sign Of Evil* . By the time *Obsessed By Cruelty* emerged in 1986, Aggressor had quit to be replaced firstly by Grave Violator, then Destructor and finally Blackfire. *Persecution Mania* followed in 1987 and marked a vast improvement over their debut. Produced by Harris Johns, it had a crisp and powerful sound and was to become their best selling release. They toured Europe in 1988 with Whiplash and recorded *Mortal Way Of Life*, the first ever double live thrash album. *Agent Orange* was released in 1989 and they landed the support slot on Sepultura's European tour to help promote it. Michael Hoffman was recruited as the new guitarist when Blackfire left to Kreator in 1990.

Albums: *Obsessed By Cruelty* (1986), *Persecution Mania* (1987), *Mortal Way Of Life* (1988), *Agent Orange* (1989).

Sojourn

This US melodic rock quintet was formed in 1983 by Kevin Bullock (vocals/guitar/keyboards) and Doug Robinson (guitar/vocals). Enlisting the services of Kevin Stoker (keyboards), Doug Pectol (bass) and Dane Spencer (drums), they secured a deal with the Mad Cat label in 1985. They debuted with *Lookin' For More*, a melodic rock album with rough edges. It incorporated abrasive guitar work within a pomp-rock framework, and drew comparisons with Triumph, Journey and at times UFO. *Different Points Of View* consolidated their style and they went out on tour with Mr. Mister to promote the work.

Albums: *Lookin' For More* (1985), *Different Points Of View* (1988).

Sortilege

This French heavy metal band was formerly known as Blood Wave. Sortilege were formed in 1981 by vocalist Christian Augustin and guitarist Stephanne L'Anguille Dumont. Adding Didier Dem (guitar), Daniel Lapp (bass) and Bob Snake (drums) they secured a contract with the Dutch Rave On label in 1983. They specialized in metallic boogie and had much in common with other French acts such as Trust and Telephone. *Metamorphose* was also released as *Metamorphosis*, complete with English lyrics, but it still failed to make any impact outside France. *Hero Tears* saw the band running short of ideas. They broke up shortly after the album's release.

Albums: *Sortilege* (1983), *Metamorphose* (1984), *Hero Tears* (1985).

Sound Barrier

Formerly known as Colour, Sound Barrier were a black heavy metal band formed in 1980 by Spacey T. (guitar) and Bernie K (vocals). Enlisting the services of Stanley E. (bass) and Dave Brown (drums), they signed to MCA Records in 1982. They debuted with *Total Control*; a highly complex fusion of metal, soul, funk and blues influences that defied simple pigeon-holing. It sold poorly and they were subsequently dropped by their label. They bounced back with a mini-album on the independent Pitbull label, which consolidated the style laid down on their debut release. This led to a contract with Metal Blade, but the resulting *Speed Of Light* was very disappointing. It adopted a simpler, more mainstream approach and was an unsuccessful attempt to widen their appeal. Emil Lech had taken over on bass by this stage, but the band splintered shortly after the album's release. Bernie K. went on to Masi, Spacey T. and Stanley E. joined Liberty, while Emil Lech teamed up with Joshua.

Albums: *Total Control* (1983), *Born To Rock* (1984), *Speed Of Light* (1986).

Soundgarden

This US Seattle-based quartet fused influences as diverse as Led Zeppelin, the Stooges, Velvet Underground and the Cult into a dirty, sweaty and sex-oriented style of rock 'n' roll. The group comprises Chris Cornell (vocals/guitar), Kim Thayil (guitar), Ben 'Hunter' Shepherd (bass) and Matt Cameron (drums). Their sound is characterized by heavy-duty, bass-laden metallic riffs that swing between dark psychedelia and *avant garde* minimalism. Cornell's vocal style completes the effect, as he rants and raves. After signing to SST Records and releasing *Ultamega OK*, they attracted the attention of A&M Records and eventually released *Louder Than Love*, one of the most underrated and offbeat rock albums of 1989. *Badmotorfinger* built on this but added Black Sabbath riffs, grungy guitar and their own comments on politics, religion and life in general. Landing the support slot to Guns N' Roses' USA 'Illusions' tour deservedly opened them up to a much wider audience.

Albums: *Ultemega O.K.* (1989), *Louder Than Love* (1990), *Badmotorfinger* (1991).

Spanos, Danny

This American vocalist/composer performed and recorded under his own name, but always preferred the services of hired hands to a conventional band set-up. He recorded three albums during the early 80s, using a variety of session musicians, including Earl Slick, Rick Derringer, Carmine Appice, Dana Strum and Frankie Banali. His style fell somewhere between Jimmy Barnes and Bryan Adams; easily accessible, hard-rock with gritty vocals and infectious hooklines. Ultimately, the songs lacked real character and he failed to break into the big time.

Soundgarden

Albums: *Danny Spanos* (1980), *Passion In The Dark* (1983), *Looks Like Trouble* (1984).

Spartan Warrior

This UK heavy metal group was formed in 1983 by vocalist Dave Wilkinson and guitarist Neil Wilkinson. Recruiting Paul Swaddle (guitar), Tom Spencer (bass) and Gordon Webster (drums), they made their debut with two cuts on the Guardian compilation in 1984. This opened the door to a contract with Roadrunner Records, which resulted in two non-descript, poorly produced metal albums. They incorporated elements of Rush, Deep Purple and Led Zeppelin into their music, but few original ideas of their own. Failing to make any impact, the band went back to their day jobs in 1986.

Albums: *Spartan Warrior* (1984), *Steel 'N' Chains* (1985).

Speedway Boulevard

This short-lived US group featured a pot-pourri of musical styles. Formed in 1979, the band comprised Ray Herring (vocals/piano), Gregg Hoffman (guitar/vocals), Jordan Rudes (keyboards), Dennis Feldman (bass/vocals) and Glenn Dove (drums). They signed to CBS/Epic Records and debuted in 1980 with a self-titled album that defied simple categorization. It featured a solid foundation of heavy-duty symphonic rock, modified by blues, funk, soul and Carribean influences. In places, it courted comparisons with Led Zeppelin's more experimental work. Sadly, the band broke up before their true potential could be realized. Feldman went on to play with Balance and later Michael Bolton. Rudes guested on Vinnie Moore's *Time Odyssey*.

Album: *Speedway Boulevard* (1980).

Spellbound

This Swedish metal quintet was assembled in 1984 by vocalist Hans Froberg and guitarist J.J.Marsh. Recruiting Al Strandberg (guitar/keyboards), Thompson (bass) and Ola Strandberg (drums), they debuted with a track on Sonet's Swedish Metal compilation. This led to a full contract with Sonet, with the band delivering *Breaking The Spell* in 1984. Their style is based on an amalgam of Van Halen, Led Zeppelin and Europe, but given distinction by Froberg's powerful vocals. *Rockin' Reckless* followed and indicated that the band were running out of ideas after just one album. It was a

virtual carbon copy of their debut, featuring regurgitated and re-processed riffs. Their association with Sonet ended in 1987, and little has been heard from them since.
Albums: *Breaking The Spell* (1984), *Rockin' Reckless* (1986).

Spider (UK)

This British boogie group was formed on Merseyside 1976 by the Burrows brothers. The band comprised bassist/vocalist Brian Burrows, drummer Rob E.Burrows and guitarists Sniffa and Col Harkness. After incessant gigging around the North West, they relocated to London and were eventually signed by RCA in 1983. They debuted with Rock 'N' Roll Gypsies, a fuel-injected collection of boogie-based rockers, identical in almost every respect to the style of Status Quo. From then on, they were regarded as a poor-man's 'Quo. The album sold miserably and RCA dropped them. Picked up by A&M Records, they released Rough Justice, a semi-concept affair concerning a courtroom trial. Spider were the defendents, being accused of playing heavy metal rock 'n' roll. Another flop, the band were without a label once more. Undaunted they plodded on, with Stu Harwood replacing Sniffa on guitar in 1986. Moving to the Mausoleum label, they produced Raise The Banner the same year. Musically they had not progressed, and the market for low-tech, three-chord boogie was an ever contracting one. Out-dated, and out of luck, they broke up shortly after the album was released.
Albums: Rock 'N' Roll Gypsies (1983), Rough Justice (1984), Raise The Banner (1986).

Spider (USA)

Prior to the formation of Spider in New York during 1978, Amanda Blue (vocals), Keith Lentin (guitar) and Anton Fig (drums) had worked together six years previously in the South African based Hammak. Adding keyboardist Holly Knight and ex-Riff Raff bassist Jimmy Lowell, they soon negotiated a contract with the Dreamland label. This was made possible by Ace Frehley's (Kiss guitarist) recommendation, following Anton Fig's appearance on the guitarists solo album. Specializing in commercial American rock, with pop-rock overtones, they released two classy albums and scored minor US single successes with 'New Romance' and 'Better Be Good To Me'. They changed name to Shanghai in 1982 to avoid confusion with the British group of the same name.
Albums: Spider (1980), Between The Lines (1981).

Spinal Tap

The concept for Spinal Tap - a satire of a fading British heavy metal band - was first aired in a late 70s' television sketch. Christopher Guest, formerly of parody troupe *National Lampoon*, played the part of lead guitarist Nigel Tufnell, while Harry Shearer (bassist Derek Smalls) and Michael McKean (vocalist David St. Hubbins) had performed with the Credibility Gap. Their initial sketch also featured Loudon Wainwright and drummer Russ Kunkel, but these true-life musicians dropped out of the project on its transformation to full-length film. *This is Spinal Tap*, released in 1984, was not a cinematic success, but it has since become highly popular through the medium of video. Its portrayal of a doomed US tour is ruthless, exposing incompetence, megalomania and sheer madness, but in a manner combining humour with affection. However, rather than incurring the wrath of the rock fraternity, the film has been lauded by musicians, many of whom, unfathomably, claim inspiration for individual scenes. The contemporary UK comedy team, the Comic Strip, used elements of Spinal Tap's theme in their two television films *Bad News On Tour* and *More Bad News*. Spinal Tap reunited as a 'real' group and undertook an extensive tour in 1992 to promote *Break Like The Wind*.
Albums: *This Is Spinal Tap* (1984), *The Soundtrack* (1989), *Break Like The Wind* (1992).

Split Beaver

This heavy metal quartet was formed in Wolverhampton, England during 1982 by vocalist Darrel Whitehouse and guitarist Mike Hoppet. Enlisting the services of bassist Alan Rees and drummer Mick Dunn, they signed to the local Heavy Metal Records label the same year. The band specialized in plodding and clichéd British rock, influenced by Deep Purple, Thin Lizzy and Wishbone Ash. They debuted with *When Hell Won't Have You*, a pedestrian and disappointing collection of uptempo rockers, after which they split up.
Album: *When Hell Won't Have You* (1982).

Spooky Tooth

Formed in 1967 as a blues group, they quickly moved into progressive rock during the heady days of the late 60s. Formerly named Art, they released a ponderous version of Buffalo Springfield's 'For What It's Worth', as 'What's That Sound'. The original band comprised Gary Wright (b. 26 April 1945, Englewood, New Jersey, USA; keyboards/vocals), Mike Kellie (b. 24 March 1947, Birmingham, England; drums),

Spinal Tap

Luther Grosvenor (b. 23 December 1949, Worcester, England; guitar), Mike Harrison (b. 3 September 1945, Carlisle, Cumberland, England; vocals) and Greg Ridley (b. 23 October 1947, Cumberland, England; bass). Their hard work on the English club scene won through, although their only commercial success was in the USA. They combined hard-edged imaginative versions of non-originals with their own considerable writing abilities. *Its All About* was a fine debut; although not a strong seller it contained their reading of 'Tobacco Road', always a club favourite and their debut single 'Sunshine Help Me', which sounded uncannily similar to early Traffic. It was *Spooky Two* however that put them on the map; eight powerful songs with a considerable degree of melody, this album remains as one of the era's finest. Their self-indulgent excursion with Pierre Henry on *Ceremony* was a change of direction that found few takers, save for the superb cover painting by British artist John Holmes. *The Last Puff* saw a number of personnel changes; Ridley had departed for Humble Pie, Gary Wright left to form Wonderwheel and Grosvenor later emerged as 'Ariel Bender' in Stealers Wheel and Mott The Hoople. Three members of the Grease Band joined; Henry McCullough, Chris Stainton and Alan Spenner. The album contained a number of non-originals, notably David Ackles' 'Down River' and a superb version of Elton John's 'Son Of Your Father'. The band broke up shortly after its release, although various members eventually re-grouped for three further albums which, while competent, showed no progression and were all written to a dated formula.

Albums: *It's All About* (1968), *Spooky Two* (1969), *Ceremony* (1970), *The Last Puff* (1970), *You Broke My Heart So I Busted Your Jaw* (1973), *Witness* (1973), *The Mirror* (1974). Compilation: *That Was Only Yesterday* (1976 - features Gary Wright with Spooky Tooth, plus solo recordings), *The Best Of Spooky Tooth* (1976).

Spy

This US, six-piece symphonic rock group was formed in 1979 by guitarist David Nelson and vocalist John Vislocky. The line-up was completed by Danny Seidenberg (violin), Michael Visceglia (bass), Dave Le Bolt (keyboards) and Rob Goldman (drums). They were a highly versatile and extremely talented band in the Boston, Styx and Kansas vein. Their self-titled debut, released in 1980, was an undiscovered classic of the pomp-rock genre. Saturated with keyboards, stunning

vocal harmonies and fluid guitar work it is still difficult to explain why the album sold so poorly. They had more songs in preparation, but CBS dropped them before they could be fully completed. Spy disintegrated as most of the band members went back to session work.
Album: *Spy* (1980).

Spys

This US pomp-rock quintet was formed in 1981 by ex-Foreigner duo Al Greenwood (keyboards) and Ed Gagliardi (bass). Enlisting the services of John Blanco (vocals), John Digaudio (guitar) and Billy Milne (drums), they signed to EMI the following year. They debuted with a self-titled album, produced by Neil Kernon (of Dokken and Michael Bolton fame). This featured some upfront, raunchy guitar work amid the sophisticated, keyboard dominated arrangements. On *Behind Enemy Lines*, they became self-indulgent and utilized a Russian male voice choir on some tracks. The album flopped and with growing legal and contractual problems, the band disintegrated in 1983. Greenwood went on to work with Joe Lynn Turner and later N.Y.C..
Albums: *Spys* (1982), *Behind Enemy Lines* (1983).

Squadron

This American glam-rock quartet was formed in 1981 by Kevin (guitar/vocals) and Shawn Duggan (guitar/vocals). With the addition of bassist Bob Catalano and drummer John Blovin, they drew inspiration from the New York Dolls, Marc Bolan and Motley Crüe. Dressed in red plastic clothes, with their hair sprayed grey, the visuals were always more interesting than the music. They released one album but disbanded soon after its release.
Album: *First Mission* (1982).

Squier, Billy

Having gained valuable experience as guitarist in the power-pop group Sidewinders; Billy Squier formed his own band under the name of Piper and recorded two albums for A&M during the late 70s. He dissolved Piper in 1979 and signed a solo deal with Capitol Records. *Tale Of The Tape* was released the following year and helped establish Squier's reputation as a sophisticated and talented songwriter/guitarist. Drawing inspiration from Led Zeppelin, Queen, Fleetwood Mac and Genesis amongst others, he has continued to release quality albums of hard-rock/pop crossover material. In the UK Squier has largely been ignored, even though he toured with Whitesnake in 1981. In the USA, he has scored major successes with *Don't Say No* and *Emotions In Motion*, both which made

Billy Squier

number 5 in the *Billboard* album chart.
Albums: *Tale Of The Tape* (1980), *Don't Say No* (1981), *Emotions In Motion* (1982), *Signs Of Life* (1984), *Enough Is Enough* (1986), *Hear And Now* (1989), *Creatures Of Habit* (1991).

Stage Dolls

This melodic power-trio emerged from Trondheim, Norway. Formed in 1983, the original line-up comprised Torstein Flakne (ex-Kids vocalist/guitarist), Terje Storli (bass) and Erlend Antonson (ex-Subway Sect drummer), the latter eventually replaced by Steinar Krokstad. Their three albums to date combine high-technology production with superbly crafted AOR. The songs are heavily infused with melody and display a keen sense of dynamics. Their sound does lack a degree of individuality though, and comes over as a sterile hybrid of Bryan Adams, Europe and Foreigner. 'Love Cries', lifted as a single from their latest album, became a minor Stateside hit in 1989. On the strength of this, they secured the support slots on the Blue Murder and Warrant USA tours the same year.
Albums: *Soldier's Gun* (1985), *Commandoes* (1986), *Stage Dolls* (1988).

Stampede

This UK melodic hard-rock quartet was formed in 1981, by ex-Wild Horses trio, Reuben Archer (vocals), Laurence Archer (guitar) and Frank Noon (drums). Recruiting bassist Colin Bond, they signed to Polydor the following year. Noon left for Torme and was replaced by Eddie Parsons before they debuted with *The Official Bootleg*, recorded live at the Reading Festival. Their music at this point, incorporated elements of Deep Purple and UFO; particularly the guitar style of Laurence Archer which appeared to be based on the techniques of Michael Schenker and Ritchie Blackmore. *Hurricane Town* followed, but was a disappointment. It featured disposable, mid-paced rockers reminiscent of Thin Lizzy. Unable to attract media attention, Stampede split up in 1983. Laurence Archer joined Grand Slam and later recorded a solo album, *L.A.*

Albums: *The Official Bootleg* (1982), *Hurricane Town* (1983).

Starcastle

This US melodic pomp-rock group was formed in Illinois, USA in 1972 by Stephen Hagler (guitar/vocals), Herb Schildt (keyboards) and Gary Strater (bass). The six-piece line-up was completed by ex-REO Speedwagon vocalist Terry Luttrell, guitarist Matt Stuart and drummer Steve Tassoer. After being championed by the local WGPU Radio Station in Champaign, Illinois, they were signed by Epic in 1974. Their music, which incorporated elements of Yes, Emerson, Lake And Palmer and Rush was characterized by multi-vocal harmonies and complex, but carefully executed time-changes. They released four albums before splitting up, but never achieved the recognition their talents deserved.

Albums: *Starcastle* (1975), *Fountains Of Light* (1977), *Citadel* (1978), *Reel To Reel* (1979).

Starchild

This Canadian hard-rock quartet was formed in 1977, by vocalist Richard Whittie and guitarist Robert Sprenger. Enlisting the services of bassist Neil Light and drummer Gregg Hinz, they debuted with *Children Of The Stars* the following year. Influenced by Triumph, Rush and Styx, the album was characterized by Sprenger's inventive guitar work and Whittie's powerful, but distinctive vocals. Hinz quit to join Helix shortly after the album's release, with ex-Lone Star drummer Dixie Lee stepping in as replacement. The band continued for a short time, but split up before any further recordings were made.

Album: *Children Of The Stars* (1978).

Starfighters

This UK hard-rock/boogie quintet was formed in 1980 by ex-Suburban Studs vocalist Steve Burton and guitarist Stevie Young (cousin of AC/DC's Angus Young). With Pat Hambly (guitar), Doug Dennis (bass) and Steve Bailey (drums) completing the line-up, they were picked up by Jive in 1981. Produced by Tony Platt, their debut album was characterized by raunchy rock 'n' roll, with abrasive, up-front guitar work from Young. At best, they were a poor man's AC/DC, specializing in second-hand riffs, hackneyed vocals and a predictable backbeat. On *In Flight Movie*, they tried desperately to move away from the AC/DC approach, concentrating instead on more traditional blues-based hard-rock. Unfortunately, this new style had even less to commend it, and they broke up soon after its release.

Albums: *Starfighters* (1981) *In Flight Movie* (1983).

Starr, Jack

After quitting the heavy metal band Virgin Steele in 1984, guitarist Jack Starr teamed up with ex-Riot vocalist Rhett Forrester and former Rods rhythm section, Gary Bordonaro and Carl Canedy. They delivered *Out Of The Darkness* in 1984, a subtle combination of aggression, melody and dynamics. Starr dissolved the band soon after the album came out, preferring instead to use a new set of backing musicians on each subsequent release. Over the next four albums he moved away from his metallic roots, towards more commercial, arena-style rock typified by Kiss, Bon Jovi and Dokken. Starr is one of the more original new style, techno-wizard guitarists, but has yet to receive the recognition his talents undoubtedly deserve. He has recently opted to record under the band name of Burning Starr.

Albums: *Out Of The Darkness* (1984), *Rock The American Way* (1985), *No Turning Back* (1986), *Blaze Of Glory* (1987), *Burning Starr* (1989).

Start

This Icelandic pop-rock group was formed in 1980 by vocalist Petur Kristjansson and guitarist Kristjan Edelstein. Enlisting the services of Eirikur Haukson (guitar/vocals), Nikulas Robertson (keyboards), Jon Olafsson (bass/vocals) and David Karlsson (drums), they signed to the Steinar label the following year. They debuted with *En Hun Snyst Nu Samt*; a predictable collection of soft-rock anthems with Icelandic vocals. They disappeared into oblivion, after representing Iceland in the Eurovision Song Contest.

Album: *En Hun Snyst Nu Samt* (1981).

Statetrooper

After leaving MSG, vocalist Gary Barden formed Statetrooper in 1986 with Martin Bushell (guitar), Jeff Summers (guitar), Steve Glover (keyboards), plus ex-Wildfire duo Jeff Brown (bass) and Bruce Bisland (drums). They debuted the following year with a self-titled album of melodic AOR, which featured the extensive use of keyboards. It courted comparisons with Foreigner, Styx and Thin Lizzy, but lacked consistency in terms of songwriting. The album sold poorly and following a short period with Brian Robertson (ex-Motorhead and Thin Lizzy) on guitar, the band broke up.
Album: *Statetrooper* (1987).

Status Quo

The origins of this durable and now-legendary attraction lie in the Spectres, a London-based beat group. Founder members Mike (later Francis) Rossi (b. 29 May 1949, Peckham, London, England; guitar/vocals) and Alan Lancaster (b. 7 February 1949. Peckham, London, England; bass) led the act from its inception in 1962 until 1967, by which time Roy Lynes (organ) and John Coughlan (b. 19 September 1946, Dulwich, London, England; drums) completed its line-up.

The Spectres' three singles encompassed several styles of music, ranging from pop to brash R&B, but the quartet took a new name, Traffic Jam, when such releases proved commercially unsuccessful. A similar failure beset 'Almost But Not Quite There', but the group was nonetheless buoyed by the arrival of Rick Parfitt aka Rick Harrison (b. 12 October 1948, Woking, Surrey, England; guitar/vocals), lately of cabaret attraction, the Highlights. The revamped unit assumed their 'Status Quo' appellation in August 1967 and initially sought work backing various solo artists, including Madeleine Bell and Tommy Quickly. Such employment came to an abrupt end the following year when the quintet's debut single, 'Pictures Of Matchstick Men', soared to number 7. One of the era's most distinctive performances, the song's ringing guitar pattern and *de rigueur* phasing courted pop and psychedelic affectations. A follow-up release, 'Black Veils Of Melancholy', exaggerated latter trappings at the expense of melody, but the group enjoyed another UK Top 10 hit with the jaunty 'Ice In The Sun', co-written by former 50s singer, Marty Wilde.
Subsequent recordings in a similar vein struggled to emulate such success, and despite reaching

number 12 with 'Down The Dustpipe', Status Quo was increasingly viewed as a *passé* novelty. However, the song itself, which featured a simple riff and wailing harmonica, indicated the musical direction unveiled more fully on *Ma Kelly's Greasy Spoon*. The album included Quo's version of Steamhammer's 'Junior's Wailing', which had inspired this conversion to a simpler, 'boogie' style. Gone too were the satin shirts, frock coats and kipper ties, replaced by long hair, denim jeans and plimsolls. The departure of Lynes en route to Scotland - 'He just got off the train and that was the last we ever saw of him,' (Rossi) - brought the unit's guitar work to the fore, although indifference from their record company blighted progress. Assiduous live appearances built up a grass roots following and impressive slots at the Reading and Great Western Festivals (both 1972) signalled a commercial turning point. Now signed to the renowned Vertigo label, Status Quo scored a UK Top 10 hit that year with 'Paper Plane' but more importantly, reached number 5 in the album charts with *Piledriver*. A subsequent release, *Hello*, entered at number 1, confirming the group's emergence as a major attraction. Since that point their style has basically remained unchanged, fusing simple, 12-bar riffs to catchy melodies, while an unpretentious 'lads' image has proved equally enduring. Each of their 70s albums reached the Top 5, while a consistent presence in the singles' chart included such notable entries as 'Caroline' (1973), 'Down Down' (a chart topper in 1974), 'Whatever You Want' (1979) and 'Lies'/'Don't Drive My Car' (1980). An uncharacteristic ballad, 'Living On An Island' (1979), showed a softer perspective while Quo also proved adept at adapting outside material, as evinced by their version of John Fogerty's 'Rockin' All Over The World' (1977). (The song was later re-recorded as 'Running All Over The World' to promote the charitable *Race Against Time* in 1988.)

The quartet undertook a lengthy break during 1980, but answered rumours of a permanent split with *Just Supposin'*. However, a dissatisfied Coughlan left the group in 1981 in order to form his own act, Diesel. Pete Kircher, (ex-Original Mirrors), took his place, but Quo was then undermined by the growing estrangement between Lancaster and Rossi and Parfitt. The bassist moved to Australia in 1983 - a cardboard cut-out substituted on several television slots - but he remained a member for the next two years. Lancaster's final appearance with the group was at *Live Aid*, following which he unsuccessfully took out a High Court injunction to prevent the group performing without him. Rossi and Parfitt secured

the rights to the name 'Status Quo' and reformed the act around John Edwards (bass), Jeff Rich (drums) and keyboard player Andy Bown. The last-named musician, formerly of the Herd and Judas Jump, had begun his association with the group in 1973, but only now became an official member. Despite such traumas Quo continued to enjoy commercial approbation with Top 10 entries 'Dear John' (1982), 'Marguerita Time' (1983), 'In The Army Now' (1986) and 'Burning Bridges (On And Off And On Again)' (1988), while *1+9+8+2* was their fourth chart-topping album. Status Quo celebrated its silver anniversary in October 1991 by entering *The Guinness Book Of Records* having completed four charity concerts in four UK cities in the space of 12 hours. This ambitious undertaking, the subject of a television documentary, was succeeded by a national tour which confirmed the group's continued mass-market popularity. The much-loved Status Quo have carried a very large niche in music history by producing uncomplicated, unpretentious and infectious rock music.

Albums: *Picturesque Matchstickable Messages* (1968), *Spare Parts* (1969), *Ma Kelly's Greasy Spoon* (1970), *Dog Of Two Head* (1971), *Piledriver* (1973), *Hello* (1973), *Quo* (1974), *On The Level* (1975), *Blue For You* (1976), *Status Quo Live!* (1977), *Rockin' All Over The World* (1977), *If You Can't Stand The Heat* (1978), *Whatever You Want* (1979), *Just Supposin'* (1980), *Never Too Late* (1981), *1+9+8+2* (1982), *To Be Or Not To Be* (1983), *Back To Back* (1983), *In The Army Now* (1986), *Ain't Complaining* (1988), *Rock 'Til You Drop* (1991). Compilations: *Status Quo-tations* (1969), *The Best Of Status Quo* (1973), *The Golden Hour Of Status Quo* (1973), *Down The Dustpipe* (1975), *The Rest Of Status Quo* (1976), *The Status Quo File* (1977), *The Status Quo Collection* (1978)), *Twelve Gold Bars* (1980), *Spotlight On Status Quo Volume 1* (1980), *Fresh Quota* (1981), *100 Minutes Of Status Quo* (1982), *Spotlight On Status Quo Volume 2* (1982), *From The Makers Of...* (1983), *Works* (1983), *To Be Or Not To Be* (1983), *Twelve Gold Bars Volume 1 & 2* (1984), *Na Na Na* (1985), *Collection: Status Quo* (1985), *Quotations, Volume 1* (1987), *Quotations, Volume 2* (1987), *From The Beginning* (1988), *C.90 Collector* (1989).

Further reading: *Status Quo: The Authorised Biography*; John Shearlaw.

Stealin' Horses

Formerly known as Radio City, Stealin' Horses were a melodic pop-rock group established in 1985 around the nucleus of Kiya Heartwood (vocals/guitar) and Kopana Terry (drums). Utilizing an impressive array of guest musicians, that included Toto's Steve Lukather and Mike Porcano, they released their self-titled debut in 1985. It comprised a commercial, pot-pourri of styles and featured blues, rock, funk, soul, R&B and even country numbers. Unfortunately, they were unable to find an audience for such derivative material and split up shortly after the album was released.

Album: *Stealin' Horses* (1985).

Steel Forrest

This Dutch quintet formed in Amsterdam during 1981 by vocalist Sunny Hays and guitarist Fred Heikens. With the addition of Appie van Vliet (keyboards), Ron Heikens (bass) and Joop Oliver (drums), they negotiated a deal with the Dureco label the following year. Debuting with *First Confession*, which comprised cliched and formularized Euro-rock, they failed to find an audience. Hays was replaced by Thijs Hamelaers (later of Sleez Beez) and William Lawson (ex-Angus) took over the drumstool after the album was released, but this line-up disintegrated before entering the studio.

Album: *First Confession* (1982).

Steeler (Germany)

This German heavy metal quintet, formerly known as Sinner, emerged as Steeler in 1981. The band were formed in Bochum, Westphalia, by vocalist Peter Burtz and virtuoso guitarist Axel Rudi Pell. With the addition of Volher Krawczak (bass), Bertram Frewer (backing vocals) and Volker Jakel (drums), they signed to the independent Earthshaker label in 1984. They debuted the same year with a self-titled album of uptempo hard-rockers, that came over as a hybrid of Scorpions and Accept. However, the strong material was discredited somewhat by the budget production. After *Rulin' The Earth*, the band moved to Steamhammer Records and replaced Krawczak with new bassist Herve Rossi. Strike Back saw the band move towards an Americanized arena-rock approach, typical of Ratt, Dokken and Kiss. Following the release of *Undercover Animal*, a series of line-up changes ensued, with Pell leaving to build a solo career. The future of the band is still uncertain.

Albums: *Steeler* (1984), *Rulin' The Earth* (1985), *Strike Back* (1986), *Undercover Animal* (1988).

Steeler (USA)

This US hard-rock quartet was formed in Nashville, 1982 by vocalist Ron Keel. Recruiting Rik Fox (bass) and Mark Edwards (drums), the line-up was completed when Shrapnel label boss, Mike Varney introduced Swedish guitarist Yngwie Malmsteen to the band. They relocated to Los Angeles and gigged incessantly on the bar and club circuit. Varney offered them a deal and they delivered a self-titled debut the following year. It was pure Americana bar-rock; chest-beating anthems, punctuated by shrill guitar work. Malmsteen quit just as the album was released, joining Alcatrazz and later forming his own Rising Force. Keel formed a new outfit under his own name, while Fox formed Sin.

Album: *Steeler* (1983).

Steeplechase

This US melodic rock quartet was formed in 1980 by vocalist Joe Lamente and guitarist Tony Sumo. Enlisting the services of Bob Held (bass) and Vinny (drums) Conigliaro, they were signed to the local BCR label the following year. Drawing inspiration from the Mid-west rock scene, their music incorporated elements of Petra, Starz, Head East and Spy. The album failed to take off and the band disintegrated soon after its release. Lamente joined Shelter and later recorded the solo *Secrets That You Keep* in 1986.

Album: *Steeplechase* (1981).

Sterling Cooke Force

This Jimi Hendrix-inspired US group was put together by guitarist/vocalist Sterling Cooke in 1983. Recruiting Gino Cannon (vocals), Harry Shuman (bass) and Albie Coccia (drums), they recorded two unspectacular albums during the mid-80s. *Force This* saw Cooke rescind the vocals to Cannon and the music adopted a more melodic and restrained style. Second-hand riffs, bridges and solos, were the order of the day, which left the band with a serious identity crisis. They seem destined to remain a minor bar/club circuit band.

Albums: *Full Force* (1984), *Force This* (1986).

Steve Steven's Atomic Playboys

Steve Stevens first attracted attention as lead guitarist in Billy Idol's band. His flash and fiery style, brought Idol's hard-rock to life. Stevens also accompanied Michael Jackson on 'Dirty Diana' and has worked with Ric Ocasek of the Cars, Steve Lukather of Toto and the Thompson Twins. He broke ranks from Idol's band in 1988, to form Steve Steven's Atomic Playboys with vocalist Perry McCarty, drummer Thommy Price and keyboard player Phil Ashley. Released in 1989, their self-titled debut was a major disappointment. With the exception of the title cut, the songs were derivative and commercial. Ratt, Kiss, Boston, Journey, Dokken and even Billy Idol nuances were included. Following an unsuccessful US club tour in 1990, the band split up.

Album: *Steve Steven's Atomic Playboys* (1989).

Steve Whitney Band

This Euro-rock group was formed in 1975 by guitarist Chrigi Wiedemeier and bassist Rolf Schlup. Recruiting Mick Hudson (vocals), guitarist Andy Lindsay and drummer Pete Leeman, they debuted with *Hot Line*, an overtly commercial melodic rock album that nevertheless lacked aggression. Gary Steimer and Rob Seales replaced Leeman and Lindsy respectively on *Night Fighting*, which marked a distinct change in direction. They dropped the poppy harmonies and switched to blues-based hard-rock in the style of AC/DC and Krokus. Mick Hudson quit and the remaining four members continued as Sergeant.
Albums: *Hot Line* (1980), *Night Fighting* (1982).

Stingray

This South African melodic rock group was formed in 1978 by vocalist Dennis East and guitarist Mike Pilot. Enlisting the services of Danny Anthill (keyboards), Allan Goldswain (keyboards), Eddie Boyle (bass) and Shaun Wright (drums), they based their style on the American rock giants such as Styx, Boston, Kansas and Journey. They released two technically excellent albums, characterized by the heavy use of keyboards and multi-part vocal harmonies. Failing to attract attention outside their native South Africa, the band split up in 1981.
Albums: *Stingray* (1979), *Operation Stingray* (1980).

Stone Fury

Moving from Hamburg to Los Angeles in 1983, vocalist Lenny Wolf teamed up with Bruce Gowdy (guitar) to form Stone Fury. Adding Rick Wilson (bass) and Jody Cortez (drums), they signed to MCA and debuted the following year with *Burns Like A Star*. The album was traditional blues-based hard-rock, very similar to Led Zeppelin. Wolf's vocals were modelled very closely on Robert Plant's, both in pitch and phrasing, which resulted in accusations of imitation. *Let Them Talk* was more restrained and employed a greater use of melody and atmospherics. Unable to make a breakthrough in the USA, Wolf went back to Germany and formed Kingdom Come. Gowdy, in the meantime, formed World Trade.
Albums: *Burns Like A Star* (1984), *Let Them Talk* (1986).

Storm

This Los Angeles-based quartet was formed in 1978 by Jeanette Chase (vocals) and Lear Stevens (guitar). Enlisting the services of Ronni Hansen (bass) and David Devon (drums), they played hi-tech hard-rock, characterized by Lear's Brian May-like guitar sound and the powerful vocals of Chase. They incorporated elements of Queen, Van Halen and Styx within complex, and at times classical style arrangements. Their second album moved more towards AOR, with the inclusion of more lightweight material and even folk influences. They never achieved the recognition, their undoubted talents deserved.
Albums: *Storm* (1979), *Storm* (1983).

Stormbringer

This Swiss quintet was formed in 1984 by vocalist Dave Barreto and guitarist Angi Schilero. Recruiting Fabian Emmenger (keyboards), Urs Hufschmid (bass) and Laurie Chiundinelli (drums), they specialized in melodic power-metal, based on the style of Rainbow, Scorpions, Deep Purple and Gary Moore. They took their name from Deep Purple's 1974 album. Their brand of Euro-rock characterized their self-titled debut album. Disillusioned by the lack of media and public response, they split up soon after the album was released. Schilero went on to play with China for a short time, before starting his own band.
Album: *Stormbringer* (1985).

Stormtroopers Of Death

More commonly known as S.O.D., the band came into existence as a one-off side project of Anthrax men, Scott Ian (guitar) and Charlie Benante (drums). Taking time out during the recording of Anthrax's *Spreading The Disease* in 1985, they asked Nuclear Assault bassist Dan Lilker and roadie Billy Milano (vocals) to join them, to make use of three days free studio time. The result was *Speak English Or Die*, a manic fusion of thrash and hardcore styles, that had both humour and considerable crossover appeal. Milano went on to form M.O.D., using exactly the same musical blueprint. However, they never captured the raw aggression and real spontaneity of the S.O.D. project.
Album: *Speak English Or Die* (1985).

Stormwitch

This German heavy metal quintet employed a strong satanic/gothic horror image. They were formed by guitarist Lee Tarot (b. Harold Spengler) in 1981, who recruited Andy Aldrian (vocals), Steve Merchant (guitar), Ronny Pearson (bass) and Pete Lancer (drums) to complete the line-up. They were all fellow Germans, who altered their names, in order to sound American. Their first three albums were undistinguished Euro-metal, reminiscent of Running Wild, and made very little impact outside Germany. Due to the lack of success, they changed direction on 1987's *The Beauty And The Beast*. Adopting a more straightforward hard-rock approach, they seem likely to remain a minority attraction within Europe.

Albums: *Walpurgis Night* (1984), *Tales Of Terror* (1985), *Stronger Than Heaven* (1986), *The Beauty And The Beast* (1987).

Stranger

This melodic pop-rock quartet was formed in Florida during 1981 by Greg Billings (vocals) and Ronnie Garvin (guitar). Enlisting the services of Tom Cardenas (bass) and John Price (drums), they signed to CBS the following year. Produced by Tom Werman (of Ted Nugent and Motley Crüe fame), their debut album was a highly impressive collection of anthemic rockers, punctuated by some fiery guitar work from Garvin. It incorporated elements of Foreigner, REO Speedwagon and Styx and had great commercial potential. The album surprisingly failed to make an impact, and little has been heard of the band since.

Album: *Stranger* (1982).

Strangeways

This Scottish quartet was put together in 1985 by the brothers Ian (guitar) and David Stewart (bass). With Jim Drummond (drums) and Tony Liddell (vocals), they debuted with a self-titled album in 1985. The blend of Americanized, melodic AOR was comparable with the work of Boston, Journey, Styx and Kansas. Produced by Kevin Elson, it surpassed all expectations, but was ignored by the UK public. Terry Brock replaced Liddell on *Native Sons*, which saw the band consolidate their style and progress significantly as songwriters. It remains today, one of the sadly neglected albums of the pomp-rock/AOR genre. *Walk In The Fire* was less immediate, with Brock's vocals sounding hoarse and less sophisticated. He left to audition for Deep Purple in 1989, but was unsuccessful. Strangeways have been inactive since.

Albums: *Strangeways* (1986), *Native Sons* (1987), *Walk In The Fire* (1989).

Strapps

This UK hard-rock quartet was formed in 1975 by Ross Stagg (vocals/guitar) and Noel Scott (keyboards). With Joe Read (bass) and Mick Underwood (drums) stabilizing the line-up, they were picked up by EMI in 1976. Drawing inspiration from Deep Purple, Thin Lizzy and Uriah Heep, they released four albums over a five-year period. These met with very limited success,

except in Japan. They never graduated from support act status in Europe, which was really a fair summation of their true potential. The band finally disintegrated in 1979, when Underwood joined Gillan.

Albums: *Strapps* (1976), *Secret Damage* (1977), *Sharp Conversation* (1978), *Ball Of Fire* (1979).

Stratus

When former Iron Maiden drummer Clive Burr joined Praying Mantis in 1985, the band became known as Stratus. The remaining personnel comprised Bernie Shaw (vocals), Tino Troy (guitar), Alan Nelson (keyboards), and Chris Troy (bass). Moving away from the formularized New Wave Of British Heavy Metal approach, Stratus employed the extensive use of keyboards and mutli-part vocal harmonies. They debuted with *Throwing Shapes*, a lacklustre pomp-rock album, that was devoid in energy and quality songs. The album fared badly and the band split up soon after it was released. Bernie Shaw went on to join Uriah Heep.

Album: *Throwing Shapes* (1985).

Stray Dog

This US blues-based, heavy metal group started life as a power-trio in 1973. Formed by the nucleus of Snuffy Walden (vocals/guitar), Alan Roberts (bass/vocals) and Leslie Sampson (b. 1950, drums), their style incorporated elements of Grand Funk, Jimi Hendrix and Led Zeppelin. Timmy Dulaine (guitar/vocals) and Luis Cabaza (keyboards) were added in 1974, with rather negative results. The aggression and power of the three-piece had been dissipated amongst needlessly intricate arrangements. *While You're Down There* was a major disappointment and following management and contractual problems, the band went their separate ways in 1975.

Albums: *Stray Dog* (1973), *While You're Down There* (1974).

Streets

This melodic heavy rock quartet was formed in 1982 by ex-Kansas vocalist Steve Walsh and Mike Slamer (guitar, ex-City Boy). Drafting in Billy Greer (bass) and Tim Gehrt (drums), they adopted a much more straightforward AOR approach than Kansas. They concentrated on infectious hooklines and memorable choruses, rather than intricate keyboard fills and complex arrangements. Their self-titled debut, was received very favourably by the music media, but failed to win over a large audience, partly due to poor promotion. *Crimes In Mind*, saw the band maturing as songwriters, but Atlantic were guilty of indifference once more,

Stryper

and the album did not take off. Disillusioned, the band split up in 1986, with Walsh and Greer joining the re-vamped Kansas.
Albums: *Streets* (1983), *Crimes In Mind* (1985).

Strife

This British, blues-based hard-rock trio formed in 1972. The band comprised John Reid (vocals/guitar), Gordon Rowley (bass/vocals) and David Williams (drums/vocals). They gigged incessantly and earned a reputation as a perennial support act, but lacked the individuality to reach headline status. Strife built up a small, but loyal cult following during the mid-70s, with their honest, no-frills, good-time rock 'n' roll. They released two average rock albums, with *Back To Thunder* featuring Don Airey on keyboards and Paul Ellison in place of Williams on drums. After one last stab at success with the EP *School*, the band gave up in 1979. Rowley went on to form Nightwing.
Albums: *Rush* (1975), *Back To Thunder* (1978).

Striker

This versatile hard-rock quartet was formed in 1977 by the multi-talented Rick Randle

(vocals/keyboards/guitar). Enlisting the services of Scott Roseburg (vocals/bass/guitar), Rick Ramirez (guitar) and Rick Taylor (drums/vocals), they signed with Arista Records the following year. Their music incorporated rock, funk, boogie, blues, and soul influences, with the result that it was difficult to pigeon-hole. They tried to please everyone, but ended up appealing to just a loyal handful. Their debut album featured impressive guitar and vocal harmonies, but ultimately lacked identity because of the varied styles employed. Failing to win an appreciative audience, Randle dissolved the band in 1979. Rick Ramirez went on to join Bruzer.
Album: *Striker* (1978).

Stryper

This Christian heavy metal quartet from Los Angeles was formed by the Sweet brothers in 1981. They were originally known as Roxx Regime and featured Michael Sweet (vocals), Robert Sweet (drums), Timothy Gaines (bass) and Oz Fox (guitar), playing standard, Americanized hard-rock. Devising a carefully constructed image and marketing strategy, they changed name to Stryper and dressed in matching yellow and black outfits. They were a band with a mission, to spread the word of God through rock music, and become the total antithesis of the satanic rock movement. They signed to Enigma Records and attracted widespread media attention. The debut *Yellow And Black Attack* mini-album featured standard hard-rock, with simple lyrics and high-pitched harmonies. Their live shows climaxed with the band throwing bibles into the audience. By their third album, they had built up a loyal army of fans and their excellently produced melodic rock widened their appeal. *To Hell With The Devil* peaked at number 32 on its three-month stay on the *Billboard* album charts. *In God We Trust* saw the band mellow with more emphasis on pop-rock singalong numbers and the resultant exclusion of hard-driving rock. The album was a commercial disappointment, failing to build on the success of the previous release. It did reach number 32, but only stayed on the *Billboard* chart for five weeks. The band took time off for a radical re-think, before entering the studio again. Oz Fox ventured into production during this time, and oversaw the recording of the debut album by fellow Christian-rockers Guardian. *Against The Law* emerged in 1990, marking a return to a more aggressive style. The yellow and black stage costumes had been jettisoned and the lyrics were considerably less twee. However, by this time, most of their original fans had moved on and the album sold poorly.

Albums: *The Yellow And Black Attack* (1984), *Soldiers Under Command* (1985), *To Hell With The Devil* (1986), *In God We Trust* (1988), *Against The Law* (1990).

Styx

This Chicago-based quintet were largely responsible for the development of the term pomp-rock. This refers to pompous, overblown arrangements, with perfect-pitch harmonies and a very full production. They evolved from the bands Tradewinds and T.W.4, but re-named themselves after the fabled river from Greek mythology, when they signed to Wooden Nickel, a subsidiary of RCA Records, in 1972. The band comprised Dennis De Young (vocals/keyboards), James Young (guitar/vocals), Chuck Panozzo (bass), John Panozzo (drums) and John Curulewski (guitar). Combining symphonic and progressive influences they released a series of varied and highly melodic albums during the early 70s. Success was slow to catch up with them; *Styx II*, originally released in 1973, spawned the Top Ten *Billboard* hit 'Lady' in 1975. The album then made similar progress, eventually peaking at number 20. After signing to A&M Records in 1975, John

Styx

Curulewski departed with the release of *Equinox*, to be replaced by Tommy Shaw. This was a real turning point in the band's career as Shaw took over lead vocals and contributed significantly on the writing side. From here on Styx albums had an added degree of accessibility and moved towards a more commercial approach. *The Grand Illusion*, released in 1977, was Shaw's first major success, peaking at number 6 during its nine-month stay on the *Billboard* album chart. It also featured the number 8 single, 'Sail Away'. *Pieces Of Eight* and *Cornerstone* consolidated their success, with the latter containing 'Babe', the band's first number 1 single in the USA. *Paradise Theater* was the band's *tour de force*, a complex, laser-etched concept album, complete with elaborate and expensive packaging. It generated two Top 10 hits in 'The Best Of Times' and 'Too Much Time On My Hands'. The album became their most successful ever, and stayed at number 1 for three weeks on the US album chart. *Kilroy Was Here* followed, yet another concept album which indicated the band were beginning to run out of ideas. Its success came on the back of their previous album rather than on its own merit; a watered down pop-rock album with a big-budget production. *Caught In The Act* was an uninspired live album. They disbanded shortly after its release. Styx re-formed in 1990 with the original line-up, except for pop-rock funkster Glenn Burtnick, who replaced Tommy Shaw (who had joined Damn Yankees). *Edge Of The Century* emerged and indicated that the band still had something to offer. It featured a diverse and classy selection of contemporary AOR, delivered with power, precision and panache. As one of the surprise cuts on the album states, this band are 'Not Dead Yet'.

Albums: *Styx* (1972), *Styx II* (1973), *The Serpent Is Rising* (1973), *Man Of Miracles* (1974), *Equinox* (1975), *Crystal Ball* (1976), *The Grand Illusion* (1977), *Pieces Of Eight* (1978), *Cornerstone* (1979), *Paradise Theater* (1980), *Kilroy Was Here* (1983), *Caught In The Act* (1984), *Edge Of The Century* (1990). Compilation: *The Best Of Styx* (1979).

Sugarcreek

This top class pomp-rock group emerged from North Carolina, USA. The band were formed in 1981 by vocalist Tim Clark and guitarist Jerry West. Recruiting Rick Lee (keyboards), Robbie Hegler (bass) and Lynn Samples (drums), they drew inspiration from the popular AOR rock artists of the day (Journey, Styx, Boston and Kansas). They made a significant breakthrough with *Fortune*, a highly melodic album swathed in keyboards and silky-smooth vocal harmonies. Michael Hough was added as a second guitarist for *Rock The Night Away*, which marked a more commercial slant to the band's songwriting. He quit shortly after the album was released and the band subsequently shortened their name to the Creek in 1986.

Albums: *Live At The Roxy* (1981), *Fortune* (1982), *Rock The Night Away* (1984).

Surface

This Birmingham, England-based, hard-rock group was formed in 1986 by vocalist Gez Finnegan and guitarist Mark Davies. With Loz Rabone (guitar), Dean Field (keyboards), Ian Hawkins (bass) and Jamie Hawkins (drums) completing the line-up, they styled themselves on the successful US, AOR rock formula of groups such as Journey. Signed to the independent Killerwatt label, they debuted with *Race The Night*, which was recorded live. The album failed and the band returned to their former part-time status.

Album: *Race The Night* (1986).

Surgin

This US melodic hard-rock group was put together in 1984 by former Rest members Tommy Swift (drums) and Jack Ponti (guitar/vocals). Enlisting the services of Russel Arcara (vocals), John Capra (keyboards), Gay Shapiro (keyboards) and Michael King (bass/vocals), they debuted in 1985 with *When Midnight Comes*. This featured the Bon Jovi track 'Shot Through The Heart', which was written by Ponti and Jon Bon Jovi, while they were both part of Rest. The album comprised infectious hard-rock anthems, underscored by strong melody lines, and was critically acclaimed at the time of release. In spite of tours supporting Aerosmith and Ratt, Surgin failed to achieve commercial success. Subsequently, Ponti concentrated on session work and composing for other artists, and Surgin became redundant.

Album: *When Midnight Comes* (1985).

Surrender

This Canadian hard-rock quintet was formed in 1978 by vocalist/guitarist Alfie Zappacosta. Recruiting Steve Jenson (guitar), Peter Curry (keyboards), Geoff Waddington (bass) and Paul Delaney (drums), they incorporated elements of Rush, Triumph and Yes in their music, but avoided accusations of imitation. Two excellent albums characterized by extended guitar-keyboard interplays were released, but they failed to find an appreciative audience. Curry and Waddington quit in 1983 and the remaining trio continued as Zappacosta.

Albums: *Surrender* (1979), *No Surrender* (1982).

Survivor

This sophisticated, melodic US rock group was put together by guitarists Jim Peterik (formerly of Ides Of March) and Frankie Sullivan in 1978. Recruiting vocalist Dave Bickler, they recorded their self-titled debut as a three-piece. This featured a pot-pourri of ideas that had no definite direction or style. They expanded the band to a quintet in 1981, with the addition of Marc Doubray (drums) and Stephen Ellis (bass). From this point on, the band were comparable in approach to the AOR rock styles of Styx, Foreigner and Journey, but never achieved the same degree of recognition or success. Their first short-lived affair with glory came with the song 'Eye Of The Tiger', the soundtrack to the film *Rocky III*. The single, with its heavy drum beat and anthemic chorus, became a worldwide number 1 hit. Unfortunately, the rest of the songs on the album of the same name were patchy in comparison. Nevertheless, the work succeeded on the strength of the title cut, peaking at number 2 and 12 on the US and UK album charts, respectively. *Caught In The Game*, released the following year, was a more satisfying album. It adopted a heavier approach and featured a more up-front guitar sound from Sullivan, but

surprisingly did not find favour with the record-buying public. Bickler was fired at this stage and replaced by ex-Cobra vocalist Jimi Jamison. Jamison's vocals added an extra dimension to the band with his powerful, and at times soulful, style. The resulting *Vital Signs* gave the band their second breakthrough. The album had a six-month residency on the *Billboard* album chart, attaining number 16 as its highest position. It also spawned two Top Ten hits with 'High On You' and 'The Search Is Over'. They recorded 'Burning Heart' as the theme song to *Rocky IV* in 1986 and achieved another international hit, which reached number 5 on the UK singles chart. Surprisingly, the song was not included on *When Seconds Count*, which pursued a heavier direction once more. The band had contracted to a three-piece nucleus of Jamison, Sullivan and Peterik at this juncture and had used session musicians to finish the album. *Too Hot To Sleep* was probably the most consistent and strongest album of the band's career, featuring a magnificent collection of commercially-minded, hard-rock anthems. The album made little commercial impact and the band finally disbanded in 1989.
Albums: *Survivor* (1979), *Premonition* (1981), *Eye Of The Tiger* (1982), *Caught In The Game* (1983), *Vital Signs* (1984), *When Seconds Count* (1986), *Too Hot To Sleep* (1988). Compilation: *Best Of* (1989).

Suzuki, Kenji

This Japanese child prodigy and virtuoso guitarist first came to prominence after winning a national competition for guitarists at the age of 14. Resembling a Japanese version of Elvis Costello, his mastery of the fretboard was quite astonishing. After a low-key mini-album of mainly Japanese-style instrumentals, he teamed up with ex-Cream bassist Jack Bruce and Frehley's Comet's drummer Anton Fig. This association recorded as a power-trio, playing Cream classics and *avant garde*, blues-based rock-fused with Japanese classical pieces.
Album: *Jack Bruce, Anton Fig & Kenji Suzuki - Inazuma Supersession* (1988).

Sweet Savage

This melodic hard-rock quartet was formed in Belfast 1979 by guitarists Vivian Campbell and Trevor Fleming. Recruiting bassist David Haller and drummer David Bates, they achieved their first break, by landing the support slots on the 1981 tours of Motorhead and Wishbone Ash. Debuting the same year with the single 'Take No Prisoners', the future looked very bright for the band. A UK tour supporting Thin Lizzy was followed by an impressive session on UK disc jockey Tommy Vance's *Friday Rock Show*. 'Eye of

The Storm' appeared on the compilation *Friday Rock Show II*. Two more noteworthy singles were released, before Campbell accepted the offer to join Ronnie James Dio. Four re-written Sweet Savage tracks appeared on Dio's *Holy Diver*. The band continued for a short time with Ian Wilson as Campbell's replacement. However, Wilson he was a poor substitute and the band folded in 1984, after the release of the single 'Straight Through The Heart'.

Sword

This Canadian heavy metal quartet was formed in 1981 by vocalist Rick Hughes and drummer Dan Hughes. Augmented by Mike Plant (guitar) and Mike Larock (bass), it took the band five years to secure a record deal. Signing to Aquarius in 1986, they released *Metalized*, which paid respect to both the early 80s British scene and older groups such as Black Sabbath and Rainbow. Sword secured the support slots on the Alice Cooper and Metallica tours in 1987. *Sweet Dreams*, released in 1988, consolidated their approach; monstrously aching riffs and gut-wrenching guitar breaks, encased within dynamic and melodic arrangements. Sword are an excellent unit, but due to a lack of image and record company backing, their commercial prospects remain questionable.
Albums: *Metalized* (1986), *Sweet Dreams* (1988).

Sye

This Canadian hard-rock group was formed in 1981 by Phillipino-born vocalist/guitarist Bernie Carlos. Based in Toronto, Carlos joined forces with bassist and fellow countryman Phillipino Gunner San Augustin. The duo joined the Metal Blade label and debuted with *Turn On The Night* in 1985. Session musician Ray Cincinnato played drums on the album, but Steve Ferguson was recruited as a permanent addition after the work was released. Sye's music features some impressive guitar parts, but is ultimately hampered by the weak and indistinct vocals. The band have been inactive since 1986.
Album: *Turn On The Fire* (1985).

T

Taffola, Joey

Beginning his career on the guitar at the age of 14, Joey Taffola served his apprenticeship with the unremarkable speed-metal outfit Jag Panzer. In 1987, he left the band and returned to California to take instruction from guitar guru Tony Macalpine. Moving to the Guitar Institute Of Technology, Taffola studied jazz, rock and classical styles alongside Paul Gilbert (later of Racer X). After recording a series of demos, Shrapnel boss Mike Varney signed Taffola to produce a guitar instrumental album. With the help of former Jag Panzer drummer Reynold Carlson and ex-Rising Force bassist Wally Voss, Out Of The Sun appeared in 1987. Although the album featured guest appearances by Paul Gilbert (guitar) and Tony Macalpine (keyboards), it lacked both direction and individuality. Taffola's style is a characterless hybrid of Malmsteen's, Macalpine's and Vinnie Moore's styles. After an aborted band project featuring ex-Rising Force vocalist Mark Boals, Taffola started work on another instrumental album.
Album: Out Of The Sun (1987).

Talas

This US hard-rock outfit was masterminded by bass virtuoso Billy Sheehan. Enlisting the services of former Chain Reaction vocalist Phil Naro, guitarist Mitch Perry and drummer Mark Miller, they specialized in melodic, guitar-oriented rock with a strong commercial edge. After the release of a self-financed debut album in 1980, the band began to build up a small, but loyal fanbase. This attracted the attention of Food For Thought Records. Enjoying a larger budget, the band delivered Sink Your Teeth Into That in 1982. This was a showcase album for Sheehan's amazing bass work and featured 'Shyboy', which he later re-recorded with David Lee Roth. At this point, the band were put on hold, as Sheehan helped out UFO on their European tour. After an unfruitful association with Steve Stevens, Sheehan put Talas back on the road and recorded Live Speed On Ice in 1983. The album did not sell and the band became redundant as Sheehan left to join David Lee Roth's Band and later form Mr. Big.
Albums: Talas (1980), Sink Your Teeth Into That (1982), Live Speed On Ice (1983), The Talas Years (1990).

Talion

This UK speed-metal quartet was formerly known as Trojan. Formed in 1988, the band comprised Graeme Wyatt (vocals), Pete Wadeson (guitar), Phil Gavin (bass) and Johnny Lee Jackson (drums). Influenced by Metallica, Megadeth and Judas Priest, they played uninspired and at times amateurish speed metal. Signed to the independent Major Records, they debuted with Killing The World in 1989. This was a fairly lacklustre recording and on this evidence, it seems unlikely that they will progress beyond pub-rock status.
Album: Killing The World (1989).

Talisman

This Swedish, melodic metal outfit was put together in 1989 by ex-Rising Force bassist Marcel Jacob. Recruiting vocalist Jeff Scott Soto and guitarist Christopher Stahl, they joined Airplay Records. Debuting the following year with a self-titled album, they incorporated elements of Europe, Yngwie Malmsteen and TNT in their music. High-pitched vocal harmonies and bursts of fiery guitar work are the band's trademarks, but they have yet to make an impression outside Sweden.
Album: Talisman (1990).

Tangier

This US hard-rock outfit have adopted a different style on each of their three albums to date. Formed in 1984 by vocalist Bill Matson and guitarist Doug Gordon, they initially played blues-based hard rock, which paid respect to Free, Molly Hatchet and Bad Company. With Rocco Mazella (guitar), Mike Kost (bass) and Mark Hopkins (drums) completing the line-up, they toured frequently but failed to make a breakthrough. After an almost five-year gap, Matson and Gordon returned with Gari Saint (guitar), Garry Nutt (bass) and Bobby Bender (drums) to record Four Winds. This was more sophisticated and leaned towards mainstream AOR, having much in common with Journey and Styx, but with blues undercurrents. Matson and Saint quit in 1990, with Mike Le Compte taking over vocal duties and the band contracting to a four-piece in the process. Stranded emerged the following year and saw the band diversifying their approach, and toughening their act. They now come across as an awkward hybrid of Tesla and Thunder.
Albums: Tangier (1985), Four Winds (1989), Stranded (1991).

Tattooed Love Boys

This streetwise UK rock quartet were formed in 1987 by vocalist Gary Mielle and drummer Mick

Ransome. With Cris C.J. Jagdhar (guitar) and Darayus Z. Kaye (bass) completing the line-up, they drew inspiration from the New York Dolls, Ramones and Hanoi Rocks. Debuting with *Bleeding Hearts And Needle Marks* in 1988, they proved they could write instant if ultimately disposable sleazy rock anthems, which posssessed a degree of naive charm. The album sold poorly and the band disintegrated in 1989. The band were resurrected in 1991 with the nucleus of Ransome and Mielle plus new recruits Dean Marshall (bass), Nick Singleton (guitar) and Chris Danby (rhythm guitar). *No Time For Nursery Rhymes* emerged on the MFN label and its attempt at a more sophisticated approach backfired totally. The result was an amateurish affair, which hinted at plagiarism of Guns N' Roses.

Albums: *Bleeding Hearts And Needle Marks* (1988), *No Time For Nursery Rhymes* (1991).

Tattoo Rodeo

Previously known as White Sister, an ultra-sophisticated funk-tinged hard-rock outfit. The band switched name and changed image somewhat during 1991, in order to land a major recording deal. With acoustic and blues influences replacing the soul/funk elements, the band aimed at the same market as Tesla, Bon Jovi and Def Leppard. Comprising Dennis Churchill-Dries (vocals/bass), Rick Chadock (guitar), Michael Lord (keyboards) and Rich Wright (drums), the band specialize in highly infectious and melodic song structures, characterized by an impassioned vocal delivery. Picked up by Atlantic, they debuted with *Rode Hard, Put Away Wet* and received a positive, if slightly guarded media response. This comprised thirteen, blues-based rock anthems that had both guts and style. Their image was rather understated and as a result, they failed to attract the degree of attention that their talents deserved.

Album: *Rode Hard, Put Away Wet* (1991).

Temple Of The Dog

This one-off project involved members of the USA, Seattle-based bands Mother Love Bone and Soundgarden. The album was recorded as a tribute to the late Andrew Wood, former Mother Love Bone vocalist. The band comprised Chris Cornell (vocals), Matt Cameron (drums), Mike McCready (guitar), Stone Gossard (rhythm guitar) and Jeff Ament (bass). Signed to A&M Records, the album received widespread critical acclaim immediately upon release. The music fused the Doors/Joy Division/Stooges fixation of Mother Love Bone with the harder, dirtier and at times funkier rhythms of Soundgarden. A moving, powerful and genuine tribute to a great vocalist in every sense.

Gossard and Ament later formed Pearl Jam. Album: *Temple Of The Dog* (1991).

Tesla

Tesla

Originally known as City Kid, Tesla are a five-piece, blues-based, hard-rock quintet from Sacramento, California, USA. Named after the scientist Nikola Tesla, the current line-up came together in 1985. The band comprises Jeff Keith (vocals), Tommy Skeoch (guitar/vocals), Frank Hannon (guitar/keyboards/vocals), Brian Wheat (bass/vocals) and Troy Lucketta (drums and ex-Eric Martin Band). They signed to Geffen Records in 1986 and recorded *Mechanical Resonance*, a universally acclaimed debut that ranks alongside that of Montrose's first album in terms of quality and setting new standards. The title was taken from one of Tesla's theories and combined raunchy metallic rock with blues and rock 'n' roll influences. Jeff Keith's impassioned vocals gave the material an added dimension, as the songs alternated between passionate, gut-wrenching ballads and crazy, fuel-injected rockers. The album eventually took off Stateside, reaching number 32 on the *Billboard* chart. *The Great Radio Controversy* saw the band rapidly maturing, with a highly polished, but no-less energetic collection of songs that were saturated with infectious riffs and subtle hook-lines. The ballad 'Love Song' became

Thin Lizzy

a Top 10 hit, while the album climbed to number 18 on the US charts. Tesla's third album created something of a precedent, a live album that was totally acoustic and included a number of inspired cover versions. It highlighted the band's humour, technical excellence and ability to entertain. *Edison's Medicine* showed they could easily switch back to power-mode, with a near 70-minute onslaught of high-energy hard-rock numbers. Tesla defy convention, have no gimmicks nor do they conform to any particular image. They have no peers; instead they remain true to their own beliefs and consequently are a very rare commodity in the rock world today.
Albums: *Mechanical Resonance* (1986), *The Great Radio Controversy* (1989), *Five Man Acoustical Jam* (1990), *Edison's Medicine* (1991), *Psychotic Supper* (1991).

Thin Lizzy

Formed in Dublin, Eire in 1969, this hard-rocking group comprised Phil Lynott (b. 20 August 1951, Dublin, Eire, d. 4 January 1986; vocals/bass), Eric Bell (b. 3 September 1947, Belfast, Northern Ireland; guitar) and Brian Downey (b. 27 January 1951, Dublin, Eire; drums). After signing to Decca, they issued two albums, neither of which charted. A change of fortune occurred after they recorded a novelty rock version of the traditional 'Whiskey In The Jar'. The single reached the UK Top 10 and popularized the group's blend of Irish folk elements and strident guitar work. The group underwent a series of line-up changes during early 1974. Bell was replaced by Gary Moore and two more temporary guitarists were recruited, Andy Gee and John Cann. The arrival of guitarists Brian Robertson (b. 12 September 1956, Glasgow, Scotland) and Scott Gorham (b. 17 March 1951, Santa Monica, California, USA) stabilized the group as they entered their most productive phase. A series of UK concerts throughout 1975 saw the group make considerable headway. 1976 was the breakthrough year with the acclaimed *Jailbreak* hitting the charts. The driving macho-celebrating 'The Boys Are Back In Town' reached the UK Top 10 and US Top 20 and was voted single of the year by the influential and discerning *New Musical Express*. In early 1977, Robertson was forced to leave the group due to a hand injury following a fight and was replaced by the returning Moore. Another UK Top 20 hit followed with the scathing 'Don't Believe A Word' from the album *Johnny The Fox*. Moore then returned to Colosseum and the recovered Robertson took his place. Both 'Dancin' In The Moonlight' and *Bad Reputation* were UK Top 10 hits and were soon followed by the excellent double album, *Live And Dangerous*. 1979 saw the group scaling new commercial heights with such Top 20 singles as 'Waiting For An Alibi' and 'Do Anything You Want To', plus the best-selling *Black Rose*. The tortuous line-up changes continued apace. Robertson again left and joined Wild Horses. Moore returned, but within a year was replaced by Midge Ure (formerly of Slik and the Rich Kids). By late 1979, the peripatetic Ure had moved on to Ultravox and was replaced by Snowy White. In early 1980, Lynott married Caroline Crowther, daughter of the television personality Leslie Crowther. After recording some solo work, Lynott reunited with Thin Lizzy for *Chinatown*, which included the controversial Top 10 single, 'Killer On The Loose'. The heavily-promoted *Adventures Of Thin Lizzy* maintained their standing, before White bowed out on *Renegade*. He was replaced by John Sykes, formerly of the Tygers Of Pan Tang. One more album, *Thunder And Lightning*, followed before Lynott split up the group in the summer of 1984. A posthumous live album, *Life-Live* was issued at the end of that year. Its title took on an ironically macabre significance two years later when Lynott died of heart failure and pneumonia after a drugs overdose. Four months later, in May 1986, Thin Lizzy reformed for the Self Aid concert organized in Eire by Bob Geldof, who replaced Lynott on vocals for the day.

Albums: *Thin Lizzy* (1971), *Shades Of Blue Orphanage* (1972), *Vagabonds Of The Western World* (1973), *Night Life* (1974), *Fighting* (1975), *Jailbreak* (1976), *Remembering - Part One* (1976), *Johnny The Fox* (1976), *Bad Reputation* (1977), *Live And Dangerous* (1978), *Black Rose* (1979), *The Continuing Saga Of The Ageing Orphans* (1979), *Renegade* (1981), *Rockers* (1981), *Thunder And Lightning* (1983), *Life-Live* (1983). Compilations: *Lizzy Killers* (1983), *The Collection* (1985), *The Best Of Phil Lynott And Thin Lizzy* (1987), *Dedication - The Best Of Thin Lizzy* (1991).
Further reading: *Phil Lynott: Dancing In The Moonlight*, Pamela McCleeve.

Thought Industry

This US four-piece band specialize in the fusion of thrash, power-metal and industrial elements. Formed in 1991, the band comprise Brent Oberlin (vocals), Christopher Lee (bass), Paul Enzio (guitar) and Dustin Donaldson (drums). Signed to Music For Nations, they debuted in July 1992

with Songs For Insects, an impressive and offbeat amalgam of Killing Joke, Birthday Party and Metallica influences.
Album: Songs For Insects (1992).

Thunder

Thunder

This British hard-rock quintet was heavily influenced by Bad Company and the Rolling Stones. Thunder evolved from the ashes of Terraplane, with the surviving nucleus of Danny Bowes (vocals), Luke Morley (guitar) and Gary James (drums) recruiting Mark Lockhurst (bass) and Ben Matthews (guitar) to complete the line-up. Moving away from the melodic power-pop of Terraplane, they teamed up with producer Andy Taylor (ex-Duran Duran), to record *Backstreet Symphony*, a stunning album of bluesy rockers and atmospheric ballads, which received widespread critical acclaim. Their style is characterized by a dual guitar attack of alternating riffs and lead breaks, with Bowes' gritty and emotional vocals adding charisma and distinction. They landed the opening slot at Donington in 1990 and were the surprise success of the day. In 1991 they concentrated on the American market, touring extensively in an attempt to make the all important breakthrough. It remains to be seen whether they can transcend the adulation heaped upon them after just one album.
Album: *Back Street Symphony* (1990).

Travers, Pat, Band

Canadian guitarist Pat Travers began his career playing in his brother's band and then in the Band. Having moved to London, Travers set up a band of his own consisting of Peter 'Mars' Cowling (bass) and drummer Roy Dyke (of Ashton, Gardner And Dyke). In 1976 they played at the Reading rock festival, and this led to greater recognition of their debut, *Pat Travers*. In 1977, Nicko McBrain, who subsequently joined Iron Maiden, replaced Roy Dyke. Travers himself

Pat Travers

turned his talents to songwriting, his music taking a more experimental turn, and being aided by other artists, including Scott Gorham. During their 1977 tour, Clive Edwards replaced McBrain, and Michael Dycke added another guitar. Guitarist Pat Thrall, who had been a member of Automatic Man, and Tommy Aldridge (drums), formerly of Black Oak Arkansas, were recruited to work on *Heat In The Street*, a very heavy, powerful sounding album. Their relationship with the band was short-lived, however; Thrall left and Aldridge departed in order to work with Ozzy Osbourne. Subsequent recordings featured Sandy Gennaro (drums) and Michael Shrieve, and were notable for their solid, blues-like sound. In 1984 the line-up of Pat Marchino (drums), Barry Dunaway (bass), Jerry Riggs (guitar) and Travers himself released *Hot Shot*, an album which was not a great commercial success. There was then a lengthy break in Travers' recording career until 1990 when he released *School Of Hard Knocks*. The following year Travers was working again with Thrall, Aldridge and Cowling, touring Japan along with Jerry Riggs and Scott Zymowski, and planning a reunion album.
Albums: *Pat Travers* (1976), *Makin' Magic* (1977), *Putting It Straight* (1977), *Heat In The Street* (1978), *Go For What You Know* (1979), *Crash And Burn* (1980), *Radio Active* (1981), *Black Pearl* (1982), *Hot Shot* (1984), *School Of Hard Knocks* (1990).

Triumph

This Canadian power-trio formed in Toronto during 1975. The band have many similarities to Rush, as they are all highly accomplished musicians and have experimented with many facets of high-tech melodic rock. Comprising Rik Emmet (guitar/vocals), Gil Moore (drums) and Mike Levine (bass/keyboards) they follow a rockier road than their fellow countrymen. Interest built slowly, but the band finally made

Triumph

the breakthrough with *Progressions Of Power*, their fourth album, released in 1980. *Allied Forces* and *Never Surrender* saw the pinnacle of their success, with both albums attaining gold status in the USA. Their music is characterized by Emmet's high-pitched vocals and intricate guitar work, supplemented by keyboard fills and a thunderous rhythm section. *Thunder Seven*, a CD only release was a disjointed collection, while the live album that followed suffered from a wooden sound and flat production. In the live setting, the band used Rick Santers as an extra guitarist to overcome the limitations of a three-man line-up. Their concerts were renowned for their sophisticated special effects rather than the actual music, and featured every conceivable pyrotechnic device available, plus the ultimate in computerised, laser-lighting rigs. *The Sport Of Kings* saw the band move in a blatantly commercial direction, but *Surveillance* marked a return to their roots: an aggressive and superbly produced hard-rock album. They have been inactive since Emmet quit in 1988.
Albums: *Triumph* (1976), *Rock 'N' Roll Machine* (1977), *Just A Game* (1979), *Progressions Of Power* (1980), *Allied Forces* (1981), *Never Surrender* (1982), *Thunder Seven* (1984), *Stages* (1985), *The Sport Of Kings* (1985), *Surveillance* (1987), *Classics* (1989).

Trojan

Formed in Wigan, England in 1982 the band's original line up consisted of Dave Kenyon (vocals), Pate Wadeson (guitar), Andy J. Halliwell (guitar), Brian Bentham (bass) and Mick Taylor (drums). The band first became noticed on the heavy metal underground scene with a hastily recorded five-track cassette. This credible offering was a blend of high speed thrashmetal with a punk attitude. The band contributed a track to a budget compilation *Metal Maniaxe* released on Ebony Records in 1982. However, due to a relative lack of record company promotion, coupled with a yearning by various members of the band to pursue other musical directions, the band dissolved. Determined to carry on, Wadeson underwent lengthy auditions to re-form the band. By 1984 a new line-up was confirmed, featuring Graeme Wyatt (vocals), Eddie Martin (bass) and Sam Hall (drums). *Chasing The Storm* was released on Roadrunner Records in 1985 and was well received. With a sound firmly rooted in the NWOBHM the band stirred up a storm utilizing catchy melodic hooklines over high speed thrash-metal riffs. The group toured extensively at home and abroad culminating in an appearance at the Whiplash Festival in Belgium in 1986. Unfortunately, owing to managerial and personal problems, the band split up in 1988 and Wadeson and Wyatt went on to form the melodic thrash band Talion.
Album: *Chasing The Storm* (1985).

Trout, Walter, Band

This highly talented and experienced blues guitarist finally formed and recorded with his own band in 1989. With the help of Jim Trapp (bass), Leroy Larson (drums) and Dan Abrams (keyboards) he debuted with *Life In The Jungle* in 1990. This showcased Trout's remarkable feel and dexterity and courted Jimi Hendrix, Robin Trower and Gary Moore comparisons. Klas Anderhill took over the drumstool on *Prisoner Of A Dream* and saw the band move in a more commercial direction. Much of the soulful passion had evaporated, leaving almost identikit Europe, Whitesnake and Bon Jovi style songs. These average songs were rescued by the occasional inspired guitar break.
Albums: *Life In The Jungle* (1990), *Prisoner Of A Dream* (1991).

Tuff

This US rock quartet were formed in 1990 by vocalist Stevie Rachelle and guitarist Jorge Desaint. Recruiting bassist Todd Chase and drummer Michael Lean, they signed to Atlantic Records and debuted with *What Comes Around,*

Tuff

Goes Around in 1991. This was an amalgam of Poison, Warrant and Bon Jovi influences, yet they displayed enough energy to maintain a level of credibility.
Album: *What Comes Around, Goes Around* (1991).

Twisted Sister

Formed in 1976, this New York quintet's original purpose was to provide the antidote to the disco music that was saturating the airwaves during the mid-70s. Featuring Dee Snider (vocals), Eddie Ojeda (guitar), Mark 'The Animal' Mendoza (bass and ex-Dictators), Jay Jay French (guitar) and Tony Petri (drums) they had a bizarre image that borrowed ideas from Kiss, Alice Cooper and the New York Dolls. Musically they combined sexually provocative lyrics and dumb choruses with heavy-duty, metallic rock 'n' roll. A.J. Pero (ex-Cities) took over the drumstool before the recording of the debut *Under The Blade*. This was picked up from the independent Secret label by Atlantic Records, following a successful UK appearance at the Reading Festival and a controversial performance on *The Tube* television show in 1982. They never lived up to their initial promise, with successive albums simply regurgitating earlier ideas. Their greatest success was *Stay Hungry*, which cracked the Top 20 album

Twisted Sister

charts on both sides of the Atlantic. It also included the hit single 'I Am, I'm Me', which peaked at number 18 in the UK. Their audience had become bored with them by the time *Come Out And Play* was released and the tour to support it was also a flop. Pero quit and returned to his former outfit, Cities; Joey 'Seven' Franco (ex-Good Rats) was drafted in as replacement. Snider steered the band in a more melodic direction on *Love Is For Suckers*. The album was still-born, Atlantic terminated their contract, and the band imploded in 1987. Snider went on to form Desperado, with ex-Gillan guitarist Bernie Torme. Albums: *Under The Blade* (1982), *You Can't Stop Rock 'N' Roll* (1983), *Stay Hungry* (1984), *Come Out And Play* (1985), *Love Is For Suckers* (1987).

21 Guns

This melodic hard-rock quartet were assembled in 1991 by ex-Thin Lizzy guitarist Scott Gorham. Recruiting fellow Americans Leif Johansen (bass), Michael Sturgis (drums) and Tommy La Verdi (vocals) to complete the line-up, the band were soon offered a contract by RCA Records. They debuted in the summer of 1992 with Salute, a highly polished melodic rock album which met with positive reviews in the rock press. Influences such as Thin Lizzy, Foreigner, Journey and White Lion surfaced regularly throughout the album but without ever being plagiaristic.
Albums: Salute (1992).

2 Tribes

This rock, funk, metal crossover band were formed in London during 1990. The racially mixed line-up gave them their name. The band comprises Ashton Liburd (vocals), Paul Gold (bass), Rod Quinn (drums) and Jon Mcloughlin (guitar) and represent the UK's answer to Living Colour. Signed to Chrysalis Records, they debuted with a self-titled album in early 1992 which met with an enthusiastic response from the music press.
Album: 2 Tribes (1992).

Tygers Of Pan Tang

This hard rock band was formed in Whitley Bay, Newcastle-upon-Tyne, England, in 1978, as part of the New Wave Of British Heavy Metal. The four-piece line-up comprised Jess Cox (vocals), Rob Weir (guitar), Rocky (bass) and Brian Dick (drums). Their debut EP was the first rock release on Newcastle's Neat label, and it quickly topped all the metal charts. On the back of their first flush of success they moved to MCA. However, after one album Cox departed to be replaced by John Deverill (from Cardiff, Wales; vocals) and John Sykes (guitar). Sykes later left (to join Thin Lizzy and then Whitesnake) and was replaced by former Penetration guitarist Fred Purser. *The Cage* broke the band in the USA, before two years of disputes with MCA held up their career, and only compilation albums were released during this period. Steve Lamb joined as guitarist in 1985, and a year later former vocalist Cox formed Tyger Tyger in order to try and recapture past glories.

Albums: *Wild Cat* (1980), *Spellbound* (1981), *Crazy Nights* (1981), *The Cage* (1982), *The Wreckage* (1985), *First Kill* (1986), *Burning In The Shade* (1987). Compilation: *The Best Of The Tygers Of Pan Tang* (1983).

U

UFO

The band formed in 1969, when drummer Andy Parker joined Phil Mogg (b. 1951, London, England; vocals), Pete Way (bass) and Mick Bolton (guitar) in Hocus Pocus. With a name change to UFO and a musical style that fused progressive space-rock and good-time boogie, they released three albums that were successful only in Germany and Japan. In 1974 Bolton quit, to be replaced by Larry Wallis (ex-Pink Fairies), followed by Bernie Marsden (later of Whitesnake) and finally Michael Schenker. Securing a deal with Chrysalis Records, they recorded *Phenomenon*, a stunning hard rock album that featured the all-time heavy metal classics 'Rock Bottom' and 'Doctor, Doctor'. Schenker's presence helped to forge their new sound, as he strangled the hard-edged metallic riffs out of his trusty Flying V. A series of excellent albums followed, and the band expanded to a five-piece in 1976, with the

addition of a keyboardist, initially Danny Peyronel (ex-Heavy Metal Kids) and later Paul Raymond (formerly of Savoy Brown). *Lights Out* and *Strangers In The Night* consolidated the band's success, the latter a superb double live album recorded on their sell-out US tour of 1977. After long-running internal disagreements, Schenker quit in 1978 to rejoin the Scorpions and later form MSG. Paul Chapman (ex-Lone Star) was offered the guitarist's vacancy, having played with the band for short periods on two previous occasions. From this point on, the band never recaptured the level of success and recognition they had attained with Schenker. A string of uninspiring albums followed, that lacked both aggression and killer riffs. Paul Raymond joined MSG in 1980, with Neil Carter (ex-Wild Horses) taking his place. Pete Way split after the release of *Mechanix*, eventually forming Waysted and ex-Eddie And The Hot Rods/Damned bassist Paul Gray took over his position.

Making Contact represented the nadir of the band's creativity, being dated and devoid of the old energy. A farewell UK tour was undertaken in 1983, but it was a sad end for what was originally a fine band. Two years later Mogg resurrected the

name with Raymond and Gray, plus ex-Magnum drummer Jim Simpson and the Japanese guitarist Atomic Tommy M. They recorded *Misdemeanor*, which unsuccessfully attempted to rekindle the old flame, with up-front guitars and hard-line melodies. Success eluded them and they disbanded again. In 1991, UFO were re-born once more. This time the line-up featured the nucleus of Mogg and Way, plus guitarist Lawrence Archer (ex-Grand Slam) and drummer Clive Edwards (ex-Wild Horses). They have tried to recapture the halcyon days of 1974-78, with *High Stakes And Desperate Men*, but only time will tell, if they have the songs and ability to compete with the current market leaders in this field.

Albums: *UFO 1* (1971), *Flying* (1971), *UFO Lands In Tokyo - Live* (1971), *Phenomenon* (1974), *Force It* (1975), *No Heavy Pettin'* (1976), *Lights Out* (1977), *Obsession* (1978), *Strangers In The Night* (1979), *No Place To Run* (1980), *The Wild, The Willing And The Innocent* (1981), *Mechanix* (1982), *Making Contact* (1983), *Misdemeanor* (1985), *Ain't Misbehavin'* (1988), *High Stakes And Desperate Men* (1992). Compilations: *Classic Tracks 1970-73* (1981), *Headstone - The Best Of UFO* (1983).

Uncle Sam

Formed in 1987, Uncle Sam were the brainchild of guitarist Larry Millar. With the recruitment of fellow New Yorkers David Gentner (vocals), Bill Purol (bass) and Jeff Mann (drums), the band signed with the independent Razor Records. Influenced by both the punk and thrash movements, their songs were short, frantic and often devoid of melody. Gentner's vocals were monotonous, while the back beat lacked depth and colour. At best they came across as an updated, but pale version of the Stooges or MC5.

Albums: *Heaven Or Hollywood* (1988), *Letters From London* (1990).

V

Vai, Steve

b. 6 June 1960, Long Island, New York, USA. Steve began his musical career at the age of 13, forming his first rock band, Rayge, while still at school. At this time he was tutored by Joe Satriani, who was to have a profound effect on his style for years to come. He studied jazz and classical music at the Berklee College of Music in Boston, Massachusetts, before relocating to Los Angeles, California in 1979. He was recruited by Frank Zappa as the lead guitarist in his backing band, while he was still only 18 years old. By 1984 he had built his own recording studio and had begun experimenting with the fusion of jazz, rock and classical music. These pieces were eventually released as *Flex-able*, and were heavily influenced by Zappa's off-beat and brilliantly unpredictable style. In 1985 Vai replaced Yngwie Malmsteen in Alcatrazz, then moved on to even greater success with David Lee Roth and later Whitesnake. *Passion And Warfare*, released in 1990, was the album that brought Vai international recognition as a solo performer. It welded together jazz, rock, funk, classical and metal nuances within a melodic instrumental framework. It climbed to number 18 on the *Billboard* album chart, earning a gold disc in the process.
Albums: *Flex-able* (1984), *Flex-able Leftovers* (1984), *Passion And Warfare* (1990).

Van Halen

The origins of one of America's most successful heavy metal bands, date back to Pasadena, California in 1973. Edward (Eddie) Van Halen (b. 26 January 1957, Nijmegen, the Netherlands; guitar/keyboards), Alex Van Halen (b. 8 May 1955, Nijmegen, Netherlands; drums) and Michael Anthony (b. 20 June 1955, Chicago, Illinois, USA; bass) who were members of the Broken Combs persuaded vocalist David Lee Roth (b. 10 October 1955, Bloomington, Indianapolis, USA) to leave the Real Ball Jets and become a member after which they changed their name to Mammoth. Specializing in a mixture of 60s and 70s covers plus hard rock originals, they toured the bar and club circuit of Los Angeles, virtually non-stop, during the mid-70s. Their first break came when Gene Simmons (bassist of Kiss) saw one of their club gigs. He was amazed by the energy they generated and the over-the-top flamboyance of their lead singer. Simmons produced a Mammoth demo, but surprisingly it was refused by many major labels in the USA. It was discovered that the name Mammoth was already registered, so they would have to find an alternative. After considering Rat Salade, they opted for Roth's suggestion of simply Van Halen. On the strength of Simmons' recommendation, producer Ted Templeman checked out the band, was duly impressed and convinced Warner Brothers Records to sign them. With Templeman at the production desk, Van Halen entered the studio and recorded their self-titled debut in 1978. The album was released to widespread critical acclaim and compared with Montrose's debut in 1973. It featured a unique fusion of energy, sophistication and virtuosity through Eddie Van Halen's extraordinary guitar lines and Roth's self-assured vocal style. Within 12 months it had sold two million units, peaking at number 19 in the *Billboard* chart. Eddie Van Halen was named as Best New Guitarist Of The Year in 1978, by *Guitar Player* magazine.
The follow-up, the imaginatively titled *Van Halen II* kept to the same formula and was equally successful. Roth's stage antics became even more sensational. He was the supreme showman and combined theatrics, a stunning voice and an outrageous sense of fun to startling effect. *Women And Children First* saw the band starting to explore more musical avenues and experimenting with the use of synthesizers. This came to full fruition on *Fair Warning* which was a marked departure from their earlier releases. *Diver Down* was the band's weakest album, with the cover versions of 60s standards being the strongest tracks. Nevertheless, the band could do no wrong and the album, as all their previous releases, went platinum. With *1984*, released on New Years day of that year, the band made a return to form. Nine originals that re-affirmed their position as the leading exponents of heavy duty melodic metal were infused with a pop-sensibility. Spearheaded by 'Jump', a *Billboard* number 1 hit single, the album lodged at number 2 in the US chart for a full five weeks during its one year residency. Eddie Van Halen was also a guest on Michael Jackson's *Beat It* the same year.
Roth quit in 1985 to concentrate on his solo career, and ex-Montrose vocalist Sammy Hagar (b. 13 October 1947, Monterey, California, USA) eventually filled the vacancy. Retaining the Van Halen name, against record company pressure to change it, the new line-up released *5150* in June 1986. The album name was derived from the police code for the criminally insane, as well as the name of Eddie Van Halen's recording studio. The lead off single 'Why Can't This Be Love' reached number 3 in the *Billboard* chart, while the album

Vai, Steve

became their first number 1 and their biggest seller to-date. *OU812* was a disappointment in creative terms. The songs were formularized and lacked real direction, but the album became the band's second consecutive number 1 in less than two years.

For Unlawful Carnal Knowledge, written as the acronym F.U.C.K., stirred up some controversy at the the time of release. However, the music on the album transcended the juvenile humour of the title, with an immaculate collection of gritty and uncompromizing rockers. The band had re-defined their identity and rode into the 90s on a new creative wave. Needless to say, platinum status was attained yet again.

Albums: *Van Halen* (1978), *Van Halen II* (1979), *Women And Children First* (1980), *Fair Warning* (1981), *Diver Down* (1982), *1984 (MCMLXXXIV)* (1984), *5150* (1986), *OU812* (1988), *For Unlawful Carnal Knowledge* (1991).

Van Halen, Eddie, Brian Setzer and Richie Sambora

Van Halen, Eddie

b. 26 January 1957, Nijmegen, Netherlands. Van Halen is highly regarded as one of rock music's more distinctive guitarists. The group Van Halen's debut album was considered by many to be one of the greatest heavy rock album ever released. A short guitar-only track, 'Eruption', epitomizes Eddie Van Halen's guitar pyrotechnics. Together with fellow Van Halen band mate, extrovert showman David Lee Roth, their stage show was an incredible spectacle. Eddie Van Halen not only proved to be a superb musician but he always exuded an air of total enjoyment. He has recorded nine albums with Van Halen the band and although they have not all been as fiery and dynamic as the first release, they all display his versatile guitar style. Matters have not, however, always gone according to plan and in 1984 he fell out with colleague Roth over musical direction, resulting in Roth departing the ranks and Sammy Hagar joining. This marked almost a new beginning for the band who continue to enjoy considerable success. To date, Eddie Van Halen has not recorded a solo album, although he has guested on several including those by Private Life (who he has also produced) and Toto guitarist's Steve Lukather. Perhaps his most famous guest contribution to date is his guitar solo on Michael Jackson's single 'Beat It' from Jackson's phenomenally-successful *Thriller*.

Vinnie Vincent's Invasion

Vincent, Vinnie

b. Vinnie Cusano. Vincent began his musical career as guitar/vocalist in the melodic rock band Treasure in 1977. In 1982 he accepted the offer to join Kiss and contributed to *Creatures Of The Night* and *Lick It Up*, the latter featuring the band without make-up on the cover for the first time. After two years with Kiss, Vincent left to form the autonomous Vinnie Vincent Invasion. Recruiting Robert Fleischman (ex-Journey; vocals), Dana Strum (ex-Ozzy Osbourne group; bass) and Bobby Rock (drums), they secured a deal with Chrysalis Records in 1985. Their self-titled debut album, released the following year, was a critical success. Fleischman was replaced by Mark Slaughter immediately the album was released, and the cohesion of the band was lost. *All Systems Go* followed a similar pattern to its predecessor, but was not picked up by metal fans in the market

Vixen

place. Frustrated by the lack of success, Slaughter and Strum left to form Slaughter. Vincent was dropped by Chrysalis, but in 1990 he teamed up with Fleischman again to work on a solo project.
Albums: *Vinnie Vincent Invasion* (1986), *All Systems Go* (1988).

Vixen

This US female rock quartet with a glossy image, was put together in 1986 by former Madam X drummer Roxy Petrucci. The line-up initially featured Steve Vai's wife Pia Koko on bass, but she was succeeded by Share Pederson before signing to EMI Records. With Janet Gardner handling vocals and Jan Kuehnemund on guitar, the band had a wealth of musical ability and a strong visual image. Their debut album included much material by outside writers, notably Richard Marx and Jeff Paris. *Rev It Up*, was virtually self-penned and it launched the band in the USA. Marketed as the female equivalent of Bon Jovi, they specialised in four-minute pop-rock anthems and the occasional obligatory power-ballads, with memorable choruses including 'Cryin' and 'How Much Love' plus the Marx-composed epic 'Edge Of A Broken Heart'.

Albums: *Vixen* (1988), *Rev It Up* (1990).

Voivod

Formed in Canada in the early 80s, Voivoid consisted of Denis Belanger (vocals), Denis D'Amour (guitar), Jean-Yves Theriault (bass) and Michel Langevin (drums). The release of their first album made them one of the first thrash metal bands to make a name for themselves world-wide. The sound of the first album was very off-the-wall, noisy and industrial, with an almost *avant garde* feel at times. *RRROOOAAARRR* continued this style and helped them become popular in the metal underground movement. Progression was evident on *Killing Technology* which showcased improved musicianship and more advanced ideas. However, it was the release of *Dimension Hatross* that really saw Voivod assume the role of pioneers and experimenters in the metal field. Leaving behind much of their thrash roots, there was now much more to their sound than that original basic attack. This trend continued on *Nothingface* which contained little that could be labelled thrash metal. The same can be said of *Angel Rat* which also saw the departure of Jean-Yves Theriault. More than ever other influences such as progressive rock, were increasing. It was the strength of their ideas and the depth of their music that helped them grow steadily and transcend their thrash metal roots while still retaining a strong fan base right across the metal spectrum.

Albums: *War And Pain* (1984), *RRROOOAAARRR* (1986), *Killing Technology* (1987), *Dimension Hatross* (1988), *Nothingface* (1989), *Angel Rat* (1991).

W

Warrior Soul

This psychotic art-rock quartet from New York was the brainchild of one-time video disc jockey, Kory Clarke. With the help of of Pete McClanahan (bass), John Ricco (guitar) and Paul Ferguson (drums), *Last Decade, Dead Century* was released in 1988. Influences as diverse as the Doors, Metallica, the Stooges and Joy Division were combined to produce a dark, intense, angst-ridden album. Lyrically, it criticised the establishment's inability to solve contemporary social problems, with references to political and police corruption, the homeless and narcotics. Mark Evans took over as drummer on *Drugs, God And The New Republic*, which built on previous themes, but increased the musical intensity of their delivery. Both works have received considerable critical acclaim, but this has yet to be converted into album sales.
Albums: *Last Decade, Dead Century* (1990), *Drugs, God And The New Republic* (1991).

Watchtower

This experimental four-piece Texan outfit married the power of Metallica, with the intricate, sophisticated and quirky arrangements of Rush. The group comprised of Alan Tecchio (vocals), Ron Jarzombek (guitars), Doug Keyser (bass) and Rick Colaluca (drums). Watchtower's musicianship was of a high order and their songs contained multiple time-changes, including Jarzombek's exemplary performances on lead, acoustic and even reverse-taping guitar. To date, the group's brand of electro-charged, techno-thrash has yet to earn them the wide-spread attention that is due to them.
Albums: *Watchtower* (1988), *Control And Resistance* (1989).

White Lion

This US group was formed in Brooklyn, New York City during 1983, by Mike Tramp (lead vocals, ex-Mabel) and Vito Bratta (guitar, ex-Dreamer). After a series of false starts, they signed to Elektra Records with Felix Robinson (bass, ex-Angel) and Dave Capozzi (drums) completing the line-up. However, the label were unhappy with the recording of *Fight To Survive* and after refusing to release the album, terminated their contract. RCA-Victor picked up the release option and the album finally surfaced in Japan in 1984. By this

White Lion

stage, James Lomenzo and Gregg D'Angelo had taken over bass and drums, respectively, on a permanent basis. The album did in fact meet with favourable reviews, some quarters comparing Mike Tramp to David Lee Roth and Vito Bratta to Eddie Van Halen, and likening the songs to that of Europe, Dokken and Journey. Signing to Atlantic Records, they released *Pride*, which developed their own identity, in particular Mike Tramp's characteristically watery falsetto style. The album catapulted them from obscurity to stardom, climbing to number 11 during its year-long stay on the *Billboard* album chart. It also spawned two US Top 10 hits with 'Wait' and 'When The Children Cry'. *Big Game* was a disappointing follow-up, nevertheless, it still made the US charts, peaking at number 19. *Mane Attraction* released in 1991, saw the band recapture lost ground with a magnificent melodic rock album. Lomenzo and D'Angelo quit due to 'musical differences', shortly after the album's release and were replaced by Tommy 'T-Bone' Caradonna (ex-Alice Cooper bassist) and ex-Y&T drummer Jimmy DeGrasso.
Albums: *Fight To Survive* (1984), *Pride* (1987), *Big Game* (1989), *Mane Attraction* (1991).

Whitesnake

This UK-based heavy metal band was led by David Coverdale (b. 21 September 1951, Saltburn, Tyne & Wear, England). The lead vocalist with Deep Purple since 1973, Coverdale left the group in 1976 and recorded two solo albums, *Whitesnake* and *Northwinds*. Shortly afterwards, he formed a touring band from musicians who had played on the records. Called David Coverdale's Whitesnake, the group included Micky Moody (guitar), Bernie Marsden (guitar), Brian Johnston (keyboards), Neil Murray (bass) and John Dowle (drums). For much of the late 70s, the group toured in the UK, Europe and Japan. The first US tour was in 1980. During this period, there were personnel changes

Whitesnake

with ex-Deep Purple members Jon Lord and Ian Paice joining on keyboards and drums. Whitesnake's first British hit was 'Fool For Your Loving' (1980), composed by Coverdale, Marsden and Moody, and the double album, *Live in The Heart Of The City* (named after the Bobby Bland song featured on stage by Coverdale) reached the Top Ten the following year. At this point, the illness of Coverdale's daughter caused a hiatus in the group's career and when Whitesnake reformed in 1982 only Lord and Moody remained from the earlier line-up. The new members were Mel Galley (guitar), ex-Back Door and Alexis Korner bassist Colin Hodgkinson and Cozy Powell (drums). However, this configuration lasted only briefly and by 1984 the long-serving Moody and Lord had left, the latter to join a reformed Deep Purple. While Coverdale remained the focus of Whitesnake, there were numerous personnel changes in the following years. These had little effect on the band's growing reputation as one of the leading exponents of heavy rock. Frequent tours finally brought a million-selling album in the USA with 1987's *Whitesnake* and Coverdale's bluesy ballad style brought Top 10 hits with 'Is This Love' and 'Here I Go Again'.

They were co-written with ex-Thin Lizzy guitarist John Sykes, a member of Whitesnake from 1983-86. His replacement, Dutch-born Adrian Vandenburg was co-writer with Coverdale on the band's 1989 album, co-produced by Keith Olsen and Mike Clink. Ex-Dio guitarist Vivian Campbell was also a member of the band in the early 90s.

Albums: *Trouble* (1978), *Love Hunter* (1979), *Live At Hammersmith* (1980), *Ready An' Willing* (1980), *Live In The Heart Of The City* (1980), *Come And Get It* (1981), *Saints 'n Sinners* (1982), *Slide It In* (1984), *Whitesnake* (1987), *Slip Of The Tongue* (1989).

Wild Horses

This melodic, hard rock quartet was formed in 1978 by bassist Jimmy Bain (ex-Rainbow) and guitarist Brian Robertson (ex-Thin Lizzy). Deriving their name from a song on the Rolling Stones' *Sticky Fingers*, they enlisted the services of drummer Clive Edwards (ex-Pat Travers) and second guitarist/keyboard player Neil Carter. The line-up never lived up to expectations; Bain's weak vocals did not give the band enough identity, while the material was too derivative of

Wild Horses

Thin Lizzy and UFO. Live, the band were a different proposition and exuded a raw energy and aggression not evident on their studio works. John Lockton and Dixie Lee (ex-Lone Star) replaced Carter and Edwards for *Stand Your Ground*. This was a marked improvement on their debut, and followed a much bluesier direction. The band fell apart in 1981, with Bain going on to work with Ronnie James Dio (in Dio), and Robertson joining Motorhead after a period of session work.
Albums: *Wild Horses* (1980), *Stand Your Ground* (1981).

Wildhearts

This innovative British hard-rock quartet were formed in London during 1991. The band comprises ex-Quireboy, Ginger (guitar/vocals), ex-Dogs D'Amour drummer Bam, CJ (bass) and Danny (drums), they have recently been consistently cited as the 'Great White Hope' for British rock by the music media. Defying convention, their music is a unique fusion of pop, hard-rock and thrash, with deft lyrics and a cool attitude. They incorporate influences as diverse as Metallica, Poison, Cheap Trick, the Sex Pistols and Kings X, but blend these into an individualistic style that bears little resemblance to anyone else. Sgned by East West Records, they debuted with Mondo Akimbo A-Go-Go, a mini-album in early 1992; unfortunately the muddy production, stifled the impact of the excellent material. However, with time their full length debut should see them achieve the recognition that their undoubted talents deserve.
Album: Mondo Akimbo A-Go-Go (1992).

Wildside

This L.A. based quintet were formed in 1991 by vocalist Drew Hannah and guitarist Brent Wood. With Benny Rhynestone (guitar), Marc Simon (bass) and Jimmy D. (drums) completing the line-up, the band model themselves on Ratt, Motley Crue and Cinderella. Contracted to Capitol Records, Under The Influence emerged in July 1992 to a lukewarm reception. Although professional, competent and technically without fault, their material is far too derivative at this stage of their career to make any lasting impact.
Album: Under The Influence (1992).

Willard

Named after a character from James Herbert's book The Rats, Willard were formed in Seattle, USA in 1991 by vocalist Johnny Clint and guitarist Mark Spiders. Enlisting the services of Steve Wied (drums), Otis P. Otis (guitar) and Darren Peters (bass) they were picked up by Roadracer Records the same year. Subtitled The Sound Of Fuck!, Steel Mill released in July 1992 was a powerful and uncompromising debut. It represented a four-way musical collision between Black Sabbath, Nirvana, Metallica and the Henry Rollins Band.
Album: Steel Mill (1992).

Wishbone Ash

In 1966 Steve Upton (b. 24 May 1946, Wrexham, Wales; drums) who had played with the Scimitars, joined Martin Turner (b. 1 October 1947, Torquay, Devon, England; bass/vocals) and Glen Turner (guitar) in the Torquay band the Empty Vessels. This trio moved to London where they took the name of Tanglewood. Glen Turner departed, and another man of the same surname, Ted Turner (b. David Alan Turner, 2 August 1950; guitar) joined the band. He had previously played in the Birmingham band, King Biscuit. Wishbone Ash was formed when Andy Powell (b. 8 February 1950; guitar) of the Sugarband joined Upton, Turner and Turner. Heavily influenced by the music of the Yardbirds and the Allman Brothers, Wishbone Ash's hallmark was the powerful sound of twin lead guitars. Their biggest commercial success was *Argus*, released in 1973. This was a prime example of the band's preoccupation with historical themes, complex instrumentals, and folk-rock. Ted Turner departed in 1974, and was replaced by Laurie Wisefield, formerly of Home. Wishbone Ash continued successfully, becoming tax exiles in the USA, returning to England in 1975 to play at the Reading Rock festival. In 1980 Martin Turner left Wishbone Ash, John Wetton, formerly of Uriah Heep and Roxy Music, serving as his replacement, and singer Claire Hammill joined the band, along with Trevor Bolder. This line-up released only one album before disbanding in 1982, and it was the recruitment of Mervyn Spence to replace Bolder that seemed to give some of its former

Wishbone Ash

vitality back to Wishbone Ash. It was in 1987 that the original quartet got back together again, recording *Nouveau Calls*. This project involved the renewal of Wishbone Ash's relationship with Miles Copeland, who was manager of the Police, and who had managed Wishbone Ash for a brief spell in the 60s. They continue to perform to a loyal and devoted following.

Albums: *Wishbone Ash* (1970), *Pilgrimage* (1972), *Argus* (1973), *Wishbone 4* (1973), *Live Dates* (1974), *There's The Rub* (1974), *Locked In* (1976), *New England* (1977), *Frontpage News* (1977), *No Smoke Without Fire* (1978), *Live In Tokyo* (1978), *Just Testing* (1979), *Live Dates Vol. II* (1979), *Number The Brave* (1981), *Hot Ash* (1981), *Two Barrels Burning* (1982), *Raw To The Bone* (1985), *Nouveau Calls* (1987), *BBC Radio 1 Live In Concert* (1991, rec. 1972). Compilations: *Classic Ash* (1981), *The Best Of Wishbone Ash* (1982).

Wolfsbane

This UK hard rock quartet from Tamworth, Staffordshire, employed a strong biker image. Featuring Blaze Bayley (vocals), Jase Edwards (guitar), Steve 'Danger' Ellet (drums) and Jeff Hateley (bass), they incorporated elements of Van Halen, Iron Maiden and Zodiac Mindwarp into their own high-energy, frantic and, at times, chaotic style. Picked up by Rick Rubin's Def Jam label, they released *Live Fast, Die Fast* as a statement of their *carpe diem* philosophy of life. The album failed to match the manic intensity of their live shows and was let down by weak production. Their next two releases saw some development on the songwriting front, with the addition of sci-fi b-movie imagery, to supplement the well-worn themes of sex, booze and rock 'n' roll. After three albums, their style remained loud, aggressive and, to a degree, derivative.

Albums: *Live Fast, Die Fast* (1989), *All Hell's Breaking Loose Down At Little Kathy Wilson's Place* (1990), *Down Fall The Good Guys* (1991).

XYZ

Xentrix

Originally known as Sweet Vengeance the band was formed in Preston, Lancashire, England, in 1986 and featured Chris Astley (vocals/guitar), Kristian Havard (guitar), Paul Mackenzie (bass) and Dennis Gasser (drums). The group had done little until signing to Roadrunner Records on the strength of their 'Hunger For' demo tape in 1988. They had already recorded the track 'Blackmail' for inclusion on the Ebony Records compilation *Full Force*, under the Sweet Vengeance monicker. It was their debut *Shattered Existence* that bought them to public attention. Combining Metallica-style power riffs with Bay Area thrash pretensions, the band became popular on the UK club circuit and recorded a cover version of the Ray Parker Jnr. track 'Ghostbusters', a band stage favourite, for their first single release. They had problems with the single as they had used the *Ghostbusters* film logo for the cover without Columbia Pictures'

permission. The resulting press did the band no harm and the single was released with a new cover in 1990. Also in that year the band released *For Whose Advantage*. Musically much the same as previous releases, it nevertheless did much to enhance their profile. With *Dilute To Taste* the band are taking a more traditional Power Metal approach which may bode well for the future.
Albums: *Shattered Existence* (1989), *For Whose Advantage* (1990), *Dilute To Taste* (1991).

Zodiac Mindwarp And The Love Reaction
(see Mindwarp, Zodiac, And The Love Reaction)

Z.Z. Top
Formed in Houston, Texas, USA, in 1970, Z.Z. Top evolved out of the city's garage-band circuit and comprises Billy Gibbons (b. 12 December 1949, Houston, Texas, USA; guitar, ex-Moving Sidewalks) with Dusty Hill (b. Joe Hill, 1949, Dallas, Texas, USA; bass) and Frank Beard (b. 10 December 1949, Houston, Texas, USA; drums) both ex-American Blues. Z.Z. Top's original line-up; Gibbons, Lanier Greig (bass) and Dan Mitchell (drums), was also the final version of the Moving Sidewalks. This initial trio completed Z.Z. Top's

Xentrix

Z.Z. Top

debut single, 'Salt Lick', before Greig was fired. He was replaced by Bill Ethridge. Mitchell was then replaced by Frank Beard while Dusty Hill subsequently joined in place of Ethridge. Initially Z.Z. Top joined a growing swell of southern boogie bands. Their debut album, while betraying a healthy interest in blues, was firmly within this genre, but *Rio Grande Mud*, indicated a greater flexibility. It included the rousing 'Francine' which, although indebted to the Rolling Stones, gave the trio their first hit and introduced them to a much wider audience.

Their early career coalesced on *Tres Hombres*, a powerful, exciting set which drew from delta music and high energy rock. The group's natural ease was highly effective and Gibbons' startling guitar work was rarely bettered during these times. However successive releases failed to attain the same high standard and Z.Z. Top took an extended vacation following their expansive 1976-1977 tour. The reasons, however, were not solely artistic, as the group now wished to secure a more beneficial recording deal. They resumed their career in 1979 with the superb *Deguello*. Revitalized by their break, the trio offered a series of pulsating original songs as well as inspired recreations of Sam And Dave's 'I Thank You' and Elmore James' 'Dust My Broom'. The transitional *El Loco* followed in 1981 and although it lacked the punch of its predecessor, preferring the surreal to the celebratory, the set introduced the growing love of technology which marked the group's subsequent release.

Eliminator deservedly became Z.Z. Top's best-selling album. Fuelled by a series of memorable, tongue-in-cheek sexist videos, it provided several international hit singles, including the million-selling 'Gimme All Your Lovin''. Additionally 'Sharp Dressed Man' and 'Legs' were gloriously simple yet enormously infectious songs. The group skilfully wedded computer-age technology to their barrelhouse R&B to create a truly memorable set which established them as one of the world's leading live attractions. The follow-up, *Afterburner*, was a comparative disappointment although it did feature some excellent individual moments in 'Sleeping Bag' and 'Rough Boy' and the cleverly titled 'Velcro Fly'. Aware of this dichotomy, Z.Z. Top undertook another lengthy break before returning with the impressive *Recycler*. One of rock's maverick attractions, Gibbons, Hill and Beard have retained their original inspirations, yet remain a contemporary force. Their eccentric, colourful image, dark glasses and stetson hats, complete with an almost casual musical dexterity have won over hardened cynics and carping critics. In addition to having produced a fine (but

sparse) canon of work, they will stay in the record books as having the longest beards in musical history (although one member Frank Beard is clean-shaven!), and always destined to be the last entry in a popular music encyclopedia.

Albums: *First Album* (1971), *Rio Grande Mud* (1972), *Tres Hombres* (1973), *Fandango!* (1975), *Tejas* (1976), *Deguello* (1979), *El Loco* (1981), *Eliminator* (1983), *Afterburner* (1985), *Recycler* (1990). Compilations: *The Best Of Z.Z. Top* (1977), *Greatest Hits* (1992).

The Guinness Encyclopedia of Popular Music

Compiled by Colin Larkin

The most comprehensive and authoritative guide to popular music that has ever been published, *The Guinness Encyclopedia of Popular Music* covers every important artist, band, genre, group, event, instrument, publisher, promoter, record company and musical style from the world of popular music in four 832-page volumes.

The product of over four years of intensive labour by an international group of more than 100 skilled writers, musicologists and advisors, its scope is truly global. Compiled in an A-Z format, it covers all forms of popular music from 1990 to 1992 and contains over 9,000 entries varying in length from 100 to 5,000 words.

A bibliography of over 5,000 entries is included along with a full index of artists' names.

For further details of this essential reference work, please write to:
Section C,
The Marketing Department,
Guinness Publishing,
33 London Road,
Enfield,
Middlesex EN2 6DJ,
England.

Proposed Titles for Inclusion in the

'Guinness Who's Who of Popular Music Series'

The Guinness Who's Who of 50s Music
The Guinness Who's Who of 60s Music★
The Guinness Who's Who of 70s Music
The Guinness Who's Who of 80s Music
The Guinness Who's Who of Indie and New Wave Music★
The Guinness Who's Who of Blues Music
The Guinness Who's Who of Folk Music
The Guinness Who's Who of R&B Music
The Guinness Who's Who of Soul Music
The Guinness Who's Who of Country Music
The Guinness Who's Who of Jazz★
The Guinness Who's Who of Heavy Metal Music★
The Guinness Who's Who of Gospel Music
The Guinness Who's Who of UK Rock and Pop
The Guinness Who's Who of USA Rock and Pop
The Guinness Who's Who of Danceband Pop
The Guinness Who's Who of World Music
The Guinness Who's Who of Stage Musicals

★ Already published

For further information on any of these titles please write to:
Section C,
The Marketing Department,
Guinness Publishing,
33 London Road,
Enfield,
Middlesex EN2 6DJ,
England

The Guinness Who's Who of Jazz

General Editor: Colin Larkin

The history of jazz is a long and varied one, from its beginnings in the whorehouses and bars of the turn of the century, to the top concert halls of today. Encapsulating the embryonic forms of New Orleans, trad, boogie-woogie, and the ragtime of Louis Armstrong, Jelly Roll Morton, Scott Joplin and Fats Waller, The Guinness Who's Who of Jazz, follows the progress of jazz through the big bands and jive artists such as Paul Whitman, Bix Biederbeck, Duke Ellington, Count Basie, Glenn Miller, Cab Calloway and Louis Jordan on to the present day, via the innovative bop sounds of the 50s and 60s with Miles Davis, John Coltrane, Coleman Hawkins, Dave Brubeck, Dizzy Gillespie and the modern sounds of Andy Shepard, John Surman, Wynton Marsalis, Elton Dean and Courtney Pine. Special consideration is given to the talent of the past decade, making this book instantly more accessible than all its rivals.

The Guinness Who's Who of Jazz also contains entries on the various noted orchestra and band sidemen, the composers, arrangers and label owners. With hundreds of entries it will become an indispensable book for aficionados of the music and will act as an introduction to its many newcomers.

This book is available from all good bookshops and selected record stores. For information on this or on forthcoming titles in the series, please write to:

Section C,
The Marketing Department,
Guinness Publishing,
33 London Road,
Enfield,
Middlesex EN2 6DJ,
England

The Guinness Who's Who of Sixties Music

General Editor: Colin Larkin

From the publishers of *The Guinness Encyclopedia of Popular Music* comes the definitive guide to the groups and artists who created the music of the 60s. From the early years of Del Shannon, Bobby Darin, Ricky Nelson, and Cliff Richard; the Beach Boys, Jan and Dean and the Shangri-Las to the beat-boom with the Beatles and the Rolling Stones; the 'swinging London' era of the Who and the Kinks, and the explosion of sound from California's west coast with the Byrds, Doors, Jefferson Airplane and Grateful Dead. Folk protest, the blues boom, psychedelia, soul, jazz, ska, Merseybeat, pirate radio plus the impact on a whole generation by Bob Dylan - it's all told here with information on the musicians, songwriters and personalities.

From those who survived to those lost in the mists of time, everything you'd ever want to know is included in this complete and accurate record of the music and major artists of the decade. With hundreds of entries written by some of today's leading rock writers, this is the definative guide to the movers and shakers of 60s music.

This book is available from all good bookshops and from selected record stores. For information on this or on forthcoming titles in the series, please write to:

Section C,
The Marketing Department,
Guinness Publishing,
33 London Road,
Enfield,
Middlesex EN2 6DJ,
England

The Guinness Who's Who of Indie and New Wave Music

General Editor: Colin Larkin

From the publishers of *The Guinness Encyclopedia of Popular Music* comes the definitive guide to the groups and artists who have moulded the shape of popular music in the 70s 80s and 90s. From the beginnings of punk in the late-70s with the Sex Pistols, Clash, Damned, X-Ray Spex and the Buzzcocks in the UK, and Television, Talking Heads, Blondie and the Ramones in the US, modern popular music was shaken to its foundations. These bands paved the way in the ensuing years for many new and varied forms of exciting music including Siouxsie And The Banshees, Joy Division/New Order, the Cure, Smiths, Cocteau Twins, Birthday Party, Jesus And Mary Chain, Happy Mondays, Stone Roses, James and R.E.M.

This book contains entries on all these bands plus many others on groups and artists who are usually, and unjustifiably, ignored in lesser encyclopedias. In all, there are hundreds of entries including contributions by some of the leading pop and indie writers today plus an introduction by Johnny Rogan.

This book is available from all good bookshops and from selected record stores. For information on this or on forthcoming titles in the series, please write to:

Section C,
The Marketing Department,
Guinness Publishing,
33 London Road,
Enfield,
Middlesex,
EN2 6DJ,
England.